Management
Information Systems

MANAGEMENT INFORMATION SYSTEMS

Third Edition

JEROME KANTER

Honeywell Information Systems

PRENTICE-HALL, INC.
Englewood Cliffs, New Jersey 07632

Library of Congress Cataloging in Publication Data

Kanter, Jerome.
  Managemant information systems.

   Rev. ed. of: Management-oriented management infor-
mation systems. 2nd ed. c1977.
  Bibliography: p.
  Includes index.
  1. Management information systems. I. Title.
T58.6.K36 1984   658.4'038   83-11245
ISBN 0-13-549543-1

Editorial/production supervision: Nancy Milnamow
Cover design: Jeannette Jacobs
Manufacturing buyer: Gordon Osbourne

Previously published under the title
Management-Oriented Management Information Systems, Second Edition

Printed in the United States of America

10 9 8 7 6 5 4 3 2 1

ISBN 0-13-549543-1

PRENTICE-HALL INTERNATIONAL, INC., *London*
PRENTICE-HALL OF AUSTRALIA PTY. LIMITED, *Sydney*
EDITORA PRENTICE-HALL DO BRASIL, LTDA., *Rio de Janeiro*
PRENTICE-HALL OF CANADA INC., *Toronto*
PRENTICE-HALL OF INDIA PRIVATE LIMITED, *New Delhi*
PRENTICE-HALL OF JAPAN, INC., *Tokyo*
PRENTICE-HALL OF SOUTHEAST ASIA PTE. LTD., *Singapore*
WHITEHALL BOOKS LIMITED, *Wellington, New Zealand*

To Carolyn
who knows what she has meant to my work and to me

Contents

Preface

Management information systems provided the "wish-fulfillment syndrome" of the seventies. The syndrome develops this way: when one has a serious problem and an approach emerges that, although only partially understood, appears to bear some relation to the problem, this approach tends to become the solution. The next phase is "nonfulfillment backlash." As this backlash occurred, writings on MIS took on negative and apologetic tones, attendance at courses on MIS dwindled, and the term itself was avoided by professionals. The backlash has tended to obscure the role of MIS in the eighties.

MIS, properly defined and understood, has untapped potential for business—indeed it may prove to be the only way to maintain a competitive industry posture. This book puts MIS in proper perspective so that business managers can understand what such systems can do and—equally important—what they cannot do.

A major problem has been the proliferation of books and magazine articles that purport to deal with MIS. The term "management information system" has been used to describe systems ranging from the preparation of an inventory report showing updated ending balances to the simulation of how new products will fare in complex marketing environments. The most rudimentary systems books, many devoted solely to describing the input, output, and processing characteristics of computers, have been titled as treatises on management information systems. In another vein, the businessman has come to think of MIS as being synonymous with the total systems concept, where one grandiose system is designed to encompass the entire operation of a company, providing meaningful and timely reports upon which managers can base immediate decision and action. This is hard for the businessman to swallow, since he wonders how a computer is going to quantify the information that he knows is subjective and psychological in nature and that often is as important as the quantitative type.

Also associated with management information systems is the idea that such a system assists management at all levels in the organization, including top management. MIS has come to mean automated board rooms where corporate executives can obtain the daily profit-and-loss picture, the current sales situation, or the instantaneous cash-flow position by pushing a button on a graphic display console.

Thus, on the one hand, MIS has meant something as basic as a simple order-processing or inventory system, and on the other hand, it has been used to refer to advanced simulation applications and direct board-room interaction with the computer. It's confusing, to say the least.

This book clarifies the situation. It provides a comprehensive explanation of what an MIS is and what it can do for management. It is intended for the technically oriented, non-data-processing manager, and it should serve well as a text for a basic course in MIS or in the design of MIS at the college or graduate level. It should also prove useful to the data processing manager who is seeking to broaden the managerial rather than the technical aspects of his job.

OBJECTIVES OF THE REVISION

While planning this third edition, I thought seriously about changing the title to "Information Resource Management." IRM represents a more global way of looking at information systems, centering on information rather than on the computer or the system. It recognizes that information is as valuable a resource as the more traditional ones of money, material, people, and facilities and should be treated and managed as such. It places emphasis on the process as opposed to the product. The product—in this case the computer—is still significant, but under the IRM concept the balance shifts to the management process. I agree with this concept and have incorporated it in the book. This edition recognizes that a successful MIS resides in the general environment of IRM. A new chapter entitled "Information Resource Management" has been added. I conclude, however, that MIS remains a valid term and, properly conceived, defines the information process that is the objective of management. In my mind, the principles of MIS in the book are not at all inconsistent with IRM—the two terms fit.

The objectives of the revision are to:

- Update sections where technology, terms, and processes have changed.
- Emphasize the concept of information resource management and its implications for managing and controlling the MIS function.

- Expand the discussion of data base, end-user languages, and the growing significance of these capabilities to MIS.
- Describe the growth and management impact of mini- and microcomputers, office automation, distributed data processing, and decision support systems—trends that are coming to the fore.
- Emphasize MIS long-range planning, the need to develop an MIS mission or direction statement, and the importance of their consistency with corporate objectives.
- Elaborate on MIS control tools such as capacity planning, structured design and programming techniques, charge-out systems, risk analysis, and security and back-up systems.
- Analyze a new survey I conducted on the involvement of management in MIS and other research focused on MIS impact on management.
- Organize for easier reading and more logical flow of information.
- Update bibliography, case studies, and references.

ORGANIZATION OF THE BOOK

The book has eleven chapters compared to ten in the previous edition, and they have been organized a bit differently. Chapter 1 defines what a management information system is and how one is built to mirror the business processes of the enterprise. Chapter 2 moves the MIS discussion into the realm of information resource management and explains why the latter is essential as the environment for successful MIS. Chapter 3 stresses the concept that before discussing information systems, the business itself must be understood. The chapter analyzes business as a system in its own right, indicating the business processes or subsystems that comprise it and then exploring the underlying information systems and data elements that support the business processes. The importance of data base is stressed in Chapter 4, while the role of communications and distributed data processing is reviewed in Chaper 5. Chapter 6 scans the history and evolution of the information processing industry. Chapter 7 describes the life cycle of MIS application development—the steps that an application goes through on its way to productive operation. Chapter 8 explores the management tools necessary to plan and control the life-cycle process. Chapters 9 and 10 swing back to the main theme and focus of the book, the emphasis on the word "management" in MIS. Finally, Chapter 11 looks at the future of MIS and information resource management.

STUDY AIDS

Study aids are provided throughout for the use of instructors and students employing the book as a text. Each chapter concludes with several short cases, which can be used as a foundation for classroom assignment and discussion. The cases elaborate on major issues discussed in the chapter and are based on actual company experiences. Pertinent questions are appended to each "case" to stimulate analysis and discussion.

A bibliography is included. In addition, there are comprehensive case studies in the appendices which can be used to stress the principles of system design, system trade-offs, and the analysis of specific application subsystems within an MIS framework. The Rolco case is particularly beneficial as an extended class assignment. I have used it quite successfully in a course I teach on MIS. Individual case histories and company experiences are embedded in each chapter.

The book is not an exhaustive treatise of management information systems. It presents a framework for those seeking understanding of MIS as well as for those responsible for the planning and implementation of MIS within a business environment. Guidelines are presented for successful employment of MIS concepts. The book explores MIS from the management and business viewpoint; its thesis is that this is the correct viewpoint. While the framework established is heavily influenced by the efforts of Anthony, Deardon, and Churchill of the Harvard Business School, Simon of Carnegie-Mellon University, Forester of MIT, and Carroll of The Wharton School, I have not followed the typical scholarly approach in writing the book. I share with other business people a discouragement in trying to wade through a book filled with references, footnotes, quotations, and critiques of other people's works. With this in mind, I have emphasized readability and understanding. The book is intended for the business manager, not the scholar, and therefore refrains from the "wordsmanship" and "quotesmanship" that characterizes many of today's business books. What others call a systems taxonomist, for example, I call simply a person who classifies systems, and others' information technology methodologist is in my book a systems person.

Tackling the subject of MIS is an ambitious undertaking. My goal is to advance the basic understanding and employment of business-oriented management information systems. My viewpoint on MIS emanates from the following background:

Manager of a data processing department in a large manufacturing and distribution company.

Assistant controller in charge of accounting and financial control operations in a manufacturing company.

Assistant to the plant manager of a manufacturing company in developing organizational and informational systems to improve plant operations.

Designer and implementor of applications, including management information systems, for use by companies in several industries.

Manager of a planning department using the output of computers to aid marketing and planning functions.

Active learner having knowledge of surveys and studies of information systems and direct contact with MIS professionals and practitioners.

Consultant to companies employing MIS in a wide variety of industry settings.

Instructor and lecturer in computer sciences at Babson College; Amos Tuck Business School, Dartmouth; Northeastern University; the Harvard Business School; and Cambridge and Oxford Universities in England.

In undertaking this book, the most important credential I possess is an emotional involvement in using, developing, and installing MIS and portions of MIS in various companies and a belief in its importance.

ACKNOWLEDGEMENTS

My appreciation to John F. Rockart, Director of MIT's Center for Information Systems Research for his aid and counsel and for ample use of his material; also to James L. McKenney, F. Warren McFarlan and James I. Cash, Jr., all of the Harvard Business School, for use of case material and for their help in conducting the survey on the impact of computers on management at Harvard's Program for Management Development, and to Dick Dooley, the consultant's consultant, for his sage advice.

I would like to thank the following Honeywell people for use of material and for their review of portions of the book: Jerome Lobel for security and privacy, John Field for project control, Jim Hannigan for MULTICS, Oliver Miles for communications and Floyd Johnson for end user languages.

My gratitude to Carol Dello Russo, Bessie Koshivas and Beverly Butters for their invaluable editing and typing assistance, to Eileen Ward for her outstanding library and research skills, and to fellow consultants John Warren, Jack Walsh, Carol Mazuy, and Frank Chen for their significant contributions during the past two years that we have worked together.

JEROME KANTER

Management
Information Systems

Chapter 1

MIS—Establishing the Framework

This chapter builds an analytical framework in order to facilitate a meaningful discussion of management information systems. Some time ago I read a provocative *Harvard Business Review* article asserting that management had not been affected by computerized information systems and probably would not be for at least another five years. A long rebuttal was printed several issues later, citing example after example of how management had been affected by the computer. In carefully reviewing both the article and the rebuttal, I saw that the two authors were talking about completely different levels of management, and I felt that there would be a surprisingly high level of agreement between the two writers if the semantic barrier were removed. Thus I think it is well worth the effort to define terms and to establish a generalized framework from which to view the often misinterpreted management information system concept.

Before dissecting each term, I will define an MIS. An MIS is a system that aids management in making, carrying out, and controlling decisions. *Decision making*, including the process leading up to the decision, can be termed planning, and *management* can be defined as the planning and control of the physical and personnel resources of the company in order to reach company objectives. This definition of management differs from others—one of which is getting things done through people—but I feel it is more definitive. Getting things done through people, plus the selecting, training, and motivating of people, is assumed part of the control function, for implementing and controlling the decisions made will obviously require the motivation of people. Referring back to the MIS definition, we can simplify it by saying that *MIS is a system that aids management in performing its job.* Later chapters will analyze the manager's job in greater detail and will indicate in which areas computerized management information systems can make the greatest impact and in which areas its impact is doubtful, even in the future. The following analysis should aid this discussion.

ELEMENTS OF A MANAGEMENT INFORMATION SYSTEM

We begin by looking at the basic elements or ingredients of a management information system. The term MIS is well conceived in that if one understands the three words or parts that comprise it, one can obtain a basic understanding of the whole. This point may seem obvious, but it is not true of certain other technical terms or the so-called buzz words that form the argot of a new industry.

The Classic Management Triangle

Figure 1.1 indicates three levels of business activities or processes carried out in operating a company. These three levels were first described by Robert B. Anthony in 1965 and are still used to portray the functioning of a business enterprise.

The first level, *operational control*, indicates processes performed to control the basic product or services produced by the company. In a manufacturing company, examples of operational control are the processes that move a product from one assembly point to the next and the actions that take place at each assembly point. In a

Fig. 1.1   Levels of business activity

bank, operational control includes the physical sorting, recording, and posting of checks.

The next level, *management control*, includes processes or functions that facilitate the management of those processes delegated to the operational control level. An example of a management control process is production scheduling, where a system is established to schedule products through the various fabrication and assembly points within a factory. The feedback from the production scheduling process enables management to control the operation.

The top level of the triangle represents strategic planning processes, the processes that determine what products to produce in the first place or, even more broadly, what markets or businesses the company should be in currently or plan to be in the future. These are brief examples or definitions of these three levels; later sections will build on this basic Anthony triangle. It represents a very useful classification schematic for establishing the proper perspective and providing a foundation for beginning the exploration of MIS.

LEVELS OF MANAGEMENT

The first term to define is management. Figure 1.2 presents the organizational chart of a manufacturing company. Company organization charts generally have considerably more detail than this one; however, it has enough to illustrate the distinction between the different levels of management.

There are several ways to describe the various management levels. Although lines of demarcation are not absolute, one can distinguish certain layers within the organization. For the most part, top management will perform the strategic planning processes, middle management the management control processes, and operating management the operational control functions.

In attempting to distinguish the layers of management, we may find it difficult to stick to only three levels when most companies have an organizational hierarchy consisting of eight or more levels; that is, some managers are eight levels or more removed from the company president. One of the purported operational advantages enjoyed by Japanese companies is an organizational structure having as few as five levels separating the factory worker from the president.

Figure 1.3 summarizes the interaction of the three levels. Top management establishes the policies, plans, and objectives of the company, as well as a general budget framework under which the various departments will operate. These factors are promulgated and passed down to middle management, where they are translated into specific revenue, cost, and profit goals, particularly if each department works under a cost or profit center concept. These are reviewed, analyzed, and modified in accordance with the overall plans and policies until agreement is reached. Middle management then issues the specific schedules and measurement yardsticks to operating management. The latter level has the job of producing the goods and services required to meet the revenue and profit goals, which in turn will enable the company to reach its overall plans and objectives.

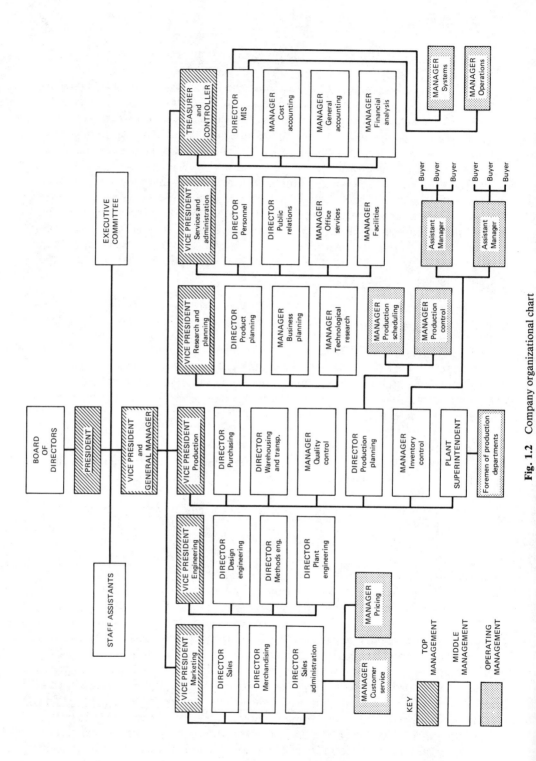

Fig. 1.2 Company organizational chart

4

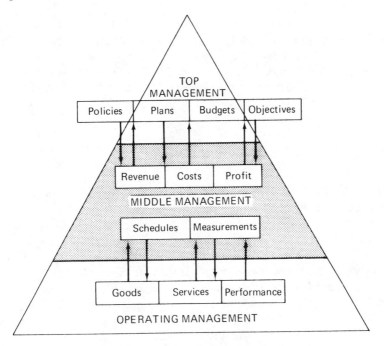

Fig. 1.3 Interaction of management levels

THE PLANNING PROCESS

Most companies have some form of a long-range plan, typically five years, which acts as the master strategy and road map tying together the processes just mentioned. The plan promulgates the major business, market, and product strategies of the company for the next five years or longer, indicating the resources in the form of facilities, people, technology, and money necessary to accomplish the strategies. In addition to the strategies, the overall company goals are stated for the long-range plan period including performance indicators such as revenue, profit, return on investment, return on assets, market share, and the like. The goals are broken down by product line or operating division or both. The yearly operating plan of the company comes directly from the long-range plan, usually being identical for the first year or the first two years.

The long-range plan and the yearly operating plan are the basis for the formulation of individual objectives and goals, both of the numeric type and of the event type. An example of a numeric goal is a specified sales or shipment volume, while an event goal might be the delivery of a new product on a specific date or the completion of a new facility. The degree to which these objectives and goals cascade through an organization is a function of the planning process and the operating style of the company; however, the trend is to continually link more lower-level management goals to the company long-range plan and operating plan. This obviously provides a more cohesive, direct, and motivated organization. The point of raising the planning process here is to emphasize that this should be the true starting point for MIS. If an MIS is to support management, and management is goaled and measured by the long-range plan, then it is obvious that the contents of the plan are vital to the overall goals and objectives of the MIS operation. Indeed, MIS must itself be a part of the long-range plan—both influencing and being influenced by it.

DISTINCTION BETWEEN MANAGEMENT LEVELS

It is significant to compare the job content of the three levels of management. Figure 1.4 contrasts the levels by reference to twelve characteristics. The first two represent the essence of management. There is a heavy planning content in top management, less at the middle-management level, and a minimum at the operating level. Control is focused on implementation, so that there is a heavy control content at the middle and operating levels but only a moderate amount at the top. In reality, planning and control take place at all levels of management, for it is difficult to separate one activity from the other. Every management job is to some extent a microcosm of the total organization. Top management can never define company objectives to the point where there is no room for interpretation. Therefore, it is necessary for lower levels of management to plan as well, although they may do so in a more restricted environment. Within each department and subdepartment, there are usually counterparts to the executive committee who meet periodically to plan the activity for the next time

Characteristic	Top management	Middle management	Operating management
1. Focus on planning	Heavy	Moderate	Minimum
2. Focus on control	Moderate	Heavy	Heavy
3. Time frame	One to five years	Up to a year	Day to Day
4. Scope of activity	Extremely broad	Entire functional area	Single subfunction or subtask
5. Nature of activity	Relatively instructured	Moderately structured	Highly structured
6. Level of complexity	Very complex, many variables	Less complex, better defined variables	Straightforward
7. Job measurement	Difficult	Less difficult	Relatively easy
8. Result of activity	Plans, policies and strategies	Implementation schedules, performance yardsticks	End product
9. Type of information utilized	External	Internal, reasonable accuracy	Internal historical, high level of accuracy
10. Mental attributes	Creative, innovative	Responsible, persuasive, administrative	Efficient, effective
11. Number of people involved	Few	Moderate number	Many
12. Department/divisional interaction	Intra-division	Intra-department	Inter-department

Fig. 1.4   Job content of management levels

period and to review techniques for implementing the plans. The individual departments have their own equivalent of top, middle, and operating management.

Top management deals with activity that has a time dimension of one to five years. It is not that they ignore shorter-term problems; rather, the executive committee focuses on the future. In some cases the span is greater than five years.

Middle management must project activity a year to enable the development of the annual operation plan, but normally the focus is on weeks or months. The key question raised at meetings of middle management is how the prior period—whether a week, two weeks, or a month—compared to plan and, if below plan, how they can take remedial action. Middle management deals with the plans and performance against plans.

Operating management's time frame is day-to-day. They have specific tasks to accomplish, and they can measure their accomplishments on a short-term basis. Their time span usually is a week.

The next three characteristics apply to the overall nature of the activity. It is already clear that the scope of top management's responsibilities is extremely broad, whereas middle management is concerned with major functional areas, such as production planning or quality control. Operating management's attention is focused on individual subfunctions, the elements of which enable a function to be accomplished. The nature of activity runs from an unstructured framework at the top to a highly structured one at the bottom. Top management is dealing with such factors as the marketplace, the products and services to offer, the competitive factors, and the timing of product introductions. Although some companies have succeeded in building a statistical market model that helps in the structuring of the outside world, much of the data on which the model feeds is qualitative and subjective in nature and has a varying probability quotient. As a result, top management's job is complex and involves numerous variables, many of which are difficult to measure. The variables at the middle-management level are better defined, for they deal with events and activities that take place within the operating environment of the company. Although some people would say that the world at the operating level is not as straightforward as indicated on the chart, it is when compared to higher management levels. A foreman may consider the reassignment of workers to expedite a rush order as a difficult task, especially if there are union restrictions on assignments. However, this activity does not approach the complexity of forecasting the profitability and impact on company operations of the introduction of a new product line.

The result or output of top management's activity consists of the plans, procedures, and strategies that the company will follow over the next year, plans that are consistent with the longer-range thinking of the company. Middle management produces, as their output, the schedules and performance measurements to accomplish the plan, while the result of operating management's activity is the end product itself. Thus the objective of a business enterprise is to evolve broad-gauged and somewhat intangible directives and plans into progressively more detailed and tangible work plans that eventually result in the tangible production of a product. As will be discussed in the next section, top management deals primarily in external information, whereas middle and operating management deal with internal and historical information. There is a greater degree of accuracy and validity in the internal brand of information.

The last three characteristics cover personal attributes of the job content. Top management's job requires creativity, innovation, and the ability to make decisions under varying degrees of uncertainty. Middle management's job entails a persuasiveness and motivational element that can get the job done. While top management can be regarded as the navigator and architect of the ship, the middle manager is the captain who barks the orders and sustains the people's effort to reach the destination. Operating management must employ efficient and effective techniques that will accomplish the job. The number-of-people characteristic reflects the hierarchical pyramid of company organization, with few people at the top and many at the bottom. Finally, each management level has interaction paths with other management levels. Top management must deal at the division to ensure that their plans are consistent with corporate goals and objectives. Middle managers of one department must interact with management of other departments because of the interdependence of one department to another. For example, an important customer needs a rush order by a certain date. In this case the sales department influences the production department and vice versa. Operating management's interaction can usually be confined to the department in which it operates.

It is important to delve as deeply as we have into the nature of the activity at different management levels. Too many system practitioners have designed (and even attempted to implement) so-called management information systems without an understanding of the management process. The results have been either abortive and costly systems that missed their mark or systems under the guise of MIS that really were aimed at the lower management levels—sometimes at the operating management but often at lower, clerical levels. Thus it is important to understand the management process and to determine the focus of MIS.

I have mentioned that every management job is a microcosm of the total organization. This holds for the MIS Director's job as it appears on the organizational chart in Fig. 1.2. The planning element of the MIS Director's job is to ascertain the activities and responsibilities of management and to develop with them an information system that assists them in carrying out their responsibilities. Too often a hasty and haphazard planning job precedes a premature plunge into the implementation phase. An understanding of the management process is a necessary prerequisite to a management information system. As will be pointed out later, difficulties remain in successfully designing and implementing an information system even when the management process is understood; and without such an understanding, there is no chance at all of success.

TYPES OF MANAGEMENT INFORMATION

Information, the second element in the term management information system, has come to be recognized as an increasingly valuable commodity required by management in order to plan and control business operations effectively. Information is the

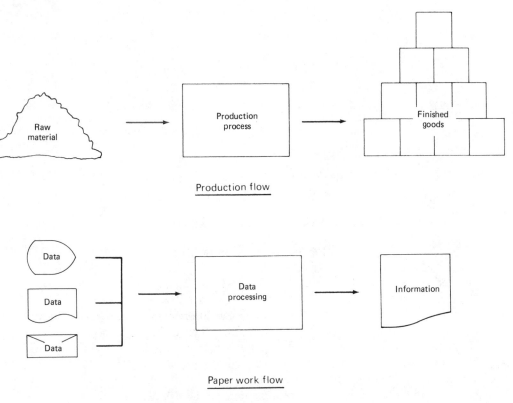

Fig. 1.5   Process flow

"stuff" of paperwork systems just as material is the "stuff" of production systems. For purposes of definition, this analogy is shown in Fig. 1.5. *Data* is defined as raw material and may enter the processing system from the keyboard of a cathode ray tube, from optically sensed documents, from writings on the back of envelopes, and so on. Processed data is called *information* and is in a form to assist management and other users. (Concerning the use of the word "data," although I realize that it is plural, with the singular being datum, I have never felt comfortable with the plural use and therefore will use data in the singular sense where it seems to fit.)

Information is now considered a resource on the level of money, material, facilities, and people; indeed the concept has been given an imposing title: Information Resource Management. Chapter 2 will elaborate on this concept and its implications for a company.

BUSINESS DIMENSION OF INFORMATION

We have noted that different levels of management utilize different types of information. There are a variety of ways to classify information. Figure 1.6 contrasts the business dimension of information over a continuum with top management at one

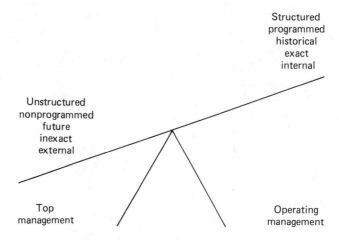

Fig. 1.6   Business dimension of information

end and operating management at the other. Middle management, as always, falls in between, having elements of both.

The factors shown in the figure obviously are related. For example, information that is unstructured is difficult to program. Structured information tends to be rhythmic in that it follows a repetitive pattern that occurs at prescribed time periods. Thus the foreman has the monthly production schedule for a particular product, which indicates that 50 units are scheduled for each of the next ten days. He will want to review the information that indicates the material cost, labor cost, and expenses incurred on a day-to-day basis to see if the schedule is being met and if it is being met efficiently. Because the information is structured, it can be programmed. Rules and procedures can be established to develop schedules and measurements that will be most efficient for the known operating conditions. This is why more computerized information systems are programmed to assist operating management than to assist top management. The nature of top management's responsibilities revolves around strategic planning, where the nature of information is unstructured and therefore difficult to program. For example, it is difficult to determine with exactness the market share of a company's products or the particular penetration in a specific market segment.

Information for planning purposes stresses the future and thus is inexact when compared to information required at the operating level. This is not to say that top management is not interested in past history and in operating results. However, past results must be reviewed in light of external conditions and the marketplace in which the company competes. The focus of top management is on future plans and policies. The matrix shown in Figure 1.7 focuses on the difference between internal and external information.

Internal information is a by-product of the normal operations of a business. For example, a recording of inventory usage for the past week is typical internal information. Internal information generally is historical or static in nature; it is after-

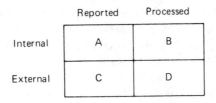

Fig. 1.7   Information matrix

the-fact data. This point is true at least in category A, information reported but not statistically processed. In the case of inventory usage, if the information is limited to prior history and no attempt is made statistically to sample or draw meaningful correlations from it, this represents internally reported data. However, if inventory usage is statistically plotted to project future usage patterns, which are used to set optimum inventory levels, it represents an example of category B or statistically processed internal information.

External information is data whose source is outside the operations of the company. An example is population growth in the market served by a company or the changes in ethnic makeup of the market. Category C reports the data but makes no attempt to analyze it statistically, and category D uses various mathematical techniques to analyze and correlate the data. A sales forecast that projects the future based on historical sales movement would be category B information, whereas a sales forecast that also includes external market statistics and trends would be a combination of B and D. The relative use of the various forms of information by a computer system is consistent with the alphabetic sequence; that is, A is found in a computer system more often than B, B is found more often than C, and C is found more often than D.

TECHNICAL DIMENSION OF INFORMATION

The concept of a data base, which is so important to a management information system, will be described in more detail in a later chapter. Simply stated, the *data base* is a unified collection of data that is utilized by the various information systems. The form, capacity, and degree of integration of the data depend on the needs to which the data is put, plus cost considerations. The technical dimensions of the data base are such elements as response time, capacity, interrelationships of data elements, security, and validity. The cost considerations involve the summation of the following three costs:

1. Cost to acquire data
2. Cost to maintain data
3. Cost to access data

Figure 1.8 describes the data-base concept, depicting three data bases or classes of data. The transaction data base includes the detailed transactions that occur in the day-to-day operation of the business, such as individual sale of items or individual receipt of inventory. These transactions are recorded against the inventory and sales files. The data at this level is voluminous and detailed. Access to the data is gained by programmers or operators whose work is dedicated to this function. Access languages are optimized for this purpose.

On the other hand, management users require only summary and cumulative information and usually not on a repetitive or instantaneous basis. Therefore the access languages are simple, easy to learn, and adaptable to intermittent use. Managers also require external data, as explained earlier, so that extractor programs are developed to move the external and transaction data into a data base accessible by management users.

The role of the system specialist in MIS will be discussed in more depth in later chapters. A few words will suffice for now. The system specialist has a major role to play in designing systems that aid the planning and control process. There is a systems expertise just as there is a financial expertise, an engineering expertise, a planning expertise, and a marketing expertise. Although it is certainly important for the system specialist to have a good understanding of the functional areas, and for the functional specialist to have a good understanding of the systems area, it is essential to distinguish between the systems and functional specialties. Too often the system specialist makes decisions that are not his prerogative to make, even if he possessed the expertise to make them. System specialists can indicate the possibilities and alternatives open to management, but it is up to management to make the decision as to what information is required to better conduct business. System specialists should avoid determining policy, the organizational structure, or the division of responsibilities within the company. The system specialist can point out the various profit margins in introducing new products; he does not decide what products to introduce. He can illustrate the potential savings of utilizing linear programming for production sched-

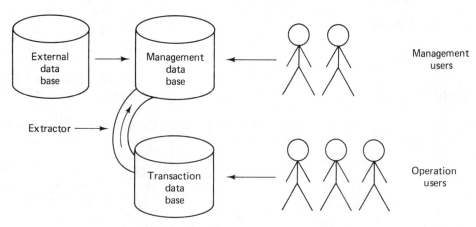

Fig. 1.8 The data-base concept

uling; he does not decide on what production control system will be implemented. The system analyst can indicate data processing benefits from a company reorganization; he is not responsible for initiating the change. Thus the company's organizational structure and the information requirements expressed by the management of the functional departments are the "givens" of system development; system design proceeds from this point.

THE SYSTEM ELEMENT

We now define the last of the three elements in management information system—the system. There are many definitions, but *Webster's Unabridged* comes fairly close to one that will suit our purposes. Webster defines system as "a set or arrangement of things so related or connected to form a unity or organization." Examples given are the solar system, an irrigation system, and supply system. Indeed, this definition is so broad that many things with which we are familiar can be termed systems. An even broader definition is suggested alternately by Webster—that a system is a regular, orderly way of doing something. For purposes of its use in management information systems, the system module of Fig. 1.9 is a useful method of describing the related things that are brought together to form a unity. The system module has the four elements of input, processing, output, and feedback/control. Every system has these four elements in common. For example, the broadest view of a manufacturing company indicates that it is a system comprised of input in the form of raw material, piece parts, and subassemblies; processing in the form of manufacturing facilities; output in the form of finished goods; and feedback/control via either internal quality control procedures or external via customer reaction.

The total economy has been viewed as an input/output matrix in a manner similar to the system module. Educational and medical institutions can be viewed as system modules with people as the prime input and output. On a more personal scale, most of us prepare our income tax returns on a systematic basis, gathering the input in the form of earnings records and deduction receipts, processing the information mathematically in accordance with preestablished rules and regulations, and producing as output the completed tax return that is mailed to the Internal Revenue Service.

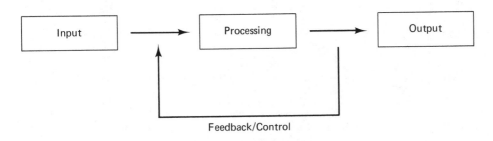

Fig. 1.9 Systems module

The feedback/control comes in the form of a notice indicating that either the mathe-matical processing is wrong or that the interpretation of the rules is in error.

Feedback/control is a very important element in system operation. Control can be automatic, such that the system is programmed to detect errors or potential errors and flag them to the operator. It is possible to correct some of the errors automati-cally based on preprogrammed logic, but others require manual intervention; the lat-ter constitute semiautomatic feedback loops. The program that doesn't encounter some foreseen or unforeseen problem during its lifetime has not yet been written. Effective system design requires careful attention to feedback/control; indeed it can be considered a separate and distinct phase of system development. Feedback/ control determines whether output measurements are outside of established toler-ances or not and, if they are, what modifications of the input will bring the output back within tolerable limits.

DISTINCTION BETWEEN BUSINESS PROCESSES AND INFORMATION SYSTEMS

Although the distinction is difficult to make, it is important to understand the differ-ence between a physical business system or process, on one hand, and an information system on the other. A *physical system* is the process itself and is concerned with the content, or "what" is going on. An *information system,* in the sense in which we shall use the term, is concerned with the form, or "how" something is being accomplished. The general schematic shown in Fig. 1.10 is a physical system that exists in an auto-mated bakery.

The dough, the principal input, enters the oven. Automatic controls continually monitor the temperature and humidity, actuating certain remedial functions if the elements fall above or below specific predetermined tolerances. This is an example of a process control system or a closed-loop industrial process. It is a physical system. For the most part, information systems try to achieve the same level of control over physical processes that are not as receptive to the closed-loop type of treatment. An example is a discrete manufacturing company as compared to a continuous-process

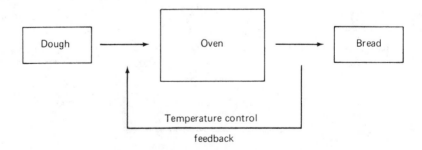

Fig. 1.10   Physical system or process

manufacturer. In discrete manufacturing, there are a number of individual work stations where raw material is fabricated and assembled into various in-process stages until a prescribed finished-goods item is produced. This differs from the process type of manufacturing, as in cement plants, petroleum companies, or bakeries, where there is a continuous process of feeding raw material in one end and obtaining a finished item at the other. An information system for a discrete manufacturer would be a production scheduling system that takes orders for particular items for a particular period of time and develops a work schedule to produce them. The information system is based on the physical facilities that are available. We have noted that the job of the system analyst is not to initiate changes in organizational structure or the information requirements of management, although he can point out the benefits of so doing. Similarly, it is not his job to initiate changes in the physical systems or processes that exist within a company. The physical systems are the givens; system analysis should concentrate on improving management control over the existing facilities and materials.

A management information system encompasses both physical and information systems. An information system can be designed to enable management to obtain a clearer view of the company's use or misuse of its facilities. It can suggest alternatives and test the potential consequences of these alternatives to improve the use of facilities. The ramifications of adding a warehouse or increasing production capacity by an additional assembly line can be better ascertained through the use of a properly designed information system. The point is not that information systems and physical systems are unrelated activities that can and should be tackled separately. Rather, the distinction is made to differentiate the role of management from that of the system analyst.

I have used the terms *physical system* and *process* interchangeably. In developing a MIS, the starting point is an understanding of the physical systems or processes that occur in a given company. Once these processes are understood and their interconnection ascertained, information systems can be developed to support the processes. The designation of the processes facilitates the breakdown of MIS into information subsystems, which we can then implement one at a time, knowing they will fit together as the phasing proceeds. It is like starting a jigsaw puzzle by filling in the border: the overall size and structure can thus be determined. Starting with the internal pieces of a jigsaw puzzle may also get you there, but it will take a bit longer. The analogy fails at this point, because starting with the pieces within MIS will never get you there.

BUSINESS PROCESSES

Figure 1.11 illustrates the business processes of a manufacturing company. It is a highly simplified schematic that suffices for our purposes here. (The processes will be described in greater detail in Chapter 3.) The boldface arrows at the bottom of Fig. 1.11 follow the physical flow of material through the factory. Raw material, piece

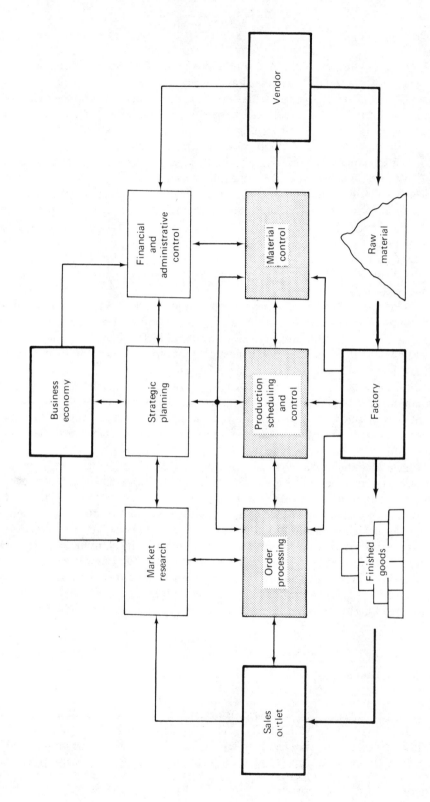

Fig. 1.11 Business processes

parts, and supplies originate from a variety of vendors and flow into the factory. Within the factory, the materials are stocked in finished stores, semifinished stores, or raw material, depending on classification and physical storage facilities. Material is then requisitioned from the inventory-holding areas to the fabrication and assembly operations necessary to turn the materials into finished products. Inspection stations at selected points in the operation check for both quantity and quality of product. Finished goods are stored in inventory areas within the main factory or in finished-goods warehouses at various locations throughout the country. As orders are received, the goods are released from the factory or warehouse and transported to the required sales outlet. Sales outlets range from large distributors to direct shipment to individual consumers.

The heavily outlined blocks (vendor, factory, sales outlet, and business economy) indicate physical entities as contrasted to the other blocks, which represent processes to control the physical flow of goods from the vendor through the factory and into the hands of the consumer. The prime business objective of a manufacturer is to facilitate this material flow in the most economical manner while satisfying customer demand to the extent that the incoming sales cash stream exceeds the outgoing cash stream. The resultant profit must produce a return on investment that meets the business goals of the company.

Turning now to the business processes that control the physical flow, the order processing process fits in at the front end. This process provides the direct contact with the sales outlets, handles the flow of orders into the factory, expedites orders, and facilitates customer payment for goods shipped. The order processing process is linked directly to the material control system. The job of material control is to ensure that there is a balanced finished-goods inventory to satisfy customer demand in the required time frame. Material control is also indirectly related to the production planning and control process. It establishes when production orders must be initiated to replenish stock levels. In addition to finished-goods inventory, the material control process controls piece parts, assemblies, raw material, and other in-process inventories. Moreover, material control is directly linked to the vendor. Items that are not manufactured must be requisitioned from outside suppliers; therefore the purchasing function is an important part of the material control process.

Production scheduling and control is undoubtedly the most significant process at the operating level. It is here that orders and forecasts for orders, which together form the gross manufacturing requirements, are screened against available stock to determine net requirements (the amount that must be produced to satisfy customer demand). Scheduling the production of net requirements while making the most economical use of the manpower, machines, and material at the company's disposal is the job of production scheduling and control. The arrows in Fig. 1.11 indicate a tie-in of production scheduling and control with the factory. This link is a most important one.

The market research process analyzes sales trends and provides both long- and short-range forecasts for the strategic planning system. The financial and administrative control process is responsible for the accounting statements of the company and plots cash positions for various time intervals. The administrative control process is responsible for the most efficient utilization of the company's personnel resources. The strategic planning process receives summary reports from the other systems, particularly market research and financial and administrative control, combines this information with that from outside sources, such as Gross National Product and political factors, and assists in making the top policy decisions for the company. These decisions include profit and budget planning, resource and capacity analysis, new product development, and general business objectives, both short and long range.

The crosshatched boxes of Fig. 1.11 represent processes that are relevant to middle- and operating-management levels. The unshaded boxes represent processes that are significant to the strategic area of operations, or mainly top management.

We have built a business model—not a mathematical model, but a process representation of what a company does. The concept of business as a system has been used to show that like any system, it is comprised of subsystems—or, in this case, business processes. It is a bit surprising that many MIS efforts begin without a thorough understanding of the business model.

ANALYSIS AND DESIGN OF INFORMATION SYSTEMS: THE DEVELOPMENT CYCLE

An assessment of the company's long-range plan, analysis of the organization, a review of what managers indicate are their information needs, the development of the business processes in the previous section, and an assessment of data-base requirements are the prerequisites of MIS development.

This section will introduce the steps in the development of the information subsystems or applications of MIS. Later chapters will deal with this cycle in detail.

Figure 1.12 illustrates the elements of systems analysis and design. The top portion indicates that application development should be in tune with the overall MIS plan, which in turn is in tune with the corporate plan. These two plans together form the "why" of MIS. At this point, application development plans materialize, as indicated by the letters A, B, and C. Each development path is similar and includes the "what" elements of specification, return on investment, and risk involved in the application's implementation. This could be termed the feasibility or "what" phase.

Next the detailed system analysis occurs, defining and breaking the application into subapplications, subprograms, and other smaller, more manageable units. The next set of activities—design, coding, and unit testing—are performed on each submodule. Then the submodules are combined and tested as one unit before being turned over to operations for productive running. These functions can be termed the "how" phase.

One important aspect of application development is the rising cost of personnel, such that procurement from an outside source becomes increasingly attractive. This is indicated in the "B" column; however, it is important that the user not abrogate his responsibility to develop the application specification and to perform final system testing.

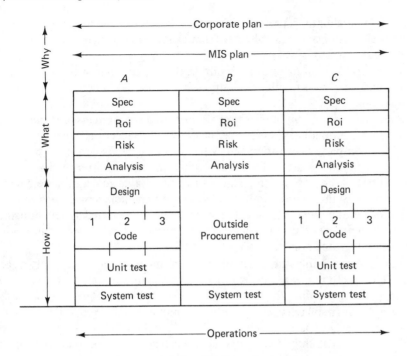

Fig. 1.12 Systems analysis and design—the development cycle

TOTAL SYSTEMS AND INTEGRATED SYSTEMS

The term management information system can be viewed in totality, now that we have defined the three words that make it up. Our earlier definition stated that MIS is a system that aids management in performing its job. Since management was defined as the planning and control of company resources to reach company objectives, MIS aids the management process. However, this is too broad a definition, which is the reason for the various categorizations of management, information, and systems made in this chapter. Too often MIS is used synonymously with the terms "total system" and "integrated system." Although a company can have a system that incorporates all three concepts, it certainly can have a system that has one concept without the other two. A total system implies that all the functional systems have been designed and implemented. Although many companies can state that they have made inroads into the major functional areas, few would even boast that they have implemented all elements of each of the functional systems listed in Fig. 1.11, not considering the functional systems that are not included. Studies of medium and large companies have shown that there is a relatively low saturation ratio of computerized applications—the saturation ratio being measured by dividing the computer time of operational applications by the running time of all existing and future applications, were they running on the computer. Survey after survey indicates that many companies have not yet tackled complete functional system areas, such as market research or financial modeling. If a prerequisite of an MIS is a total system, then there is good reason for the disillusionment with MIS that exists in many quarters today. However, MIS is not synonymous with a total system. Although it may be a long-run goal to establish a total system or at least to aim in that direction, MIS can be directed at specific functional areas with very impressive results. It is certainly not an all-or-nothing proposition.

An *integrated system* implies that all the functional systems are linked together into one entity. Individual systems may be designed to meet the needs of a restricted area of the company's operation but with the needs of the whole organization in mind. Functional areas are tackled not in isolation but only after realization of their relationship with the total system. This is a most desirable goal and represents a characteristic of MIS; however, an integrated system and a management information system are not synonymous. It is possible to develop an integrated system aimed not at the management level but at the clerical and operating levels. The result could be a completely integrated system, but not an MIS.

MIS does not imply that it aids all levels of management. Frequently a computerized MIS is taken to mean a system that reacts instantaneously to top-management requests, pouring out data that shows the status of the company at 60-second intervals in graphic form on television screens. A company can employ MIS concepts that focus on middle and operating management rather than top management. As will be shown in subsequent chapters, it may be more feasible to approach MIS from this point of view. It will also become clear that top management operates in a longer-range and more strategic framework, thus eliminating the need for real-time access to information.

CHARACTERISTICS OF MIS

It should be apparent that MIS is not an easy concept with which to deal. It can be viewed and analyzed from many sides. The first step in understanding its potential impact on business operation is to break through the semantic barriers, as we do in this chapter. This section will summarize the pertinent characteristics of MIS.

1. Management Oriented

This is the most significant characteristic of MIS. The system is designed from the top down. This does not mean that the system will be geared to providing information directly to top management; rather, it means that the system development starts from an appraisal of management needs and overall business objectives. It is possible that middle management or operating management is the focus of the system, such that their needs are the cornerstone on which the system is built.

A marketing information system is an example. Basic sales-order processing, the shipment of goods to customers, and the billing for the goods are fundamental operational control activities. However, if the system is designed properly, this transaction information can be tracked by salesman, sales territory, size of order, geography, and product line. Furthermore, if designed with strategic management needs in mind, external competition, market, and economic data can be created to give a picture of how well the company's products are faring in their marketing environment and to serve as a basis of new product or marketplace introduction. The initial application can be geared to the operational and management control areas, but in such a way as not to preclude its integration into a strategic planning subsystem for upper management.

2. Management Directed

Because of the management orientation of MIS, it is imperative that management actively direct the system development efforts. Involvement is not enough. In terms of the preceding examples, management must determine what sales information is necessary to improve its control of marketing operations.

It is rare to find an MIS where the manager himself, or a high-level representative of his department, is not spending a good deal of time in system design. It is not a one-time involvement, for continued review and participation are necessary to ensure that the implemented system meets the specifications of the system that was designed. Therefore, management is responsible for setting system specifications, and it must play a major role in the subsequent trade-off decisions that inevitably occur in system development. An important element of effective system planning is the process for determining the priority of application development. Management must control this process if a management information system is the objective. A company without a formal application approval cycle and a management steering committee to determine priorities will never develop an MIS.

3. Integrated

Although not synonymous with management information systems, the integrated concept is a necessary characteristic. Integration is significant because of the ability to produce more meaningful management information. For example, in order to develop an effective production scheduling system, we must balance such factors as (a) setup costs, (b) work force, (c) overtime rates, (d) production capacity, (e) inventory levels, (f) capital requirements, and (g) customer service. A system that ignores one of these elements—inventory level, for example—is not providing management with an optimal schedule. The cost of carrying excess inventory may more than offset the other benefits of the system. Integration, in the sense intended here, means taking a comprehensive view or a complete picture look at the interlocking subsystems that operate within a company. One can start an MIS by attacking a specific subsystem, but unless its place in the total system is realized and properly reflected, serious shortcomings may result. Thus an integrated system that blends information from several operational areas is a necessary element of MIS.

4. Common Data Flows

Because of the integration concept of MIS, there is an opportunity to avoid duplication and redundancy in data gathering, storage, and dissemination. System designers are aware that a few key source documents account for much of the information flow and affect many functional areas. For example, customer orders are the basis for billing the customer for the goods ordered, setting up the accounts receivable, initiating production activity, sales analysis, sales forecasting, and so on. It is prudent to capture this data closest to the source where the event occurs and use it throughout the functional areas. It is also prudent to capture it once and thus avoid the duplicate entry of source data into several systems. This concept also holds in building and using master files and in providing reports. The common-data-flows concept supports several of the basic tenets of system analysis—avoiding duplication, combining similar functions, and simplifying operations wherever possible.

The development of common data flows is an economically sound and logical concept, but it must be viewed in a practical and pragmatic light. Because of a company's method of operation and its internal procedures, it may be better to live with a little duplication in order to make the system acceptable and workable. MIS and integration are more important for their ability to blend the relationship of several functional areas of a business and to produce more meaningful management information, rather than for producing that information more economically. Effectiveness gets the nod over efficiency in MIS.

Given the track record and experience to date, one should look closely at the degree of integration of common data flows. Although benefits exist, the degree of difficulty is high, and many would-be implementers have failed because they underemphasized the complexity and amount of time or did not possess the necessary system-design skills. What is being questioned is not the desirability of building the concept of common data flows into the system; rather, it is the degree to which the concept is used. Building a system that cannot operate unless *all* data springs from a common data path is usually an unwise design concept—as many companies have discovered to their detriment.

5. Heavy Planning Element

Management information systems do not occur overnight; they take from three to five years and longer to get established firmly within a company. Therefore a heavy planning element must be present in MIS development. Just as a civil engineer does not design a highway to handle today's traffic but to handle the traffic five to ten years from now, so the MIS designer must have the future objectives and needs of the company firmly in mind. The designer must avoid the possibility of system obsolescence before the system gets into operation. Needless to say, sound system planning is an essential ingredient to successful MIS.

A phasing plan is an essential ingredient to MIS planning. While an enlightened management will see the future benefits from implementing systems in an integrated fashion around a data base, it can't tolerate a complete hiatus during the transition phase. Plans must include some new development while going toward the integrated new MIS. The practical philosophy is that MIS is a compass. While the final goal is never completely reached, MIS provides a meaningful direction toward which one strives. A phasing plan with intermediate benefits accruing like time capsules is an appropriate way to proceed.

6. Subsystem Concept

In tackling a project as broad and complex in scope as a management information system, one must avoid losing sight of both the forest and the trees. Even though the system is viewed as a single entity, it must be broken down into digestible subsystems that can be implemented one at a time. The breakdown of MIS into meaningful subsystems sets the stage for a prioritized implementation. Although the functional areas of sales-order processing, material control, and so on, as illustrated in Fig. 1.11, have been referred to as systems, in reality they are subsystems that, in turn, can be broken down into additional subsystems. This subsystem analysis is essential for applying boundaries to the problem, thus enabling the designer to focus on manageable entities that can be assigned and computerized by selected systems and programming teams.

7. Flexibility and Ease of Use

Despite a careful analysis of future management information needs, it is impossible to predict what is desired three to five years hence. This is true in most industries, and especially in industries with rapid change patterns. It is naive to think that anyone possesses the omniscience to predict the future.

With this as a premise, the next best thing an MIS developer can do is build in the flexibility to incorporate as many future nuances as possible. Even then, future happenings will sorely try the flexibility boundaries of the system. Building an MIS on a solid data-base foundation is a good starting point for flexibility. On the lighter, but realistic side, expect Murphy's law and Reilly's law both to occur. Murphy's law states that anything that can happen, will, and Reilly's law states that Murphy is an optimist.

A feature that often goes with flexibility is ease of use. This means the incorporation of features that make the system readily accessible to a wide range of users and easy to use once they are ready to try it. One of the major information systems trends is the broadening base of users, consistent with evolving end user languages and MIS access methods. The MIS should be able to incorporate the best of the improving user windows into the MIS data base.

8. Data Base

As explained earlier, the data base is the mortar that holds the functional systems together. Each system requires access to a master file of data covering inventory, personnel, vendors, customers, general ledger, work in process, and so on. If the data is stored efficiently and with common usage in mind, one master file can provide the data needed by any of the functional systems. It seems logical to gather data once, properly validate it, and place it on a central storage medium that can be accessed by any system. However, it is not unusual to find a company with multiple data files, one serving one functional system and another serving another system. This is obviously not the most efficient way to operate. Data-base concepts will be discussed thoroughly in a subsequent chapter. Although it is remotely possible to achieve the basic objectives of MIS without a data base, thus paying the price of duplicate storage and duplicate file updating, more often than not the data base is the sine qua non of management information systems.

9. Distributed Data Processing

The majority of companies implementing MIS have a geographic network of sales offices, distribution points, manufacturing plants, divisions, subdivisions, and so on. Some of these entities are operated in a completely independent fashion and therefore may not be a part of the integrated MIS. More often than not, the remote sites do have a connection with each other and with a host operation. In order to create an effective MIS with geographic boundaries, some form of distributed data processing (DDP) is necessary. DDP will be covered in a later chapter, but for now it means that two or more information subsystems in different locations act in a cooperative fashion. This is a simple definition for a concept that is vital to effective MIS. DDP can be thought of as the delivery system, placing information in the hands of those who need it when they need it. Teleprocessing, networking, or just plain communication systems are an important part of DDP, and DDP is an important part of MIS.

10. Information as a Resource

Chapter 2 will discuss the information resource management (IRM) concept. Suffice it to state here that in MIS, IRM is an overriding philosophy. Pervading the entire organization must be the concept that information is a valuable resource, particularly in the management control and strategic planning areas, and must be properly managed. This is a subtle but important change in thinking. It was common in the past to view data processing as an entity into itself doing its own thing. The new outlook is that data processing, MIS, is more than a support for the business; in many instances it is inextricably bound up in the business itself. One of the manifestations of IRM is that MIS will have a higher reporting relationship in the organization and will become more a part of its executive committee.

SUMMARY

In order to put the concept of a management information system into proper context, this chapter has presented an analytical framework from which to view the subject. Each term in the word has been discussed, and various categorizations have been made. Three levels of management were distinguished, and the salient job characteristics and responsibilities of top, middle, and operating management were contrasted. Information was viewed from the business dimension and the technical dimension. The types of information required by the three management levels were discussed.

A basic system module introduced the discussion of different types of systems. A physical system or process was distinguished from an information system with the statement that the system analyst is responsible for the information and not the physical system. The development of a business entity comprised of processes was developed using a manufacturing company as a model. The steps in developing an information system were presented, beginning with the establishment of a system specification and ending with the actual programming and testing of the programs. This development cycle will be presented in more detail later in the book. Finally MIS was compared to the total system and integrated system. Ten basic characteristics of MIS completed the chapter.

The chapter established the viewpoint and perspective of MIS, introducing and defining the elements that will be explored in later chapters. Because of the heavy dependence of subsequent chapters on this one, the reader should have a good understanding of the analytical framework described here before proceeding.

CASE STUDIES

EXPERIENCE OF A SMALL INTEGRATED
STEEL COMPANY*

Several years ago, we came to the conclusion that any company big enough to afford a computer that does not have one either functioning or in its planning for the immediate future is not going to grow in the competitive business world of today. Everything we've learned during our first year as a computer user has served to reinforce that conviction.

If we were willing to spend the money, we could manually prepare most of the reports our computer is giving us today.

*From "A Small Company Turns to the Computer" by Daniel A. Roblin, Jr., *Management Thinking*, Harvard Business School Association.

Five years from now this will not be true. We will then have a management information system pervading all phases of our corporate activity, and we will be achieving the growth and earnings objectives we have set for ourselves, which we could not hope to achieve without the computer.

A small company dedicated to growth thus can utilize the benefits of a computer more fully and in a shorter period of time than a large complex corporation. The complete management information system we are installing here, for example, will be accomplished in five years or less.

To ensure that the computer has no adverse effect on the company and to hasten its full utilization, it is necessary to properly indoctrinate all of the management group to its use. The procedure is the same as the indoctrination program after the purchase of a new piece of sophisticated machinery. You have a training program for those who are to be involved with it. The only difference is that in this case the computer is a tool that is used by the whole management group, not by just a handful of operating people, so the whole management group is included in the educational programs.

Prior to the installation of the computer we began our indoctrination program with a three-day seminar at Cornell University for our whole management group to discuss what we hoped to accomplish with our new computer. We then formed a committee of operating people who analyzed every piece of paper in the use of the entire corporation. After the committee completed its work, we held a second seminar to talk about what we had accomplished in the course of that year—but no longer were we talking about just a computer. We were talking now about our business, its progress, and its goals. At this second seminar, we introduced the management information system concept, explaining that such a system had always existed, but in a very crude form. All of those pieces of paper we had worked with every day were part of this system; for that matter, information written on a paper napkin would be part of it.

We try to manage this business by objectives. In order for us to do this, management people must make commitments on how they are going to operate each unit of the company. The computer is beginning to play a big part in helping them to set these goals and to reach them.

For example, one new plant manager faced with setting his standards for the year was able to make a massive analysis of past operations to secure some particular data he felt he needed that would have been impossible to get with our old tab equipment. Furthermore, with some corrections and revisions, this same system is helping him now to attain his objectives by supplying him with a weekly status report. Soon he may be able to have updated information on a daily basis as part of our complete management information system.

In another instance, the sales department was able to use a very detailed sales analysis of past performance provided by the computer to predict what they will sell to each customer this year, not just in dollar volume, but by product, broken down by specific chemistry and size. This in turn permitted our manufacturing people and purchasing people, who formerly had to base their cost objectives on groups of products, to determine more accurately the specific alloys they will require and the amount of material they will have to produce in various sizes, and therefore to forecast more accurately what the cost of sales will be. The more accurately you can predict, the more effectively your costs can be reduced.

Because we do measure management people by their performance relative to the objectives they themselves have set, they also determine what information they want and what the computer can do to help them. Manufacturing applications, for example, are developed by manufacturing people assisted by the people in the computer department—and not the other way around.

I do not know what possibilities we will uncover in the future, when more data becomes available. We are contemplating a complete random access system, with terminals in all of our operating departments. I foresee people, for example, in order processing, production scheduling, or sales, with a computer inquiry station at their desks being able to press a button when a customer calls and have instantly displayed all information needed to give an immediate answer to questions about delivery, pricing, and so on.

I can envision a computer-controlled continuous steelmaking process in which a scrapped automobile will go in at one end of a plant and a finished steel product will come out the other end. It is possible that this kind of thinking eventually will cause a complete revision of the operating systems we have now.

As my function is more planning and looking to the future, I do not need information in the detail or with the frequency that people involved in making our day-to-day decisions do. But I would like to have on my desk each morning a summary report of corporate activities up through the day before—cash balance, accounts receivable, accounts payable, shipments, production, and the like—for each segment of the business. This can not happen for a long time, of course, but eventually it will be possible.

STUDY QUESTIONS

1. How important is an information system that can grow along with the company—will it take five years to develop?

2. Do you think it relevant that members of the management group drifted from just talking about a computer and started discussing business goals and objectives?

3. Do you see indications that the computer is becoming woven into the basic fabric of the company's operation—is this the correct approach?

4. Do you think the view of the future is realistic in light of the company's experience and viewpoint to date?

HARRIS MANUFACTURING INC.

Harris Manufacturing Inc. with four plants, sixteen assembly departments, about that many fabricating centers, and more than 200 machine centers has installed an integrated information system.

The operations are characterized by a nationwide distribution network. The product moves through 38 branch offices and 312 authorized distributors—all of which maintain some inventory. Authorized distributors generate 37 percent of the orders but account for only 24 percent of the sales. Most of the business is done through the branch offices.

The product line is large. Products are classified into 176 family groups, representing 12,000 finished goods (listed in catalog), of which 3600 are carried in inventory and 8400 are made to order. Approximately 1500 new items enter the product line annually, and a similar number are discontinued.

These 12,000 finished goods require 25,000 component parts, of which 6600 are carried in inventory and 18,400 are made to order.

The integrated system already has paid off substantially, and refinements continue to increase the benefits. In the seventies, Harris was achieving an 80 percent customer service level (i.e., 80 percent of the orders were being delivered according to original customer requests with no delays or adjusting of dates). The sales/inventory ratio was a respectable 4.2. However, the production-cost variance averaged 16.3 percent. Clerical expenses ran 3.6 percent of sales.

This was not good enough in a highly competitive business. Since the primary asset a company has (in addition to high-quality, reliable products) is customer service, an improvement in customer service was given top priority.

Three areas of cost control also were given high priority:

1. Production costs must be controlled within tight tolerances. This is especially true in a business where prices are negotiable at field sales level.
2. Distribution costs, especially those associated with a nationwide disbursement of inventory, must be controlled within reasonable limits relative to needs for customer service.
3. Clerical costs in a growing business must be contained, and if possible reduced.

A computerized integrated management information and control system was instituted. By the early eighties performance in the four areas of high priority was greatly improved.

1. *Customer service.* Fully 97 percent of orders were filled as requested, a substantial improvement.
2. *Inventory turnover.* The sales/inventory ratio was 6.2, a 50 percent increase over the previous performance. More improvement was expected.
3. *Production-cost variance.* This category had all but disappeared, being controlled within a 1 percent tolerance. This was possible because timely, accurate information now was available when needed.
4. *Clerical expense.* The ratio of clerical expenses had dropped to 2.8 percent, an unusual achievement in a rapidly growing business that had to face increasing rates of clerical labor.

STUDY QUESTIONS

1. Are you impressed with the improvements in customer service, inventory turnover, production-cost variance, and clerical expense?

2. Do you think all these improvements can be related to the MIS?

3. Which areas would be more affected by the integrated approach?

4. Do you think these gains could be achieved if a company were not growing and expanding?

5. Do you know of any situations where the results of MIS were measured?

6. Which activity areas were the focus of MIS—operational control, management control, or strategic planning? Do you agree with the emphasis?

7. How would you go about evaluating the benefits of MIS? Are there reliable and realistic measurement yardsticks?

BIBLIOGRAPHY

Anthony, R. N., *Planning and Control Systems: A Framework for Analysis.* Cambridge, MA: Division of Research, Graduate School of Business Administration, Harvard University, 1965.

Churchill, N. C., J. H. Kempster and M. Uretsky, *Computer-Based Information Systems for Management—A Survey.* New York: National Association for Accountants, 1968.

Guilbaud, *What Is Cybernetics?* New York: Grove Press, Inc., 1959.

Optner, Stanford L., *Systems Analysis for Business Management.* Englewood Cliffs, NJ: Prentice-Hall, Inc., 1960.

Chapter **2**

Information Resource Management

This chapter will focus on the concept of information resource management, a subtle but important shift in the way MIS is viewed within a company. This change is characterized by the progression of titles under which the MIS function has operated. In the fifties the department head of MIS was called a *computer manager* or *computer center manager*. This implied that the central focus was the computer and that the manager was the custodian of this new electronic device. In the sixties the term data processing came into vogue, and the manager was called the *manager of data processing* or *manager of electronic data processing* (EDP): now the department was called by the function it performed rather than the principal device that performed it. The late sixties brought increasing use of the word *system*, an acknowledgement that an EDP department was comprised of more than a computer and that indeed the principal tool being managed was a system. A system consisted of a computer, but also a host of input and output equipment, storage devices, software, applications, and the people that make the whole thing work. The emphasis shifted from the computer to the system.

The seventies ushered in the term *information* as opposed to *data*. Data is defined as raw numbers and files; thus, to be useful to management, data must be processed into meaningful information. The term *information systems* more closely characterized the function performed by the computer or EDP manager. To this term, the word *management* was then appended. Though MIS groups did exist in the sixties, the concept really took hold in the seventies. This addition of the word management was significant, because it indicated a heretofore missing element in the equation. It was becoming apparent that information systems were falling short of their objectives because of a lack of top and user management involvement and a lack of management perspective in operating information systems departments. MIS today is a valid and meaningful term, placing emphasis on the elements that are the most significant.

The eighties brought a further shift to a new and imposing term— information resource management. *Management* and *information* remain, but *system* has been replaced by *resource*. The concept is that information should be treated as a resource the same as the more traditional ones of money, material, facilities, and people. MIS, powered by sophisticated computer hardware and software with responsive communication to and from a variety of remote terminals to an integrated data base, has reached the stage where information has become a valuable—or perhaps invaluable—resource in maintaining a competitive business. Whether the head of the IRM function is called an MIS director, an IRM director, or just the CIO (chief information officer), the concept is the same: that of viewing information as a valuable company resource and planning and controlling that resource with the same concern as cash and facilities.

Along with the evolutionary title change of MIS, the role of MIS within the organizational hierarchy has been elevated. Starting from a reporting position within the controller's function, the MIS operation now reports to the financial or administrative vice-president, to an executive vice-president, or directly to the president.

The title, too, has gradually evolved from manager to director to vice-president. The realization that information is a resource has brought the acknowledgement that its manager should be on the same level as managers of other equivalent resources.

MIS STAGES THEORY

Richard Nolan, the head of a successful consulting firm, has developed a staging theory to explain how companies have evolved their MIS function over the years. The premise is that companies progress through six stages of growth, each stage being characterized by unique elements. Adapted over the years, the stages theory now provides a framework that works surprisingly well for most companies. The companies I have consulted for over the past five years bear this out. The stages-theory approach is useful in analyzing where a company is in its MIS evolution, where it appears to be headed, and the management practices required to make the evolution most effective. It also points out mistakes made in previous stages that should be avoided in future stages.

Figure 2.1 represents my adaptation of the stages theory. The horizontal axis lists the stages of growth, the vertical axis the elements or essence of that growth. The curved line represents the MIS budget over the six stages. The shape of the curve will become more meaningful as the stages are explained, but it is roughly S-shaped, with budgets rising rapidly during stages 1 and 2, leveling off in stage 3, rising steeply again in stage 4, and beginning to level again in stages 5 and 6.

Stage 1 begins with a company's purchase of a computer system. Since most medium to large companies already have computer systems, this stage is history as far as the majority are concerned. A company may, however, start a new division or purchase a new company that does not have a computerized information system. If the lessons learned from the stages discussion are not heeded, it is possible to go through the entire painful cycle again; indeed, reinventing the wheel remains a popular pastime with many.

Stage 2, contagion, involves a rapid proliferation of applications without a growth plan or a controlled framework. Most companies proceeded through this stage in the late fifties or early sixties, when unbridled technical excitement and management laxity permitted proliferation of computers and applications, only some of which were directed at areas of real payoff.

Stage 3 usually begins with a management awareness that their computer systems are out of control, that computer budgets are growing at a rate of 30 to 40 per-

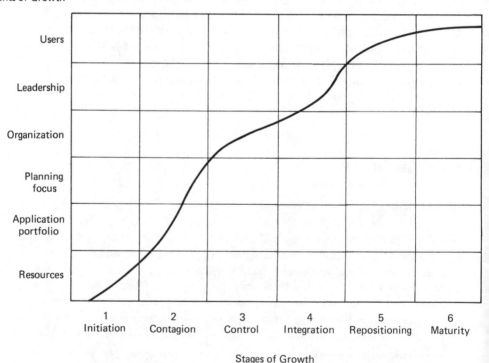

Fig. 2.1 The stages theory (Adapted from Richard Nolan's stages theory)

cent a year and more, and that the return on investment is in serious question. A period of free-wheeling or what Nolan calls "management slack" is replaced by a period of strict control, often so strict that it is damaging to future growth. Somehow out of stage 3 the realization emerges that applications have not been aimed at the management levels and that those aimed at the operational control areas lack the required responsiveness and flexibility.

Stage 4 initiates a retooling and a redesign of applications to the on-line responsive mode, built around an integrated data base; thus this stage is called integration. Another rapid budget buildup occurs because of the massive retooling required. Stage 4 establishes the foundation of the previously described concept of information as a resource and leads to what is called the repositioning stage, where a major change occurs in the role of MIS. The management process and responsiveness to users are emphasized over technical expertise.

Finally a utopian stage 6, termed maturity, is realistically striven for but never really attained. Nolan originally depicted four stages, which over time became six. While the six stages described here appear more realistic than the original, it may well be that they eventually become eight. It is difficult to predict the cycles of a discipline, the commercial history of which spans only thirty years. In general, stages 1 and 2 can be viewed as where MIS has come from, stages 3 and 4 as where it is, and stages 5 and 6 as where it is headed. We turn now to the elements of growth within the six stages.

ELEMENTS OF GROWTH

The first element of growth refers to the MIS resources a particular company employs. Figure 2.2 brings out that in the early stages, the principal storage device is tape and secondary storage disk, but even with disk the prevailing mode is sequential. The computer system operates on one application at a time, starting with a single-shift operation, but as applications grow in stage 2, round-the-clock operation is more the norm. In stages 3 and 4, the major resource is a large, centrally based computer system. Stage 3 still employs large tape files, but as the need for fast response increases, on-line disk files become the predominant storage vehicle. Stages 5 and 6 usher in the concept of distributed data processing (DDP), where the processing work is off-loaded from the central mainframe to a bevy of off-site mini- and microcomputer systems and terminals. DDP represents one of the most significant industry trends. Generally speaking, computing resources, the major concern and focus of early stages thinking, give way to the other growth elements in later stages.

One of the principal benchmarks of the stage a company is in is its application portfolio. During the early stages, applications are batch oriented; that is, transactions are collected and grouped before they are processed. In stages 3 and 4, the evolution is most definitely toward on-line applications built around an integrated data base. Transactions are processed as they occur rather than being batched and processed after the transaction. Stages 5 and 6 still maintain some batch applications (it will probably always be more efficient and effective to process certain applications in a batch mode), but the predominant mode is on-line.

Another dimension of the application portfolio is activity focus. During stages 1 and 2, applications are developed from the bottom up and focus on operational control activities, the basic lower-level operational tasks. During stages 3 and 4 the focus shifts to management control applications, as on-line data from an integrated data base permits applications that aid management in controlling the operation tasks. Cumulative, summary, and exception information are used in this process. Finally, in stages 5 and 6, data external to the company is combined with internal historical data to provide application assistance to upper and strategic management levels.

The third element of growth is the planning focus, where the stages are characterized by a progressively longer-term planning horizon. During stages 1 and 2, applications are developed one at a time on the basis of short-term opportunity, rather than that of relative priority and fit with an overall, longer-term strategy. The planning perspective shifts from a three- to a nine-month horizon during stages 1 and 2, to twelve to 24 months during stages 3 and 4, to three to five years in stages 5 and 6. Also, stages 5 and 6 mark the beginning of the change of emphasis from the computer

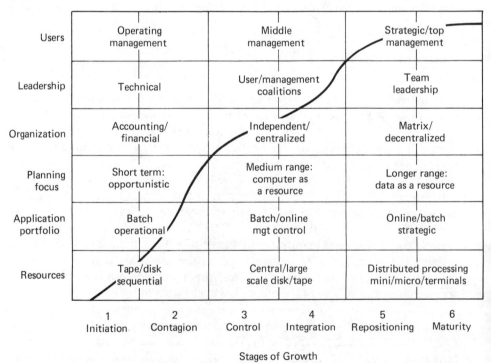

Elements of Growth

	1 Initiation	2 Contagion	3 Control	4 Integration	5 Repositioning	6 Maturity
Users	Operating management		Middle management		Strategic/top management	
Leadership	Technical		User/management coalitions		Team leadership	
Organization	Accounting/ financial		Independent/ centralized		Matrix/ decentralized	
Planning focus	Short term: opportunistic		Medium range: computer as a resource		Longer range: data as a resource	
Application portfolio	Batch operational		Batch/online mgt control		Online/batch strategic	
Resources	Tape/disk sequential		Central/large scale disk/tape		Distributed processing mini/micro/terminals	

Stages of Growth

Fig. 2.2 The stages theory (Adapted from Richard Nolan's stages theory)

as a resource to information as a resource. This latter concept will be elaborated on throughout the chapter.

The fourth growth element refers to the organizational positioning of the MIS function. In the early stages the function resided under the accounting or financial arm. The computer was considered an adjunct to existing accounting and bookkeeping machines and as such became part of the controller's bailiwick. This rather natural but shortsighted view is changed in stages 3 and 4, where MIS spins off from the controller, evolves into an independent activity, and is given full department status. The function is highly centralized, with systems analysts, programmers, and operators reporting directly to the MIS director. They may be doing work for specific operating departments, but they are part of the MIS department. In stages 5 and 6 a shift to a decentralized, matrix style of organization occurs. With the trend to distributed data processing, operating departments become much more involved in MIS. At this stage, it makes sense to assign systems analysts to specific operating departments, reporting on either a straight- or dotted-line basis. It may be that control of MIS operations (running the hardware and software) remains under the MIS director; more often than not, however, application development becomes the responsibility of the department employing the application.

The fifth growth element refers to leadership style. During stages 1 and 2, technical leadership is prevalent. Computers are complex, highly technical devices and must be managed by people with the requisite technical skills. However, concomitant with the other change elements, users and top management become more aware of MIS impact and seek more involvement in managing it. MIS directors realize they can't completely manage the expanding scope of activity and take on a consultant role rather than direct management. Often the initial involvement by users is a reactive one, fueled by disappointment with the service or response level and the increasing application backlog built up by the central MIS organization. During stages 5 and 6, however, team leadership evolves to a point where users, top management, and MIS management jointly determine strategy and establish implementation priorities; the *we* and *they* is replaced by *us*.

Finally, the sixth growth element portrays the change in the principal users of MIS. This element is a natural by-product of the other growth factors. As data is integrated and applications focus on management control and strategic areas of the business, progressively higher-level managers become interested and dependent on system output. At this stage, the upper levels of management not only are receiving the results of MIS but are actively engaged in specifying their individual information needs—in many instances initiating and directing a particular system themselves.

Dick Nolan's stages theory presents a useful perspective by which to synthesize the changes that have been and are taking place in MIS. Some professional MIS observers see the stages a company goes through not as six, but as two alternating cycles of growth and control or ingestion and digestion. In whatever way the cycle is viewed, it is generally agreed that those companies employing the style and practices of the later stages will have the more effective MIS operation. A key lesson to follow is to build in a greater degree of planning and control during periods of rapid growth, so that integration and repositioning can evolve more naturally and effectively. The greater the fragmentation, the more difficult it will be to achieve control and integration—elements that are necessary prerequisites to information resource management.

THE CHANGING NATURE OF THE MIS DIRECTOR'S JOB

Though this book focuses on MIS from the user or developer viewpoint, we should also consider the characteristics of the MIS director's job, the MIS organization, and the people who work in the MIS department.

It has been said that the growing demands on the MIS director have created an impossible job description that only a superperson can fulfill. The preceding section described the evolving nature of the job and hinted at its pressures. The MIS director thus finds himself in a challenging, if not precarious, position within his company. He must understand the challenge and tackle it effectively in order to survive. The prominent writers on this subject—Withington of A. D. Little, "Coping With Computer Proliferation," Nolan of Nolan, Norton & Company, "Managing The Crisis In Data Processing," and Rockart of MIT, "Critical Success Factors For The Information Systems Executive," have all focused on this topic.

To my thinking it is a survival issue, with MIS directors facing the most crucial crossroad of their careers. The reason is that most MIS directors have exploited their technical and professional MIS skills in arriving where they are. What they need at this point are managerial, organizational, and strategic skills. The user coalitions, often supported by top management, have been waiting in the wings, repressing their hostility; and now they have reemerged, waving the industry-accepted banner of distributed data processing. It is a bit uncomfortable to be forced away from one's strengths to deal with the opposition on unfamiliar terrain. But that is exactly the challenge for the MIS director. The issues are not technical; they involve strategy, planning, organization, human communication, and leadership.

TWO-CULTURE MILIEU

I was privileged to hear C. P. Snow discuss the two-culture milieu concept in the Godkin lectures he delivered at Harvard in the early sixties. Snow, an Englishman trained in physics with a doctorate from Cambridge, was a scientist and worked in a variety of government agencies; he also was a prolific author, writing more than a dozen novels. He was knighted in 1957 and died in 1980. He was a man for many seasons.

Figure 2.3 illustrates his basic concept: a continued confrontation between the scientist and the humanist. He referred, for example, to the decision on strategic

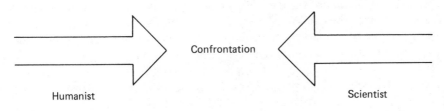

Two-culture milieu

Fig. 2.3

bombing in World War II, wherein the thinking was that bombing a city's population centers as well as its military and support centers would remove the will of the people to resist. This thinking proved to be incorrect. Snow used this issue to show the danger inherent when a prime minister (in this case Winston Churchill) relies almost completely on a single scientific source (F. A. Lindemann) on which to base a complex technical decision with such far-reaching effects. Snow elaborated on the necessity for the humanist and scientist to reach the proper level of communication and understanding.

The two-culture milieu is most appropriate in discussing the role of the MIS director versus that of the general manager. Often, the MIS group develops a culture of its own that is inconsistent with that of the company in which the function resides. This can prove most dangerous, because it is the generalist who must make the final decision. An MIS director, proceeding without management awareness and concurrence, particularly on major strategic issues, can run blindly into disaster. Pursuing a course of innovation and risk taking in a company that is in a cash bind and a cost-cutting mode, for example, will soon lead to the confrontation suggested in Fig. 2.3. In accordance with the C. P. Snow philosophy, the outcome will be far from desirable.

At this point it is pertinent to look at the type of people who form the MIS culture. The MIS director must be aware of the types of people he or she is dealing with and must apply leadership and direction to blend that culture with the culture of the company.

Several studies suggest that MIS people are a bit different from the operating people whom they serve. Gerry Richardson, an industrial psychologist from Denver, administered a test to 6000 people (half MISers, half others) over an eight-year period. The general profile of MISers indicates they are more cool and impersonal, more serious and reserved, more persevering, more dogmatic, and more perceptive. Other generalizations drawn from the profile show the MISer as preferring to be aloof, accustomed to dealing in precise and exact terms, and preoccupied with detail. The question arises as to the MISer's loyalty to his company versus that to his profession; evidence points to a greater loyalty to the profession. Also the MISer likes to work on things he considers challenging and advanced in nature.

A study reported by J. Daniel Couger of the University of Colorado brings out that MISers have a low social need strength (SNS) and a high growth need strength

(GNS). The implication of the low SNS is that MISers do not feel the need to meet or communicate with their fellow MISers and particularly the users whom they serve. They may not be prone to develop the important interfaces and relationships that are so important to successful systems development and implementation. The high GNS implies a need for strong personal accomplishment and the avoidance of anything that gets in the way. This develops a low tolerance level for meetings and discussion with users. Attending meetings is a good way to fill social needs, but since MISers have a low social need, they have a dual barrier against meetings.

I was involved myself in such a survey of character and personality traits of MISers and emerged with similar observations. This situation presents a real challenge to MIS leadership. The following approaches may reduce the potential for conflict of MISers and users.

Rotation of MIS-User Personnel

One of the best remedies is the interchange of people within the MIS and operating areas of a company. It makes good sense to staff the MIS department with personnel from operating departments who show an aptitude and an interest for systems work. Similarly, systems analysts should receive a tour of duty outside of MIS, in order to appreciate the problems of the actual business world and understand the difficulties of putting an advanced new system into productive operation.

This rotation of people must not become a way of dumping the marginal performers within a department. Management should recognize the long-term benefit of transferring proven performers in key support departments such as MIS. Many companies have filled key MIS management positions with individuals with records of success in operating departments who possess a system outlook but lack direct computer experience. Transfer of people from MIS to key operating department positions should also be encouraged.

Education and Training

Professor Couger feels that the SNS and GNS factors can be balanced by larger doses of human and organizational behavior courses in the MIS curriculum in colleges and universities. He suggests a program stressing the importance of interpersonal and group behavior skills and also the development of courses or laboratories where students majoring in human and organizational behavior would interact and have joint projects with MIS students.

I concur, and I suggest that this approach also be followed within a company. MIS people should be trained in organizational behavior and should attend the same courses with users. They should also be trained in specific business areas outside the MIS functions, as users should be trained in MIS subjects.

Interarea Activities

Whenever possible, MIS and operating personnel should be assimilated in everyday business activities. At conferences, work sessions, or business get-togethers, the groups should be encouraged to work together and to take every opportunity to discuss and explore things together. If possible, MIS people and operating people should travel together, engage in social activities together, and develop an awareness of each other's standpoint on business matters. Most people are prone to stay with employees of their own department and to discuss matters with people of similar background. Following this tendency does nothing to facilitate the understanding and resolution of problems; it merely reinforces one's predetermined judgments. Another opportunity to work together is presented by special projects that require interdisciplinary participation. Mutual confidence and respect are built up when a task is accomplished by such a group.

INFORMATION RESOURCE MANAGEMENT

John Diebold coined the term *information resource management (IRM)* in explaining the concept that information is a valuable and costly asset that must be preserved, protected, controlled, and planned as are other valuable assets within the corporation, such as money, material, facilities, and people. This may not seem like anything new, but the fact is that companies have not treated information with this perspective.

The Diebold Research Program report (No. 187545) on the Administration of Information Resources states that "The ultimate goal of IRM is to put in place mechanisms (the IRM program itself) to enable the company to acquire or produce the data and information it needs, of sufficient quality, accuracy and timeliness, and with minimum cost. This is accomplished by creating conditions whereby all levels of the organization come to look upon information not as a free good, but rather as a costly and valued asset that must be treated with the same management discipline as is currently afforded financial assets, human resources, material assets and other resources the company utilizes to achieve its aims. In so doing, a major shift from a preoccupation and focus on the power of the technologies, to a focus on the power of the information content, must occur."

The Diebold report goes on to point out the similarities between information as a resource and other corporate assets or resources.

- It possesses fundamental value, as does money, capital goods, labor, or raw materials (e.g., a mineral such as coal).
- It has identifiable and measurable characteristics such as method, difficulty, and cost of acquisition; purpose for which used (utility); and different forms and media by which generated, handled, and processed.

- It comes in various degrees of "purity" and utility.
- It must be refined and processed in order to enhance its value.
- It passes through many hands that transport and exchange it from point of collection, to point of enhancement, to point of use.
- Synthetic substitutes are available—some cheaper, some more expensive.
- Information functions can be integrated vertically by buying and processing raw materials. Alternately, costs can be cut by buying processed materials.
- Consumption of the resource can be either expensed or capitalized, depending on management's goals.
- It is an expenditure for which standard costs can be developed and cost accounting techniques employed to help control outlays.
- A cost/benefit equation is possible at each point in collection, handling, enhancement, dissemination, and so forth, which helps manage the efficiency and effectiveness of utilization.
- A variety of deployment choices are available to management in making trade-offs between different "grades," types, and prices.

The report sees the IRM concept and function as important enough to warrant a separate corporate information officer, who would have the responsibility for establishing policies and procedures concerning the information resource. Policies would include a statement of the company's attitude and view of the information it collects, processes, and produces, a procedure to indicate who should have access to different classes of information, the methods of safeguarding and protecting the confidentiality of information against physical disaster, sabotage, or fraud, and an expression of the rights of different groups to information, such as an employee's right to see his own personnel file or a government's right to specific information.

While these issues are real, I do not see the need for a separate information officer or group to oversee this process. I think the MIS director has the responsibility to view information as a resource and incorporate the necessary measures within his operation. Setting up a separate entity in an already complex MIS world is, to my way of thinking, counterproductive. IRM is too fundamental a concept and too integral to the operation of MIS to be embodied in an outside agency.

Figure 2.4 illustrates the role of information in company operations alongside that of money, people, facilities, and material. The concept of looking at a business as a system has been covered earlier. In this illustration, raw material and piece parts are fabricated and assembled into whatever products the company produces. The product process utilizes the necessary resources owned by the company. During the planning phase for any new product, an assessment is made of the resources' availability, cost, and adequacy. More often than not, a similar assessment of the information resource is lacking—and I have seen situations where products were seriously delayed as a consequence. The point is that information is a resource of the company and MIS has become part of the business rather than just supporting it. Information must be considered in planning any major company changes.

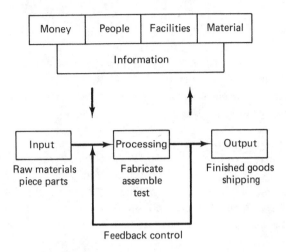

Fig. 2.4 Information as a resource

SCOPE OF INFORMATION RESOURCE MANAGEMENT

The concept of IRM broadens the conventional definition of MIS. In reality only a small fraction of the information used throughout a corporation is under the control of MIS, as MIS has traditionally been understood. Information more broadly conceived includes the letters and memos typed by secretaries, the copying process, the mailroom, telephone service, manuals and catalogs, files and records, and so on. Many firms are using this broader definition to reorganize functions within the company. The thinking is that management of information should not be confined to that portion that is currently in electronic form. The full benefit of integration is not realized unless all information is managed as an entity.

Significant efficiencies can be achieved by optimizing the total flow of information. A simple example should illustrate the point. An executive writes a report, which is typed, edited, corrected, copied, and sent to twenty people within the company. Each recipient has a different time frame in which the information is valid, so each reads and/or files the report for later reference according to his or her need. If the report were produced initially in electronic media, it could be accessed by each executive on a need-to-know basis. When called for, the report could be delivered electronically over a communication line either as hard copy or as a video display. Teleconferencing, too, can be used to augment the communication process. The point is that by integrating and coordinating all the information and its communication, we can make it both more effective and more efficient.

Mobil Oil Corporation is experimenting with this type of organization and presented a model (Fig. 2.5) at a conference sponsored by Business Week in early 1981. A typical MIS organization performs the duties in the boxes entitled System Support

Services, Planning Controls and Technology, and Processing Services (sometimes not including text processing). Though some MIS groups have a few of the information responsibilities listed under Communications and Distribution Services, Reprographics Services, and Records Services, usually these are separate entities managed by other organizations. However, there is much to commend in a plan that phases these functions under the MIS director. The concept of IRM broadens the scope of MIS and causes a healthy rethinking of what constitutes information and how it should be controlled.

This integration has come to be called the *convergence of technologies.* James McKenney and Warran McFarlan, writing in *Harvard Business Review,* termed it the *information archipelago,* the three islands that comprise it being data processing, communication, and office automation. These started as individual islands or entities within a company, often controlled and managed under separate departments. The authors state their case for providing bridges or links to connect these islands

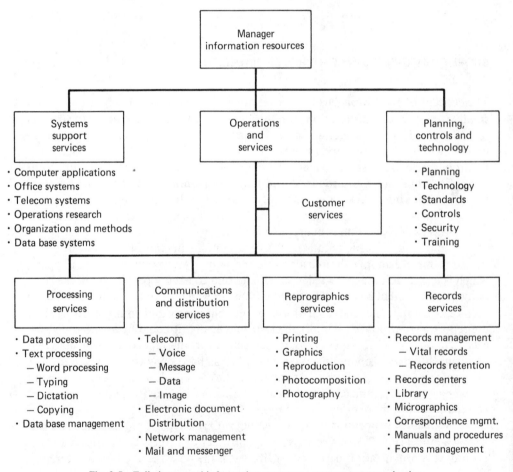

Fig. 2.5 Fully integrated information resources management organization

because they must play an integrated role within the operation of a business. Whether they fall under the same direct management is less important than whether plans, controls, and general management of the functions are integrated by cross-function standards, policy, and strategy.

CRITICAL SUCCESS FACTORS

John Rockart, director of MIT's Center for Information System Research, has written extensively about a concept he calls *critical success factors (CSF)*. By analyzing a variety of companies and executives, he has found that a relatively few elements determine whether a particular company or executive will be successful. CSF's are those key areas where high performance is necessary to achieve personal and company goals. For example:

School of Business Management
1. Quality faculty
2. Quality students
3. Reputation

Supermarket Company
1. Product mix
2. Inventory
3. Sales promotion
4. Pricing

Dr. Rockart's objective is to enable the MIS director to understand what is important to executive MIS users and then to develop the information systems to measure, control, and support CSF achievement. It is a top-down approach to defining information needs.

Further research analyzed CSF's for the MIS director. Dr. Rockart interviewed directors who, by company and industry standards, were considered highly successful. The objective was to bring out those elements or characteristics that appeared to produce success. Synthesis of the data indicates what the nine successful MIS directors thought was important to them. The following is my interpretation and summary of Dr. Rockart's study. In general, the successful MIS director is a business manager, a leader who is aware and concerned with the business, is politically astute in dealing with top management and user management, and recognizes the concepts of information resource management. He is more marketing oriented than production oriented and begins to promote MIS services through newsletters, annual reports, and the like, taking in general a more outward or proactive approach.

1. *Customer service*
   - Perception by users is the key.
   - Mechanisms installed to influence perception (user performance index, independent audit, user sign-off, complaint box).

- Spends increasing amount of time with users.
- Possible charge-out system based on customer-understood and oriented method (charge per transaction or report).

2. *User relations/communications*
   - Knows customers, their CSF's, corporate political leanings, etc.
   - User/top management involvement in setting application priorities.
   - Viewed as a leader.
   - Develops clear, concise user interfaces and respective responsibilities.

3. *People resource*
   - Ensures maximum utilization of this high-quality component.
   - Attention to career development and training.
   - Emphasizes management/business focus.
   - Interchanges people with line departments.
   - Controls turnover.

4. *Repositioning of MIS*
   - Reports to president or very high in organization.
   - Views himself as a manager versus a technician.
   - Sees a constantly evolving structure; more responsibility to users.
   - Focuses on effectiveness versus efficiency.

A COMPANY WITHIN A COMPANY

An earlier chapter indicated that activities within a business conform to a triangle (see Fig. 1.1) with the layers of operational control, management control, and strategic planning. Using this focus to describe the MIS function, the operational control activities cover the gathering of input, the processing of data through the computer shop, and the production of output in the form of reports or terminal display screens. This level of activity is quite similar to a factory operation and follows the model illustrated in Fig. 2.4. Operators key in data, load and unload tapes and disks, and monitor the activity much like production foremen. In carrying out these functions, the MIS operation, like the business it supports, utilizes the resources of money, people, facilities, material, and information. It is enlightening to realize that MIS is a user as well as a provider of its own services. It is also enlightening to realize that the "shoemaker's children" syndrome holds true: MIS does not often produce information to optimally manage itself.

Management control activities include such things as scheduling computer operations, monitoring hardware utilization, reviewing performance and costs, and managing application development projects. Strategic planning involves the development of an MIS mission or direction statement as well as a long-range plan to project future hardware, software, application, and people resource requirements.

Thus it is true the MIS is literally a business within a business, operating as a microcosm of the company it supports. This perspective establishes the importance of the MIS director as a business manager using information to control his or her own operation as well as providing information to support the business in general.

MIS ORGANIZATION

Figure 2.6 presents a typical MIS organization. The top MIS executive is commonly given the title of Vice-President. While some MIS executives report directly to the President, most still report to either an Executive Vice-President, a Financial Vice-President, or an Administrative Vice-President.

A word about the reporting relationship within the MIS department: With the advent of distributed processing, much of the computer hardware is located at user sites. Though the hardware is outside the physical confines of the computer center, it is usually prudent to maintain direct control of the people operating the equipment. Users do not seek this responsibility, as they neither possess the skills nor see benefit in controlling the function. It is a different story in the application development group. Users are very much interested in the applications being developed for their operational area, and matrix type organizations are cropping up. Application developers are assigned by particular business function (e.g., Engineering, Manufacturing, Finance, Marketing) and become specialists in a particular area. I think this is important in order to establish user involvement and satisfaction rather than to use an expert of a particular function as a requirement for effective system development. To my thinking, the skills of a competent systems analyst are transferable between functional areas. If the user is responsible for establishing the specs of the system (as he should be), then the system analyst's job is to translate them into the

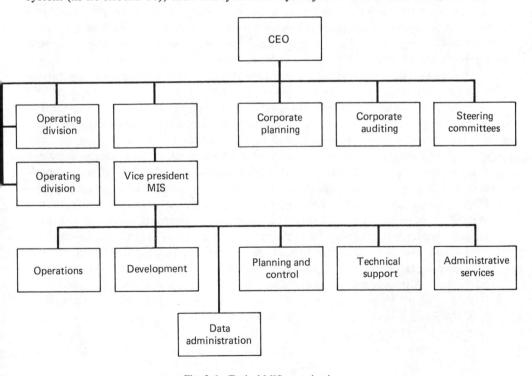

Fig. 2.6 Typical MIS organization

most efficient system he or she can design, given time and resource restraints. He or she need not be a marketing or engineering specialist to accomplish this.

The application developers can either report directly to the operating departments with a dotted-line relationship to the MIS function, or the other way around. This depends on the local environment, but it is becoming more common to have the solid-line relationship with the operating department.

Figure 2.7 lists the functions that must be planned and controlled by the MIS organization. Subsequent chapters will focus on the techniques and procedures for effectively carrying out these functions.

I have placed corporate planning, steering committees, and corporate auditing on Fig. 2.6, since these are the critical outside departments for the MIS executive. The importance of proper integration of MIS plans with corporate plans will be emphasized throughout the book. It is appropriate here to mention the role of MIS planning, steering committees, and the corporate MIS audit function.

MIS PLANNING

Planning a job or a project before launching it is logical and practical. While individuals and companies realize the worth of planning specific tasks and projects, the application of planning to a major and complex function of a business is not as readily seen. Projects usually have a one- or two-year time horizon, while planning for a major department or function such as MIS requires a longer time horizon, usually in the three- to five-year range. Examples of effective, comprehensive five- year MIS plans are not as prevalent as they should be.

Planning has gone through a stage evolution consistent with the stages-theory concept of information system growth within most companies. It is not just an MIS issue but a corporate one as well. Managers have always been leery of planning. Planning is hard work, not much fun, ill defined, not immediately rewarding, and can detract from time devoted to the day-to-day operations of the business. Also the classic profile of the type A executive indicates a natural block to the planning function. Type A executives are action-oriented, aggressive leaders with short attention spans who are impatient with activities that don't promise concrete and immediate payoffs. Planning does not fit the natural mind set of the type A manager. As a result, during the late fifties and early sixties, there was a negative corporate environment for planning. Since any MIS planning methodology must match and fit the company culture, it was obviously not a good time to do much serious thinking about developing an MIS long-range plan.

The late sixties and most of the seventies might be characterized as a complacency era, with corporate leaders exhibiting a laissez-faire attitude toward planning. Executives realized that planning was necessary, but they really didn't know how to do it—and whatever was entailed, it certainly didn't require much of their personal attention, so they conjectured. During this period, managers gave lip service to planning, perfunctorily nodding whenever the subject came up. A sharp dichotomy be-

OPERATIONS

- Data input
- Computer operations
- Tape/disk library
- Report distribution user services
- Load forecasting/scheduling
- Technical support—HW/SW/data comm.

PLANNING AND CONTROL

- Long range planning
- Operations planning
- MIS policies and procedures independent systems review process
- Systems strategic/tactical plan coordination
- Internal training and education
- Back-up and security plans

DEVELOPMENT

- Systems analysis
- Systems design
- Computer programming
- Systems maintenance DP requirements forecasting
- Systems testing/installation
- User training/support

TECHNICAL SUPPORT

- Product evaluation/selection (hardware/software)
- Systems design standards
- Technical standards
- Quality control standards

DATA ADMINISTRATION

- Data standards/policies
- Data base administration
- Data base design standards
- Transaction processing administration and standards
- Data processing management/control

ADMINISTRATIVE SERVICES

- Telecommunication services
- Document transmission/mail
- Word processing services
- Cost charge outs to users
- Budgetary review and control

Fig. 2.7 MIS organization functions

tween planning and doing was drawn, with planners assigned full time to the task but assigned in an ivory-tower environment where they would work separately and not interfere with the nonplanners (the workers). Massive documents were produced and put on the shelf, where they gathered dust, except when withdrawn to display to visiting consultants, auditors, college professors, or planners from other companies. These thick tomes were quite impressive but did not really direct the strategies and actions of the company. They gave management a warm feeling and assuaged a planning guilt complex, but did little more.

The eighties initiated a firm belief in a new concept—*action planning*, planning that is jointly conducted by executives and planners, that addresses the key business directions of the company and is followed and modified as market changes dictate. The plan is the basis for action, not a book that's put on the shelf for review by the intelligentsia.

What prompted this new and serious look at planning is a bit obscure. It may have been the inflationary economy and its impact on future growth, it may have been the political changes in regulation, taxes, and budgetary direction, it may have been the emergence of foreign competition and particularly the Japanese model of doing business based on a long-term planning foundation, or it could have been just an awakening by executives to the importance of looking out further and the realization that they had to be involved in the process. Whatever the cause or causes, it has become evident that a manager's job and the success of his enterprises depend on a dual responsibility: to perform to meet the current year's goals and to plan to meet future years' goals. This establishes a healthier and more receptive corporate environment for MIS planning.

Evolution of MIS Planning

In the early stages of MIS, applications were initiated and implemented as separate entities without much attention to integration. The aim was to get a specific application up and running to satisfy a particular user's need. The first emergence of planning was project planning, for it was found that many of the earlier applications did not really satisfy user needs, once the implementation was completed. Users would say, "That isn't what I told you" or "You should have done what I meant, not what I said." Projects typically were behind schedule and took more resources than were comtemplated—and by an order of magnitude or worse. It soon became clear that identifying the project milestones, gaining user sign-off on specifications, and scheduling management reviews throughout the cycle produces better products.

The proliferation of applications during what has been called the contagion stage resulted in heavy demands for computer time. This initiated the second kind of MIS planning, capacity planning. Though capacity planning remains, to this day, more art than science, MIS managers had to find a way to project future computer hardware requirements in an era of growing application backlogs. Capacity planning permits the modeling of the current workload in order to project future volume levels and the need and time frame for added capacity.

With the increase in computer resources, management became alarmed over the sharply rising cost of data processing services. This led to a third type of planning, resource or budgetary planning. MIS managers began developing annual operational plans, which necessitated looking ahead at least a year to project what hardware, software, people, and facilities were required to run the operation and handle the growing portfolio of computer applications. This ushered in the third or control stage of MIS development.

At the advent of stage 4 (integration stage), an assessment of management needs showed a requirement for integrated data files in order to provide meaningful management information to run the business. This established the need for another type of planning—long-range planning—to formulate the direction and strategy of the MIS function to support the business in the next three- to five-year period.

Long-Range MIS Planning

In considering an MIS long-range plan, we need to keep several precepts in mind.

- *Planning is a verb, not a noun*—Planning is not a once-a-year function that produces a report and gets management blessing. Rather it is a continuous process that takes place throughout the year. The report is reviewed and updated continually; it is a living document. Most planners and executives would agree that the effectiveness of planning is in the process rather than in a particular document that becomes the final output.

- *The MIS plan must be consistent with the corporate business plan*—The MIS plan must dovetail with the corporate plan. Since the MIS plan supports the future business, the future business direction of the company must be known before any meaningful MIS plan can be developed. This usually means that the planning cycle of the MIS plan is in sequence with the corporate planning cycle. A set of corporate strategic guidelines will kick off the planning cycle for the year. The MIS cycle should commence at that point and coincide with the key management review points of the corporate schedule.

- *Management involvement and commitment are essential*—Involvement and commitment go hand-in-hand, in that commitment without involvement is usually lip service, rather than arising from understanding and participation in the review process. In order to achieve this participation, an information steering committee is usually required. Since each manager is involved in his or her own department plan, conservative and sensitive use of managers' time is important. Meetings should be well structured and focused on broad strategic issues rather than short-term tactical ones. The makeup and operation of the management review board or steering committee is extremely important. The plan's content obviously is crucial, but its perception by management can be equally as crucial.

- *Planning is everybody's job*—Though a specific individual or department is responsible for developing the MIS plan, they are the catalysts or agents, chartered to select a planning methodology and to ensure that the planning process takes place according to that methodology and is consistent with corporate guidelines. They can contribute to the plan's content but are not responsible for it. The key department managers and the MIS executive bear the responsibility for providing the strategic directional content. Planning is not a function to be delegated.

    Organizational behaviorists point out that it is difficult for a manager to successfully implement a plan that was dictated from the top without his or her involvement or commitment. Grass-roots planning, where the people responsible for implementing the plan are also involved in the planning process, has proven more workable than ivory-tower planning.

- *It takes several cycles to institutionalize a planning process*—We noted earlier that planning is not an easy task and runs against the grain of the action-oriented, hard-driving manager. Therefore, no matter how sound the methodology chosen or how efficient the techniques for developing the plan, it will take more than one iteration to establish the process firmly within a company. Planners instituting the process should not be discouraged the first time around. Often the first year's plan is not completely understood by either the MIS people implementing it or the MIS users supported by it. An assessment should be made at the completion of the first planning cycle in order to improve the process during the next cycle. Modifications may include items such as an off-site half-day workshop to review the final version, a different composition of the steering committee, or a change in the scheduling of various milestones. Remember that planning is a verb; it is a continuous process.

Contents of a Long-Range Plan

Figure 2.8 segments the contents of an MIS long-range plan into fifteen categories. The contents answer six basic questions:

1. Where are we?
2. Where do we want to go?
3. How do we get there?
4. When will it be done?
5. Who will do it?
6. How much will it cost?

While the contents will vary between different companies, MIS groups, and stages of development, Fig. 2.8 presents a good starting point. Some sections will be emphasized one year and deemphasized in another. For example, at a particular development stage, the establishment of MIS management control techniques (section 10) may be of principal significance, while being downplayed in subsequent years. This is true also for other areas such as policies or transition strategies. Often planners feel that if a plan doesn't change dramatically each year, it is not a good one or they are not doing their job. This is not the case, because if a good solid vision of the future is established and if meaningful, well-founded strategies are put in place, they may hold with but minor fine tuning for several years to come. An extremely useful technique is to develop a difference document which summarizes the key changes of this year's plan from that of the preceding year. Management is particularly interested in this focus.

The fifteen sections of the plan include the following:

1. *Corporate guidelines*
   (a) Strategic—markets/products
   (b) Volume indicators
   (c) Functional/organizational changes
2. *Environment*
   (a) Industry trends
   (b) Technology scan
   (c) Government regulations
   (d) Work-force composition
   (e) Customer/supplier relational changes
3. *Current operations*
   (a) Budget/organization
   (b) Strengths/weaknesses

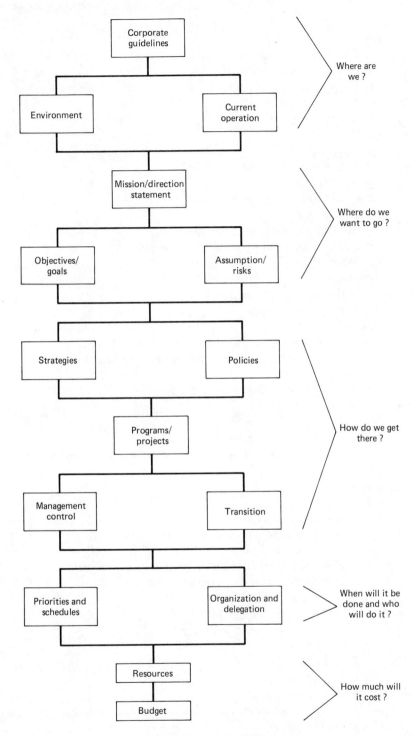

Fig. 2.8 Content of an MIS plan

      (c) Strategy/projects

      (d) Opportunities/potentials

4. *Mission/direction statement*

      (a) Purpose or reason for MIS

      (b) Main business of MIS

      (c) Objectives of MIS

      (d) Scope of users

5. *Objectives/goals*

      (a) Targets and time frame

      (b) Results expected

      (c) Qualitative and quantitative goals

6. *Assumptions/risks*

      (a) Internal and external constraints

      (b) Assumptions and potential consequences

      (c) Major risks

7. *Strategies*

      (a) Major strategies to reach objectives

      (b) Timing of strategies

8. *Policies*

      (a) Major current policies (internal and external to MIS)

      (b) Projected policy changes required and time frame

9. *Programs/projects*

      (a) Current program/projects in process

      (b) New ones required

10. *Management control tools*

      (a) New procedures/methods needed

      (b) Timing and approach to develop new control techniques

11. *Transition plans*

      (a) Old environment

      (b) New environment

      (c) Plan to go from old to new

      (d) Necessary user and operational conditioning

12. *Priorities and schedules*

      (a) Ranking and prioritization of programs and projects

      (b) Timing and schedule of programs/projects

13. *Organization and delegation*

      (a) Organization to manage MIS

      (b) Delegation of authority and responsibility

14. *Resource projections*

      (a) Equipment projections

      (b) Software projections

      (c) Facilities projections

      (d) Personnel requirements (hiring, maintaining, training, developing)

15. *Operating budget*

      (a) Incremental budget by new program/project or zero based

      (b) New budget projected for each of planned years

Steering Committees

The MIS steering committee has become quite significant in many companies and, if properly utilized and administered, can be an effective tool in developing good user relations. The steering committee is comprised of a group of key users of information services whose duty it is to act as a review or overseeing body for MIS plans and development. A steering committee helps formalize the concept of user involvement that is so necessary for successful systems. It provides a higher-level control that can break log jams or give direction when for one reason or another the MIS activity bogs down. A properly comprised steering group can present a broader business perspective to a situation and can help keep system objectives in balance.

Another important function is to sign off on the specifications of a new major application area. Often the specs or requirements of a new application either are not stated at the outset or are not clear to the eventual users, so that they are major surprises once the application is in operation.

Output and response time of the system should be reviewed at the outset and referred to throughout the production process to ensure the project will meet its objectives. Things inevitably change during the course of a development cycle. The steering committee can assess the impact of these events and assist in making the most beneficial trade-off decisions.

Deployment and organization of steering committees vary within a company. Sometimes there is only one general information advisory group, while in other situations a hierarchy of steering committees exists. Figure 2.9 illustrates a hierarchical arrangement of an overall MIS steering group and three decision-level groups focusing on the key operating areas of the company—marketing, manufacturing, and engineering. The top group is responsible for approving the business plan for the entire management information system. The basis of this application plan will undoubtedly be the information system model or MIS framework described in Chapter 1. The group is headed by a prominent member of top management who must be able to devote a good amount of time to the program; in this case it is the executive vice-president. The heads or key decision makers of the departments to be affected by MIS are also members of the steering group. The director of MIS and the manager of systems and programming represent the MIS department. This group meets periodically to update the MIS business plan as well as to review the status of the three advisory groups working under it.

An advisory group is formed for each of the major application subsystem areas—in this case marketing, manufacturing, and engineering. The group is chaired by a top executive of the department concerned and includes key people within the department as well as the key MIS personnel involved in system development. Note that in each group there is a system analyst representing the department affected. His or her inclusion is extremely important; it ensures that the department's interests and objectives are represented in the detailed implementation steps as well as in the overall planning. The key system designers within the MIS department, called the marketing, manufacturing, and engineering project leaders, are also members of the group. They are the MIS personnel responsible, together with the department's system analyst, for the full-time direction of the particular application area. Note, also, that

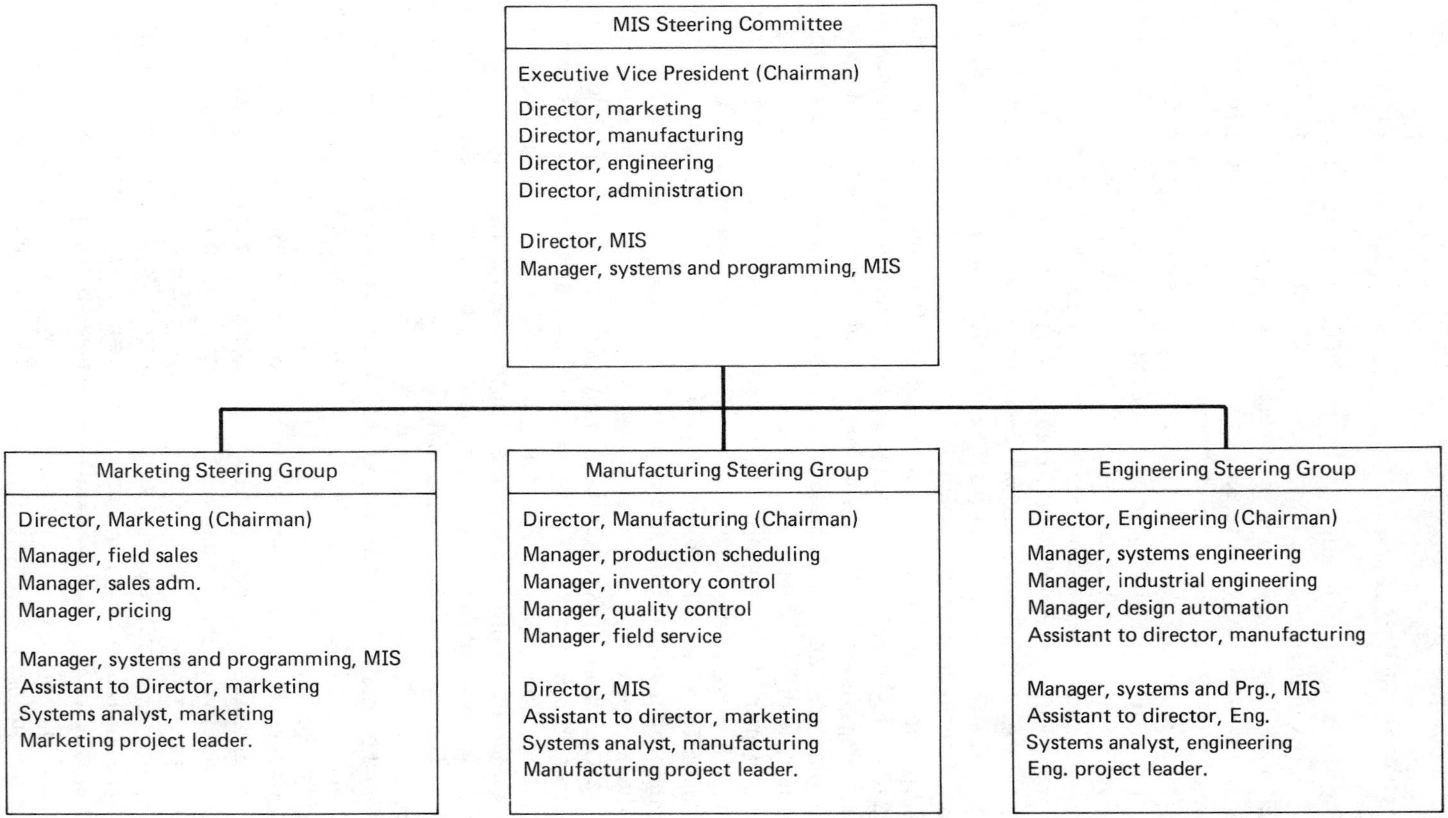

MIS Steering Committee

Executive Vice President (Chairman)

Director, marketing
Director, manufacturing
Director, engineering
Director, administration

Director, MIS
Manager, systems and programming, MIS

Marketing Steering Group

Director, Marketing (Chairman)

Manager, field sales
Manager, sales adm.
Manager, pricing

Manager, systems and programming, MIS
Assistant to Director, marketing
Systems analyst, marketing
Marketing project leader.

Manufacturing Steering Group

Director, Manufacturing (Chairman)

Manager, production scheduling
Manager, inventory control
Manager, quality control
Manager, field service

Director, MIS
Assistant to director, marketing
Systems analyst, manufacturing
Manufacturing project leader.

Engineering Steering Group

Director, Engineering (Chairman)

Manager, systems engineering
Manager, industrial engineering
Manager, design automation
Assistant to director, manufacturing

Manager, systems and Prg., MIS
Assistant to director, Eng.
Systems analyst, engineering
Eng. project leader.

Fig. 2.9 Steering committee organization

there is cross-representation on each of the committees. The directors of manufacturing, marketing, and engineering are on the steering group, and they also head one of the advisory groups. The director of MIS and the manager of systems and programming also sit on advisory groups. Thus there are continuity and tie-in.

The example above illustrates the ultimate in the use of steering committees. It may well be that a less formal structure will suit a particular situation. Whatever the scope, it is important to follow certain procedures. First, because members of the steering groups all have full-time jobs, every effort must be made to make the meetings crisp, well organized, focused, and pertinent. The purpose of the steering committee is not to cover details or do the work of the MIS department, but to review direction, progress toward objectives, and fit of systems to the company culture. The subject matter should emphasize questions of "what," not "how." The group should include respected people from the various organizations and not just those who happen to be available. This is probably the most important success factor of steering committees: the people selected should be able to speak for their division or organization.

While the expanding scope of MIS makes cross-functional steering groups essential (see "Managing Information Systems by Committee," *Harvard Business Review,* July-August 1982) the following pitfalls should be avoided if the committee approach is to be effective.

- Group is too large and diverse (six to eight is optimum).
- Meetings deteriorate into vague, wandering discussion.
- Subject matter becomes too detailed and specific rather than focusing on broad direction, strategy, and priority.
- The necessary staff work is not accomplished before meetings.
- Frequency and length of meetings are greater than management can tolerate.
- Substitutes and substitutes for substitutes begin to show up at meetings.
- Low-level chairmanship or MIS domination of the meeting occurs.

Corporate Audit Function

Companies have been expanding the role of their corporate audit function to include MIS auditing. Previously, the MIS audit function concentrated on financial auditing, checking those areas that were involved with cash intake and cash disbursements such as purchasing, order processing, and payroll. However, the role in many instances has expanded to include the overall workings of the MIS function. The role of working around the computer—that is, inspecting what goes in and what goes out—is changing to include what goes on inside the computer and inside the MIS department. One company lists the following functions under its corporate audit department.

- Review data center procedures and standards
- Check for operational compliance

- Security audits
- Recovery and back-up
- Performance measurements
- Postimplementation audits
- System effectiveness reviews
- Review internal controls
- Ensure auditability of new systems
- Quality assurance
- Review documentation
- Evaluation and verification

The philosophy of some organizations is not to give the responsibility for these functions to a separate audit group, but to include them in the charter of the MIS department. This is similar to combining the quality control department with the production department. Each approach has its obvious pros and cons. However, if the company adopts the separate audit function, it behooves the MIS director to work with this department, to agree on a set of goals and guidelines, and to perform and be measured against this agreed-to set. The audit group becomes a very important corporate interface.

SUMMARY

This chapter has introduced the important concept of information resource management (IRM), indicating that it does not replace MIS, but provides the managerial umbrella under which MIS operates. The stages theory of Richard Nolan was presented to give a life-cycle portrayal of the evolutionary progress of MIS within a company. It is a good starting point for a review of the MIS function. It also establishes a perspective for planning future evolutionary steps. The changing nature of the MIS function was then analyzed in light of the pressures bearing down on the MIS executive.

This led into a definition and discussion of the IRM concept based on the work of the Diebold Research group. IRM changes the way a company thinks and acts about its information resource and also broadens the scope of MIS by including in its purview information that is not currently in electronic form within the company. A proposed organization by Mobil Oil Corporation illustrated this broadening perspective on information. Introduced at this point was the critical-success-factor concept developed by John Rockart as applied to MIS directors. This facilitated an understanding of the elements that appear to correlate with successful management of the MIS function.

The approach of looking at MIS as a business within a business was reviewed. The organization that develops information systems is itself a business and performs the same operational control, management control, and strategic planning activities.

This provides the framework for reviewing the types of business practices that are needed to manage the MIS operation. Particularly attention was given to MIS planning, steering committees, and the corporate audit function.

CASE STUDIES

NATIONAL INSURANCE COMPANY

The environment at National Insurance Company is growth, growth, and more growth. A late starter in the business, National has grown through acquisition of new lines of business and new companies. Its MIS activity has mirrored the company's business activity. The first major computer complex was installed just ten years ago. Proliferation has been the name of the game since then, with applications being added to handle the new lines of insurance and new hardware being acquired as capacity has grown. The MIS department's budget has grown an average of 50 percent per year over the past five years. The company now finds itself with three different computer configurations representing four vendors. On the software side, an opportunistic approach has been employed with the purchase of application software packages from a variety of software houses. Though there are substantial amounts of disk files and on-line storage, the major operation mode of MIS is batch, and data bases exist on a variety of media.

The president of National has been concerned for some time with his company's MIS function. Customer complaints have grown, primarily because it has taken sometimes as long as six months for a new customer to receive his or her initial policy. Also loan processing is slow, and they have encountered a large number of mistakes in regular premium billing. The president realizes that MIS is an integral part of the insurance business and has brought in a consultant to thoroughly review his operation and to make recommendations for improvement.

The president was reviewing the consultant's report and wondering what his next steps should be. The consultant had made a stages-theory assessment and concluded that National was in early stage 3—just beginning to concern itself with computer control, documentation, and the like. His recommendations were far reaching and called for sweeping changes in the way MIS was managed within National. He strongly suggested the development of a long-range plan and the employment of an executive information steering committee to guide the overall direction and strategy of MIS. The consultant found the MIS group lacking in control tools and recommended an adoption of project management, risk assessment, and a method of prioritizing application selection and development. Further, the report brought out the need for an integrated data base around which the MIS group should build its applications. The consultant concluded with a long discussion of a concept called information resource management, which was a bit confusing to the president.

As the president reviewed the situation, he knew that changes had to be made but he thought the consultant had laid on every available technique, using a lot of fancy consultant terms and nomenclature from the literature. His big question was how much of this to buy and how to phase it into National's way of doing business. He knew his company was a late starter in MIS and was behind its competitors, but taking on too much too soon could have damaging effects.

The recommended approach would cause at least a temporary hiatus to new developments while the shop was put into order. An analogy came to mind. He drove to work every morning from the suburbs over the major commuter circumvental highway. Crews were always working on the road, adding lanes and improving others. A balance had to be achieved—keeping the heavy traffic going while creating a proper thoroughfare for the 1980s and beyond. His MIS operation appeared to be in the same state.

QUESTIONS

1. Is the president over-reacting to the situation?

2. How did National get into this situation? Is it a natural evolution? Who is responsible for it?

3. What do you think of the approach suggested by the consultant. Is it practical? Is it necessary?

4. Will the consultant's sweeping recommendations fit the culture of National? Is a company in this position ready for strict controls?

5. Can a company progress from stage 2 through stages 3 and 4 simultaneously? That is, can they institute the proper control mechanisms while instituting the integrated data base, long-range plans, steering committees, and so on that are the elements of information resource management?

BROWN AND GORDON AUTO PARTS

Brown and Gordon Auto Parts (B&G) is the third largest auto parts manufacturer in the world. It is an autonomously run division of a large conglomerate, RST Inc. Their headquarters and principal manufacturing facilities are in Cleveland, Ohio, but they operate plants in East Chicago, Illinois; Indianapolis, Indiana; Columbus and Cincinnati, Ohio; and South Bend, Indiana. Total annual revenues are close to $2 billion, but profits have been reduced dramatically the last two years because of the recession and particularly because of the decline in automobile sales. Plant capacity has dropped to 60 percent, with a slight pick-up in the fourth quarter of this year. RST Inc. has turned in record profits in the past two years, with all divisions save B&G performing beyond plan.

Most of B&G's management team are old-line managers who have proven themselves in operational jobs and have worked their way up the hierarchy. They don't believe in frills or fancy procedures; rather it is to get the job done as quickly and simply as possible. It's a tough, no-nonsense management style. Because of the highly competitive nature of the business, accentuated by the recent business downturn, management has adopted a cost-cutting mode. Almost all investments or expenditures must be justified by tangible cost savings, and this usually means people savings. This is particularly true within MIS, where expenditures are not approved until the number of the job eliminations is verified.

MIS ORGANIZATION

The MIS Division is headed by R. L. (Buck) Steubens, Assistant Controller, who reports to W. W. Johnson, V.P. of Finance, who reports to the President of B&G, T. J. Baker.

It is generally accepted that Johnson delegates the MIS responsibility totally to Steubens and is not himself a factor in decision making on MIS matters. The two key MIS directors are Tom Mansfield and Harry Crowley. Mansfield is in charge of the application development for all operations. Development personnel located in outlying plants develop applications for these plants but report to Mansfield. Operations reports to Harry Crowley. The outlying plants have their own operators, who report to local line management. MIS operations are highly centralized, however, such that no processing is done locally, but via remote batch, remote job entry, or time sharing on Cleveland's central systems.

Buck Steubens was concerned about the way his MIS group was organized and was reviewing the following report, which was sent to him by a consulting firm he had asked to look into the matter.

CONSULTANT REVIEW OF
BROWN AND GORDON INFORMATION SYSTEMS FUNCTION

Organization

B&G has a rather unique organization with two directors managing the entire information systems function. Missing is a third or coordinating element found in most organizations. This third element is responsible for integrating services that span the MIS division—services such as standards, planning, education, project management, and often database administration. While where is nothing that says the B&G organization cannot work, interviews suggest that major application developments have been implemented without complete awareness of their fit with existing or future subsystems. Also there is a lack of emphasis on planning and education, two functions that are vital to future progress.

To make this dual-directorship concept work, standards and protocols must be better established to facilitate proper communications and integration at the working levels. It is conceivable that the Assistant Controller can be the integrating force, but this is too high a level in the organization, particularly in light of the expanding duties of the office. The integration must occur at lower levels.

The stated management organizational style at B&G is heavily people oriented. Thus, the primary criterion for assigning a job is the track record of the individual in getting jobs accomplished rather than an assessment of where the function best fits into the organization or where there is the necessary expertise. The design of complex integrated applications is a difficult task, and while the ability to get a job done is probably the number one attribute, it is not the only one.

Another expressed organizational style is adversary management, the theory being that pitting two competent managers against each other will result in a competitive drive to get the work accomplished. The question raised here is: does this approach work in a functional area of the business that needs integration and communication so desperately?

QUESTIONS

1. What is the company culture at B&G? What are the pros and cons of this culture?

2. What does the consultant report tell Buck Steubens? What action should he take?

3. Do you think the cost-cutting mode is a "given" for MIS? Is it wise to justify MIS expenditures on the number of job eliminations?

4. Do you link the organizational issues with the consultant's statement that there appears to be a lack of systems integration at B&G?

BIBLIOGRAPHY

Administration of Information Resources, Report 187545 (Sept. 1980), New York: The Diebold Research Program.

Alloway, Robert M., *Defining Success For Data Processing*, WP 1112-80, Cambridge, MA: Center for Information Systems Research, Sloan (MIT), March 1980.

Blumenthal, Marcia, "Mobil Considering IBM as Separate Line Entity," *Computerworld* (Feb. 9, 1981).

Bullen, Christine V. and John F. Rockart, *A Primer on Critical Success Factors*, Cambridge, MA: Center for Information Systems Research, June 1981.

Couger, Daniel J., "Low Social Need Strengths (SNS) of Computer Professionals and the Impact on Curriculum Design," *Proceedings of the First International Conference on Information Systems* (Dec., 8–10, 1980), Philadelphia, PA.

Couger, J. D., and R. A. Zawicki, *Motivation and Management of Computer Personnel*. New York: Wiley-Interscience, 1980.

Diebold, J., "Information Resource Management—The New Challenge," *Infosystems* (1979), 50–53.

Honeywell Consulting Services, *A Planning Method, Instructional Guide*, 1982.

IBM, "Business Systems Planning: Information Systems Planning Guide," Doc. GE20-0527-2, Technical Publications, White Plains, NY: IBM Corp., 1978.

IBM, "Business Systems Planning: Information Systems Planning Guide (Application Manual), 2nd ed.," Doc. GE20-0527-2, Technical Publications, Dept. 824, White Plains, NY: IBM Corp., 1978.

Matlin, Gerald L. "IBM: How Will Top Management React?," *Infosystems* (Oct. 1980), 40–48.

McFarlan, F. W., "Management Audit of the EDP Department," *Harvard Business Review* (1973), 131–142.

McFarlan, F. Warren, "Problems in Planning the Information System," *Harvard Business Review* (1971), 75–89.

McKenney, James L. and Warren F. McFarlan, "The Information Archipelago—Maps and Bridges," *Harvard Business Review* (Sept./Oct. 1982), 109–119.

McLean, E., and J. Soder, *Strategic Planning for MIS*. New York: Wiley-Interscience, 1977.

MIS Planning for 1981–1983. The Diebold Research Program Working Session 80-2 (1980).

Nolan, R. L., "Business Needs a New Breed of EDP Manager," *Harvard Business Review* (1976), 283–293.

Nolan, R. L., "Managing the Computer Resource: A Stage Hypothesis," *Comm. ACM 16*, 7 (1973), 399–405.

Nolan, R. L., "Managing the Crisis in Data Processing," *Harvard Business Review* (1979), 115–126.

Nolan, R. L., "Managing Information Systems by Committee," *Harvard Business Review* (1982), 72–79.

Nolan, R. L., "Plight of the EDP Manager," *Harvard Business Review* (1973), 143–152.

Rockart, J. F., "Chief Executives Define Their Own Data Needs," *Harvard Business Review* (1979), 81–93.

C. P. Snow, *Science and Government*. Cambridge, MA: Harvard University Press, 1961.

C. P. Snow, *The Two Cultures and the Scientific Revolution*. Cambridge, England: Cambridge University Press, 1959.

C. P. Snow, *The Two Cultures: A Second Look, 2nd ed*. Cambridge, England: Cambridge University Press, 1963.

Stevens, Barry A., "Probing the DP Psyche (Report on Study by Gerry Richardson, a Denver Industrial Psychologist)," *Computerworld* (July 21, 1980).

Withington, F. G., "Coping With Computer Proliferation," *Harvard Business Review* (1980), 152–164.

Chapter 3

Building A Business Model: Business Processes

The contents of this chapter fit between the MIS long-range plan and the design phase of the application development cycle. The methodology of building a business model and understanding the business are essential prerequisites to establishing application priorities and then implementing them.

This chapter will explore in more detail the business processes first described in Chapter 1. Figure 1.11 depicted the basic processes that are the building blocks of a management information system. We will now delve deeper into these processes, illustrating how they can be identified, classified, and placed in proper perspective to one another.

The way to approach MIS development is to look first at the broad road map and then break it down into progressively finer and finer detail until individual milestones are established. In actual practice, the development involves working at the problem from both ends. It is similar to establishing an annual plan for a business operation. Theoretically, the best approach is to work from the top down, with top management expressing the basic strategies and goals of the organization and then passing them down to lower levels of management for use as guidelines in establishing lower-level plans. In reality, time pressures and feedback requirements necessitate simultaneous work plans. These plans, worked both from the top down and the bottom up, are correlated at various stages in the planning cycle. Thus, while the general flow is top down, there are a series of iterative feedback loops before finalization of the plan. This is true with management information systems. Although the approach suggested will be a sequential one where the establishment of management objectives, strategies, and goals is the first step, it becomes obvious that this approach is difficult to achieve in practice. This fact should not detract from the basic requirement of MIS that it be management oriented. Perspective is required to determine at what point management's points of view are known well enough to be used as a basis for action. To wait for 100 percent clarity and certainty is unrealistic. The wise MIS developer is able to make this distinction, to proceed accordingly, but to seek management feedback continually as a check and balance.

BUILDING THE BUSINESS MODEL

The approach to MIS is first to develop a business model comprised of the business processes or activities that are the essence of the business. This is not a mathematical model, but the portrayal of a business as one large system showing the interconnection and sequence of the business subsystems or processes that comprise it. The procedure to accomplish this is described in Fig. 3.1. The arrows denote that the planning

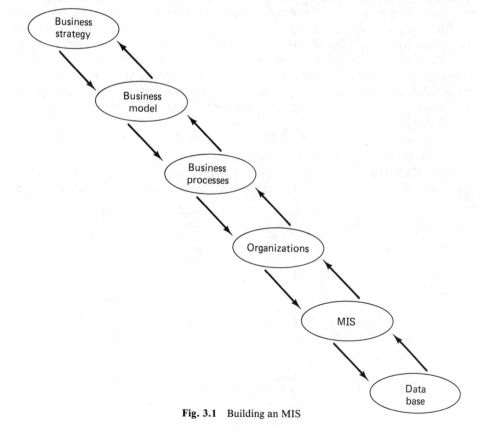

Fig. 3.1 Building an MIS

is accomplished from the top down while the implementation is from the bottom up. Based on business strategy and objectives (the long-range plan), a business model comprised of business processes is developed. These processes are managed and controlled by various individuals in various organizations. The MIS is developed to provide the required information to the organization to manage the processes that are part of the business model. The data base is the source of information and drives the MIS.

As we have seen, business can be viewed as a system itself, pumping products or services through its operation while deploying money, people, facilities, and material as its resources. Information is not listed as a resource, as this is the area on which we will concentrate in building MIS. It will be added as we go. Figure 3.2 shows the concept of business as a system.

The easiest way to understand the processes that underlie a management information system is to use an example. The example we use here is a typical company in the food-distribution business. We could equally well have chosen a distributor of any type of product or group of products, a manufacturer, an insurance company, a bank, an educational or government operation, a hospital, or a service company. The type of company is relatively unimportant; the general principles of business-process analysis and classification, the methodology of looking at a company's information system to support a series of interlocking subsystems, is applicable and pertinent across industry lines. We will now build a business model of a distributor.

Our business-process model will begin with the sales activity or sales process. It has been often stated that "nothing begins until something is sold." This point is certainly valid, and we will see that sales-order processing is a primary process interconnected to other processes that comprise our model. Figure 3.3 is the starting point of the business model.

It is obviously important to satisfy customer demand, for doing so is the principal reason for being in business. Management should continually strive to give the customer the best product at the best price and at the same time should realize a profit in line with the product being offered. The basic cycle starts here, because what goes

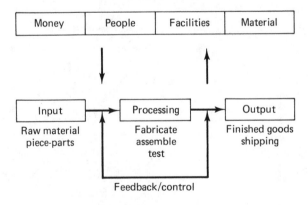

Fig. 3.2 Business as a system

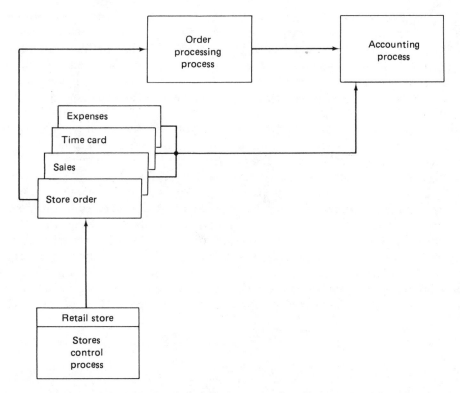

Fig. 3.3   The order-processing, stores-control, and account processes

out of the stores must be replaced. As the shelves in the store are depleted, certain store-order operations are put into play that result in the reorder of goods to replenish the shelves. The store will reorder goods on the basis of turnover and the lead time required to replenish the item. The store order is one of the basic source documents that initiates a long series of activities throughout many departments. This document enters the first of the processes—that of order processing. This process will screen the orders for errors in omission as well as commission and ensure that the order is valid before it proceeds further into other processes. The connecting arrow to the accounting process indicates that the order is the basis for setting up accounts receivable and eventually reconciling the cash payment for the goods.

Another source document is the record of sales or the movement of items from the store. This source document will eventually produce meaningful sales statistics and analyses as output from the accounting and marketing processes.

In addition to the store and record of sales, it takes people to run a store, and they must be paid according to services rendered. A time record represents the medium for recording hours worked; in Fig. 3.3 it is shown entering the accounting subsystem. Similarly, the expenses of store operation (heat, light, and maintenance) are recorded and entered into the accounting process. This would be the case only if the company controlled its own stores (as in a chain operation).

The stores-control process has not been greatly affected by automated information systems. However, this is beginning to occur. Checkout-counter devices can optically read imprinted prices and item numbers on products, automatically producing the customer sales total and recording as a by-product the item and quantity sold as input into the order-processing subsystem. Another activity within the stores-control process is the scheduling of checkout personnel based on a simulation of activity through the store as a reflection of historical sales patterns and known conditions. For example, a study can indicate the requirement for a Thursday and Friday when Saturday is a holiday; also it is known that about 70 percent of the business for the week is done on Thursday, Friday, and Saturday. These factors can be reflected in a queueing model to assist in the scheduling of personnel.

Figure 3.4 adds the inventory-control subsystem as well as the materials-control and transportation processes. After the store order has been validated by the order-processing process, it moves to the inventory-control process, where it must be screened against the current inventory in the warehouse. This process is indicated by the two-way arrow connecting the order-processing and inventory-control processes. If there is sufficient inventory on hand, the order-processing process produces a store-order picking document for the warehouse and an order invoice for the retail store. Since employee labor and operating expenses were recorded at the store level,

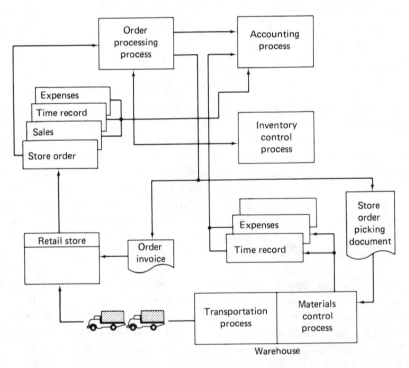

Fig. 3.4   Addition of inventory-control, materials-control, and transportation processes

they must be recorded at the warehouse level. These items can be seen entering the accounting process in Fig. 3.4. The blank record will be explained in Fig. 3.5.

The materials-control and transportation processes are excellent examples of how integrated processes operate. For example, the basic information on orders and movement from the warehouse can be used to lay out warehouse space more efficiently. Similarly, the information on each order, such as the cubic content and weight of items comprising the order, can be used to load and route trucks. These valuable by-products can often be real payoff applications. Thus the same basic raw data is processed in a little different way to help in the handling of another functional activity.

Figure 3.5 adds another process to the overall integrated model—the purchasing process. This process depends on the strength of the inventory-control process. A well-conceived inventory-control process provides for automatic ordering based on such considerations as customer service, economic order quantity, and lead time. Orders were screened against inventory records in Fig. 3.4. When the inventory of particular items reaches a predetermined reorder point, the inventory-control process directs the purchasing process to write a purchase order. The purchase order is made out and sent to the respective vendor or manufacturer. The vendor in turn fills the order, ships the product to the warehouse, and submits his invoice for entry into the account process. This process initiates accounts-payable activity and the eventual reconciliation of cash payments. The arrow indicates the connection of the accounting and purchasing processes.

The blank record of Figure 3.4 can now be identified as a receipt record. This record enters the inventory-control process to update pertinent inventory records; it

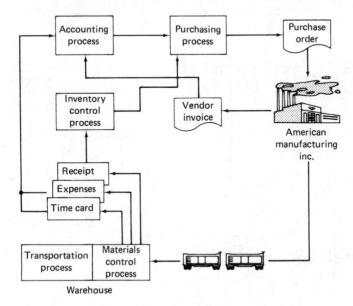

Fig. 3.5   Adding the purchasing process

is also passed through to the accounting process to form the basis for vendor payment.

Figure 3.6 brings together the processes that have been mentioned up to this point. Two additional arrows have been added to the illustration. The first connects the inventory-control and accounting processes. This step is necessary because inventory data is a requirement of accounting reports. The second arrow shows the important output of the accounting process. Accounting acts as the scorekeeper of all the processing mentioned thus far. It accumulates such data as store orders, cash sales, expenses, receipts, and vendor invoices, and from this basic source information produces a host of meaningful management reports. Three of these reports are noted in Figure 3.6—profit-and-loss statement, inventory statistics, and sales statistics. These reports might show, for example, profitability by region, by store, or by department; or they might show sales by salesman or item grouping. They might also indicate inventory turnover or return on inventory investment.

The processes discussed thus far are basic ones common to most businesses. They cover the operational control and management control activities discussed in

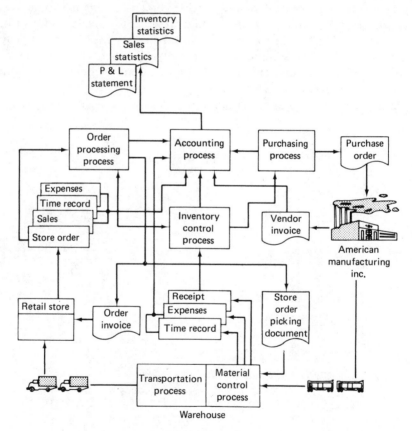

Fig. 3.6   Basic processes

Chapter 1. Figure 3.7 shows more advanced processes that can build on the basic ones already described.

Marketing and strategic planning are the processes that produce the real pay-offs for a company. As a by-product of the basic processes, the marketing process uses the basic source data that has been collected and filed. However, the data is processed in different ways to answer specific management questions—questions such as the effect of promotion on sales, the effect of pricing changes and product mix, the comparative advantages of a limited as compared to a full product line, the significance of store layout and shelf allocation on profit, and the desirability of introducing new items or product lines.

Another key output of the marketing process is the sales forecast. The forecast is based on historical sales movement (information coming from the accounting process) as well as on projected external events (buying trends, economic factors, and so on). The sales forecast is significant to all aspects of the business. It is shown in Figure 3.6 entering the inventory-control process as a basis of establishing inventory policy and entering the strategic planning process as a basis of influencing total company goals and objectives.

The strategic planning process is the core of the business model. It is here that the major company decisions are made. Reports produced by the accounting subsystems are digested, reviewed, and analyzed. Overall company policies are determined and promulgated. In addition to the historical or internal data, the strategic planning

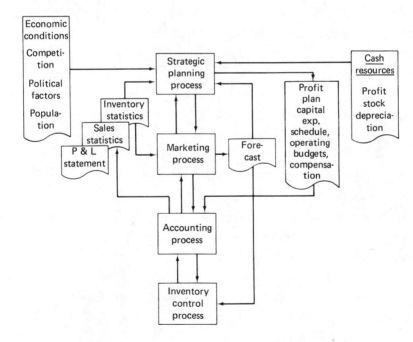

Fig. 3.7 Addition of marketing and strategic planning

process uses external data gathered from outside sources. On one side are the basic economic factors, such as trends in Gross National Product, political factors, and population growth; on the other side are the available cash resources, such as profit plow-back, new stock issues, and depreciation. The results of the strategic planning process are marketing policies as well as the profit, capital-expenditure schedule, and operating budget. These figures enter the accounting process to form the basis of measuring actual operation. They form the yardstick for measurement. The cycle is thus completed. Figure 3.8 presents the complete integrated business model that we have been building in stages.

Figure 3.8 shows nine processes that comprise a business model. These nine are major processes, each of which can be further subdivided. For example, the financial

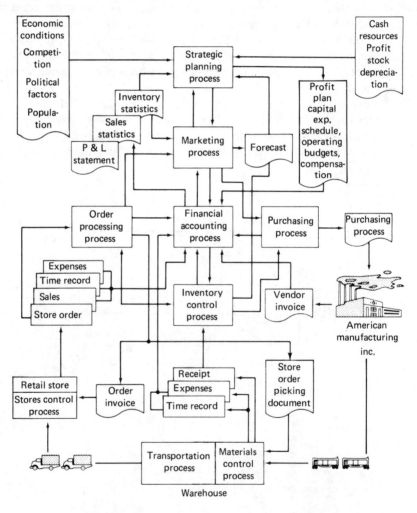

Fig. 3.8   Business model for a distribution company

and accounting process includes subprocesses for accounts receivable, accounts payable, general ledger, payroll, cost accounting, and the like. A significant point to bear in mind in planning an MIS is to lay out the overall road map or model first. It is true that the initial focus may, for example, be on improving the sales-order processing process; however, this should be undertaken in light of where that particular process fits into the whole.

Middle and top management can understand a framework similar to that illustrated in Fig. 3.8. Too often the first thing they are shown is a detailed flow chart of the order-processing cycle. This is discouraging to them, for they are unaware of where order processing fits into the overall process network and what part it will play in a management information system. Although interested and vitally concerned with improving the order cycle, thereby improving inventory turnover and reducing capital requirements, they would like to get a "feel" of how the by-product data from this application can help them pinpoint unfavorable sales trends by product line and store location, plus suggesting action to improve the situation. Developing a business model for your company in your industry is an important first step in developing and gaining the benefits of MIS.

INTEGRATION AND INTERRELATIONSHIP OF PROCESSES

At the beginning of the Industrial Revolution, business was run by individual entrepreneurs who did the planning, selling, producing, accounting, and other necessary jobs. The basic data and information needed to carry out these duties were filed in the entrepreneur's head. His data processing system was integrated, because there was a central source of information from which sprung all policies, plans, and decisions. However, the tasks began to grow more complex until he could no longer handle all of them himself. He hired people to help him, and he set up functional responsibilities, such as accounting, production, and engineering, and assigned people to these various functions. In the beginning there was a good deal of overlap in the assignment of individuals to functions; functional specialization would be a later development. But as business evolved, the entrepreneur found he could not train people himself. Colleges and universities offered to assist in the task. As university curricula were developed, fences began to appear that were to become the functional boundaries within a business—the accounting profession was formed, the advertising profession, and so on.

This is not to say that these functional boundaries were logical in nature; it just happened to be the way they were recognized within a business organization. With the entrepreneur we had a natural integrated system, but the growth of functional boundaries determines the kind of data utilized by the various groups and tends to limit the scope of problems and the vision of individuals tackling these problems. This explains, to a great extent, why many data processing systems still emphasize accounting applications. The computer is under the control of the accounting department, and the functional boundaries of accounting perpetuate applications like payroll, accounts receivable, and accounts payable.

This situation suggests a real challenge for management. The top executive must somehow get the various functional heads to coordinate their activities— to achieve the same effectiveness as the single entrepreneur. The integrated model or system concept is a prime vehicle for accomplishing this step, emphasizing that although the whole is made up of parts, the parts must not be so specialized and unique that their function as part of the whole is forgotten.

Obviously management cannot play a passive role in the design and development of an integrated system. Since the system crosses all functional boundaries, only top management can ensure that the computer will best serve the overall needs of the company and not be used for parochial interests.

Figure 3.8 enables the system analyst or business manager to see the interrelationships of processes. The tracing and interaction of key source data will illustrate the necessity and practical implications of designing systems that avoid redundancy and take advantage of common data flows. The sales forecast is a prime example. The forecast is a key strategic tool in the operation of any company. First of all, a sales forecast is crucial to the planning process. It is the basis for determining whether a new item should be introduced or an entirely new product line developed. It forms the rationale for establishing plant capacity and long-range facility needs. It is a key determinant for budget preparation and profitability projection. In the operational and control area, the sales forecast determines purchasing policies (how much to order, when to order), manufacturing policies, work levels, hiring, training, quota setting, machine loading, inventory levels, and the like.

It would appear prudent to recognize the commonality and significance of the sales forecast and to take these elements into account in designing a management information system. It is common to have a variety of forecasting systems in use within a single enterprise, some of which are mutually inconsistent. Thus the manufacturing manager may be formulating his production schedule on forecast A while the materials control manager, who is responsible for supplying raw materials to enable forecast A to be met, may be ordering on the basis of forecast B. This seems a strange way to operate, but some companies do operate this way. It is a classic example of the lack of system integration.

The preceding discussion does not imply that the same forecast should be used in every instance. Indeed, there may be logical reasons for using different forecasts. For example, it may be wise from an inventory standpoint to use a higher or more optimistic forecast, thus risking a chance of overstocking at a time when particular products are hard to procure. On the other hand, it may be logical to use a lower or more realistic forecast in setting sales and quota goals for salesmen lest their motivation and performance be adversely affected. The important point is that the concept of integration should be recognized: there should be a single function dedicated to sales forecasting. Forecasting should be accomplished by the group having access to the most current and meaningful data and having the ability to best process that data. All forecasts should emanate from the same quantitative data. If adjustments are desired to reflect various probabilities and risks, these adjustments should be made by the same group. Thus a forecast could consist of a most likely, most optimistic, and most pessimistic outlook. The various departments could then select the forecast that represented the level of risk and management judgment that they thought best under the circumstances. However, in no case should the situation arise where the manufacturing manager and the material manager use different forecasts—one second-guessing the other. In this case, they should get together, jointly agree on a forecast, and proceed to provide the necessary resources to meet it.

It is surprising, when reviewing a business model, to discover that almost all the information needed to drive it emanates from a rather small number of common source documents. It is also surprising to see the interconnection of processes that were thought to be entities in themselves but that are really connected by a common flow of data. A prime example is a purchase requisition. This document initiates a long series of activities, starting with the writing of a purchase order by the accounting department, and including the physical receipt of the goods, the quality control check, the paperwork updating of inventory records, the establishment of accounts payable, and eventual vendor payment. Thus the purchase requisition affects the accounting, financial, quality control, receiving, purchasing, and inventory-control functions. An integrated system approach recognizes rather than ignores these interrelationships. The system may begin with the automation of a specific function, but only after the total picture is studied. Then subsystems can be added later with minimum effort and duplication.

MANUFACTURING BUSINESS MODEL

Figure 3.9 adds six processes to the distribution model to produce a manufacturing model. Since all manufacturers perform the distribution function, the major difference between the two operations is that the distributor orders all manufactured items from a vendor while the manufacturer produces the items himself and orders only raw materials, assemblies, and piece parts. The physical facilities now include a factory as well as a warehouse.

The manufacturing model adds the engineering and research process (E&R), which is a vital one to a manufacturing operation. The engineers design the products the company produces and develop bill-of-material and routing-sheet information. Basically, the bill of material indicates the components and assemblies (and quantities of each) required to build an end item, whereas the routing sheet indicates the type and sequence of production operations necessary to transform the raw material and components into finished goods. The E & R process is also responsible for establishing requirements and standards for quality control and machine maintenance.

Figure 3.9 indicates the interrelationship of the E & R process with quality control, maintenance, production scheduling, and requirements generation. Let us see how these subsystems are tied together with the distribution processes described earlier.

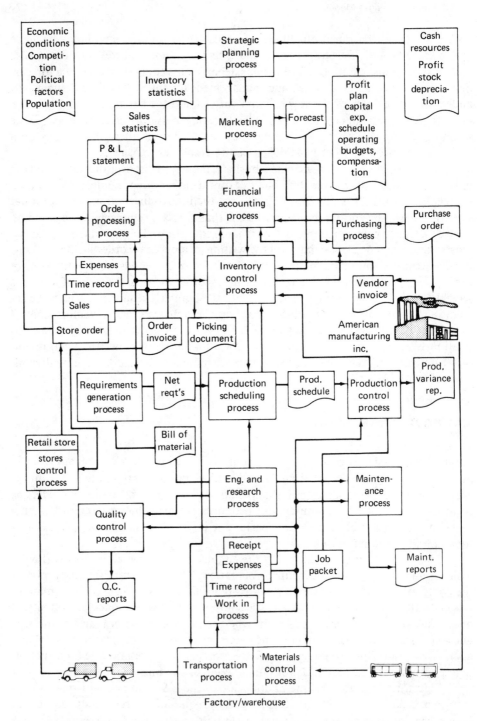

Fig. 3.9 Business model for a manufacturing company

The requirements-generation process takes finished-goods requirements (sales forecast, plus sales orders, minus finished-goods inventory) from the inventory-control subsystem and, utilizing the bill-of-material information from the E & R process, determines the requirements for subassemblies, piece parts, and raw material by multiplying the number of finished-goods items by the components that constitute each end item. The total for each subunit is then measured against inventory records to produce net requirements.

This netting process is direct input into the production-scheduling process. The routing data, also supplied by the E & R process, is combined with the net requirements to produce a production schedule. The production-control process deals with the day-to-day implementation of the production plan by issuing job packets to the factory (telling them what jobs to work on, the sequence and scheduled completion dates), accepting feedback (including labor, material, expense, and work-in-process data), and producing a variety of quality-control and maintenance reports and analyses. The result of these six manufacturing processes is to maintain an availability of finished-goods items in the warehouse to satisfy customer demand and interface to the distribution process (order processing, inventory control, accounting, and transportation), which has been described previously.

BUSINESS PROCESSES

Now that the business processes have been described and their interconnection illustrated, let us categorize or classify them. Doing so helps the MIS designer determine where to start, what resources are necessary, what capabilities are required, the degree of difficulty to be expected, and the potential benefit to various levels of management. Figure 3.10 further classifies the fifteen processes illustrated in the manufacturing information model. The three major categories are supportive, mainstream, and administrative. The supportive category includes marketing, strategic planning, and engineering and research. The supportive processes differ from the mainstream processes in that the latter control the physical line operation of the business, the flow of raw materials through the plant into the hands of the ultimate consumer.

The supportive processes are obviously most significant in establishing the plans, budgets, and facilities, as well as the basic decision rules embedded in the mainstream processes; however, they differ from the line or mainstream functions. The administrative processes involve the accounting for facilities, activities, and people necessary to run the business. These processes satisfy the external requirements of a business placed upon it by various government and regulatory agencies. Thus taxes must be paid, profitability reported to the Security and Exchange Commission, and the business operated within the framework of proper licenses and contracts.

Figures 3.11, 3.12, and 3.13 further characterize the processes on the basis of twelve criteria. An example will explain how to read the charts. The sales-analysis

SUPPORTIVE

Marketing
Sales analysis
Sales forecasting
Advertising
Sales administration

Strategic Planning
Econometric models
Market models
Simulation
Decision theory
Investment analysis
Facilities planning

Engineering and Research
Design automation
Project control
Numerical control
Configuration management
Industrial engineering
Bill of material generation

MAINSTREAM

Sales Order Processing
Customer billing
Order filling
Transportation

Inventory Reporting and Control
Stock status reporting
Statistical replenishment.

Requirements Generation
Gross requirements generation
Net requirements generation

Production Scheduling
Fabrication and assembly scheduling
Shop loading
Issuance of job packets

Production Control
Performance vs plan analysis
Variance reporting

Purchasing
Receiving
Quality Control
Maintenance

ADMINISTRATIVE

Financial
Accounts receivable
Accounts payable
General ledger
Cost accounting
Fixed asset accounting
Budgeting
Financial models
Key rated analysis
Profit and loss statements

Personnel
Payroll
Payroll reports
Wage and compensation analysis
Performance appraisals

Legal

Fig. 3.10 Business-process classification

Process	Type of function	Major management focus	Cycle	Form of processing	Processing complexity	Data base	Type of data	Time demand	Transaction volume	Typical mode of operation	Frequency of implementation	Difficulty of implementation
Sales analysis	Mktg. supp.	Opert'g & middle	Weekly	Structured	Low	Customer & sales files	Internal	Medium	Heavy	Batch	High	Low
Sales forecasting	Mktg. supp.	Middle	Monthly	Structured	High	Sales history	Internal	Low	Heavy	Batch	Med.	Med.
Advertising	Mktg. supp.	Middle	Monthly	Unstructured	High	Sales history	Internal external	Low	Light	Batch	Low	High
Sales administration	Mktg. supp.	Opert'g & middle	Daily	Highly struc.	Med.	Customer & inventory	Internal	Med. to high	Heavy	Direct & Batch	High	Low
Econometric models	Plan'g supp.	Middle & top	Monthly	Structured	High	Gen. Ledger accounting	Internal	Low	Light	Batch	Low	Med.
Market models	Plan'g supp.	Middle & top	Monthly	Unstructured	High	Sales history	Internal external	Low	Med.	Batch	Low	High
Decision theory	Plan'g supp.	Middle & top	Weekly	Unstructured	High	— —	Internal external	Med.	Low	Batch	Med.	High
Investment analysis	Plan'g supp.	Middle & top	Monthly	Structured	Med.	Gen. Ledger accounting	Internal	Low	Low	Batch	Low	Med.
Facilities planning	Plan'g supp.	Middle & top	Monthly	Structured	Low	Gen. Ledger accounting	Internal	Low	Low	Batch	Low	Med.
Design automation	Engr'g supp.	Opert'g & middle	Daily	Structured	High	Product file	Internal	High	Med.	On line	Low	High
Project control	Engr'g supp.	All levels	Weekly	Structured	Low	— —	Internal	High	Med.	On line	Med.	Med.
Numerical control	Engr'g supp.	Operating	Weekly	Structured	High	Product file	Internal	High	Med.	On line	Low	High
Configuration management	Engr'g supp.	Opert'g & middle	Weekly	Structured	Low	Product file	Internal	Low	Med.	Batch	Low	Med.
Industrial Engineering	Engr'g supp.	Opert'g & middle	Daily	Structured	Med.	Personnel file	Internal	Med.	Med.	Batch	Low	Med.
Bill of Mat'l generation	Engr'g supp.	Operating	Daily	Highly struc.	Med.	Product file	Internal	Med.	Heavy	Direct & batch	Med.	Med.

Fig. 3.11 Supportive-process characteristics

Process	Type of function	Major management focus	Cycle	Form of processing	Processing complexity	Data base	Type of data	Time demand	Transaction volume	Typical mode of operation	Frequency of implementation	Difficulty of implementation
Customer billing	Mainstream	Operating	Daily	Highly struc.	Low	Customer file	Internal	High	Heavy	On line	High	Low
Order filling	Mainstream	Operating	Daily	Highly struc.	Low	Customer file	Internal	High	Heavy	On line	High	Low
Transportation	Mainstream	Operating	Daily	Highly struc.	Med.	Cust.& vehicle	Internal	High	Heavy	On line	Med.	Low
Stock status reporting	Mainstream	Opert'g & middle	Daily	Highly struc.	Low	Inventory file	Internal	Med.	Heavy	On line	High	Low
Statistical replenishment	Mainstream	Operating	Daily	Structured	High	Inventory file	Internal	Med.	Heavy	On line	Med.	Med.
Gross Requirements gen.	Mainstream	Operating	Daily	Highly struc.	Med.	Inv. & product file	Internal	Med.	Med.	Batch	Med.	Med.
Net requirements generation	Mainstream	Opera-ing	Daily	Highly struc.	Med.	Inv. & Prod file	Internal	Med.	Med.	Batch	Med.	Med.
Fabrication & Ass'y scheduling	Mainstream	Operating	Daily	Structured	High	Inv.Prod.& facil.file	Internal	Med.	Med.	Batch	Low	High
Shop loading	Mainstream	Operating	Daily	Structured	High	Inv.prod.& facil.file	Internal	High	Med.	On line	Low	High
Issuance of job packets	Mainstream	Operating	Daily	Structured	Med.	Inv.prod.& facil.file	Internal	High	Med.	Online	Med.	Med.
Performance vs plan analysis	Mainstream	Opert'g & middle	Weekly	Structured	Med.	Inv.work in process	Internal	Med.	Low	On line	Med.	Med.
Variance reporting	Mainstream	Opert'g & middle	Weekly	Structured	Med.	Inv.work in process	Internal	Med.	Low	On line	Med.	Med.
Purchasing	Mainstream	Operating	Daily	Highly struc.	Med.	Vendor file	Internal	Med.	Med.	On line	Med.	Med.
Receiving	Mainstream	Operating	Daily	Highly struc.	Low	Inventory file	Internal	High	Med.	On line	Med.	Low
Quality control	Mainstream	Opert'g & middle	Weekly	Structured	Med.	Product & facilities	Internal	Med.	Med.	On line	Low	Med.
Maintenance	Mainstream	Opert'g & middle	Weekly	Structured	Med.	Prod. & facil.file	Internal	Med.	Med.	On line	Low	Med.

Process	Type of function	Major management focus	Cycle	Form of processing	Processing complexity	Data base	Type of data	Time demand	Transaction volume	Typical mode of operation	Frequency of implementation	Difficulty of implementation
Accounts receivable	Admin. finan.	Operating	Daily	Highly struc.	Low	Customer	Internal	Med.	Heavy	Batch	High	Low
Accounts payable	Admin. finan.	Operating	Daily	Highly struc.	Low	Vendor	Internal	Med.	Med.	Batch	High	Low
General ledger	Admin. finan.	Operating	Weekly	Highly struc.	Low	Acct'g	Internal	Low	Low	Batch	Low	Low
Cost accounting	Admin. finan.	Opert'g & middle	Weekly	Structured	Med.	Inv. & gen.ledger	Internal	Med.	Low	Batch	Med.	Med.
Fixed asset accounting	Admin. finan.	Opert'g & middle	Weekly	Highly struc.	Low	General ledger	Internal	Med.	Low	Batch	High	Low
Budgeting	Admin. finan.	All levels	Monthly	Structured	Med.	General ledger	Internal external	Med.	Low	Batch	Med.	Med.
Financial models	Admin. finan.	Middle & top	Monthly	Structured	High	General ledger	Internal external	Low	Low	Batch	Low	High
Key ratio analysis	Admin. finan.	Middle & top	Monthly	Structured	Med.	General ledger	Internal	Low	Low	Batch	Low	High
Profit and loss statements	Admin finan.	Middle & top	Monthly	Structured	Low	General ledger	Internal	Low	Low	Batch	Med.	Med.
Payroll	Admin. pers'l	Operating	Weekly	Highly struc.	Low	Personnel file	Internal	Med.	Med.	Batch	High	Low
Payroll reports	Admin. per'sl	Operating	Weekly	Highly struc.	Low	Personnel file	Internal	Med.	Med.	Batch	High	Low
Skills inventory	Admin. pers'l	Opert'g & middle	Weekly	Structured	Low	Personnel file	Internal	Low	Med.	Batch	Low	Med.
Wage and compensation analysis	Admin. pers'l	Opert'g & middle	Weekly	Structured	Low	Personnel file	Internal	Low	Med.	Batch	Low	Med.
Performance appraisals	Admin. pers'l	Opert'g & middle	Weekly	Structured	Low	Personnel file	Internal	Low	Med.	Batch	Low	Med.
Legal	Admin. legal	Middle & top	Weekly	Structured	Low	Specially prepared	Internal external	Low	Med.	Batch	Low	Med.

Fig. 3.13 Administrative-process characteristics

79

process is marketing supportive and aimed at operating and middle management. Sales-analysis reports are usually produced on a weekly basis; the decision rules required by the process are well understood, straightforward, and highly structured; and the complexity level of mathematics or computer processing required is low. The principal data-base elements from which the necessary information is extracted are the customer and sales files. The type of data is internal to the company's operation (sales history) as contrasted to external data (economic trends, buyer profiles) and the time demand is medium: that is, the information must be timely, but normally it can be produced on a scheduled basis. The transaction volume is heavy because the analysis is built from customer orders. Because the sales analysis can be scheduled and because it requires a compilation of data, the mode of operation is batch, though it could be on-line to improve responsiveness. The historical frequency of implementing this process is high, and because of the composite of characteristics, the degree of difficulty in implementing is low.

Additional study of the characteristics chart can help establish a priority analysis of processes based on the relative weights placed on the various criteria. Thus it may be wise to start with processes that are easy to implement; conversely, if the systems capability is present, the company may choose to tackle processes that are aimed at higher levels of management, thereby going after the bigger payoff and benefit.

SUPPORT ELEMENTS FOR THE BUSINESS MODEL

Referring back to Fig. 3.1, we see that once the business model and business processes are identified, an MIS is built to support the organization that performs these processes. A typical organization was reviewed in Chapter 1. Figure 3.1 also indicates that a data base underlines the MIS. Data base will be the subject of Chapter 4. The next step in understanding MIS is to go through the following type of analysis.

A series of matrices are produced to show the connection and relationship of organizational entity, specific information system, and data base in relation to business processes. A series of four matrices or cross-comparisons are developed as indi-

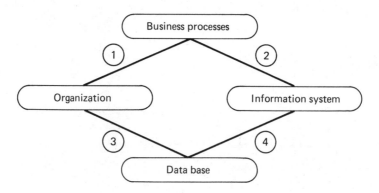

cated by the numbers 1 to 4. The four matrices are (1) business process by organization, (2) business process by information system, (3) organization by data base, and (4) information system by data base.

1. Business Process by Organization

Figure 3.14 lists organization entities across the top and business processes down the side. An asterisk indicates that the particular organization has major re-

Organization / Business process	Controller			Marketing			Production					
	Cost accounting	Accounts receivable	Accounts payable	Sales administration	Sales	Sales planning	Inventory control	Production scheduling	Transportation			
Order processing												
Order entry		●		*	●							
Order processing		●		*	●	●		●				
Billing		*		*	●							
Shipping		●			●	●	●					
Inventory control												
Inventory accounting	*				●		*	●	*			
Inventory control	*						*	●	*			
Costing	*						●					
Product build												
Production scheduling	●				●		●	*				
Material req's							*	*				
Shop control							●	*				

Fig. 3.14

sponsibilities for the business process while a solid dot indicates involvement in the process. In implementing an MIS, people who are responsible for the process are the principal recipients of the MIS support. We do not start with the people, since people and organizations show a great deal more volatility than processes. Since we want to build our MIS on a long-term basis, we want to ensure first that the processes are supported before we look at the departments and individuals responsible for carrying them out. This chart identified the key departments from which we can find out more about the processes and the information needs. It also points out potential overlap (several departments having a major responsibility for a process, e.g., billing) or underlap (no department has a major responsibility) for a specific process. In establishing interdepartment MIS priorities or in gaining specification sign-off for a particular application, we would certainly want to use this chart.

2. Business Process by Information System

Organizations developing MIS's usually are not starting from scratch. They have existing systems in place that are supporting business processes to some degree. Figure 3.15 indicates by a cross (**x**) where current information systems (the horizontal axis) are supporting business processes (the vertical axis). This brings out the current coverage of systems and indicates areas that are not supported. For example, the market research process is not supported by an information system. This is not surprising, because this process relies heavily on external data that is difficult to capture in electronic form. This schematic also shows potential overlap and redundancy. For example, the inventory-accounting and inventory-control processes are each supported by five information systems. Further analysis is needed to ascertain if there is duplication (file redundancy and the like). The redundancies, voids, and gaps are leading indications of future MIS plans and implementation.

3. Organization by Data Base

Figure 3.16 shows data base mapped against the organization. We have already stated that data is a valuable resource. This chart shows which organizations rely on information, the source of which is the data base indicated. In this instance there is no data base for sales history or competitive sales. Creation of the data base may assume a high priority status, as these areas usually are critical to the marketing department. This analysis brings out the reliance of information users on common data files, emphasizing the importance of organizing and creating a data base that is easy to access from a multiplicity of vantage points.

4. Information System by Data Base

As we have noted and will examine in greater detail in Chapter 4, the data base is the crucial reservoir for providing information for MIS and for the organization.

Information system ▲2 / Business process	Order processing	Order billing	Accounts receivable	Inventory control	Purchasing	Production scheduling	Bill of material	Shop floor control				
Order entry	X											
Order processing	X											
Billing	X	X	X									
Shipping	X	X	X									
Inventory accounting	X			X		X	X	X				
Inventory control	X			X		X	X	X				
Costing				X								
Production scheduling	X			X		X	X					
Material req's				X		X	X					
Shop control				X		X	X	X				
Market research												

Fig. 3.15

This matrix and the previous one relate data to these entities. Figure 3.17 places a cross where the data base provides information to support a particular information subsystem. In this instance we see two voids, in that a data base does not exist for the product-planning or market-research systems. This is not unusual, but it may pinpoint an area of future development if management gives it a high priority and there are resources to implement. This matrix also shows that certain data-base files (e.g., product) have broad across-the-board utilization in many information systems. The

Organization / Data base (3)	Controller			Marketing			Production					
	Cost accounting	Accounts receivable	Accounts payable	Sales administration	Sales	Sales planning	Inventory control	Production scheduling	Transportation			
Customer		X		X	X			X	X			
Product	X			X	X		X	X				
Vendor			X				X					
Employee					X			X				
Price				X	X							
Parts							X	X				
Sales history												
Competitive sales												

Fig. 3.16

need for unity and integration is apparent in these situations. This analysis adds another important insight into the future development of MIS.

These four matrixes are key analytical tools for beginning the development of MIS to support the business and the business model developed earlier in the chapter. The role and influence of management is crucial in determining the ultimate requirements and in establishing the priorities for development. The business model and matrices provide an excellent framework for gaining the necessary management involvement in the process.

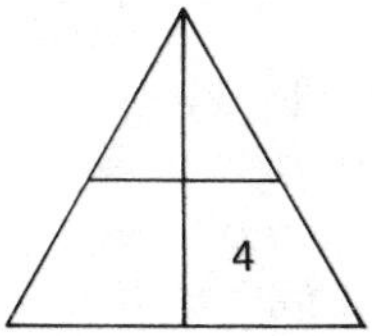

Information system / Data base	Order processing	Order billing	Accounts receivable	Inventory control	Purchasing	Production scheduling	Bill of material	Shop floor control	Product planning	Market research	
Customer	X	X	X								
Product	X	X		X	X	X	X	X			
Vendor					X						
Employee											
Facilities						X					
Price	X	X	X								
Parts						X	X	X			

Fig. 3.17

SUMMARY

This chapter has emphasized that a thorough and comprehensive understanding of the business processes precedes the planning and implementation of MIS. The sequence of MIS development emanates from the building of a business model. The business model in turn is comprised of a group of interlinking or integrated processes. A distribution-company model was developed to illustrate the concept followed by the addition of processes pertinent to a manufacturing company. The resultant processes were then analyzed via a series of characteristics that will assist in the selection and priority setting of MIS implementation.

The business-model methodology was then expanded as a basis for looking at the underlying organization, existing information systems, and data-base requirements. Four matrices were developed to help us comprehend the interaction of these elements with the business processes. The purpose is to build an MIS that mirrors the business processes and provides the information necessary to run a competitive business and meet the operational goals of the enterprise.

Throughout the chapter the word *management* appears; the repetition has the purpose of providing the desired degree of emphasis. This theme has been and will be carried throughout the book.

We next turn to a discussion of data base, the integrating element undergirding the MIS model developed in this chapter.

CASE STUDIES

MERK INDUSTRIAL PRODUCTS

The corporate planning vice-president and MIS vice-president of Merk Industrial Products agreed that a major planning effort was required to plot the future direction of the company's MIS efforts. Their only question was the way to go about it and the time to allow for its completion. After a month's study of various planning methodologies, including a review of what consultants offered as well as computer vendors, they decided on a technique called Process 1. This would take a concerted three-month effort by a team of eight people working full time. The Process 1 team would be headed by the president's hand-picked staff assistant, a bright, energetic MBA who had built an excellent reputation in his six months with the company. The team was comprised of a mixture of non-MIS managers, an individual from corporate planning, and several key people from the MIS shop. A letter from the corporate planning vice-president explained the project:

> June 23, 1983
> From: R. L. Preston, Corporate Planning
>   B. J. Harrison, MIS Division
> To: Management Distribution List
> Subject: PROCESS 1 PLANNING STUDY
> cc: J. P. Wharton, President
>
> I am sure all of you are aware of the dynamic nature of our business. Our success in the future will depend greatly on how we plan and react to the business environment. I am pleased to inform you that we are initiating a major effort to analyze our current and future information needs. I have authorized a study group that will conduct an in-depth study on

how we use information and its relation to our business, and to recommend a systems architecture which will guide us in the development of the information systems we will need to manage Merk Industrial in the future. Our goal is to complete this project by September 30, 1983.

A steering committee comprised of the department heads of Engineering, Manufacturing, Finance, Marketing, and Field Operations will be responsible for reviewing progress and approving direction.

A study team will be directed by John Parks, Assistant to the President, with our divisional personnel involved on both a full-time and part-time basis.

We will be using a methodology called Process 1, which has been helpful to other companies in evaluating and planning for their information requirements.

Process 1 involves a thorough review of our business and the business processes that are performed. This is followed by a formal analysis of current and future data needs and how our information systems meet these needs; gaps and voids will be pointed out. A full report with recommendations for action will be presented to each of you at the conclusion of the study. Please give your full cooperation in the conduct of this important planning effort.

_____   _____

R. L. Preston   B. J. Harrison

QUESTIONS

1. What do you think of Merk's approach to MIS planning? Are they going about it the right way?

2. What are the major obstacles to carrying out the study?

3. Do you think eight people working three months on a full-time basis is too much to ask? Do you think Preston and Harrison can gain the cooperation and endorsement of the key department managers and the assignment of their key people to the study?

4. Do you think the letter will serve its intended purpose? Is that the way to launch the program? Are there other approaches, or should the letter perhaps be supplemented by other actions?

5. What are the benefits of undertaking this planning effort?

WARBURTON CHEMICAL

Paul Buchanan, Director of MIS at Warburton Chemical, had called a meeting with his staff as a first step in developing a new MIS strategy. Sam Warburton, the chairman and CEO, thought his company could be getting more from their computer investment and directed Buchanan to present him a plan of how to do it. The triggering event was a discussion Warburton had with a respected fellow executive. Though his firm was only a fraction of the size of Warburton Chemical, the executive had described the meaningful reports that he personally received from his MIS group. Sam Warburton had never seen a computer printout.

Warburton Chemical had been a Sam Warburton creation since its founding some 25 years earlier. It had grown rapidly under the owner's entrepreneurial reins and now had sales in excess of $100 million. There were strong rumors that Warburton was considering an acquisition offer from a large oil company.

Buchanan opened the meeting by indicating that their systems must be more user-oriented. They had emphasized the operational, lower-level applications and had spent an inordinate amount of time and money fine-tuning, rewriting, and upgrading the old programs when there were far more important management applications. The rest of the meeting was spent on a review of the Warburton organization, the various departments, and the individual department managers. It was obvious that Sam Warburton ran the company with his unique personal style and the organization had developed in an unorthodox way. For example, though planning was not a strong function with the company, the planning director reported to the vice-president of engineering, who was one of the most influential executives. It was also an anomaly that Finance had responsibility for purchasing and inventory control— two functions normally in the bailiwick of manufacturing. All this surprised the MIS group, because it was the first time they had really thought about it. Also they wondered what its relevance was to them anyway, and why an entire meeting was spent reviewing people and their organizations. Each person present had a huge backlog of work, and this type of meeting wasn't helping them get at it. Buchanan knew that the talk of the possible acquisition had reached them all, and he concluded the meeting by asking what impact such a move would have on their systems efforts and particularly their future direction. The consensus was that this was for the higher echelons to worry about; their job was to continue with their current applications and to make them run as efficiently as possible.

Buchanan mulled over the meeting in his mind and pondered his next step. His background had been technical; an engineer by education with a sharp computer bent, he had joined Warburton five years earlier and had always impressed the executives with his grasp of the job and his quick answers to technical questions. Now he wondered whether it was a new ball game and whether he had the skills or background called for in this new arena.

He was uneasy, too, about his staff's reaction to the meeting. Though they were conscientious and attentive, he sensed a real concern on their part. Planning, strategy, and organization were all new terms to them. He didn't want to stretch them too much, because he considered them one of the best technical groups in the industry, a group that knew programming and how to get something up and running on a computer. Turnover in his group had been low—in a market where good system analysts and programmers were in great demand.

QUESTIONS

1. Is this a good time for Buchanan to introduce his new idea?

2. What is the significance of Warburton's organization to the MIS group?

3. Is there a danger in developing systems aimed at particular individuals rather than at specific business processes? What happens when changes occur in organizations?

4. What do you think of the attitude of Buchanan's staff? Do you think it is a normal one? a desirable one?

5. What is it going to take to satisfy Sam Warburton? What should be Buchanan's reply to his comment about getting more from MIS?

6. What should be Buchanan's long-range strategy for MIS? How should he go about developing it?

BIBLIOGRAPHY

Honeywell Consulting Services, *A Planning Method, Instructional Guide*, 1982.

IBM, "Business Systems Planning: Information Systems Planning Guide," Doc. GE20-0527-2, Technical Publications, White Plains, NY: IBM Corp., 1978.

IBM, "Business Systems Planning: Information Systems Planning Guide (Application Manual), 2nd ed., Doc. GE20-0527-2, Technical Publications, Dept. 824, White Plains, NY: IBM Corp., 1978.

Chapter *4*

The Mortar of MIS: Data Base

The preceding chapter made it obvious that data is the key element that drives information systems. Data was defined in the very first chapter as the raw material of MIS. The objective of MIS is to transform that data into meaningful management information, which is defined as the finished goods in the process. The business processes are supported by information that emanates from a data base; the business model is built on a data-base foundation: it is the glue or mortar of MIS. An important lesson from the previous chapter is that data often must be integrated or linked in order to provide the requisite information to the many classes of MIS users.

DATA-BASE DEFINITION

This chapter will explore the key attributes and requisites of an integrated data base. A simple definition of a data base is given by James Martin, a leading authority: "A data base is a collection of data that is shared and used for multiple purposes." Data is organized around files arranged such that duplication and redundancy are avoided. Information concerning ongoing activities is captured once, validated, and entered into the proper location in the data base. The key element in a data-base concept is that each subsystem utilizes the same data base in satisfying its information needs. Duplicate files or subsets of the data base are avoided.

In the development of systems, companies typically implemented applications on a one-by-one basis, giving little or no thought to the integration of data files. This is the root of the problem in the development of on-line, integrated, data-oriented applications. The perception of need for a data base usually follows the realization that as much as 80 percent of the system development dollars are spent in maintaining old applications as opposed to the development of new applications. Fragmented development results in each application having its own independent data file. Even minor changes to either the file or the application have serious rippling effects on the operation. With this burden, application backlogs grow and users become disillusioned, seeking information help outside the channels of their internal MIS operation.

Another development has been the demand for and shift to applications that support management control and strategic planning as opposed to operational control. In order to serve middle and upper management levels, data must be accessible in both a vertical and horizontal mode. The vertical mode permits access to an individual data file, where the desired information emanating from the file is summary, cumulative, or selective. Thus, a sales manager wants a report showing sales by region by salesman, sequenced in descending order by salesman's performance to quota. The horizontal mode allows information to be derived across file boundaries. An example is a banking application where data is captured and stored for various customer files, e.g., a file for each demand deposit account, savings, loans, trust, and so on. A manager wants to know the names and balances of customers who have three or more individual accounts with the bank. This involves the horizontal linking across boundaries usually indexed by customer name or account number. Fragmented data storage facilities do not permit this type of operation; both vertical and horizontal file access are extremely limited and cumbersome at best.

Figure 4.1 superimposes a data base alongside the activity triangle introduced in Chapter 1. The data required for operational control activities is built around transactions. Thus, in a distribution environment, orders are the principal transaction, with order-processing systems managing individual orders against a customer and inventory file. In banks, a basic operational control application is demand-deposit accounting, where customer accounts are maintained, updated by checks either debited or credited to the individual account. The checks represent transaction data, and the magnetic coding of checks has enabled this process to be carried out automatically.

The data files of these applications, however, with their origin in the fragmented development era, have not permitted the timely and meaningful extraction of data that, when combined with other data, such as performance criteria, enables the information system to support management needs. Strategic planning requires the combination of external data—e.g., competitive trends, inflationary pressures, productivity figures—with transaction and management data to support upper levels of management.

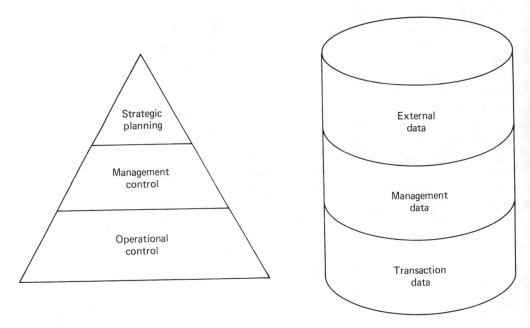

Fig. 4.1   Data-base support of applications

DATA-BASE REQUIREMENTS

Figure 4.2 lists the basic data files, the type of data contained in each, and the various time demands on information emanating from the files. Some applications or uses of the file require fast response, defined in seconds; others require medium response, defined in hours; while still others require only slow response, defined as several days to a week or even a month. This type of analysis is necessary to select the type of storage media best suited to the MIS requirements. While it is obvious that the principal data used in MIS will be computer-based, the concept does not preclude the use of other forms of data such as text, manual files, or even data carried in a person's head. To use the customer file as an example, it may be desirable to make a credit check at the check-cashing booth of a supermarket. This could be accomplished by inserting the customer's credit card into a device linked via a communication line into a computer storage device. Similarly, if a store is out of a special sale item, it may be necessary to deliver an emergency order to the store within an hour. This is not to say that complex computerized on-line systems are necessary to effect fast response time. For example, a daily listing in credit-card sequence of customers with credit problems might suffice in this instance. A chart similar to Fig. 4.2 does help to establish the necessary computerized storage hierarchy. The use of the word hierarchy implies that all data need not be accessible in the same amount of time; certain data (possibly entire files) can be stored on sequential, slow-access (but cheap) magnetic tape, while other data can be stored on high-capacity, high-speed random-access devices.

Data base element	Type of data	Fast response time	Medium response time	Slow response time
Customer file	Name Address Credit information Contract terms	Credit check Emergency orders	Normal order processing	Accounts receivable Cash collection Check reconciliation AR aging
Inventory file	Price, cost, weight Status and location of inventory items	Stock position in/out	Order processing Order point analysis Truck loading	Inventory status Obsolete inv. report Inventory value analysis Turnover ratio
Personnel file	Name, address, Wage rate Personnel status Deductions of all employees	Paychecks for bankers and part time people	Job accounting Labor analysis Overtime report	Weekly/monthly payroll Payroll register Internal revenue reports
General ledger file	Debits and credits Status of each account in general ledger	No requirements	Proforma - profit and loss and balance sheet	Profit and loss statement Balance sheet Account status
Sales history file	Units and dollars sold by region by division by store	No requirements	Forecast	Sales analysis Trend analysis Budget comparisons
Vendor file	Name, address Status, amount owed, Vendor rating Open orders for each vendor	No requirements	Purchase order	Vendor analysis Accounts payable Cash payments Check reconciliation

Fig. 4.2 Data-base requirements

The data-base concept is a most logical approach to the paperwork explosion that has hit many business areas. However, management should not overlook some important considerations in developing the data base as part of an integrated system. A fairly obvious problem is that erroneously entered data has an immediate influence on other subsystems and departments utilizing the data. Of course, this can be a desirable factor in that the errors will be noticed more quickly, and the feedback should help purify the data and ensure that necessary input controls are established and adhered to.

Another problem in building an integrated file is the interdepartmental cooperation needed to arrive at the pertinent data element in the file. One department may need a degree of detail that may burden the reporting source such that the quality of all input suffers. The solution to these problems normally means discussions, meetings, and eventual compromise if the implementation time frame is to be met.

Another problem in developing a data base is information security. When individual departments maintain their own data files, security of file information is not a problem. They know that other departments will not have access to confidential facts about their operation. In a highly centralized organization, the confidential nature of the data base is not of primary concern, but in a highly decentralized organization where divisions are autonomous, the centralization of data in one central file can represent a serious obstacle. The divisions are skeptical about the information they submit; they wonder how it is going to be used. They do not want their performance figures to be known by other divisions.

The suspicion generated by the security aspects of the data base can have a significant effect on the validity of what is supplied by the various users. It is true that certain quantitative data can be checked for obvious errors, but there is little or no check on the qualitative data—and this data can be extremely significant in the planning and analysis functions. Qualitative data can take the form of how the customer is currently using the product or how he plans to use it in the future. It also takes the form of information on customer complaints and problems in an effort to improve the product and service. The real measure of the success of the data-base concept is the input going into the system. The psychological considerations of submitting confidential data must be carefully considered.

Problems might also arise from the fact that there is a time dimension as well as a content dimension to information. In a particular situation, for example, it might take two to three months from the time an order is placed by a customer to validate the terms of the order officially. From the point of view of the sales office, the sales effort for this particular order is completed. They would like to see the results reflected in the particular period in which the customer placed the order. Their thinking is that in 90 percent of the cases, the contractual negotiations are a formality and do not change the basic terms of the order. This may not be the feeling of the production or accounting departments. Each of these departments has a different date at which they would like to see the order reflected as part of the customer and sales data base supplying reports to their departments.

Unless the new system satisfies the requirements of each user, the user is compelled to maintain his own system, which, of course, defeats the purpose of the central-data-base concept. The longer the user runs his old system in parallel, the more difficult it is to get him to supply accurate data to a new system that is not serving his needs.

Instituting an integrated system built around a data base brings to light deep-rooted management problems—problems that would continue to grow if left unattended. These are the "quiet problems," the problems of company communications, organization, and control. The development of the data base acts as the catalyst in bringing the "quiet problems" to the surface. The concerns mentioned are just a few to illustrate the challenge of data-base development. Others will be brought out later in the chapter.

USER VIEW OF DATA BASE

Before discussing the workings of a data base, it is appropriate to review the variety of data-base users, since this is the real end product and the reason for its being. Figure 4.3 depicts the gamut of end users ranging from the MIS specialist on the right-hand side to the management generalist on the left. The chart is split in two with MIS users on the left and MIS providers on the right. It is obvious that the middle- and top-management users on the left have a completely different perspective and view of the data base than the systems analysts and programmer/operators on the right. Not only are their needs different, but the methods of access to the data base are of an opposing nature.

A key difference between the users on the left and right is that of ad hoc usage versus dedicated or productive usage. The systems analysts spend full time develop-

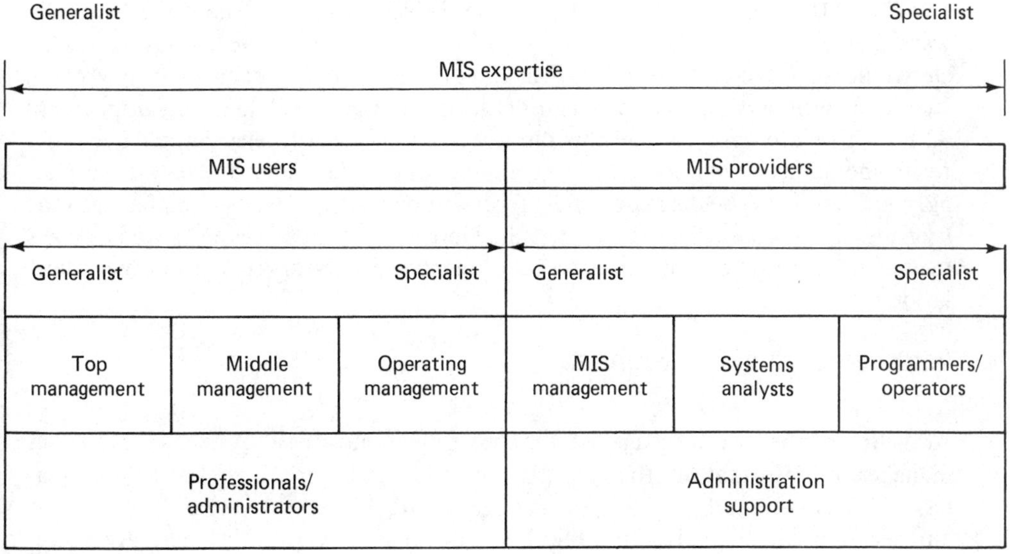

Generalist					Specialist
MIS expertise					
MIS users			MIS providers		
Generalist		Specialist	Generalist		Specialist
Top management	Middle management	Operating management	MIS management	Systems analysts	Programmers/operators
Professionals/administrators			Administration support		

Fig. 4.3   Data-base users

ing production programs and applications that will be used on a repetitive basis. Therefore, their objectives are more oriented to efficiency. They are able to learn a language or interface technique that produces an acceptable response time and turnaround time for the ultimate users. Since they are spending full time with the language, they can sacrifice ease of use for more efficient operation, and it is true that one does add resource overhead and execution time, the further one gets from the native mode instruction set of the computer.

On the other hand, the ad hoc or nondedicated user's principal need is to have a language that is easy to learn and simple to use. Since the information is a support function for accomplishing his job (his job is not to produce information), he does not want to spend an inordinate amount of time in learning new skills. His attention span is short when it comes to writing out instructions to access a computer data base.

The comparison of these two classes of usage, ad hoc and dedicated/repetitive, brings up the classic trade-off of effectiveness versus efficiency. The management user is more interested in effectiveness—that is, the end product rather than the degree of efficiency with which it is produced. Within reason of course, he doesn't care how many translation instructions are executed when he gives an inquiry to a data base; he doesn't spend that much time at it; but when he does need the information, it is vital that he gets it. Today's trend, with the reduction in hardware cost and the increase in personnel cost, is that the trade-off, even at the systems analyst/ programmer level, is shifting toward effectiveness.

Figure 4.4 depicts the variety of end-user languages or data windows through which information is obtained. These users represent only the left-hand side of Fig. 4.3. Several examples of user languages will be illustrated. With the range and number of data-base users expected to expand in the years ahead, end-user languages are most significant.

The MIS tools are to the right of the figure, representing the hardware and software interfaces and the data storage media for the data base. Note, in addition to the electronic storage media of on-line disk and off-line tape, the inclusion of microfilm storage as well as filing cabinets and data stored in an individual's memory bank. Although we are concerned in this discussion primarily with electronic data, other forms should not be overlooked. The computer operating system and data-base management system (to be discussed later) represent one layer of translation between the user and the data base. The various terminal interfaces, the devices employed by users in gaining access to the data base, and the language processors represent other translation vehicles.

VOICE AND NATURAL LANGUAGES

At the top of the user language list is the instrument most used by executives to gain management information: the voice. Ultimately, it represents a goal of future database systems—the ability of the system to recognize directly the verbal commands of an executive and to deliver the required information. Currently, there are voice-

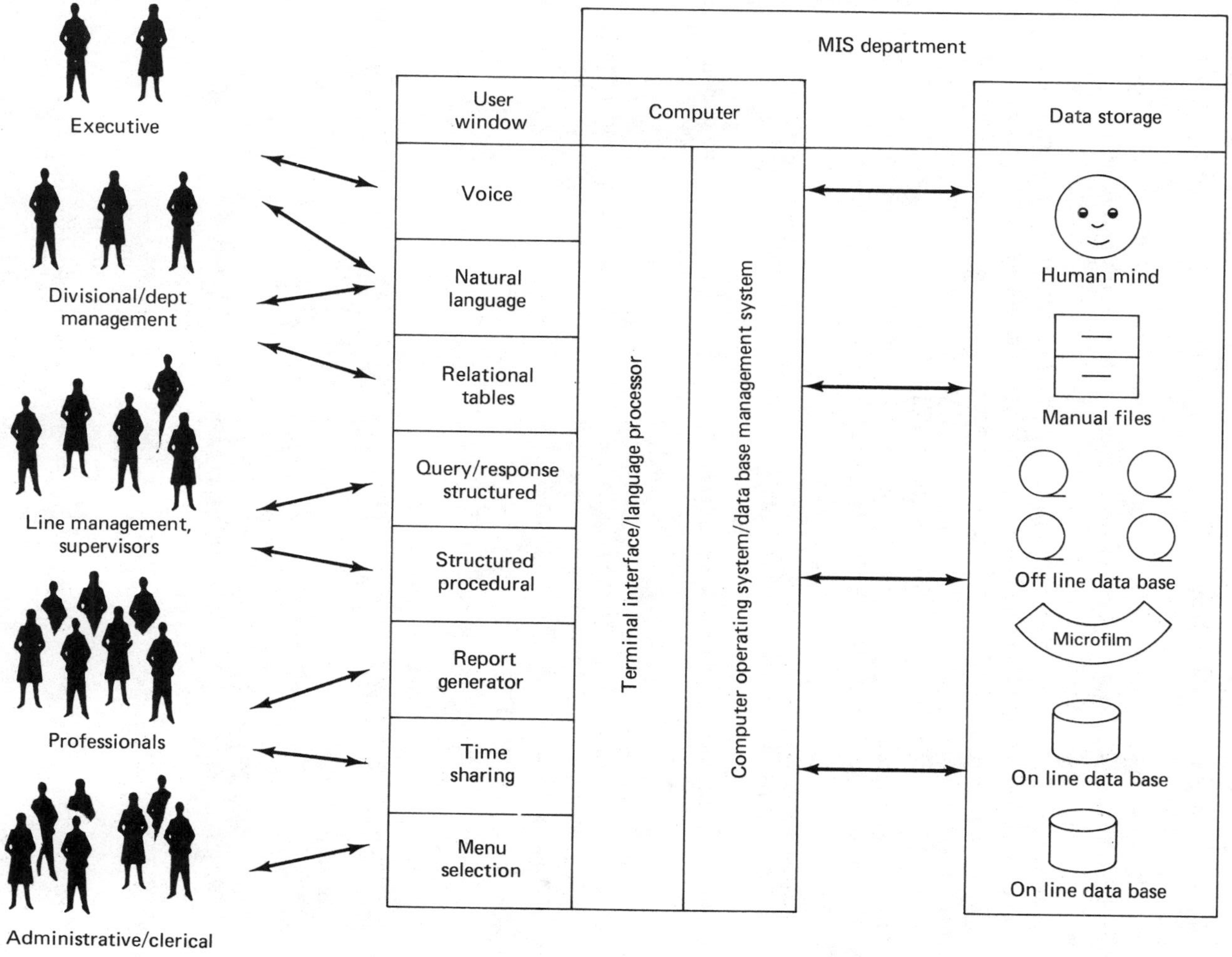

Fig. 4.4 End-user data windows

recognition systems that can comprehend a limited vocabulary, but it will be some time before an executive can use a machine the same way he can use an administrative assistant—and even with the machine, his management style may still favor the assistant.

The first language considered is natural language. A system called INTEL-LECT is an example of an English-language query system where commands can be given in complete sentences or in sentence fragments to manipulate a data base and to format meaningful reports. Numeric data can be counted, summed, divided, multi-plied, correlated, averaged, selected based on minimum and maximum ranges, and so on, while alphabetic data, along with the arithmetic data, can be produced in a vari-ety of report formats.

The following is an example of how the INTELLECT system is used. This is a simple data-base request, but the reader should be able to see the power of the tool and its possible extensions for management use.

Intellect Sample

System: In a few moments you will be conversing with INTELLECT. The file for this demon-stration consists of an employee file. Feel free to ask any questions phrased in any way you wish about this data. INTELLECT will try to answer your questions.

System: You will first be asked for your name and company affiliation. This information will be maintained on log files. You may begin asking questions when the system prompts you.

System: This is INTELLECT.
I'm ready to answer your questions pertaining to:
The employee file.
Please type in your name and affiliation.

User: John Doe, Acme, Mfg.

System: State request.

User: What's in the files?

Answer: Fields of the employee file

FIELD NAME	SEARCHABLE	SORTABLE	FORMAT	LENGTH
NAME	YES	YES	ALPHABETIC	20
CITY	YES	YES	ALPHABETIC	15
STATE	YES	YES	ALPHABETIC	2
JOB	YES	YES	ALPHABETIC	20
PHONE	YES	YES	ALPHABETIC	8
SALARY	YES	YES	ALPHABETIC	6
SEX	YES	YES	ALPHABETIC	1
AGE	YES	YES	NUMERIC	2
FAMILY STATUS	YES	YES	ALPHABETIC	10

System: Next request.

User: Print a report of salaries broken down by city within state.

System: Continue or punctuate.

User: For the New Hampshire and Connecticut people earning over 4000 and show names.

System: Print a report of state, city, salary, and name sorted by state and city of employee with salary over 4000 and state = New Hampshire or Connecticut.

Answer: The number of records to retrieve is 5.

System: How many records do you want listed?

User: All.

Answer:

STATE	CITY	SALARY	NAME
CONNECTICUT	STAMFORD	$48,000	VAN DUYN
		$ 6,000	MORRISON
CONNECTICUT	STAMFORD	$54,000	
CONNECTICUT	TOTAL	$54,000	
NEW HAMPSHIRE	HANOVER	$24,000	SAMUELSON
		$ 4,200	RUSSEL
		$ 5,500	SCHRIBER
NEW HAMPSHIRE	HANOVER	$33,700	
NEW HAMPSHIRE	TOTAL	$33,700	
GRAND TOTAL		$87,700	

RELATIONAL TWO-DIMENSION TABLES

We shall not illustrate each language mentioned in Figure 4.4, because they overlap and elements of one language appear in another; however, the examples given should facilitate an understanding of the scope and use of the entire list.

Relational data bases are now prominent, and an illustration will be used to explain this type of approach. To the user, relational means that he or she can define what data is desired by thinking in two-dimensional tables, which is a way many of us see and think of data reports. Thus, a report has a number of columns proceeding vertically down the page and a number of rows proceeding horizontally across the page. Figure 4.5 illustrates a simple report of salesmen grouped by selling region, in this case South, listed in sequence in descending order by the percentage of actual sales to their planned sales. A summary of the four salesmen completes the report.

To produce a report similar to the above, an executive would indicate on a terminal screen the columns and rows of the desired report and the relationship of the data to be displayed. If past-year sales were a factor, the executive could so indicate, and actual-to-last-year could be calculated on a percentage basis the same as actual-to-plan is on the current report. The theory behind the relational two-dimensional concept is that we tend to think this way and that it is more direct in requesting information to use this method rather than the free-form English-language format of IN-TELLECT.

Salesman	Region	Plan	Actual	Actual to Plan
Jones	South	100	120	120%
Johnson	South	150	160	107%
Higgins	South	100	90	90%
Black	South	100	85	85%
Total	South	450	455	101%

Fig. 4.5   Relational representation

Another very interesting offshoot of the tabular form of representation is the use of the electronic worksheet. The example in Fig. 4.6, a profit-and-loss statement, will be familiar to anyone who has a yearly operational plan or budget. The rows in the illustration are labeled A through G, the columns A1 through A3, with sub standing for subtotal. The relationships that produce the P&L are indicated in the first unlabeled column; thus cost of sales is 80 percent of sales while research and development is 10 percent and general and administrative expenses 5 percent. By filling actual values for sales and expenses, the model can calculate the gross margin and net profit on a monthly basis. More significantly, changes can be automatically reflected—for example, the result of decreasing cost of sales to 75 percent or of increasing sales by 10 percent during the second quarter. Thus, "what if" questions can be simulated and quickly calculated by the model. It is a very useful tool for managers and illustrates a powerful, but simple, user language.

		A^1	A^2	A^3	Sub
Sales	(A)				
Cost of sales	(B)				
	.8A				
Gross margin	(C)				
	A − B				
Expense	(D)				
R & D	(E)				
	.1A				
G & A	(F)				
	.05A				
Net profit	(G)				
	C − (D + E + F)				

Fig. 4.6   Electronic worksheet

STRUCTURED QUERY/RESPONSE AND STRUCTURED PROCEDURAL

Structured query/response is quite similar to the natural language explained above, but it is a far more structured language for obtaining simple ad hoc reports. Line managers and supervisors require more repetitive access to specific data files and are able to learn a more structured form of interface. This language falls somewhere between natural language and relational tables. For example, the notation used would be LIST ALL EMPLOYEES WITH SALARY > 8000 WITH CODE 1 THROUGH 8 AND DEPENDENTS < 4. Thus the language is a shorthand form, more congenial to middle or lower levels of management than to those at higher levels.

The structured language is similar to the above but is used for repetitive reports and routines rather than for short ad hoc requests. Thus, it results in the development of a procedure that can be repeated over time. Because it is repeated, the language is richer and a bit harder to learn, but it results in more efficient use and is more conservative of system resource. Structured procedural languages are being used more by systems analysts and programmers. They lie somewhere between the easier ad hoc languages and the more cumbersome programmer languages such as Pascal and COBOL. As mentioned, the declining cost of hardware in relation to salaries makes this an increasingly attractive approach.

REPORT GENERATION AND TIMESHARING

A report generator is a system analyst/programmer language for producing reports; it is equivalent to the natural language or structured query language used by managers. It has a far richer report formatting capability, which is necessary because the reports are used repeatedly and are seen by a wide audience. The commands and instructions must be learned, so that people using report generation usually are dedicated to the task.

Time-sharing facilities involve the use of a highly structured language and methodology that facilitate access (usually by professionals or administrators) to a shared computer facility at a remote site. The more common usage is scientific or number-related problem solving, such as mathematical equations involving a large number of iterations; however, other business-oriented uses are also found. In a typical application, a professional will develop an equation to solve a mathematical problem that needs resolution in the routine performance of his job. A common language used for this process is BASIC, and the following sample mathematical program illustrates the type of language and interaction employed.

Log-On Procedures to Time-Sharing Facility

System: User ID

User: Jones

System: Password

User: Engineer

System: System?

System: Old or new

User: New

System: Ready

The user has indicated his user ID and code name, that he wants to write a new program, and that he is now ready to begin. The following is a program using multiplication (∗) and addition (+). The reader should be able to see how complex mathematics can be performed by repeated arithmetic operations, including square roots and the like. The numbers 10, 20, and so on are TAGS to indicate the specific statement in case the user wants to save the program for later execution and/or modification or enhancement.

System: Ready

User: 10 let A = 10 ∗ 3
            20 print A
            30 let B = A + 5
            40 print B

User: 50 END

System: Ready

User: Run

System: 30
            35

MENU DRIVEN

This type of data-base interaction is primarily for relatively unskilled clerical operators who are using the system on a repetitive basis. It is a tutorial dialogue, where the system asks questions in the form of a menu selection. In this way the operator is walked through the process in a straightforward and simple fashion. A rudimentary example is Fig. 4.7, which could be used by a travel agent or an individual in his or her office or home to get a price on a trip to Phoenix, Arizona.

We have run the gamut of end-user languages from verbal and English language to highly structured query, time-sharing, and menu driven. Each has its strengths and weaknesses, the trick being to optimize language selection to the particular user and

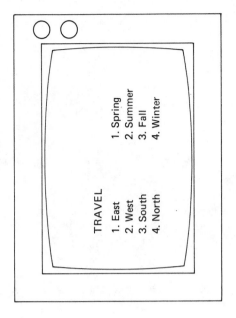

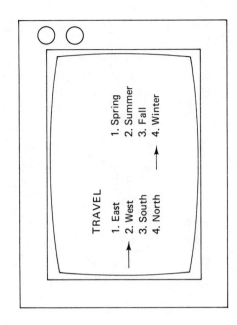

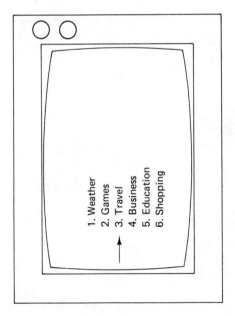

Fig. 4.7 Menu-driven dialogue

103

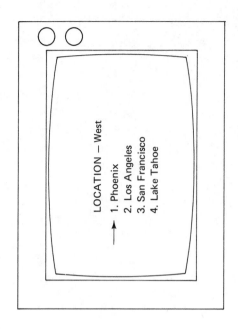

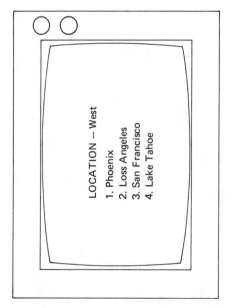

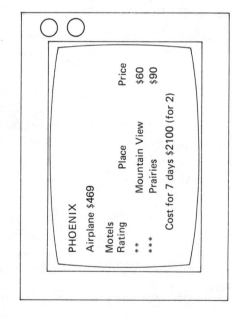

Fig. 4.7 Menu-driven dialogue (continued)

particular usage. In some cases the user is accessing an already created common data base, in others he or she is using a personal data base previously created or is creating a data base to be used only on the job at hand. Suffice it to say, the data base and the language to access it are powerful management tools.

LANGUAGE FOR MIS PROVIDERS

Figure 4.4 does not include languages employed by MIS providers; however, the trend in electronics/people cost trade-off is leading to increased use of the languages employed by MIS users. Figure 4.8 indicates a series of application development tools on a two-grid matrix of specificity versus time to develop. *Specificity* means the degree of tailoring of the solution to fit a specific problem. Some jobs, because of efficiency demands or job uniqueness, require such specificity that packaged solutions are either not available or not usable. The previous section discussed the tools in the center of the figure. An additional tool included in Fig. 4.8 is something called an *application generator.* Because product applications have to be run continually and wil have to be maintained and updated over their life span, a language that has the flexibility to include audit controls, check routines, testing monitors, and the like must be em-

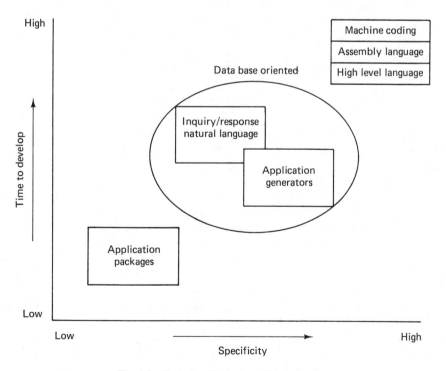

Fig. 4.8   Tools for developing MIS applications

ployed. Application generators have this capability, but are easier to use and take less time than the traditional machine assembly languages and higher-level languages on the lower right.

Of even greater attractiveness, because of the negligible time to develop, are *application packages*. If there is a fit between a specific user need and an available application package, packages represent a desirable solution. Obviously, in order to make money, application-package developers must work on generalized problems that have generalized solutions, so it behooves the user to ensure that there is a fit before he invests in a package.

Armed with a description of the data-base user languages, we can now turn inward to the workings of the data base itself and the employment of data-base software systems.

DATA-BASE SOFTWARE

The information resource management (IRM) concept, discussed in Chapter 2, emphasizes the significance of the information resource on a par with money, facilities, and personnel. It asserts that the same disciplines applied to the more traditional resources should be applied to the information resource. The elements applicable to managing a valuable resource are control, organize, plan, safeguard, measure, and protect. Data-base software, usually called *DBMS* or *data-base management systems*, represents a key tool to managing this important resource.

The move to on-line applications and management's burgeoning appetite for information pose problems for conventional data processing techniques. Demands for short-lead-time, one-time, or irregularly required reports, requests for data from several files, and the need for predicting future management needs all pose quite a challenge, for few managers can look ahead and predict with any degree of certainty what they will need in the way of information. It is difficult enough to get a clear picture of what information management wants today. Moreover, different managers on the same level often require quite different reports. This uncertainty is often discovered by a system analyst, once he develops a system and produces a report that he thought was the one the manager said he needed and then finds it is not what the manager wanted at all. The only way the system analyst can improve the situation is to follow the precept, "Don't give the manager what he *said* he wanted but what he *meant* he wanted." Needless to say, this situation presents a real problem for MIS designers.

Conventional methods of file design and acquisition have not been responsive (turnaround time for requests for data has been days or hours when it should have been seconds), have not been flexible enough to cope with the inevitable business changes that affect information systems, and have placed too great a burden on the system analyst's time. Many systems are built around a file structure that is embedded in each and every program written to process or access that file. This means that each time the file changes, the programs utilizing that file must also be changed. For example, the Social Security Administration had to modify hundreds of existing programs when a change in social security benefits affected the file structure of recipients. The result cost hundreds of thousands of dollars. This situation could have been avoided had the file structure not been embedded in each program using the file. The interleaving of file structure and programs has been a major contribution to high reprogramming costs and inflexibility to changing conditions. Data-base software solves this problem by utilizing a common file-description interface between the program and the data file, as shown in the diagram below.

An example will illustrate how the separation of files and programs facilitates change. A change occurs in the data file; for example, a company's product line may expand to the point that a five-digit item number is needed where a four-digit number previously sufficed. If there is no common file description serving as the link between the many programs that utilize the data (in this case, program 1 and program 2) and the data itself, each and every reference to that file within each program must be altered. Because of the magnitude of the change, and to ensure that all data references are flagged, program retesting and checkout are required. With the file descriptor, only the description itself is changed to indicate that the full size of the item number is now five digits. The data file, of course, must be updated to change the item numbers from four digits to five.

Data-base software has caught the attention of MIS designers because its purpose is to resolve the problems described. It attacks the problem with three major techniques: (a) data dictionaries to classify and define the various elements that become part of the data base, (b) file structures to increase the usefulness, flexibility, responsiveness to change, and accessibility of data, and (c) data-base languages to facilitate ease of access to the data base for managers, system analysts, clerical workers, and programmers. The latter topic has already been addressed.

Figure 4.9 lists the functions that must be performed upon data to create an effective DBMS. The first two functions are handled by the data dictionary. The next three fall under the file-structuring portion of the DBMS, while the latter two are covered by the data-base languages associated with the DBMS.

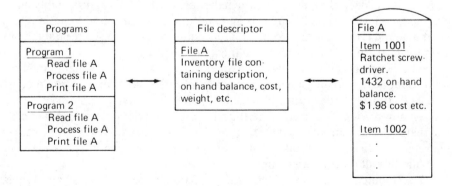

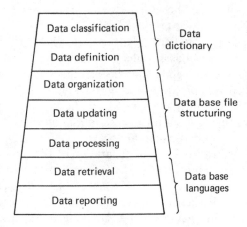

Fig. 4.9   Data-base functions

DATA DICTIONARY

The heart or hub of a data-base management system is the *data dictionary*. A multimillion-book library is useless without an index; the encyclopedias of the world are inert storehouses of knowledge without a guide to their organization and use; the largest collection of legal briefs and precedents lies fallow without access keys—and so it is with a data-base system without a data dictionary.

The files of data previously mentioned are broken down into *data fields* or *elements*. The key to a data dictionary is to define and tag each element so that it can be accessed for a specific use. People call the same thing by different names, and conversely the same name may refer to several things. A data dictionary avoids this confusion and redundancy, or at least plans for the redundancy, by defining each data element and giving it a name or identifier. A data dictionary is similar to a bill of material in a manufacturing operation. The bill of material indicates for each end product the parts and assemblies that came together to form the finished item and the sequence and order (relationship) in which they are used. A part and assembly may be used in several end products, and this must be known by the bill of material. As the bill of material is the heart of production scheduling and control, so the data dictionary is the heart of information scheduling and control.

The dictionary aids users by letting them know what data is available and how it can be obtained. A management user or an application programmer would consult the data dictionary to determine if the data required was already captured and, if so, to assess how to identify and access it; thus they avoid developing a program to collect data that is already collected, labeled, stored, and ready to use. Users write programs that refer to data structures that in turn contain the data elements. The data dictionary maintains all these relationships.

Development of a comprehensive data dictionary can help clear up organizational irregularities as regards data. Some departments or persons may be taking an ownership role as regards certain data files within their purview. They may regard the data as their proprietary possession, when in reality it may have significant value for other functions and departments within the company. A customer file, for example, may be viewed by the marketing department as their sole possession, although it can be of extreme value to various product and strategic planning activities. For the most part, data should be viewed as a resource of the total company; particular departments should be given custodial responsibility for specific files but not control over who has access to it. This is a different decision level. The development of a data base around a data dictionary brings to the surface these organizational data irregularities.

The dictionary also provides a much needed standardization mechanism. Data is continually changed, updated, modified, processed, combined, collated, sorted, and so on. Standardization, as provided by the data dictionary, abets the proper functioning of these transactions. The data dictionary can be viewed as the corporate glossary of the ever-growing information resource.

DATA INDEPENDENCE AND SCHEMAS

In the pre-data-base era, each application often had its own data base associated with it. Application A would use data base X, while application B used data base X and Y. Then along came application C, which used parts of X and Y and also a bit of its own data base. Serious problems arose when a change occurred in an application program or a change in the data-base structure. For example, a change in data base X would necessitate changes in all three applications (sometimes quite extensive). A change in any of the applications might affect its ability to access the various data bases.

This spawned the concept of data independence, which is a requisite of integrated data-base systems. Data is structured to be independent of the applications that use it. The technique that accomplishes this is called *maintaining logical and physical data independence*. The logical view of data is that of the application programmer. His or her concern should not be where the data physically resides but only what content is necessary to feed the application. To accomplish this, a data-base organization is established, built around a software data-base management system, and administered by a data-base administrator that provides what might be thought of as a data mapper, linking the logical view of data with the physical view in such a way that neither view must be known by the other. The translation takes place every time an application program accesses a piece of data, but it is transparent to the person writing the program.

Of course, the purpose of all this is to enable programs to be changed simply and efficiently without worrying about the data and vice versa. This is no trivial advantage, as a large MIS department can spend several million dollars each year to maintain existing programs.

Another set of terms used in data-base parlance is schemas and subschemas. The overall global view of a data base, similar to the view used by the mapper referred to above, is called a *schema*. The application programmer's view is referred to as a *subschema*, or sometimes the *local view* as compared to *global view*. Figure 4.10 illustrates the concept of data independence and schemas. Application programmers, referring to data in the local, logical, or subschema form, interface to the global view or schema, which provides the mapping and conversion to the physical data stored in on-line disk files.

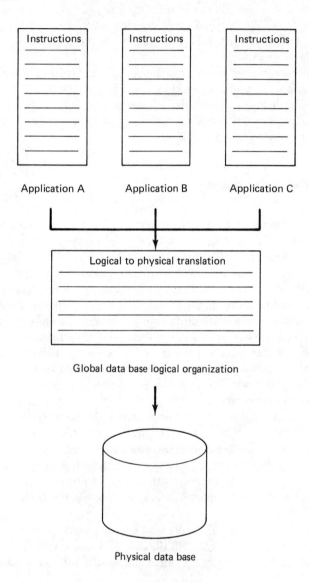

Fig. 4.10   Data independence

FILE STRUCTURE

The purpose of the file-structure element of data-base software is to facilitate the functions of data organization, updating, processing, and retrieval. A key characteristic is to allow cross-indexing or the chaining of related items so that they can be retrieved in a manner consistent with application and user needs. In simple sequential file structures, the information concerning a particular inventory item is stored on an inventory file, while the information concerning a particular customer is stored on a customer file. An additional open-order file will list the detail of each customer order that has not been delivered. This file combines information (actually duplicates it) from both the customer file and the inventory file. Although perhaps tolerable under batch sequential approaches, this method is not feasible either economically or in terms of time demand on systems utilizing direct-access storage. Features of data-base software allow data to be stored once on a direct-access file with the appropriate elements linked or chained for rapid access. Storage duplication is thus avoided. For example, Fig. 4.11 indicates two files of nonredundant data, one an inventory file indexed on item number and the second a customer file indexed on customer number.

The purpose of this example is to give the reader some feeling for the complexity of file design—the need to access information by different keys and indexes and the need to link together files and information. The subject of data-base management is a far-reaching one that deserves in-depth study and analysis on its own. This section serves only to point out the degree of difficulty and attention that must be paid to maintain, update, and retrieve information from a data base.

The data-base system establishes a chain that provides a link to all the orders for a particular item while at the same time linking that same order data to the relevant customer record. By utilizing these chaining techniques, the file can be reorganized, alternate chains can be developed, and updates can be made with minimum effort and program reworking. In addition, the system provides the ability to express associations between different files without redundant data storage.

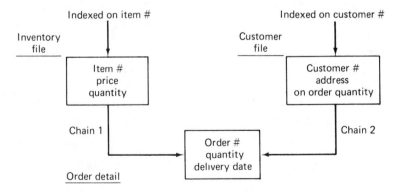

Fig. 4.11   Example of file linkage

File retrieval is aided by a technique of multiple indexing that allows data access by any of several keys. Figure 4.12 is an example of a payroll file where multiple indexing is desired. The requirement is to set up an employee information file in such a way that data can be retrieved by employee number or by employee with particular job codes or with specified length of service. The illustration shows a sample file with four employees indexed by employee number, job code, and length of service.

The indexes consist of key values that occur in the file, together with record addresses of records containing the values. It is apparent that retrieval by any of the three keys—employee number, job code, or years of experience—is equally efficient. In addition, this file structure can handle multiple-condition retrievals very efficiently. An inquiry requesting all employees who have two years experience at job code 12 can be handled by comparing the lists of addresses for job code 12 and two years experience and finding equalities; in this case, the record at address 30 is the only one that meets both conditions.

A more pertinent example would be a banking customer file where it is desirable to link savings, loan, and deposit accounts by individual, to be able to access the information by one of several keys, including customer account number or name, and to retrieve data such as savings accounts with over $1000 or accounts with no activity for 60 days or longer. The file-structuring element of data-base software enables the system designer to accomplish these requirements in an efficient and economical manner.

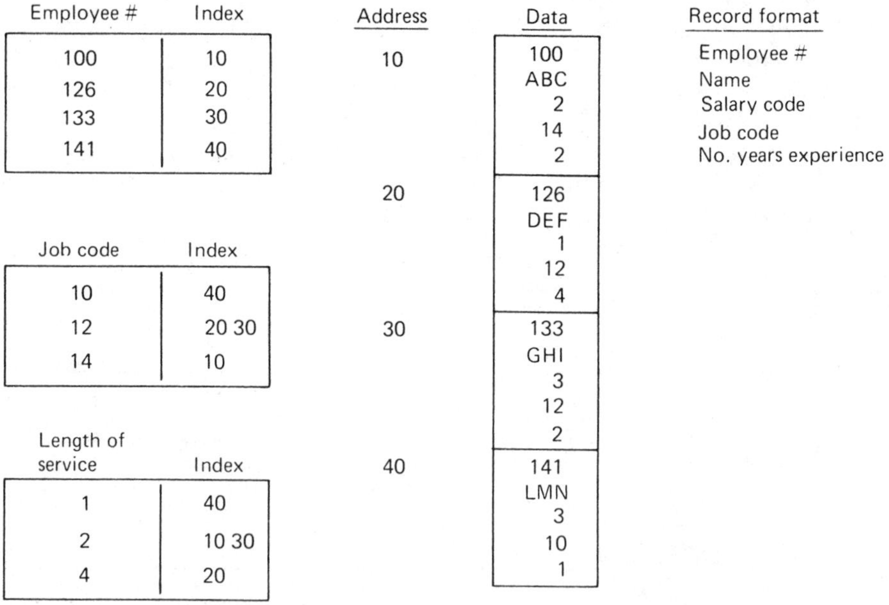

Employee #	Index
100	10
126	20
133	30
141	40

Job code	Index
10	40
12	20 30
14	10

Length of service	Index
1	40
2	10 30
4	20

Address	Data
10	100
	ABC
	2
	14
	2
20	126
	DEF
	1
	12
	4
30	133
	GHI
	3
	12
	2
40	141
	LMN
	3
	10
	1

Record format

Employee #
Name
Salary code
Job code
No. years experience

Fig. 4.12   Sample payroll file

THE GEOGRAPHY OF DATA BASE

In the early days of MIS, the term "total system" was popular. This meant that all the information functions of a business would be integrated and linked such that the business would operate as a single entity, humming along like a Swiss clock. Too deep a belief in this utopian goal can be damaging. One repercussion may be to hold off actions simply because they don't fit exactly into the defined master plan or total system. The more prudent developers of information systems realized that the total-systems concept, while a useful framework or goal, is in reality unattainable in the fast-changing business environment in which the systems operate. The same is true of what has been called a completely centralized data base. This concept implies that all data is captured and placed in the same physical storage area. This is the origin of the term *data bank*, a huge monolithic storehouse of the data used by a corporation or enterprise. While centralization has its advantages—certainly it avoids the need for communication linking of data that are in several locations—it has major disadvantages that in most cases predominate.

The first factor to be considered in centralization/decentralization is the economic trade-off of communication costs to access the data from remote spots versus the costs of subsetting the data base at remote spots where the vast majority of the activity takes place. A second factor is the improvement in response time and control when an operation is decentralized. Techniques for shared data base are still not in widespread use, but they are coming, and this development will have an additional positive influence on dispersed data bases. A shared data base is required when some transactions can be handled remotely, but a few require access to a central data base for their completion. The shared data base facilitates this handling, the objective being that service-level objectives are fully met, while the user does not know whether the access is local or remote. It goes without saying that if there are separate product lines, or completely independent entities of a company that do not share data, it is probably best to separate the local data bases from the centralized one.

Another aspect of centralized data base is that sheer magnitude and complexity often cause the concept to fall short of its objectives in actual practice. Despite the advances in teleprocessing, speed of access to data, operating systems, dedicated data base back-end processors, the storage media, and so on, sooner or later the central file becomes a bottleneck. Call it Murphy's Law, Parkinson's Law, or whatever, the point comes when the divide-and-conquer approach must be called in to save the day. The divide-and-conquer concept in this case is the shared geographically dispersed data base. Often a dispersed data base is preferred even if the sharing is not quite perfect. For example, it is usually a fact that 80 percent of the transactions are addressed to 20 percent of the data-base files. It may make sense to strip off this 20 percent each morning and place it on a separate storage medium. Transactions can be processed against the stripped file, with the exceptions going to the central file. This is a bit of a duplication, but it represents an extremely good trade-off in some instances. This form of data base can be called *controlled redundancy*. A practical approach, it may strike at the systems purity of some, but on balance it is a businesslike way to operate.

ORGANIZING FOR DATA BASE

Many MIS organizations have a data-base administrator reporting directly to the MIS director. This position, filled by the properly qualified individual, is one of the more important facets of successful data-base implementation. This individual must have not only technical expertise, but also a business and management orientation, since he or she is responsible for administering a resource vital to the needs of all management levels. The data-base administrator (DBA) is the keeper of the data dictionary and provides guidance and direction for new application development. It is often the DBA who makes the trade-off decision on shared data or controlled redundancy to serve a specific and important user need.

Another important function of the DBA is to ensure that proper training courses are available and utilized by the various levels in the organization. A data-base consciousness must pervade the organization, and properly directed courses are a principal tool in accomplishing this.

Finally, in order to succeed, a top-level and companywide commitment to the data-base concept is necessary. Management must understand and realize the significance of the information resource management concept. This must be more than a perfunctory nodding or a broad-scale blessing of IRM; it must involve a participative role—attending a data-base class, acting on an information steering committee, or taking part in an information system project that has immediate impact on a manager's specific job function.

COST OF DATA-BASE DEVELOPMENT

It should be apparent at this point that the cost of developing a data base is not inconsiderable. When one considers the benefits, one should also consider the cost side. First, there is the people cost of the data-base administrator and any associates who are needed to initially set up the files. Second, there is the cost of establishing the files. This procedure usually involves both transforming manual data into electronic media and converting existing electronic media into the new format. Also involved is the cost of converting, modifying, or rewriting existing programs, which may use the old file formats. Depending on the situation and the phasing plan, this might well run into six figures or more.

Not to be overlooked are the costs of hardware and software additions necessary to implement an integrated data base. At a minimum, additional data storage devices are required, and if there is an increase in processor and peripheral activity, it may necessitate equipment upgrade or addition. Also the cost of data-base software must be taken into account. A major switch to a data-base-oriented approach is a far-reaching decision and should be viewed as a long-term company investment. A careful design and phase-in plan must be employed, and the total project should be considered a multiyear effort.

DATA BASE: PERTINENT QUESTIONS AND ANSWERS

To summarize and complete the discussion of data base, I would like to refer to an excellent manual written by Westinghouse Tele-computer System Corporation and described by William E. Bender of Westinghouse Electric Corporation in *Management Informatics*, Vol. 3, No. 2. The manual covers, in question-and-answer form, five general areas and is aimed at "providing a clear understanding necessary to realistically evaluate benefits of the data base approach." I think it succeeds. The five areas covered are (1) definition, (2) technical aspects, (3) data-base environment, (4) CODASYL Data Base Language Task Group (I have not included questions in this area, and (5) Assessing benefits and risks. I have excerpted questions that I think are appropriate for the level of discussion aimed at in this book.

1. The Problem of Definition

Q. What does data-base management really mean?
A. Ambiguity surrounding its definition together with misunderstanding of its purpose have helped surround data-base management with mystery.

  The use and description of data-base management systems have covered both ends of the spectrum: some describe them as the panacea for all data processing problems, others consider them little more than present-day file-maintenance systems.

  In its simplest form, a data base is a collection of data from which a company would like to establish and maintain certain relationships. A data-base management system structures and maintains these relationships. Complex structures and relationships are not necessary, and all corporate data need not be included in one data base. Through use of data-base management systems, a company's data are now structured and related and therefore obtainable in a more orderly and logical fashion.

Q. Does a data-base management system encompass all corporate data?
A. It is impossible to state in all cases what data may be processed through a data-base management system, but two key points can help answer this question. First, the user must define what the system is to provide (a subset of what it can provide); and second, he must define relationships among data according to the way he views the operating environment of this company.

For certain applications with their associated files of data, data-base management techniques may be too sophisticated and cannot be beneficially applied; however, many other applications, which may appear quite complex by conventional standards, can be simplified through data-base techniques. Each situation is unique and requires an individual analysis and approach.

Q. Is data-base management synonymous with management information systems?

A. No. Management information systems are groups of application programs capable of taking raw data and from it producing information meaningful for the planning, operation, and control of a business.

Data-base management and management information systems are quite dissimilar, yet one may depend upon the other. For example, a data-base management system can maintain raw data for an MIS. Or, more simply, a data base may provide the necessary data which an MIS translates into meaningful reports.

Q. Does a data-base management system imply an on-line or communications capability?

A. No. This is a popular misconception stemming from the fact that some data-base management systems feature a communication or teleprocessing front end. In most of these systems, however, the data-base management portion is separable from the teleprocessing portion, and each is often marketed and sold separately. Even if they are part of the same product, the user should consider the two separately. Both require a certain amount of user training and development and/or conversion programming, and parallel installation may cause unnecessary disruption of day-to-day production. In most cases, the data-base management portion is installed first so that data files can be built and accessed through batch processing prior to on-line processing, although both the sequence and timing must be determined by local priorities.

Most data-base management systems are ideally suited to the management of on-line as well as batch-processed data files. There are, however, some teleprocessing applications that do not require data-base management, and many applications ideally suited to the data-base environment do not require teleprocessing.

2. The Technical Aspects of Data-Base Management

Q. What does a data-base management system do?

A. A data-base management system performs the following functions:

1. Organizes data. Data is organized or structured according to the specifications of the data definition language. These specifications are introduced by the data-base administrator at the time the data base is established and may be reintroduced as the data-base configuration

changes. Data is organized in the manner most suitable to each application.

2. Integrates data. Data is interrelated or linked together at the element (named field of data) level and can, therefore, be assembled in many combinations during execution of a particular application program. The data-base management system is the vehicle used to collect, combine, and return a portion of the available data to the user.

3. Separates data. A data-base management system serves as a filter between application programs and their associated data. It separates application logic from the input/output logic needed to calculate addresses, follow chains or links, block/unblock data, locate records, and select data elements. In addition, it separates the logical description and relationships of data from the way in which the data is physically stored. The data base remains secure and intact even though it is processed by different programs which describe the data in different ways and which may be written in different programming languages.

4. Controls data. A data-base management system appears to an application programmer to be an extension of the operating system software. As it receives data storage requests from host programs, it controls how and where data is physically stored. On data retrievals, it locates and returns requested elements of data to the programs.

5. Retrieves data. A record of data can be obtained via a data-base management system: (1) serially (in its physically stored sequence), (2) sequentially according to the value of a user-specified key, (3) randomly by key, (4) randomly by address, and (5) by structural link. All or any portion of the data record can be returned to the user.

6. Protects data. A data-base management system protects and secures both the content of a data base and the relationships of data elements. Data is protected against access by unauthorized users, physical damage, operating system failure, simultaneous updating, and certain interruptions initiated by a host program.

Q. How does a data-base management system work?
A. A data-base management system is generally composed of three subsystems, which operate as follows:

1. Data-base definition. In this subsystem, the schema (complete description of the data base) is specified through use of a special language known as the data description language (DDL). It is generally not necessary to specify a complete description of the data base at one time, especially when the data base is subdivided into named areas of addressable storage (files). In this case, the data base can be defined or redefined one file at a

time for maximum flexibility. For each file, a specified organization technique governs the file's mode of processing. Many data records, data elements, and linkages with other files can be defined within a file structure.

2. Data-base communication. Once the data base has been defined, elements of data can be stored and subsequently retrieved and/or updated through a data manipulation language (DML). In a host-language database management system, the DML is a set of CALL statements or CALL macros contained in application programs and processed by the communication subsystem. Through this communication subsystem, each application program can receive the particular elements of data it needs (the subschema) in a variety of sequences.

3. Data-base support. The support subsystem performs data-base utility or service functions which generally include: change file capacities, list files, alter file passwords, print file statistics, change record lengths and blocking factors, dump and restore files, and unlock files.

3. The Data-Base Environment

Q. How can I guarantee the integrity of my data base?
A. A data base is susceptible to five phenomena, each of which can destroy its integrity. Each is described below, together with the appropriate corrective action:

1. Access by unauthorized personnel. One of the four techniques or combinations of them can be used to isolate classified or proprietary data from unauthorized personnel:

   (a) Password security. For any user to read or update a file, he must know the password for the file.

   (b) Access by element name. To retrieve or update an element of data, the user must know the name of the element.

   (c) Data break-out. Highly sensitive data can be broken out into a separate file which can be stored off-line.

   (d) Access list. A list of program names with authority to retrieve and maintain elements of data can be stored by the data-base management system and accesses can be checked against the list.

2. Simultaneous update. In a multiprogramming environment it is possible for two users to update the same file concurrently. Whenever dependent updates are made by more than one program at the same time, unpredictable results may occur. These simultaneous updates can be prevented by locking out other maintenance transactions to the files while one transaction is being processed.

3. Host program interrupt. An abnormal end (ABEND) processing module can be provided to trap user interrupts, write current buffers to their respective files, and close the files. Changes to the data base can be written to a log file and this log can be applied to the data base, at the user's discretion, to return the data base to the exact form it had prior to the run of the application program. These two features permit the user to continue execution from the point of the error or to restore the data base and rerun the entire job.

4. System error. The ABEND processing module cannot trap system errors; therefore, a data base must be restored to the exact form it had prior to the current run of the application program. When such errors occur, the data base can be recovered by applying the transaction log or by rebuilding the individual files of the data base using a sequential back-up copy of them.

5. Physical damage. If information cannot be retrieved from a file because of a defective track or physical damage to a disk pack, the file should be rebuilt from the latest back-up. Utility programs supplied by the hardware manufacturer may be applied to recover from these errors.

Q. Who should design a data-base system?
A. The design of a data-base system requires commitments from both user management and data processing management. Because the design of a data-base system specifies how information will originate, who will use it, and how it will be used, functional users should participate in its design. Without functional user participation, there is no real assurance that the logic of the system and its output will be of value to the users.

Equally important, however, is the assistance and advice on technical matters from data processing. Again, without their technical guidance, there is no assurance that the system is technically feasible.

The key in designing a data-base management system is to have the right people assessing the right problems. Let the functional user assess the economic and functional problems and let data processing assess the technical problems.

Q. What are the management implications to be considered when installing a data-base management system?
A. Initially, organization politics may cause resistance to the installation of a data-base management system because its installation may cross organization lines. Data files that are the responsibility of one functional area may become accessible to other functional areas. Files may become part of a larger unit (a data base) where data is shared. While this is usually advantageous because it reduces data redundancy, it may cause functional departments to feel that their ability to control data is restricted.

Q. How will a data-base management system affect the role of the functional user?

A. Since the value of any system and data processing application is measured by its benefit to the functional user, the possibility of greatly increased capability in the data-base systems environment brings a strong focus on the role of the functional user.

The principles of good systems design are equally applicable within the data-base systems environment. The joint effort of users, systems analysts, and programmers to achieve optimum systems design is still a valid approach.

In addition to the traditional participation in the design and operation of a data processing application, a new perspective for the functional manager emerges. To fully benefit from the increased capabilities offered, the user must be prepared to participate in the selecting of facilities and in designing a system that satisfies his requirements. Identifying the trade-offs and justifying the cost of implementation require a user to accurately assess the relative merits of the different possibilities. User acceptance and support during implementation are vital to ensure that transitional problems are minimized and adjustments to user interfaces are made as required. Without user support, an excellent system can fail; with total user commitment, even a mediocre system can at least partially succeed.

Q. Can a data-base management system be used to measure the overall organizational performance?

A. The expanded capabilities for greater latitude in designing data processing applications provide more opportunity to measure performance.

The framework of the data-base environment, with its expanded roles for all components, provides an excellent opportunity for all activities to include performance measurement and evaluation as an integral part of their respective functions. Performance measurement and evaluation must become a more formal procedure than it has been in the past. Techniques for performance measurement can be developed and refined through use in a planned program.

The development of new techniques indicates in the data-base systems environment, the redefined roles with new activities emerging, and the more precise managerial practices required can all support a well-defined performance standard, measurement, and evaluation program.

4. CODASYL Data-Base Language Task Group
Data-Base Management Software

5. Assessing the Benefits and Risks of
Data-Base Management

Q. What can a data-base environment provide that a company cannot obtain now?

A. A company will reap two significant benefits by moving into a data-base environment: (1) maximizing the information the company collects and uses about products and customers and (2) tailoring the MIS department to more adequately meet the needs of the company.

Until the advent of the data-base environment, there had never been an easy way for business management to structure and relate corporate data in order to obtain the maximum amount of information. Each time management wanted to see data related in a different way, new programs had to be written, files tailored, and special computer runs made. The result was often a disillusioned management, unable to understand why an expensive computer and a talented professional and technical staff could not relate data.

In the final analysis, a data-base environment will provide centralized management of a company's most valuable resource—the data used in day-to-day operation. This centralized management provides convenient expansion and integration of applications with minimal data redundancy; reduced data and program maintenance; and smaller, more manageable programs.

This leads directly to the second most important benefit—the ability of the data processing department to respond more effectively to the unique reporting demands which most businesses require. Data processing can work more closely with functional users and more closely tailor its needs to the overall needs of the business. The result is a data processing department able to respond to unique requirements without sacrificing service to individual functional users.

Q. *What are some of the important aspects to be considered in assessing the potential usage of a data-base management system?*

A. One of the most important aspects is a thorough understanding and analysis of the information flow among the functional departments. This understanding of information flow is vital to the construction of a data base and implementation of data-base management system, since it forms the basis for the data relationships. A lack of knowledge in any area can result in an inadequately structured data base.

It is also important to know exactly what the data-base approach is to accomplish and to define measurable objectives. Too often the objectives are as general as "to improve information for decision making" or "to provide more timely information." Each of these objectives is fine as far as it goes, but neither is specific enough to be achieved practically. The key is to have very precise objectives which are supported by a detailed and thorough plan.

Q. *What are some of the benefits of a data-base management system?*

A. There are many benefits to be derived from installing a data-base management system. Some of the more tangible ones are:

1. Reduced programming costs. Because many of the input/output (file definition and file maintenance) routines normally coded by the programmers are now handled through the data-base management system, the

amount of time and money spent writing an application program is reduced.

2. Reduced development and implementation time. Because programmers
   spend less time writing applications, the amount of time required to implement new applications is reduced.

3. Reduced program and file maintenance costs. Nearly sixty percent of the
   programming dollar is spent on maintenance. Data-base management
   systems reduce this expenditure by performing file maintenance in a more
   convenient and more efficient manner. Program maintenance is also reduced because the volatile areas of programs, input/output, and file descriptions are handled via the data-base management system.

4. Reduced data redundancy. Redundant data items cost money in storage
   space, programmer time, and data maintenance. With a data-base management system, data items need only be recorded once and are available
   for everyone to use. Programmers do not spend time coding file descriptions that contain the same data elements found in other files, since each
   element of data is maintained by a single source.

5. Increased flexibility. Data-base management systems will make the data
   processing organization more flexible and enable it to respond more
   quickly to the expanding needs of the business. Unique reporting requirements are more adequately met, because special files do not have to be
   created or redesigned, and programming changes are minimized.

Q. How can I minimize the risks in introducing a data-base environment?
A. One sure way to minimize any risk is through careful and intelligent
   planning.
      A second way is to start small. Don't try to create a totally integrated
   data base in the first go-round. A step-by-step approach is best.
      A third way is to deal with a company whose product has a good repu-
   tation, whose financial status is good, and who will be around in the future
   when support is needed.
      A fourth way is to select good people to staff the data-base administra-
   tion and planning functions.
      The fifth and probably the most underestimated is education of the
   individuals who must function within the data-base environment. If they do
   not understand data-base concepts and do not believe in the data-base management software product, problems are likely to occur.

Q. How do I evaluate data-base management software?
A. Six areas must be considered:

1. Compatibility with CODASYL specifications. Does the product meet the
   CODASYL specifications sufficiently to be considered a standard implementation? If it does not, substantial conversion costs may be incurred in

the 1980s, when data-base compilers are more numerous and pressures from the federal government and other large users require the suppliers to conform to a standard. If it doesn't appear compatible with the CODA-SYL specifications, another reliable source must be used to measure the product's technical comprehensiveness.

2. Hardware considerations. Another important point is the impact of the data-base management system on the current hardware configuration. The system should be independent of the unique characteristics of the direct-access storage devices on which it operates. It should support processing during a transition period when files of data are being converted from one device to another. Also, memory requirements must be considered. Despite the introduction of virtual memory and substantial reductions in the price per kilobyte, memory continues to be a relatively expensive commodity. If the installation of a data-base management system results in the rental or purchase of additional memory, then this cost must be considered as part of the price of the product. Equally important is the length of time the memory is tied up. For users of small machines, it should be possible to roll the product in and out of memory so that it is resident only when needed.

3. Protection of data. Data-base management software should also be evaluated on its ability to protect data from misuse and destruction. Data must be protected from unauthorized personnel, computer operation errors, and even from errors in the data-base management system itself.

4. Ease of program conversion and product use. A data-base management system must be as applicable to existing application programs as it is to newly designed systems. It should be possible to apply data-base techniques to a single file of data and later expand to an integrated data network with minimal conversion programming. The data-base management product should be easy to use and understand. It should require minimal training of personnel and minimal "fine tuning" and reorganization of files of data.

5. Product price. How much for how long? The obvious question to consider when evaluating the price of a product is: do the benefits derived from the use of the product offset its price? The price of a maintenance contract and the price of future enhancements must be factored into the analysis. Certain software suppliers who lease their products on an indefinite basis (i.e., the product is never owned by the user) may make the price justification impossible. Also, it may be convenient to have a contract with the supplier that enables you to apply all or a portion of the monthly rental payments toward a future purchase.

6. Supplier's stability and level of support. The supplier of a data-base management system should keep the product operational with each new re-

lease of the operating system. Also he should be continuously enhancing the product to the current level of technology. He should make himself readily available whenever an error in the product is detected, and should be willing to provide, perhaps on a fee basis, extra assistance whenever needed.

Q. *What is the most important factor in implementing a data-base management system?*

A. The most important factor to consider in the installation of a data-base management system is *education.* Personnel must be trained in the data-base area, the software product, and the application techniques. Training must include top-management-level presentations to ensure the company's business plan is consistent with the information systems plan, thereby committing management to the data-base approach. Functional management must understand the applicability of the new techniques to their departments the role they must play in working with the data-base administrator to define specification requirements. Finally, the programmer/analyst must feel comfortable working with the software, knowing in general how it operates, how to use it, and when and how to back up the files of data. If education is emphasized and a company considers data-base management as an evolutionary process which follows realistic schedules, then the system will have a very positive influence on the business.

SUMMARY

The subject of data base was mentioned in parts of several chapters in the previous edition of management information systems. However, with the evolution and acceptance of the concept of information resource management, the role of data base has become so vital that it warrants a separate chapter in this new edition.

Management's appetite for information has reached a stage where the fragmented data bases of the earlier developments do not suffice. Data must be organized in such a way as to permit management browsing across heretofore self-contained and bounded data files. This is the perspective of the chapter. The user's view of data was described, running the gamut from the top-executive to lower-management levels to MIS systems analysts. This outside-in approach facilitated an understanding of what was required in the way of information before the how of data-base use was discussed. A variety of access methods or user languages was reviewed, emphasizing the concept of user-friendly systems. Data bases can lead the horse to water, but easy-to-use data-base languages are what make him drink.

Data-base software was then reviewed, and a description was given of the techniques of the data-base dictionary and file structure that are the essential underpinnings of the software. Despite the improvements in software, practical trade-offs must be made to satisfy the variety of company needs. In this regard, the subjects of geographically shared data bases and controlled redundancy were introduced. The need was then mentioned for developing a strong data-base administration function led by a data-base administrator reporting to the MIS director.

Data base is the mortar of MIS, but, because of historical application evolution, the development of a data-base management system may require significant retooling and reconstruction. It may be possible to bridge from your current system to an integrated data-base approach, or it may be necessary to start from scratch. In either case it is going to take time and resources. The strategy and conversion plan is a vital consideration. Obviously management cannot and will not countenance a plan where additional applications must be postponed for a matter of years. At the same time, continued building on a shaky foundation can prove very dangerous. The answer rests with business-oriented trade-offs, the development of a staging plan that arrives at an integrated or unified data base, but phased such that a moratorium on new development is not necessary. The best minds of the company should be put to bear on this data-base implementation plan. If the concept of information as a vital company resource is valid, there is no other way.

CASE STUDIES

MIDWEST BANK

In April 1982, Midwest Bank decided to launch a comprehensive review of their MIS operations. An eight-person team spent ten weeks, full time, to review the basic business processes, organization, information users, information systems, data classes, and data processing organization. The information was then synthesized into a report to management, recommending an overall systems architecture and strategy and application development based on user priority assessment. The effort at Midwest had top-management commitment; the resultant document was well received and, in essence, was accepted as the statement of the MIS direction of Midwest Bank for the next five years.

It was apparent to Midwest that they had developed applications in a fragmentary way, lacked an integrated data base, didn't know in what direction they should be headed, and were facing increasing demands on the part of their users. This scenario was typical of many data processing operations the size of Midwest.

An initial recommendation was to evaluate and select a data-base system that would enable Midwest to integrate its data files, so that operating management could derive the management information they said was imperative. A Data-Base Selection Committee was formed, selection criteria quickly agreed upon, and the following letter sent to three leading vendors of data-base management systems.

Dear Vendor:

I am pleased to announce the approval of the Data-Base Management System Selection Project for Midwest Corporation. This project will select the Data-Base Management System software that will become the basis for data-base development within
Midwest. Your Data Management system has been selected as one of the three products
that will be evaluated by this project.

Enclosed you will find a copy of the project plan document, which describes the
project tasks, the methodologies to be used, and the project participants. There are several
formal vendor interface points such as:

— Review and respond to the Criteria Document.
— Supply detailed technical information to be used to evaluate your project.
— Supply product-user names for us to contact in our data gathering.
— Review and comment on the findings document.

Your prompt response at these interface points will be necessary for us to meet the
project schedule. However, your contributions throughout the project are invited, and we
will be happy to consider any pertinent input at any time.

Sincerely,

QUESTIONS

1. How do you think Midwest was wise in conducting the comprehensive MIS review? Do you
   think the study-team size and time frame excessive?

2. Would you anticipate that data fragmentation would be a finding in a study conducted by a
   bank?

3. How would you evaluate the way Midwest is going about selecting a data-base system?

4. Are they too restrictive in limiting the study to three vendors?

5. What should be the criteria for bid invitations in view of the fact there are more than 50
   competent data-base systems on the market?

6. What do you think some of the key decision factors should be in Midwest's selection of a
   data-base system?

NATIONAL TELEPHONE

National Telephone, a leading independent carrier, has developed over the past six
years a large data base that they called NMDB (National Marketing Data Base). This
4-billion-character file is the basis for a diversified number of marketing analyses and
reports used by sales managers, product managers, administrators, forecasters, and
planners. The reports range from a simple request for sales by particular customers to
complex modeling, projecting a full P & L statement for a proposed new product line.
Users of the data base range from clerical personnel to department vice-presidents.

Input to NMDB emanates from the billing file, which records individual sales
transactions. The billing file is organized by customer, since billing is its principal

application. The billing system was the first to be computerized by National Telephone in the late 1950s. Over the years it has evolved from a batch/tape to an on-line system; however, the original system design has been carried forward through the series of conversions that have taken place. While the billing data base satisfied the order-processing and accounts receivable functions quite well, the marketing and planning departments have found it progressively more difficult to reformat the data base into NMDB. One major reason is that the company's strategy is placing more emphasis on product-line performance. Therefore, sales by product and product line are essential. NMDB is oriented to product but can also produce analyses keyed by customer. Current billing procedures result in a considerable time lag between the time a transaction occurs and the time it can be transferred to NMDB by the required product categories. For years the systems analysts of NMDB have been trying to have the billing system analysts rectify the situation, but without success. They know that maintaining two huge and somewhat redundant files is an expensive proposition, but somehow they have been unable to reach a solution.

The problem would soon surface anew, because the new vice-president of product marketing, Ralph Lesser, was preparing a presentation for the president of National that would indicate it was becoming impossible to manage a product line without current and accurate product-line results. Lesser knew this was going to irritate the vice-president of MIS, Bob Frank, but he felt also that Frank's people had not been able to resolve the problem and hadn't given it the priority he knew it warranted.

QUESTIONS

1. How did this problem come about? Do you think it could have been avoided?

2. Could Bob Frank have recognized the problem and put a plan in place to rectify it before Lesser brought the issue to the president?

3. Should the billing file have been constructed with the flexibility to effectively handle product information or any information required by management?

4. Do you think Lesser is acting in a responsible manner?

5. What should Frank do to resolve the problem? Is a redesign necessary, a new data-base structure, faster data-base reporting, or what?

BIBLIOGRAPHY

Date, C., *An Introduction to Database Systems.* Reading, MA: Addison-Wesley, 1975.

Kreitzer, Lawrence W., "Data Dictionaries—the Heart of IBM," *Infosystems* (Feb., 1981), 64–66.

Martin, J. *Computer Database Organization, 2nd ed.* Englewood Cliffs, NJ: Prentice-Hall, 1977.

Martin, J., *An End User's Guide to Database*. Englewood Cliffs, NJ: Prentice-Hall, Inc., 1981.

Martin, J., *Strategic Data-Planning Methodologies*. Englewood Cliffs, NJ: Prentice-Hall, Inc., 1982.

Nolan, R. L., "Computer Data Bases: The Future Is Now," *Harvard Business Review* (1973), 98–114.

Synott, William R. and William H. Gruber, *Information Resource Management*. New York: John Wiley, 1981.

Ullman, J., *Principles of Database Systems*. Woodland Hills, CA: Computer Science Press, 1980.

Chapter 5

Communications
and Distributed
Data Processing

Chapter 4 discussed data base and its importance to MIS. Another major trend is distributed data processing (DDP). Communications and DDP provide the delivery system for MIS and data base. Data is gathered, organized, and integrated into an electronic storage medium. DDP is the vehicle for connecting remote sites to the data on both the input and the output side.

Companies have gone through cycles of MIS architecture, the first being the use of small computers in multiple geographic sites. Then the trend was to centralization and the more-bang-per-buck syndrome—based on the principle that the larger computer systems were the most economical on the basis of processing power or storage capacity per dollar of expenditure. The mini and micro revolution has reversed that trend, offering an economical way to disperse resources; therefore, the trend today is most definitely toward decentralization.

Communication in MIS terms has come to mean the transmitting of data from one site to another, usually via telephone lines, but now including microwave and satellite facilities. With the advent of office automation and the development of word processing, electronic mail, and executive terminal work stations, the need for communicating data inside a building has become increasingly significant. In this chapter, therefore, we will discuss both external and internal communications. After reviewing communications and the basic elements that comprise it, we will analyze the concept of distributed data processing and give examples of its use.

TYPES OF LONG-RANGE COMMUNICATION

Communication is defined in the *American College Dictionary* as "the imparting or interchange of thoughts, opinions or information by speech, writing or signs." Without the ability to transmit knowledge and ideas, there is no civilization. What we are concerned with here is how information in the form of "speech, writing or signs" can be communicated through time and space. This is the objective of computer-based teleprocessing systems—to send and receive information from one location to another (space) so that the activity can be carried out quickly (time).

The techniques of transmitting messages (see Fig. 5.1) from one location to another can be seen as a key element in a civilization. Primitive societies developed long-distance communications using drums and smoke signals. We can begin to see trade-offs that must be considered in evaluating teleprocessing systems. A smoke signal has a much longer range than a drum but is ineffective where dense forests, mountains, or overcast skies obscure vision. Every means of transmitting messages—runners, men on horseback, automobiles, and airplanes—has strengths and weaknesses.

Telegraphy

The era of electronic communications began in 1844 with the invention of the telegraph. In October 1832, sailing home from Europe, Samuel F. B. Morse discussed with other passengers a recent publication by Michael Faraday on electromagnetism. Morse planned to make a telegraph recording instrument and devised a dot-dash code based on the absence or presence of electrical pulses.

In March 1838, after a successful demonstration before President Martin Van Buren and his cabinet, Congress appropriated funds for a practical test of the telegraph. Morse's transmission in 1844 of "what hath God wrought" from the Supreme Court chamber in Washington to his partner in Baltimore over a 40-mile line was a landmark in communications.

A company was organized to extend the line to Philadelphia and New York City. By 1851, 50 companies using Morse patents were operating in the United States; a decade later, Morse systems were operating in Europe.

The majority of the messages in the early days concerned train dispatching. The telegraph line shared the right-of-way with the rail line, while telegraphy and railroads supported each other's growth.

Automatic telegraphy, defined broadly to mean those systems where signals are transmitted by machine and recorded automatically, was the next major development. This development replaced the telegraph key and the dot-dash Morse code with the teleprinter and the five-pulse Baudot code. With this code, it is possible to represent 32 different combinations: 26 for the alphabet and six for special functions. It is much more efficient than the dot-dash code. The pulses are delivered by a keyboard device to the telegraph line; at the receiving end they activate a teleprinter to print the

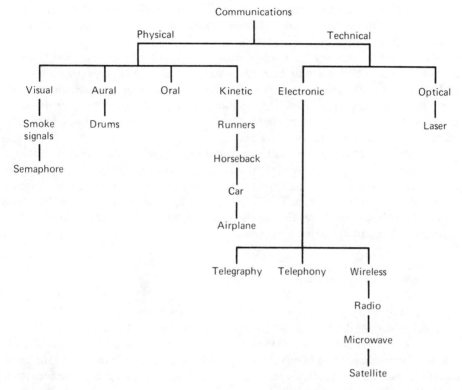

Fig. 5.1 Methods of communication

message. Automated telegraphy introduced transmission and reception of messages punched on paper tape. These automatic methods were the forerunner of today's tele-processing systems.

Telegraphy still provides low-cost data transmission where low speed is not a drawback, but its use has declined with the advances in telephony and microwave communication.

Telephony

Another major development took place in Boston on June 2, 1875, when Alexander Graham Bell heard the twang of a steel spring over an electric wire. Earlier, Bell had described an apparatus that could transmit speech. It consisted of a strip of iron attached to a membrane. When activated by a voice, the membrane vibrated before an electromagnet, inducing an electric current. Bell filed an application for a patent, and in March 1876 transmitted the first complete sentence. It was not quite as grand as Morse's message. He called to his assistant at the other end of the line, "Mr. Watson, come here; I want you."

The first commercial telephone was put into operation in May 1877, and by 1879 there were more than 50,000 telephones within the United States. Today there are more than 175 million.

Advanced technology has made it possible to conduct many conversations simultaneously over a single pair of wires. Coaxial cables and relays permit sharing hundreds of conversations. The first commercial manual telephone switchboard allowed the alternate switching of telegraph and voice communication over the same line. Dial systems were in use by 1892. More recent innovations include automatic switching systems and direct distance dialing.

Telephony advanced voice communication and provided the vital technology breakthrough for (nonverbal) data transmission. Telephone facilities carry data between computers and remote terminals, and between computers, in volumes that increase astronomically each year. The Bell System, which now can handle half a billion conversations daily, estimates that in the future more than half the volume will be digital data going to and from computers.

Wireless Communications

The ability to communicate long distances without wires came in 1895 when Guglielmo Marconi developed the first wireless telegraph. Reginald Fessenden, an American physicist, demonstrated the first radio transmission of voices in 1900. Until then radio messages had been sent using the Morse's dot-dash code. In 1901 Marconi transmitted a radio message across the Atlantic. Commercial broadcasting began in the United States in 1920.

Television transmitting is similar in principle to radio but it is modified to handle the very wide frequency bands required for the video signal.

Microwave is a short radio wave. Microwaves came to notice during World War II with their use in radar. Microwave networks can carry thousands of conversations simultaneously. Since microwaves travel in straight lines, relay towers must be constructed in the line of sight. Because of the curvature of the earth, towers are usually no more than 30 miles apart.

Recently, communication satellites have assisted the communication of data within the United States and between continents. They serve as a microwave relay station. The satellite must be in a line-of-sight position from both relay points on the earth.

Independent companies have been formed whose objective is to provide communicative services via satellite links in competition with AT&T long lines and satellite service. One such facility is Satellite Business Systems (SBS), a consortium put together by IBM, Aetna Insurance, and Comsat. Western Union and RCA also have satellites in space. Thus the company that has a large volume of data to be communicated between a variety of points within the United States will have a choice of using AT&T's long lines or satellite service provided by companies such as those described above.

Fiber Optics

Probably the most important advance in wired communication service is that of fiber optics. Fiber optics is a new process utilizing silicon rather than copper as the base element for communication lines. Silicon, a nonmetallic chemical element, is more prevalent than any other element except oxygen, and one of the benefits of fiber optics is lower cost. Light-emitting diodes are employed to send signals via these fiber lines, which are no thicker than violin strings. Thus this medium offers the potential of lower cost, higher speed, and greater capacity. There is no question that fiber optics will play an important role in future communication systems.

ELEMENTS OF A COMMUNICATIONS SYSTEM

The best way to explain a communications system is to describe a typical configuration and the elements that comprise it.

A schematic diagram of a typical communications module is shown in Fig. 5.2. The terminal device at the remote outlet is linked to a communication line. Device intelligence and/or a multiplexor is used when several terminals share the same line. The modem device converts the keyed-in characters to electronic pulses for transmission over the communication line. At the receiving end another modem unscrambles the pulses from the different terminals. The host computer interface converts the pulses into binary code and delivers the data to the memory of the host computer.

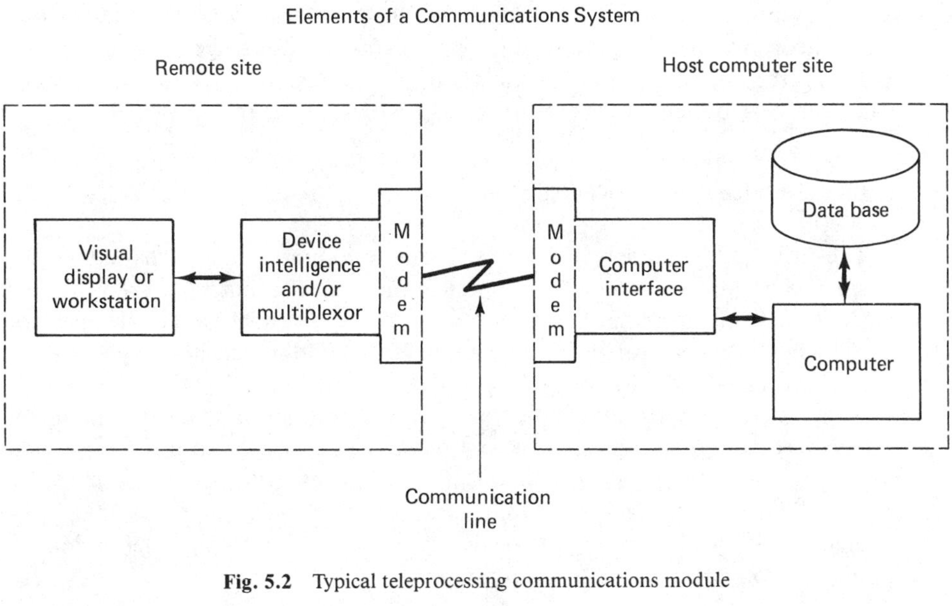

Elements of a Communications System

Fig. 5.2   Typical teleprocessing communications module

When the entire message—for example, an inventory file inquiry—is delivered, the computer has been instructed to seek out the appropriate inventory record from the data base, determine whether the requested quantity can be filled, and send back an appropriate message. The computer must reduce the available inventory balance of the item so that the correct response can be made for any subsequent orders.

The schematic of a typical communications system in Fig. 5.2 has six elements:

1. Terminal device
2. Device intelligence and/or multiplexor
3. Modem
4. Communication line
5. Host computer interface
6. Host computer

TERMINALS

The growth of the terminals segment of the information processing industry in a word has been extraordinary. The overall trend of computer "extensibility," with the provision of computer power first to diverse locations within a building, then to remote locations in outlying plants and offices, and finally to service points and offices in industries such as retailing, banking, airlines, and the like, has accounted for this amazing growth. A television screen or a CRT (cathode ray tube) has become almost as commonplace in the office as a telephone. The proliferation of terminals, along with the incorporation of low-cost microprocessor-based intelligence, represents a propelling force in the industry. Terminals come in all sizes, shapes, and functionality, but they can be grouped into several types as follows:

CRT (Cathode Ray Tube) Terminal

The basic building block or unit in any remote communication subsystem is the CRT. It is the workhorse in today's communication field. The unit has a 12- or 15-inch screen that can display alphanumeric characters. It has a keyboard to handle operator input. The keyboard can range from a simple 10-key adding machine type to a full alphanumeric set with a host of special-purpose or function keys. Usually present is some local functional capability in the form of microprocessor-based logic and memory that offers the operator a variety of options and ease-of-use features. This is usually a very low level of intelligence, and thus this form of CRT is termed an *editing terminal*. The word terminal implies that the device is not useful until it is linked to a computer, which usually is located some distance from the terminal, either within the building, in another facility, or in another city.

Intelligent Terminal

Though even the editing terminal has a degree of intelligence, it is not considered smart or intelligent unless it is equipped with enough memory and processing power to allow the user to write his own programs and thereby specialize the unit for a specific use. There are obvious degrees of intelligence, and that is the reason for the terms *intelligent terminal* and *brilliant terminal*. The latter has enough processing power and memory to enable it to perform the functions of a small-scale computer system and sometimes even more. The brilliant terminal must have an array of peripheral devices to support it, and it follows that terminals are built with the capability of interfacing to printers and storage devices. When a terminal is so connected, it is more appropriate to call the configuration a *terminal subsystem* or *work station*.

Graphic Terminal

In many applications it is necessary to display graphic material in the form of charts, pictograms, design models, and the like, and some terminals are geared to handling just that type of application. There are two general types of graphic terminals—business graphics and design graphics. The latter are beyond the scope of business operations, since they are used primarily by design engineers and model builders to design automobiles, buildings, printed circuit-board layouts, and the like. Business graphics become important to management users of information systems who want to see business results and projections in chart and graphic form (pie charts, bar charts, or regression curves). A color capability also becomes important in graphic terminals.

We should note that special-function terminals such as graphic, optical, or voice need not be treated as separate units, since these functions can often be provided as options to general-purpose terminals.

Optical and Voice Terminals

Optical terminals can sense special machine-readable numbers, letters, and special symbols and can send this data to the computer. This eliminates the need for an operator to manually key the data. Effective applications include utility bills, insurance premium invoices, or other turnaround documents produced by a computer. Another version of the terminal senses magnetic ink that is printed on the bottom of bank checks.

Voice synthesis employs devices that can comprehend a limited verbal vocabulary as input to a system. An individual voice print is established to allow for the idiosyncrasies of speech patterns. The individual is thus identified and is permitted to input commands and data to the system. On the output side, a voice synthesizer facilitates verbal commands and data as system output. Credit checking is an example of an application using verbal output.

Work Stations

Office-environment and factory-environment work stations will be covered in Chapter 6. Here we will simply note the increase in computer source data being recorded at the point of the transaction. This transaction-oriented approach updates the computer data base as the action occurs, speeds up the processing of the data, reduces errors, and eliminates redundancy in data recording. One example is the on-line banking terminal, which is quite prevalent throughout the banking industry. A savings bank teller terminal allows a branch bank to verify a customer's savings account, compute the interest, and record the new deposit or withdrawal, all in a matter of seconds. Another device used in banking (and other industries) is the audio response unit. The computer selects and activates the proper track(s) on a voice record, combining the appropriate words into a message that is sent over the communication line, or the voice is synthesized electronically. The message "order accepted" might come across the line.

Likewise, point-of-sale devices are increasing in the retailing and distribution industries. An optical reader senses the special item code on a can or a bread label, and via a computer link, automatically calculates the price, tax, and any special allowances. When all purchases are made, the completed tape is ready for the consumer—without the need for the checker to manually key the amounts on a cash register. The grocery store has a continuous record of item movement (on an hour-by-hour basis, if required). It can initiate the reordering cycle automatically to ensure the availability of products.

Another example is the hand-held terminal used in applications such as inventory audit or store ordering. A store supervisor can record, via a ten-key adding machine, the item number and quantity of either the inventory being audited or an order being taken. The device has a memory unit that can be used to transmit the data over a communication line to a host computer. It is conceivable that such transmission will become wireless, as in walkie-talkies or citizen-band radios.

DEVICE INTELLIGENCE AND/OR COMMUNICATION MULTIPLEXORS

As communication networks develop, the number and variety of terminal devices invariably increases. New applications are initiated and transaction volume expanded. One way to reduce communication costs is to provide a buffer between the terminals and the line to ensure that the best possible use is made of the line. So-called *dumb controllers* do not possess programmable logic and memory. They accomplish a specific task, such as collecting messages from low-speed terminals and preparing them for transmission over a communication line. *Intelligent multiplexors* actually contain a mini- or microcomputer. They have memory and can be programmed to accomplish functions such as error checking, data validation, message formatting, and simple processing. The trend is toward intelligent clusters of terminals linked to a host via an intelligent mini- or microcomputer.

MODEM

The name *modem* stands for modulator/demodulator. On the transmission end, the modulator converts the computer codes to tone signals for transmission over a telephone line. (Data signals are transmitted as tones.) On the receiving end, the demodulator converts the tone signals back to computer code.

COMMUNICATION LINE

The job of selecting the proper balance of communication lines is very difficult. This section will merely describe some of the selection criteria. The key criteria are set in boldface type.

Bandwidth determines the maximum transmission speed possible. Which bandwidth should be used depends on the volume and peak loads of the particular application. Narrowband transmission uses the telegraph-grade line, while voice-grade uses the telephone line. Broadband transmission depends on wireless types of transmission (such as microwaves) or special television-quality coaxial cable. In the past, the common carriers (AT&T, Western Union, General Telephone, and the independent phone companies) have controlled the telegraph and voice-grade lines. However, the Federal Communications Commission has approved the requests of private concerns such as SBS (Satellite Business Systems) for development of private satellite communication. This has paved the way for added competition in the communication area.

Data communications techniques tend to distort signals in a variety of ways that can cause loss of transmission or loss of the message. A process called **conditioning** adjusts the frequency and response elements in order to remove these distortions. Conditioning amounts to tuning a specific communication line for peak performance. Various conditioning services are available to ensure higher validity of data transmission and fewer line losses.

Another consideration in selecting communication lines is whether you require **simplex, half duplex,** or **full duplex capability.** Simplex mode allows communication only in one direction; that is, a terminal may receive data but it cannot transmit (or vice versa). Half duplex allows communications in both directions, but only one direction at a time. Full duplex allows simultaneous communication in both directions over the line.

Two classes of timing schemes are used in transmitting data, **asynchronous** and **synchronous.** In the asynchronous mode, special timing signals called start/stop bits are transmitted with each character. In the synchronous scheme, timing signals are sent much less frequently—for example, once per hundred characters transmitted.

The asynchronous scheme is used most often with low-speed terminals (up to 1200 bits per second) operating over voice-grade lines. The synchronous scheme is used with more sophisticated terminals on higher-speed lines (2400–56,000 bits per second). The higher-quality line requires less timing information to keep it in step, permitting more message information to be transmitted per unit of time.

Whether an application should employ a **dial-up (switched) network** or a **private (leased) network** is a function both of the volume of communications and of the traffic patterns of the communication network. Most large companies find they require a combination of dial-up and private lines. The Bell System offers WATS (Wide Area Telephone Service), a flat rate service for long distance calls, and TWX (Teletypewriter Exchange Service) for teleprinters and low-speed messages. Data Speed is offered for higher-speed transmission requirements. Western Union provides TELEX (similar to TWX) for low-speed communications and Broadband Exchange Service for higher speeds and more flexible service.

Another emerging service is that of VANS or Valued Added Networks. Companies such as GTE Telenet and Tymnet in addition to AT&T have established services for communicating digital data that provide data processing services such as message store and forward, forms creation, and data storage in conjunction with communication handling.

The two most significant **transmission codes** commonly in use are the Baudot five-level code and the American Standard Code for Information Interchange (ASCII) seven-level code. The selection of a code depends upon requirements such as compatibility, speed, error checking, validity, the software being used, and the terminal being used.

HOST COMPUTER INTERFACE

Between the incoming data and the computer stands an interface device usually referred to as a *front-end processor (FEP)*. It can, in fact, be a minicomputer itself. The FEP acts as buffer for the computer. It receives and sends messages to the central processing unit. It does a pre-edit and it formats and arranges the messages before passing them along to the central computer for processing. It allows for a speed imbalance between the relatively slow communication line and the high-speed processing unit. The FEP also orders messages based on a preconceived priority scheme. Thus the FEP is able to offload the central computer, specializing in the preparation, editing, error checking, and formatting of messages prior to their being sent or received.

HOST COMPUTER

The *host computer* is the nerve center of the entire communication network. It has processing power, stored programs to process the messages, and the data-base reference for the messages. In addition to the hardware required for a communication system (such as the necessary array of peripheral devices), high internal speed, program interrupt capability, and the required input/output speed and capacity, an advanced communication-oriented software operating system is essential.

Communication-oriented operating systems are needed to implement advanced teleprocessing. A computer can be thought of as similar to a production-line machine center in a manufacturing plant. The machine center is there to turn out a quality product in the most economical manner—and a computer center has the same goal. The input (raw material) consists of cassettes, diskettes, keyboard input, and the like. The product of the computer consists of useful printed or visual output. The computer center also has in-process inventory in the form of intermediate data tapes or transactions stored on disk.

To expand on the analogy, the computer operating system is similar to the production scheduling system, and the computer operating staff is similar to the machine-tool operators who feed the machine and keep it in productive operation with minimal interjob interruption or down-time. Just as the production-center operator is assisted by machine tools that automatically position and direct the machine's actions, so the computer operator is assisted by a computer operating system that automatically runs a series of programs without manual intervention. The computer operating system has two major functions: to schedule computer program operation based on the jobs to be run and the resources available; and to monitor the execution, ensuring that the resources continue to be optimally allocated, based on priority of job execution and changes unforeseen at scheduling time.

The foregoing are the six basic elements that make up a telecommunications system. Though the configurations may differ widely, every system must consider and be built from these six elements. Obviously, much added detail and analysis must be considered in order to implement an advanced teleprocessing system. The description presented here, however, should give the reader an overview of the general steps in the development of a communications system.

THE MULTICS SYSTEMS

As an illustration of a communications system at work, we shall look at the Multics system. The use here is the dedicated one of developing software, but the same system is used for many diverse purposes in other installations throughout the country. It emphasizes two very important capabilities of communication systems—high uptime and availability, and data security. This system, ten years in the making, has some unique features beyond the six elements just described.

Multics (Multiplexed Information and Control Service) is an advanced time-sharing system developed by Honeywell Information Systems in conjunction with the Massachusetts Institute of Technology and Bell Laboratories. The system is designed to operate without interruption seven days a week, 24 hours a day, the same way telephone or power systems do. Multics meets a wide range of user applications: scientific programs, checkout and testing of new programs, sharing of common data and program files, and basic batch jobs such as accounting and payroll.

The full list of system objectives is:

- Convenient remote-terminal access
- Continuous operation analogous to telephone service
- Wide range of capacity for growth or contraction
- Reliable internal file system
- Controlled access to allow selective data sharing
- Hierarchical storage of information
- Efficient service to both large and small users
- Ability to support variety of human interfaces
- Flexibility to incorporate future technological improvements and user expectations

The Multics ring protection system employs unique file-protection techniques and safeguards to prevent unauthorized access to data files and programs. Combined hardware and software barricades protect sensitive data. The different levels of security are in the form of concentric rings. Particular passwords and conditions must be met each time a user requests access to a more secure ring. Thus there may be certain program files accessible only to the system designers. Other files that exist outside this inner ring have less restrictive conditions of access. Each user determines how secure the material he controls shall be, and what other users can share it.

The system also features the concept of virtual memory. While the system has limited main memory, the hardware and software provide backing storage that can be rolled in and out of memory automatically if the contents are required by the user. The roll-in/roll-out procedure is transparent to the user; that is, the user does not have to request it. If six users are using the system and another user dials up, user seven's programs can be retrieved from backing storage, placed in main memory, executed, and rolled out again in time to let the other users continue. The procedure happens in milliseconds; thus to each user the machine seems to be entirely his. This is the concept of virtual memory.

Figure 5.3 is a schematic of the Multics system installed at the Honeywell facility in Billerica, Mass. It is similar to the Multics system employed by MIT, but it is dedicated to the design and testing of software. Several hundred programmers using teleprinters and CRT's compile and test advanced computer software. The system is connected to Tymnet, a value-added service network, and is available throughout Europe. Indeed, programming groups in England, France, and Germany currently utilize the Multics facilities.

The system is built in a very modular fashion. The core of the system is four modules of 1.25 million bytes of memory (a byte is 4 data bits) linked to dual high-speed central processors. The clock allocates time to users on a priority basis and calculates usage for purposes of cost allocation and billing. The virtual memory backing storage consists of high-speed disks connected to the memory units through a disk controller. The general input/output controller ties in the peripherals and com-

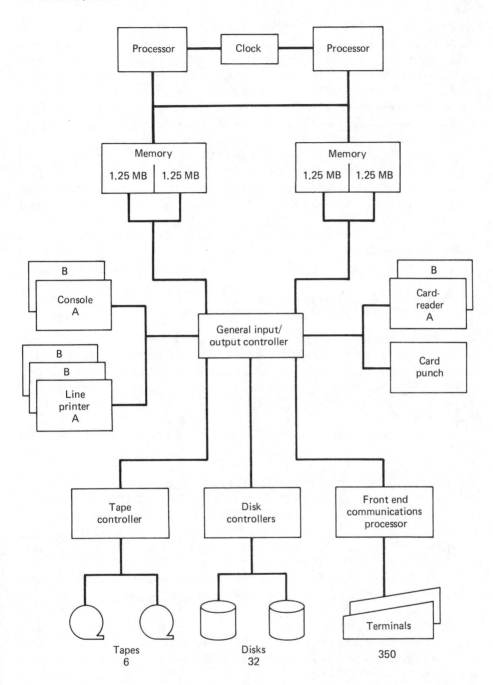

Fig. 5.3 The Multics system

munication terminals to the memory units. The peripheral complement includes two operator consoles, three line printers, two card readers, and a card punch. Also, there are six tape drives and 32 disk drives, the latter providing about a half billion characters of on-line file storage. Some 350 terminals and teleprinters are hooked to the system. The maximum number that can be attached at any one time is virtually unlimited. The terminals are located throughout the Boston area, as well as in Europe. As an interesting aside, a number of portable terminals are taken home by programmers who work in the evening and on weekends. These terminals are easily attached to a standard telephone by a snap-on acoustic coupler.

The modular design is one element in providing round-the-clock uninterrupted service. If one memory module is inoperative, the system will run using the remaining memory module until the other module is repaired. This is also true of the processing units and peripheral devices. The hardware modularity and backup plus the constant monitoring activity of the software provide a capability that approaches the goal of uninterrupted operation.

INTERNAL OR LOCAL COMMUNICATIONS

Significant changes are occurring in the internal communications world. Currently, most internal or local communications are conducted via telephone lines supplied by AT&T. However, the trend is toward the installation of PBX's (private branch exchanges), which can utilize either existing telephone wiring or new *data highways* consisting of coaxial cable, which (like cable TV) does demand a fairly radical new installation.

The PBX, which can be supplied by AT&T or independent companies such as ROLM or Western Telecom, is actually a computer that can not only switch messages like an existing switchboard but also store call messages, collect, sort, forward, switch, optimally route, retrieve, and so on. The PBX, because it is a computer and can be programmed, can also perform other functions such as heat and air conditioning control, lighting utilization, and other office-related activities. Also the PBX is a digital switch, which means that both voice and data are carried by the same signals, thus eliminating the modems that were needed in our external communications model to condition digital data for transmission across voice lines.

There are cost trade-offs in using a PBX rather than conventional message switching. The data highway or coaxial cable is more costly to install, but it does offer more capacity and higher-speed transmission, which may be demanded by a particular internal communications system. The concept—and the trend—is to provide a single digital communications network in which voice messages and data messages are transmitted over the same line without buffering or modulating devices. This affords far more options and flexibility and also, eventually, lower costs—or at least costs that are less sensitive to volume increases. Among companies offering local networks are Wang Laboratories with Wangnet and Xerox with what is called Ethernet.

Wangnet is based on a broadband network (cable television technology) that has the capability and capacity to handle high-rate data transfer and includes voice and video. Ethernet is a baseband network providing only a single cable channel on which all the equipment attached to it must contend.

Figure 5.4 depicts an internal PBX communications system. The first floor houses the host computer, similar to that of Fig. 5.2, which communicates to both the internal and external worlds. The second floor depicts an office environment, which has batteries of facsimile machines, word processors, copiers, office terminals, and phones all linked via the PBX. There is also a local data base that stores the data unique to the particular office floor, such as personal letters, personal phone messages, and personal data files. The devices mentioned are also linked via the PBX to the host computer on the first floor and to other computer systems in the outside world.

The company's executive offices are on the third floor, which, like the second floor, has its phones, word processors, and local data base. There are also graphic terminals for supplying executives with charts and graphs of business activity, and personal computers for developing reports and processing data from an executive's own personal file. This personal computing can be accomplished independently of the host computer on the first floor. Conversely, the executive can tap the host data base if it is required. Teleconferencing and video conferencing are other capabilities controlled by the PBX to the outside world (employing satellite transmission because of the high data/voice volume) and connected to the PBX's of the linked facility. There are predictions that with the high cost of travel, from 25 to 50 percent of current business travel will be replaced by tele- and video conferencing.

The potential uses of an internal/external communications system are quite exciting. For example, an executive committee of a company might be contemplating the introduction of a new product line into a new marketplace. Calling on the host data base on the first floor, they view a presentation of historical movement of product lines with similar characteristics on the graphic terminal. External market data from a linked market research company's data base is also obtained. The internal and external data are then modeled and optimal bottom lines are produced based on a variety of interacting variables. A risk assessment is also produced. Finally, a video conference is held with the executive committee of the division who are to be responsible for financing and marketing the new products. This approach is not yet in common use, but the technological elements, at least, are there to permit it to happen. As the book stresses throughout, it is not the technological elements but the managerial ones that set limits in such a scenario.

DISTRIBUTED DATA PROCESSING

Distributed processing is built around an approach that distributes the data base and processing capability to remote sites based on the type, number, and variety of work stations, their data processing requirements, the degree of control desired, the type of business organization, and overall economic considerations.

The term "distributed" is a bit of a misnomer, because, while functions and resources are distributed, there is still a central discipline or control over the remote

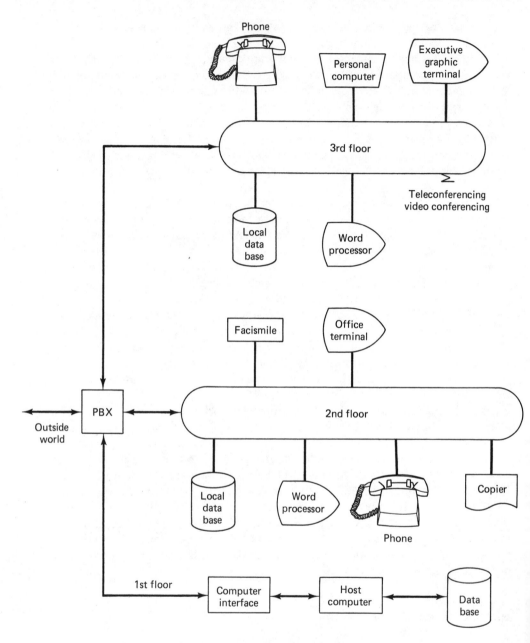

Fig. 5.4 Internal communications system

processing units. The key to DDP is that the host computer and distributed processing nodes are cooperative; that is, they are designed to be able to communicate with
each other for those applications that require it. We shall look at two examples of
a DDP network—the first a generic or general illustration and the second a specific one.

Figure 5.5 is a schematic of a generalized DDP. A DP center or host computer is the integrating element of the entire system. A front-end communications processor (FEP) handles all the remote communications entering and leaving the host. The FEP is connected to a variety of remote processors via one or a combination of the communication media that have been described. The company's home office utilizes graphic terminals for its executives, who have access to a local data base as well as to the central data base at the host site. Administrative offices perform word processing and other office automation functions while being tied to the host system for distribution of messages (electronic mail) and a variety of inquiries to the central data base. Distribution or sales centers are also linked to the host but perform a good deal of their own local processing of order taking, invoicing, and collections.

The remaining two distributed functions, the retail store and the production area, are not found as frequently in DDP as the other subsystems. The retail store or point-of-sale (POS) area is usually a free-standing subsystem, not linked on-line to the host but using a local processor in the store or in a local warehouse. However, there is no reason why it cannot be linked if there is benefit to be realized. The same holds true for the production-area subsystem. Historically this has been a free-standing entity, in some cases delivering data to the host computer but on a batch basis after a shift has been completed. In this example, sensor-based processors are monitoring an automobile assembly process. The types of data fed to the host are defects found per car, material used, and cost information. Process-control or sensor-based computers historically have been acquired and operated by engineering management rather than data processing management, and pressure to link the two activities has been lacking. However, the trend is toward closer cooperation between the two systems and the integration of their respective functions as an overall part of a company's DDP system plan.

This, then, is a generalized illustration of a DDP network. It is a bit utopian in scope, for very few companies have tied both point-of-sale and production areas into their DDP plan. The trend, however, is definitely toward this type of integration.

Loosely Coupled vs. Integrated Networks

It is helpful at this stage to view two contrasting system approaches to distributed data processing. The first, termed loosely *coupled*, is used by many small to medium-size companies who have simple communication needs and probably will not require much more in the immediate future. Most of their operations stem from a single plant or complex of plants that require simple terminal communications from the remote sites to a host. Transactions consist mainly of data entry or data inquiries related to a central inventory or sales files. Orders are taken at the remote site, usually batched and communicated to the central site at the end of the day. The major remote applications are order entry, remote batch transmission, and a small amount of on-site processing. Interface protocols (rules or conventions of data representation) between the host machine and remote terminal substations are specific, finite, and well structured. Many small to medium-size companies fall into this mode of communication processing, and it is not necessary to develop a complex integrated network architecture to satisfy their requirements.

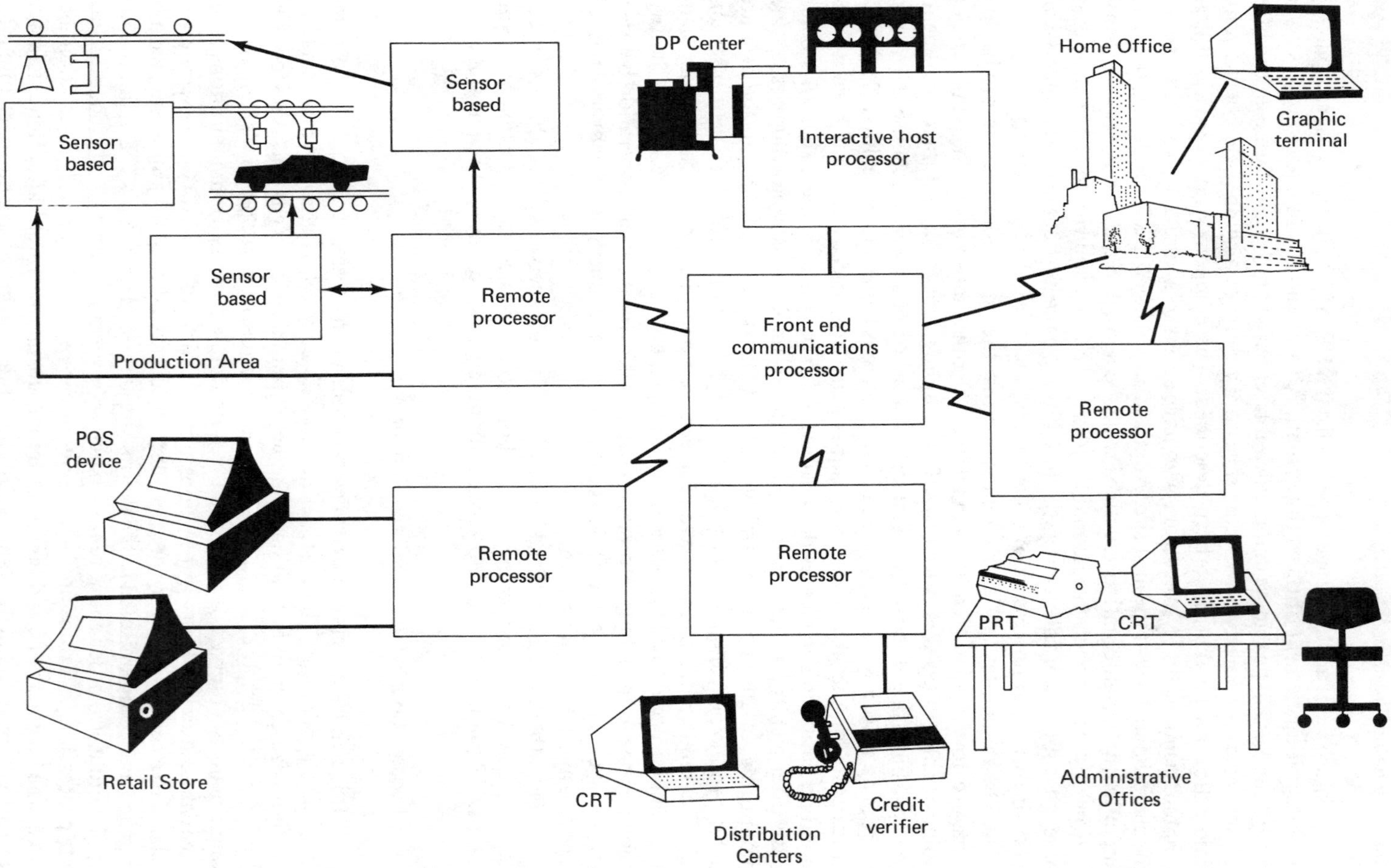

Fig. 5.5 Generic DDP schematic

Home Office

Graphic terminal

Remote processor

CRT

PRT

Administrative Offices

DP Center

Interactive host processor

Front end communications processor

Remote processor

Credit verifier

Distribution Centers

CRT

Sensor based

Remote processor

Sensor based

Production Area

Sensor based

Remote processor

POS device

Retail Store

146

On the other hand, many larger companies have a myriad of remote operations, many of a hierarchical nature—that is, suboffices or branches reporting to other sub-offices or regions, which in turn report to districts and ultimately to the home office. In addition a multiplicity of plants, factories, and other facilities are located through-out the country. This type of organization presents a far different type of data pro-cessing challenge.

In order to satisfy communication and data processing requirements in systems with complex interaction, a communication framework or distributed architecture must be established. Also, because the degree of data interaction (volume) is heavy, communication costs will be a significant factor in the total DP budget. The availabil-ity of private satellite communications and value-added networks, as described ear-lier, warrants the establishment of communication protocols that enable a company to take advantage of these services. In an integrated network, message and data stream across communication lines via microwaves or satellites between terminal sub-stations and host computers. Sometimes the network is hierarchical, and, where branches report to regions and so on, as stated above, or it may be a ring structure where branch offices communicate to each other as well as to higher-order offices.

This degree of communication complexity is far more integrated and inter-active than in the loosely coupled model, requiring a well-thought-out long range plan with established standards and disciplines to enable the total system to function as a network. Future growth and direction must be considered as well as industry and international standards and conventions. The standards and protocols you plan to use must interface with the broader-based standards.

A network system is a way for remote data processing units to work in a cooper-ative fashion to exchange information. Standard delivery-service rules are estab-lished so that a variety of devices and systems can communicate with each other. A *network* consists of a number of nodes joined by links. The nodes are computers, microprocessors, multiplexors, or terminal stations, while the links are communica-tion lines, coaxial cable, or microwave. Modern networks use what is called a *layered architecture*. The three general layer categories are applications management, mes-sage management, and communications management. The end objective of a layered architecture is to translate a message from one system into a physical code structure that can be sent over the available communication link and then translated back into a meaningful message at the receiving end. We shall not attempt here to fully describe network architecture, which is an entire discipline in itself; we note simply that net-work architecture is very important in the type of distributed data processing applica-tions that are covered in this chapter.

Mini and micro developments have made it economically feasible to have local processing capability; thus the trend is to distribute processing to remote subunits while maintaining the ability to talk to the host computer system and to other sub-units via an established network protocol. Two examples are presented below to give an overview of how these networks function. The first is a modern distributed data processing operation in a large international bank, the second a U.S. company in the distribution business.

International Bank

International Bank, a fictitious name for a real bank, is one of the largest in Europe. It is organized such that each branch renders total banking services to a specific geographical territory. A group of branches in turn is directed by an area general manager. Each area has an average of 200 employees under its management; as business and areas grow, the company has a policy that a new division is formed when the number of employees exceeds 200 people. The current number of areas is 250, with 350 expected in the next five years as the bank continues its rapid expansion. International Bank believes in a decentralized mode of operation, leaving major decision authority in the hands of the area general manager, each area functioning as a cost and profit center.

International Bank evolved to a totally centralized system in the late sixties and early seventies; they started with their current distributed data processing approach in the late seventies. The rationale for switching was (1) the ability to better serve the company's needs while being consistent with the prevailing decentralized mode of operation, (2) improved performance geared to higher throughput and turnaround time, and (3) improved system availability translated into higher up-time and ability to serve the growing number of users. The current work load is that the 250 areas currently serve 2000 branches with a total of 7000 terminals. It is expected that in five or ten years there will be 350 areas with 2500 branches and 10,000 terminals.

The distributed data processing system envisioned by International Bank is illustrated in Fig. 5.6. There are four levels of distribution in the network. The first level is the home office, which has the master central data base, maintaining the names, identification, key subtotals, and summary information of every account within the network. A back-up processor is present in case of failure of the first processor. The second level is the area office, which communicates to the central system via a miniprocessor tied into a communications front-end processor of the host system. Each area processor has a data base of the accounts within its geographical territory. The third level is the branch, which utilizes concentrators, similar to those described in the advanced teleprocessing system, to collect, edit, and prepare for transmission the data required for second-level processing. The fourth level is the terminal work stations. These work stations are a combination of cathode ray tubes, keyboards, bank teller units, printers, and the like, depending on the specific activity performed by the branch. Thus you can see the networking effect of one home-office large processor and data base communicating to area offices, which in turn communicate to concentrators at the branch, which control the variety of terminals in various locations within the branch.

The estimated total cost of this system is the approximately $125 million purchase price of the hardware complement plus about $20 million per year to operate. The latter costs include personnel, facilities rental, communication lines, power, hardware maintenance, supplies, operators, and so on. Although the distributed system is not yet in full operation, the bank feels the cost will be about equal to that of

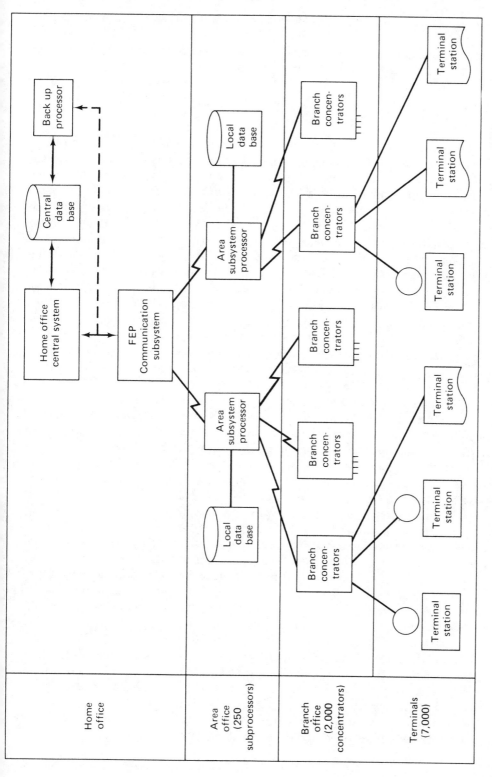

Fig. 5.6 Distributed processing network of International Bank

their previous system; the benefits result from improved customer service by virtue of greater system availability, capacity, and response time.

National Distributors

National Distributors distributes three lines of products, which are not related to each other—electronic products, plumbing and building supply products, and automotive parts. The management strongly believes in a decentralized organization and in giving maximum authority to divisional managers. They also feel the same about their MIS organization, and in 1982 they embarked on a program of decentralized DDP. So strong is their belief in decentralization that they prefer redundancy rather than telling a division manager that he has to do something a certain way.

The corporate office has a single computer system (see Fig. 5.7) that provides information services to its electronic products division and also takes care of the corporate applications, which mainly involve the consolidation of financial reports from the three operating divisions. The computer facility is operated as a service facility. There is complete independence of application development; one group works for the corporate controller and is responsible for corporate applications, another works for the general manager of the electronic products division. The reason for the single computer center is that the electronic products division operates only in the three states contiguous to the corporate office.

The plumbing and building supply division has two regions. While each region has complete autonomy in its operations, the East and West warehouses do cooperate in filling orders of customers when one warehouse does not have the inventory of a particular item. Thus, the building and supply central MIS group maintains an inventory data base, which is updated each night by the East and West MIS groups. The central group defines the common item identifiers and data-base organization, but has no authority over the MIS operations of either of the two regions.

The auto parts division operates without a central inventory data base; each of the three regions maintains its own inventory and its own inventory records and fills orders only from its own stocks. If the East division is out of an item, and the Central division has an overstock of the same item, this information is not known by either of them. On occasion a phone call is made from one region to the other to see if inventory of a particular item is available. Each region has its own autonomous MIS group, the only connection to the corporate office being the communication of summary operating data for consolidating financial reports.

National Distributors is illustrative of a highly decentralized DDP operation. The three divisions have independent MIS groups; the only connection is via the communication of financial data. There is no data-base sharing or centralized inventory control. The plumbing and building supply division does maintain a central inventory file, but the regions of the auto parts division maintain their own data base. It is most definitely an example of a loosely coupled operation, in contrast to the strictly controlled, hierarchical operation of International Bank.

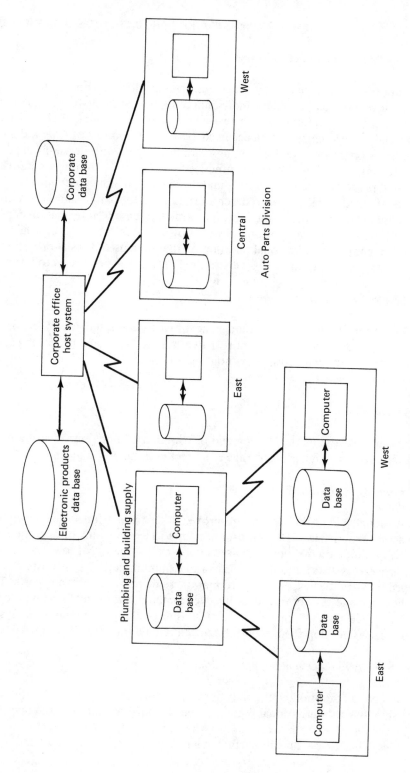

Fig. 5.7 National Distributors network

Why Distributed Data Processing?

Data processing, like many other business activities, seems to run in cycles. Thus the advent of computers saw individual computers at individual company sites. There was little, if any, interaction between computers and computer sites. Then the strong trend toward centralization occurred, based on economies of scale and the fact that business operations were becoming more integrated, with decisions depending on optimizing or balancing many functional activities within a company. The distributed-processing concept takes a middle course, possibly combining the benefits of centralization with those of decentralization. In the bank example, economies of scale are obtained while maintaining a central data base of information pertinent to overall company operations, and passing down to area offices (decentralized under the company's organizational philosophy) that data used in local operation.

The basic benefits claimed by distributed data processing are as follows:

Less Risk of System Breakdown.

In central systems, a power outage, act of God (flood, hurricane), act of sabotage, or strike can shut down the entire network. In a distributed processing system, the local operations can continue without major service interruption; only the summary or period reports are affected.

Availability.

Again, because of the sharing and distribution of functions, distributed data processing claims a higher percentage of system up-time over a given period.

Economy of Operation.

Although I find this difficult to prove, either from a functional viewpoint or from actual experience, DDP enthusiasts claim there is economy of operation. They base their opinion on the more balanced approach and the use of low-cost mini- and microprocessors throughout the network. Communication unit costs have not dropped, nor are they expected to drop, at the same rate as processing costs. Therefore the cost trade-off favors processing over communication and thus favors distributed data processing. Of concern, too, is the rising cost of programming and systems, as remote sites develop their own staffs, often redundant to the host staff.

Flexibility to Fit Organizational Philosophy.

To my way of thinking, this may be the most important rationale for distributed processing. In the International Bank example, the information files and operational control are vested at the area office level where the cost and profit center responsibility resides. This can be quite important in gaining management support and involvement in the system—vital factors that can often scuttle an otherwise well-conceived approach. Also data security and privacy are enhanced by having each area responsible for securing the data and files under its control.

Less Complexity of System Design and Implementation.

This is a strong attribute of the distributed concept. Completely centralized systems have literally choked on the complexity entailed in accomplishing the myriad of functions required when one central processor is responsible for accessing on-line data files for the entire network. The divide-and-conquer theory is the root of the distributed approach, where jobs are offloaded to processors specialized for handling the various subfunctions. However, reduced complexity may be a bit illusory, because complexity of another sort is introduced—the complexity of ensuring that the entire network is linked from level to level and the proper interaction pathways are maintained.

Whether one's approach is centralized or distributed, a strong system discipline and control is a prerequisite for success. In either case, one must have a full understanding of the interaction patterns and information relationships in order to determine where decision and action optimization or suboptimization occurs.

Level of Expertise Required.

Though some distributed-processing proponents would say the divide-and-conquer theory holds in establishing the level of expertise required of systems designers and implementers, it would seem that about the same experience level is required whether the system is centralized or distributed. While the central-system approach requires a core of highly trained and skilled practitioners, the decentralized approach requires that the system be constructed such that the disbursed personnel operating and using the system find it straightforward and simple to utilize. This adds a new challenge to system design. Languages and inquiry methodology must be flexible enough to accommodate the different class of users; thus the application programs, the operators, the area users, the branch work station users, and the management users must all find interaction with the system effective, efficient, and easy to learn.

What Functions to Distribute

We have stressed that the degree of DDP depends on the information requirements and organizational composition of a particular company. Though economic and organizational trends seem to favor equipment decentralization, this does not imply that other MIS functions should be decentralized as well.

Figure 5.8 indicates three patterns of function decentralization, the first the most centralized, the third the most decentralized, and the second in-between. Be-

	MIS Planning	Data Base Administration	Application Development	Operation
Most Centralized	C	C	C	C
Hybrid	C/D	C/D	C	C
Most Decentralized	C/D	C/D	D	D

C = Centralized
D = Decentralized

Fig. 5.8　Distributed MIS functions

cause even the most decentralized forms of DDP require some interaction and some cooperation, centralized planning is still a necessity for effective DDP. The figure indicates that in the hybrid and most decentralized instance, planning is a joint responsibility of both the central and decentralized groups, but the predominant force is still the centralized MIS planning group. Of course that group must carefully consider and reflect in their plans the needs of the decentralized groups.

Data-base administration follows the same pattern. An analysis is made of what data is unique to a specific operating unit. If data is unique, the data-base administrator places that data base completely in the control of the local entity. If data is shared, it must come under the control of the central MIS group; otherwise, serious redundancies will occur or the ability of specific groups to access data will be impaired.

The last two categories, application development and operation, usually involve a matrix type of organization. In the centralized mode, the developers work for the central group but are strongly aligned with the department or function they are servicing. In the decentralized mode, the opposite matrix relationship holds—there is a direct reporting relationship to the decentralized group with a dotted-line relationship to the central organization. Questions of critical mass, MIS personnel motivation, and advancement opportunities arise in determining the distribution of functions. However, the trend is toward the decentralized model, with the perceived advantages of MIS people being associated more closely with the business and operations than with the MIS profession.

In conclusion, the distributed-processing approach is gaining momentum, spurred by mini- and microprocessor developments that can provide intelligent, cost-effective front-end processors and intelligent work stations. The approach must be carefully evaluated by companies to see if it fits their mode of operation and their organizational environment. For most it will mean converting an existing communication system, rather than starting from scratch. This will present an added challenge, since it is more difficult to restructure a going system than to initiate a new one. However, this challenge has been faced by system designers since the beginning of data processing.

Feasibility Criteria

There is no questioning the potential benefits of advanced teleprocessing systems. At this point, however, I would like to consider some elements often overlooked in the planning process. I feel that too much attention is paid to the technology of teleprocessing, emphasizing the hardware and software aspects of line speeds, modems, multiplexors, concentrators, front-end processors, and terminals, but grossly neglecting the nontechnical elements.

In general there are three considerations of information system feasibility: technical, economic, and operational. The technical aspects have received the most attention from systems designers. Operational aspects have received the least. More emphasis must be given to the economic and operational elements of feasibility if advanced distributed data processing systems are to be installed successfully by more companies. David J. Farber (in *Datamation* magazine, "Networks: An Introduction,") describes seven typical computer networks with advanced teleprocessing. Six of the seven systems are projects sponsored by research or educational organizations. Considerations of economic feasibility are not as important to nonprofit organizations as they are to commercial businesses.

Dartmouth College has been a pioneer in using computers in its curriculum. John G. Kemeny, president of the college until 1981, developed a specialized language that simplified direct communication with the computer from terminals around the campus.

No doubt having access to a computer in college extends the range of problems a student can tackle. For example, access to a computerized simulation model adds a new dimension to a mathematics or physical science course. I also believe students should realize that a cost/benefit analysis is needed to justify the value of remote terminals and computer processing in a profit-oriented organization. Several years ago I was invited to Dartmouth's Tuck School of Business as a guest lecturer. My host asked me to direct my remarks to the cost/benefit and business considerations underlying the installation of time-sharing systems like those at Dartmouth. He, too, was concerned with the gap between technological and economic understanding.

Operational Considerations

I am even more concerned about the gap between the technological and operational considerations. A particular application may be both technically and economically feasible and still fail to produce the predicted benefits because a company is unable to make it work. A perplexed management cannot understand why a well-conceived and designed system is not successful in the operating departments. Some reasons for such failure are motivational and psychological. These often can be resolved by proper training and indoctrination. Other reasons, however, are serious enough to warrant placing a lower priority on a particular application area until the problem is resolved.

Such a situation might occur, for example, when a sales administration function performed by local sales branches becomes part of a distributed data processing system that processes orders and bills customers. The new system is designed and installed with little or no local participation at the sales branches. The branches try to circumvent the system, because they fear that account control is being removed from them. The new system develops a billing backlog, customers become irate, management becomes disillusioned, and the whole system eventually fails.

Before an application is instituted, it is necessary to assess management and general operational considerations. The impact of the application on top, middle, and operating management must be analyzed carefully. For example, a system like the one in Fig. 5.5 links process-control minicomputers to a general-purpose computer in order to control the production process. This approach will have a direct impact on the production manager and supervisors. A production manager who is very conservative, or has been antagonistic toward computerized production systems, is definitely a negative consideration with regard to operational feasibility. Unless this problem can be resolved, a lower priority should be given to this phase of the teleprocessing system.

A company's organizational philosophy may be extreme centralization, extreme decentralization, or something in between. When a company is centralized, well-defined policies and procedures are developed at the headquarters level. Local offices and plants follow these regulations to the letter; any deviations must be approved by headquarters. This type of operation usually is effective in a highly structured marketplace, and where products have long production runs and fairly stable life cycles.

The decentralized philosophy places maximum leverage and decision-making responsibility in the hands of local offices or plants. This aims to heighten an individual's motivation to succeed and develop an entrepreneurial style of operation. This approach is effective where markets and products differ according to the local environment and where quick decisions and flexibility are required.

In most cases a company's organization philosophy falls between these extremes. Also, an organization may change over time, moving from a decentralized to a centralized mode, and then possibly back toward decentralization. The changes result from normal organizational maturation, from different management styles, as well as from changes in a company's marketplace and products.

The design of distributed systems must take into account the organizational mode of a company. Although theoretically a centralized system can be effective in a decentralized company, in practice a system has less chance of success if it runs counter to the existing organizational philosophy. Furthermore, a system must be amenable to change as the company moves from one stage of organizational development to another. Flexibility and modularity are important criteria in designing distributed systems.

Timing is another consideration when a new system is planned. For example, if a company is planning to move to a more decentralized organizational structure, but hasn't yet done so, it might be wise to begin with a more centralized approach that has the flexibility to move toward a decentralized mode later on. Note that the decision to implement a centralized or distributed system does not depend on whether the company's control style is centralized or decentralized.

Key systems trade-offs must be considered during the design of any system. These should not be based strictly on technological and economical considerations. Should a completely centralized data base be developed, for example, or should subsets of the central file be maintained locally? From technological and economic viewpoints, the centralized data base might appear to be the way to go. On the other hand, operational considerations may dictate that some redundancy in file storage is necessary for the system to work. Also, corporate management may consider too rapid a move to decentralization as usurpation of their prerogatives and authority before decentralized management has earned the right to local authority.

The claim is sometimes made that advanced DDP systems solve a company's organizational and people communications problems. Experience shows that if such problems are not resolved before installing the DDP system, the new system might make them worse. If strict discipline is a prerequisite for successful implementation of DDP, it must be achieved before system installation, not afterward. The system will not create the needed discipline. Moreover, installing a new system and simultaneously implementing a new operational philosophy increases the risk that neither will succeed. The best approach is to get one's house in order before superimposing a major change. The DDP system may be the catalyst, but it alone cannot resolve underlying company organizational and operational problems.

Other Management Considerations

Implicit in teleprocessing is a real-time response capability—the capacity to respond immediately, whether or not immediate response is indeed necessary. Is it really necessary that the customer receive an immediate answer—or could it be sent hours, or perhaps even days, later? In a few special circumstances real-time response is vital. But in many business applications, such immediate response rarely will be required.

On-time systems, therefore, represent a much broader and more flexible approach, and probably a less costly one, to most business applications. Such systems are intended to respond to information demands, whether the demand is for immediate answer-back, or for answer-back an hour, a day, or a week later.

A basic criterion is that the review frequency must be matched to the response capability of the system. Before plunging into an expensive real-time system, examine what will be done with information once it is obtained. Your objective should be responses available *as they are needed*.

As an example, there is quite a difference between a military control system's need for frequent review and immediate response and a grocery buyer's need to know the amount of instant coffee in the warehouse. If the course of a missile traveling at 25,000 miles per hour is not changed in a split second, it will never hit the target. However, when a warehouse has space for large quantities of instant coffee and a buyer purchases coffee once or twice a month, the split-second status of the item is not very significant. A daily inventory status report normally satisfies the on-time criterion.

The trend is not toward universal adoption of real-time operation. Rather, executives will find better ways of analyzing the objectives of their business and determining what information is needed (and not needed) to form the basis of action. The system to satisfy these objectives will be on-time; that is, it will respond as required to meet the needs of the business. If there is cost justification for split-second responses, only then will real-time be used.

SUMMARY

This chapter covered the principles of communications, describing its history and evolution and the elements that comprise a communication system. External communications involves the linking of geographically dispersed facilities via telephone lines, microwaves, or satellites. Internal communications were also covered, where PBX's or data highways transmit voice and data within a building. Advances in telecommunications and the advent of distributed data processing are creating the need for added emphasis on these areas within the MIS organization. A separate teleprocessing group is often the result, taking over voice as well as digital transmission. Heretofore some MIS executives may have considered telephones beneath their dignity—for, after all, how could telephone directories, switchboard operators, or call buttons possess enough high-technological content to be relevant? The broadening scope of communication and the development of the digital switch places voice communications squarely in the MIS domain. The Multics system was used as an example of a centralized communications utility emphasizing the previously described elements of a communications system.

The remainder of the chapter centered on distributed data processing, defining and categorizing its different manifestations. Examples contrasted a centralized form of DDP with a more decentralized type. Management considerations in implementing such systems were then presented.

There are two major forces behind the trend to DDP. The first is the technological phenomenon that provides economical but powerful processing capability in small units. This is characterized by the microprocessor. Prior to this development, it was more economical to maintain processing power at a central site and allow remote facilities to tap the power. The second force—and, I think, the more important one—is the management tenet that decentralized authority motivates people and establishes the entrepreneurial spirit that drives businesses. As managers begin to realize the power of information and that it is indeed a valuable resource, they want more and more to direct its employment in their operations. They want control over their information in the same way they want control over their people, facilities, and products. Distributed data processing speaks to this need.

Chapters 4 and 5 represent the essence of MIS. The data base holds the relevant data that drives the transactions of the business and also provides the meaningful management data that abets the planning and control of the business. DDP is the delivery system for the data. Data base and DDP are both integral to MIS. These two functions were previously embedded within other functions in the MIS organization. As we saw in Chapter 2, where information resource management (IRM) was reviewed, these two functions become separate and vital MIS entities.

In this wondrous era of distributed data processing and electronic communication, we need to maintain perspective. Toward this end the following preteleprocessing dialogue is presented to close the chapter.

The Medium Is The Message, Mr. Lincoln

WPS (Word Processing Salesman):   Mr. Lincoln, you're going at it the wrong way.

Lincoln: Could you elaborate quickly? I must continue to work on my speech for Gettysburg next week.

WPS: I've seen your draft. First, it's scribbled on scrap paper and is hardly legible.

Lincoln: What would you suggest?

WPS: Transform your speech onto electronic media. Then we can use such things as the paragraph insert feature. Your speech is far too short; looks like about three to five minutes. We can add some stock paragraphs and produce a more traditional and respectable 45-minute address. You don't want to face that crowd with so brief a message.

Lincoln: That's interesting. And what else can you do?

WPS: Once in electronic form, we can easily edit it for you. For instance, I note your first sentence reads, "Four score and seven years ago." In your next draft, I'm sure you'll want to tighten that to 87 years. We can quickly and efficiently accommodate functions of that kind.

Lincoln: I begin to see your point.

WPS: And one last thing. Once we've captured the final text, we can reproduce thousands of copies and transmit to every city in the country; we call it electronic mail. Believe me, if you do it your way, your three-minute handwritten speech will be forgotten in 24 hours.

CASE STUDIES

BARTON MANUFACTURING, INC.

Sam Jones was the vice-president and general manager of Barton Manufacturing, a producer of lawnmowers, garden tools, and lawn furniture. Barton had warehouses and manufacturing plants throughout the 22 midwestern states in which the company operated. Jones had been a forceful proponent of computerized information systems and had thought for a long time that Barton could and should be linking all its warehouses and plants into a computer network.

There was a great disparity in the information support rendered to each location. The general approach was a centralized system and central data base providing services to the remote locations. The plant and warehouse managers had gone to one extreme or the other. In one set of plants, they had become complacent and passive, accepting whatever the central MIS unit could deliver even when they knew it was inadequate. In the other set of plants, the managers had taken a proactive approach, demanding additional reports and analyses and, when the lead time was too long, trying to do it themselves or utilize outside help.

Jones called in Wallace Barnstone, MIS director, and indicated his desire to move toward a network approach. Jones was aware of the trend toward distributed data processing and the moves of his competitors in this direction and indicated it was time for Barton to make its move.

Barnstone was a little chagrined, because he knew that with the rather basic system currently in operation, it would take a complete new design and approach to get anywhere near what Jones was demanding. He had been through an attempt to completely resystematize and develop a communication-based integrated DDP system and the effort had been disastrous. This was one of the reasons he took the Barton job—their MIS operations seemed straightforward, uncomplicated, and built on a solid foundation.

Jones went on to indicate he was dead serious in his request—he knew it would be expensive and would take time, but he intuitively knew the benefits were there to justify the added cost. The Barton company was profitable and had the required cash to invest in this type of venture. It was for this reason that Jones wanted to move on the system now, while things were going well, not when Barton was in a weak defensive position. He could see competition moving toward distributed data processing and he wanted Barton to retain its competitive edge.

After discussing the philosophy and general benefits of developing such a system for about an hour, Jones turned to Barnstone and said he wanted an initial report on the proposed new system presented to his monthly staff meeting in three weeks. He wanted Barnstone to take personal charge of this project, at least at this stage, and to give him weekly updates of the direction he was taking prior to the staff session. Jones indicated they were embarking on what could be the most significant step in Barton's long history and that he, Jones, would want to be involved personally in designing and developing the new approach.

Barnstone's head was whirling as he left Jones' office. He knew the general manager was a forceful man and meant what he said, but he wondered whether Jones had any idea of the scope of what he was proposing. Barnstone thought of his previous experience and wondered whether he could go through it again—and he had to admit to himself that there was a growing concern over the degree of decentralization that was optimum for Barton. Jones might have oversold the approach in order to gain support for it. Barnstone knew he had some deep reflection ahead of him before he would meet again with Jones.

STUDY QUESTIONS

1. Do you think Barton should go to such a system?

2. Is Barnstone the man to lead the development effort?

3. How practical and realistic is Jones' approach? How important is his commitment?

4. What should be Barnstone's next steps?

5. How much can be done prior to the staff meeting?

6. Outline the contents of what you think Barnstone's report and presentation should be.

NATURAL CONTAINER INDUSTRIES*

Typical of the differing opinions concerning distributed data processing are those expressed by Arthur Connelly, manager of systems at National's turbine division, and Arthur Seymour, president of the computer division for the last ten years.

In the late 1960s, concerned both by the rapid proliferation of computer expenditures and staff in the company, and some virtual disasters in systems design development effort, the president had directed that a centralized computing center be established in St. Louis and organized as a separate division within the corporate structure. At the same time the decision was made to locate all systems programming and computing power in the central computing facility while virtually all applications systems and programming would be done in the divisions. This pattern had been maintained, essentially unchanged, until the present.

Arthur Seymour, president of the computing division, noted in discussing his company's mission in 1980: "Our basic competitive advantage is our ability to produce reliable, cheap computing power for our sister divisions. If we fail in this dimension, we have, in fact, no reason for our existence." He noted the increased pressure his department had been under in the past two years and commented at some length on what he perceived as a growing incursion of minicomputer power. Deeply distressed at this development, he observed that it was his job to hold the line on these devices and make sure that "none of those damn little black boxes get into the hands of users." He noted that the users and the software companies they hired had little understanding of internal control systems, operations documentation, and other elements of good data processing hygiene. He further noted that his company, in the short term, was a largely fixed-cost one and that the acquisition of minicomputers by sister divisions was clearly increasing the corporation's negative cash flows. The only sensible way to manage minicomputers, he said, was to have them all approved and evaluated by the computing division organization. Otherwise, a whole series of apparently individual correct decisions could add to one large mistake. He cited the six minicomputers acquired in the Turbine Division in the last year as evidence of this type of myopia.

Arthur Connelly, manager of the systems and programming group of the Turbine Division, had a very different perspective. He noted that four times in the past year there had been major problems with the operating system on the central computing activity and that during the month-end and quarter-end closes, there had been

*Excerpted with permission from a Harvard Business School case study.

such severe capacity crunches as to sharply delay his receipt of vital management reports. He noted that these six minis had bought him independence from the reliability problems of the central data processing activity and given him the flexibility to develop new and improved systems with better service to the Turbine Division. "The best control for minicomputers, at this stage, is no control. Later on, when we get more experience in these issues, we can then begin to be more rigorous on a corporate basis."

The conflict between these two executives eventually reached the chief executive officer's ears, and, looking at the growth trend in both data processing costs and the number of computers, he decided that the subject warranted a serious investigation. Accordingly, he established a computer priorities committee, composed of the presidents of each of the three major divisions and of two of the small divisions. As their first assignment he charged them with evaluating this particular subject and developing a recommendation.

QUESTIONS

1. What do you think of Seymour's attitude toward minicomputers?

2. Is Connelly justified in his perspective?

3. How can this issue be resolved? If both parties persist, what can be done and by whom? Did the president act properly?

4. Do you think this is a typical situation in many companies?

5. Is it conceivable that some companies would be better off in operating their MIS on a centralized basis? Or is DDP the inevitable trend for everyone?

BIBLIOGRAPHY

Booth, Grayce M., *The Distributed Systems Environment*. New York: McGraw-Hill, 1981.

Buchanan, J. R. and R. G. Linowes, "Understanding Distributed Data Processing." *Harvard Business Review* (1980), 143–153.

Honeywell, "Distributed Processing System 8/Multics," no. AK 27 (1982).

Honeywell, "Distributed Systems Architecture," no. CY 28 (1982).

Kanter, Jerome and Richard S. Wells, "Teleprocessing Systems Perspectives," *Journal of Systems Management* (March 1975), 10–15.

Martin, James, *Design and Strategy of Distributed Data Processing*. Englewood Cliffs, NJ: Prentice-Hall, Inc., 1981.

Martin, James, *Future Developments in Telecommunications, 2nd ed.* Englewood Cliffs, NJ: Prentice-Hall, Inc., 1977.

Martin, James, *Telecommunications and the Computer, 2nd ed.* Englewood Cliffs, NJ: Prentice-Hall, Inc., 1976.

Martin, James, *Telematic Society: A Challenge for Tomorrow.* Englewood Cliffs, NJ: Prentice-Hall, Inc., 1982.

Mertes, Louis H., "Doing Your Office Over—Electronically," *Harvard Business Review* (1981), 127–135.

Perry, George M., "An Information Systems Approach to Telecommunications," *MIS Quarterly* (Sept. 1980), 17–29.

Sherman, K., *Data Communications: A Users Guide.* Reston, VA: Reston Publ. Co., 1981.

Tanenbaum, A. S., *Computer Networks.* Englewood Cliffs, NJ: Prentice-Hall, Inc., 1981.

Theirauf, R. J., *Distributed Processing Systems.* Englewood Cliffs, NJ: Prentice-Hall, Inc., 1978.

Thurber, K., "Tutorial: A Pragmatic View of Distributed Processing Systems," Los Alemedos, CA: EEE Comput. Soc., 1980.

Chapter 6

A Historical Perspective: Mainframes to Micros

The emphasis of this book is most definitely on MIS and specifically its management aspect. This chapter departs a bit from the main theme to discuss the technology and industry trends that provide the operating environment for MIS. Though proper management perspective has become the most important force in successful MIS, the technology has made MIS more cost effective and has changed the people-cost/hardware-cost trade-off decision. After taking a brief historical look at the industry evolution and industry uses of MIS, the chapter will focus on specific hardware, software, and support services trends.

EARLY HISTORY OF COMPUTERS

In his widely read book, *Future Shock,* Alvin Toffler points out that almost as much has happened since we were born as happened before we were born. This barrage of change, scientific acceleration, and technological turnover is causing a psychological shock wave throughout society. Toffler indicates that if the last 50,000 years of human existence were divided into lifetimes of approximately 62 years each, there have been about 800 lifetimes. Of these 800, fully 650 were spent in caves. Only during the last 70 lifetimes has it been possible to communicate effectively from one lifetime to another—as writing made it possible to do. Only during the last six lifetimes did masses of people ever see a printed word. Only during the last four has it been possible to measure time with any precision. Only in the last two has anyone anywhere used an electric motor. And an overwhelming majority of the material goods we use in daily life was developed within the present, the 800th, lifetime. This type of analysis holds for computers and the science of information processing. Certainly computers have been characteristic only of the 800th lifetime—in fact, the last third of the 800th lifetime, if you consider computers on the commercial scene.

You should view the progress of computers with this perspective to avoid reaching the conclusion that computers are overrated and their impact limited. The learning curve has been rapid despite the experience of some, particularly those in the EDP business or those using computers, who have borne the brunt of abortive attempts to reach out too far, too fast. The Toffler "lifetime" concept places the computer in its proper framework in time and projects a sobering view of its potential.

Although the abacus is not a computer, the history of computing really began with this device. The abacus is a manual device combining two fundamental concepts. It uses objects (small beads) to represent numbers, and it uses one object to represent several numbers. On an abacus the number nine is represented by one "five" bead and four "one" beads. In the hands of a skilled user, the abacus makes extremely rapid arithmetic calculations. The abacus is still the most widely used computing device in existence.

The first machine to add numbers mechanically was invented by Blaise Pascal, the French mathematician and philosopher, in 1643. Pascal used geared counter wheels that could be set to any of the positions zero to nine. The geared tooth was used for carrying one to the next position when nine was reached. Following Pascal's lead, G. W. Leibnitz, a German mathematician, invented a machine in 1671 that could control the amount of adding. This was the first multiplying machine. These early machines are the direct ancestors of the electric-powered, but hand-operated adding machines and desk calculating machines that are still very much part of the business scene. These adding machines and calculators accomplish only one operation at a time and are key driven; that is, they are activated by depressing a key.

Charles Babbage, a professor of mathematics at Cambridge University, England, attempted in 1812 to build a difference engine—a machine that could add, subtract, multiply, divide, and perform a sequence of steps automatically. The last function is the forerunner of the stored program. Babbage called his machine a difference engine because he intended to use it to compute mathematical tables by adding differences such as the time between the high and low tides. For example, if the moon rises exactly one hour later each day, and the high and low tides are 6½ hours apart, and if on August 14, high tide is at 12:00 A.M., then low tide will be at 6:30 P.M. On August 15, high tide will be at 1:00 P.M., and low tide at 7:30 P.M., and so on. A table was to be built by adding differences. Babbage failed to get the necessary funds for his machine, and in 1833 the project was dropped. Babbage also was thinking of making an analytical engine with three parts: store (memory), mill (arithmetic), and sequence mechanisms (control). These parts are very similar to the elements of a computer. Babbage didn't gain the necessary funds and support for this project either, but his concepts were sound in every respect. It is generally stated that the technology in Babbage's time just didn't permit the development of instruments with the precision required by his analytical engine.

At this point we are introduced to one of the few romantic figures in computer history, Ada Lovelace. Ada was the only legitimate daughter of Lord Byron. Unlike other ladies of her time and background, who occupied themselves with light studies, recreation, and serving tea, Ada took to mathematics and at age 15 had covered Paisley's geometry text on her own as a diversion. She became known to Charles Babbage through a translation she did of a French work that helped the development of the difference engine. Ada, described as brilliant, charming, and feminine, became a vital assistant to Babbage. Molly Gleiser, computer historian, writes that at her death at age 36, at her own wish, she was buried at the side of Lord George Gordon Byron (also dead at age 36), "all passion stilled, passionate and noble daughter of a passionate and noble father." Sometimes an emotion or two crops up even in a book on computers and information systems.

A major development occurred in 1886 when statistician Herman Hollerith was working on the 1880 census of the United States. After six years of constant work the census still had not been calculated. Obviously, a new way to handle large amounts of data was needed if this census were to be completed before the next one came around. For 80 years, cards with punched holes representing numbers had been used to control the weaving of cloth on Jacquard looms. Hollerith had the idea that these holes could be sensed by a machine that would then sort and manipulate the arithmetic sums represented by the holes. The punched card has withstood the rapid innovations in computer technology for nearly 90 years. Today, the Hollerith punched cards and punched-card number code are still the basic computer input medium.

The same Herman Hollerith became the chief asset of the Tabulating Machine Company (as William Rodgers wrote in his book *Think,* a biography of the Watsons and IBM). Thomas J. Watson left NCR in 1913 and in the following year, through a holding company called the Computer-Tabulating-Recording Company (C-T-R) headed up by a noted American financier, Charles R. Flint, became general manager of one of the component companies, the Tabulating Machine Company. In 1924 C-T-R became known as IBM, with Tom Watson its eventual president. Rodgers points out that Watson never got along with the volatile inventor Hollerith, who was to drive Watson literally out of his senses. Out of his senses or no, Watson parlayed Hollerith's concept of the punched card and the punched-card machine into an empire that today employs more than a third of a million people and has sales of over $25 billion per year. Appropriately enough, the formation of C-T-R in 1914 corresponds almost exactly to the beginning of Toffler's 800th lifetime.

The first automatic digital computer that worked was constructed at the Bell Telephone Laboratories in New York in 1939 by George Stibitz. Stibitz, an engineer, faced the problem of performing arithmetic operations on complex numbers. He decided that ordinary telephone relays could be wired together to do this time-consuming job. Stibitz represented each decimal digit by a code of ones and zeros (the beginning of binary notation), such that four relays arranged in a pattern of being energized or not could represent a number. The machine was completed and successfully demonstrated in 1940. It is interesting to note that mathematicians at Dartmouth College sent problems to the machine via teletype and received answers. This was the beginning of on-line communications to the computer.

The first general-purpose, automatic digital computer was the Harvard/IBM automatic sequence-controlled calculator called the Mark I. It began operations in 1944, under wartime pressure. It was developed by Professor Howard Aiken with the help of engineers from IBM. The Mark I performed about three additions per second and had 72 internal storage registers. This is a modest capability compared to the millions of additions per second and the millions of registers of internal storage available in today's computers. The slow operation was caused by the use of the relay, an electromechanical device, as the major component.

At the same time a group of engineers at the University of Pennsylvania, headed by John W. Mauchly and J. P. Eckert, was working on an automatic electronic digital computer using radio tubes, which function at higher speed than relays. The ENIAC (Electronic Numerical Integrator and Automatic Calculator) was completed in 1947. It had only 20 storage registers but it could accomplish 5000 additions per second, which made it the fastest computer in operation.

At this point, it would be inappropriate to proceed without at least the brief mention of three men, who though not necessarily associated with specific computer hardware development, were instrumental in the introduction of logic and programming elements enabling the computer to execute complex instructions and to control a wide gamut of business and scientific operations. These men are George Boole, Norbert Weiner, and John von Neumann.

George Boole lived in Babbage's time (early and mid 1800s). Though not involved in hardware development, he used his genius in mathematics to lay the groundwork for the theory behind computer logic. Modern computers operate with a binary or two-stage operating logic; each instruction or piece of data is converted to this two-stage form before entering the computer and being processed. The data is then converted back to decimal and alpha mode at output time. The binary representation and internal arithmetic manipulation are called *Boolean algebra,* after George Boole, and this indeed represents a most significant contribution to computer development.

Norbert Wiener, who received a Ph.D. in 1913 at the age of 19, reincarnated the word *cybernetics* from the Greek *kubernetes* (steersman) in the 1940s. The science of cybernetics is defined as that of how automatic machines or computers function, including the elements of input, output, processing, communications, and feedback loops. Wiener's work helps us understand the basic concept of a system and indeed underlines the description of the systems module described earlier. Wiener's writings develop an analogy of automatic feedback systems to the human nervous system. Thus intension tremor and Parkinsonism are impairments of the normal feedback loops between brain and motor functions. Wiener's work assists us in comprehending the overall science or body of thought in which the computer plays a prominent part.

John von Neumann (1903–1957) is a prominent name to people familiar with the early development of computers in the United States. In a book entitled *The Computer From Pascal to Von Neumann,* Herman Goldstine, who worked with von Neumann, cannot say enough about the latter's contribution in the computer field. Von Neumann, a brilliant mathematician, had a profound influence on the development of early hardware but he concentrated on the memory and software side, the latter being an area that to this day has not been fully understood nor properly emphasized. Von Neumann showed earlier hardware developers how to store instructions and what these instructions should do. His initial concept of storage in a mercury delay line is the forerunner of core memory and today's semiconductor memory. Prior to von Neumann, paper tape was the accepted vehicle for getting instructions to the processor. John von Neumann's contributions are immense.

From 1946 to 1951 the computer field was dominated by the government, universities, and small companies working with government on university grants. It was five years before the world's first commercial computer was produced by Remington Rand (now the Sperry Corporation). Remington Rand had purchased control of the Eckert-Mauchly Computer Corp., developers of the ENIAC. The first commercial computer, UNIVAC I, was delivered in 1951 to the same U.S. Bureau of the Census that first spurred Dr. Hollerith to use punched cards in calculations. The first non-government installation of a UNIVAC I was at General Electric's appliance plant in Louisville, Kentucky, in 1954.

THE COMMERCIAL ERA

The installation of UNIVAC I's at the Census Department and at General Electric opened up the commercial era of computers, and few could forecast what was to come. Several prominent prognosticators of the time proclaimed that no more than 100 of these machines would be needed to handle the computations for the entire country.

This section will review the commercial developments over four decades, beginning with the fifties and ending with the eighties.

The First Computer Decade — 1950 to 1959

During the fifties, the so-called mainframers—IBM, Remington Rand, Honeywell, and RCA—predominated. The term *mainframe,* which was not coined until the advent of minicomputers, connoted the large, high-power, high-cost nature of these first computer products.

Remington Rand completely dominated the market during the five-year period between 1951 and 1956. The situation then shifted radically, and by 1957 IBM controlled the computer field as it had the office-machine and punched-card fields. Other companies—Honeywell, General Electric, Control Data, NCR, Burroughs,

Digital Equipment Corporation, and RCA, to name some of the larger ones—also began manufacturing computers. General Electric subsequently was bought out by Honeywell in 1970. Sperry Rand purchased the remains of the RCA computer business after RCA left the field in 1971. IBM still dominates the market with about 60 percent of all computers installed.

The fifties can be characterized as the era of the engineer. The demands of engineers, mathematicians, and scientists for raw calculating power created the need for computers. The iterative mathematical process is immense if you want, for example, to solve a complex equation involving hundreds of calculations by assigning values x and y ranging from 1 to 100 in gradations of 0.1. Thus the first computers were big "number crunchers." They also were expensive, as well as difficult to maintain and use.

Early machines were supported by government and educational funds; cost effectiveness was not the primary focus. This is, of course, not all bad in the infancy of a burgeoning new technology, for constraining the scope of research and development too early can hinder progress. Since much of the work given to computers had not been done before, it was hard to determine whether computer benefits offset costs. Cost justification is particularly difficult in experimental R&D.

There were many abortive attempts to build new machines and to improve existing ones. The builders received little help from equipment users. At first there was no great interest in the use of computers for business purposes. Business was not aware of the computer's vast potential in business operations. Also, there were no company planning groups or special-interest organizations to give guidance or direction to computer manufacturers. Frequently a product was developed before its market potential, if any, had been determined. An already developed product sought a suitable market, instead of being determined by marketplace needs. The fifties were completely dominated by the mainframes, as there were about 4000 systems installed by the end of the decade.

The Second Computer Decade—1960 to 1969

As the first computer decade was the era of the engineer, the second decade was that of the marketeer. Large well-financed companies, led by IBM, and including Honeywell, Sperry Rand, Burroughs, and NCR, developed powerful marketing and sales forces in this new growth industry. Thousands of sales and systems personnel were sent out to convince the marketplace that the "chicken in every pot" idea applied to computers. These marketeers were young, ambitious, enthusiastic, intelligent, and wrapped up in their new product. Perhaps as a result, they oversold it on a grand scale. The sixties marked the era of mainframe computer proliferation, with the number of installed computers increasing from 4000 to over 50,000.

While mainframes were proliferating, the minis were entering the scene, led by DEC (Digital Equipment Corporation), who had achieved over $100 million sales by the end of the decade. During the sixties, minis hardly dented the installed computer base, but the potential was ominous, to say the least.

This decade also marked the end of the unit record equipment market. These punched-card workhorses produced by IBM and Univac were the backbones of payrolls, order processing, accounting, and the like, pumping out cards and listings by the millions. The unit record or accounting machines now gave way to computers that could accomplish in one integrated step what formerly took multiple steps of passing punched cards through EAM (electronic accounting machine) units. It was a major breakthrough.

What the marketeers failed to understand was the practical company environment in which computers had to operate, and they vastly overestimated their customers' ability to use the equipment. Computer users, however, have to share the rap for this unwise proliferation. Very few users understood the role the computer should play in a company: they didn't select the areas where it should be used; they didn't establish priorities or determine schedules; future systems planning was almost nil. Upper management didn't understand computers and didn't take the time to learn, either because they didn't think they could or because they thought computers were merely another accounting tool that belonged in the controller's shop. So they turned over the computers to the technocrats: systems and programming priesthoods ran the show and managed the new machines.

The advanced-systems or innovative approach was "in." Systems analysts had a tendency to be too cute or too sophisticated. The value of something became a function of its uniqueness or complexity, not its worth to the user: the means justified the ends. Vendors and users alike were subject to a wish-fulfillment syndrome: when a new technique or product on the market bears some relationship (however remote) to a problem, there is a tendency to apply it, regardless of relevance. The computer and the various concepts of management information systems, central data bases, operations research, management science, and the like were facets of this wish-fulfillment syndrome.

This was also the decade of advertising, seminars, general- and special-interest groups, trade shows, press conferences, and educational institutes. Computers were talked about as never before.

In perspective, however, the sixties represent the essential phase of growth and expansion of the computer industry. Successful marketing is as important as product development (perhaps even more so). Many experts feel that the demise of GE and RCA in the computer industry resulted principally from their lack of effective marketing organizations.

Early mainframes were built from vacuum tubes and carried $3-million-plus purchase prices. Costs were reduced in the sixties with transistors and integrated circuits. There was, however, a limit to the cost effectiveness of the new machines. The inherent design had a top-down focus; that is, the basic architecture was optimized for large-scale computing. It is difficult to subset a system whose design point is at the upper end of the power curve. Also, the architecture was geared to batch processing, the principal operation mode in the fifties and sixties. Mainframe manufacturers did introduce new families of small machines, but these remained batch oriented and carried over a good deal of large-machine mentality, including complex systems software, which required excessive amounts of memory. Only in recent years have main-framers incorporated a transaction-oriented design philosophy to handle individual transactions in an on-line mode with quick turnaround to the waiting user—a requirement of most small business systems.

Mainframe companies built up large user bases, where the inherent software lock-in and vendor loyalty (about 80 percent of all mainframe vendors each year make decisions to upgrade or replace their systems with another model from their current vendor) motivate the manufacturer to provide compatibility and ease of upgrade to its existing base. This constrains, to a certain degree, innovation and the improvement of cost effectiveness. Another important element is that a good portion of the mainframe business is rental rather than outright purchase. For this reason, cash flow, especially in the early part of the product life cycle, does not allow for both reasonable levels of development funds and maintenance of acceptable profit rates.

To summarize, the evolution of the mainframe vendors with emphasis on large-scale computing power, product-line compatibility, batch-application orientation, and protection of their customer base left a niche for a new breed of computer vendor. The minicomputer vendor entered the scene with a high-technology product optimized around transaction processing and an interrupt-driven architecture. The minicomputer era started first with special-purpose uses in the mid and late sixties, but with the advent of general-purpose/commercial use, really took off in the seventies.

The Third Computer Decade—1970 to 1979

The third computer decade began with the business downturn in the early seventies. With business volume down, companies found themselves underutilizing their computers, or having excess capacity because of the oversell and overbuy of the late sixties. For the first time since computers appeared on the commercial scene, MIS managers were forced to cut computer operating budgets. The data processing industry had experienced a kind of chain-letter effect: everything growing at an exponential rate. One system this month became two next month, four the next, and eight the following. Similarly, software and services companies proliferated, terminal and peripheral devices multiplied, and the market for trained systems analysts, programmers, and operating personnel expanded. The business recession ended all that. The computer industry was not immune to depressions after all.

This era, characterized by more judicious selection and use on the part of the user community, marked a maturing of the mainframes. However, this was the era of minicomputer proliferation, and extensibility became a popular buzz word. The less expensive minis led to their use in remote offices and facilities of large companies as well as lowering the entry threshold for small businesses acquiring their first computer. This decade also marked the start-up phase of the microcomputer.

In the late sixties, few could see the inroads that minis would make in the information processing business in the decade to come. Minis grew at a rate three times that of mainframes (33 percent per year to 12 percent) over this decade. By 1977, Digital Equipment Corporation (DEC), the leading mini producer, became a $1 billion company. What is the reason for this growth, and what does it mean for the businessman/manager? The explanation requires dividing the minicomputer period into two phases.

In the sixties, minis could be characterized as follows:

- Selling price under $25,000
- Maximum 16-bit architecture
- Limited input/output capability
- Limited general-purpose software
- Limited storage capability
- Specialized software, mostly scientific
- Special-purpose usage
- Architecture optimized for interrupt-driven applications

The market for minis was primarily in the industrial OEM (original equipment manufacturer) marketplace. A paper or chemical company requires computer-based control of production operations. A third party buys a minicomputer, adds special hardware/software, and develops a packaged system for a specific task. The industrial OEM then sells the package to the end user, who is usually not aware even of the embedded computer's brand name. It is a solution sell. Thus, during phase one, the minis served a specialized industrial use. Other uses included communication message switching, laboratory statistical number crunching, computerized simulation models, and the like. The minis were not, at this juncture, employed in the commercial business marketplace dominated by IBM and the other mainframers.

During phase one, the mini companies were able to concentrate on technology, and they succeeded in implementing cost-effective solutions for specific problems. It was only a matter of time until the mini vendors began to see the growing market potential if they could adapt their product to commercial business data processing. The hardware was there; what was lacking were the important ancillary peripheral and software capabilities. It was fortuitous for the mini vendor that the data processing world was changing from a batch orientation to a transaction-processing environment (the architecture of minis). The same type of real-time response required in industrial process-control applications was carried over to the business data processing arena. This became the focus of phase two of the minicomputer era.

During phase two (the seventies) minis were complemented with an expanded array of peripheral equipment. Business data processing requires a wide range of storage devices for applications such as inventory control and order processing. Storage capacities ranging from low-cost removable diskettes (one million characters) to large fixed-disk devices (billions of characters) are commonplace in business applications. Likewise, line and serial printers are required, and the scope of terminal and communications equipment broadens. From a hardware sense, it becomes difficult to tell a mini from a small or medium mainframe, and today some of the large superminis even begin to compare to large mainframes.

But, as many users are beginning to realize, the name of the data processing game has shifted from hardware to software. Here, too, the mini vendors have been diligent in producing the requisite commercial software—the programming languages, operating systems, data-base software, and query languages. Application software is also in evidence, much of it developed by third-party software/system houses and marketed as a package along with the hardware.

What is the difference between a business system emanating from a mini vendor and one emanating from a mainframe vendor? Very little. The products must be evaluated in the perspective of a company's individual needs and the overall cost effectiveness of the system solution (*system* solution, not *hardware* solution). The elements of software, applications, service, support, and maintainability become increasingly important decision criteria as the system choices multiply at an almost exponential rate.

The third decade of computers belonged to the businessman and to management, as the first belonged to the engineer, and the second to the marketeer. Although this outlook shows increasing maturity in a rapidly growing and changing industry, it should not be used to stifle product innovation and expansion. Rather, it should be used to direct the thrust of product development to ensure the greatest return from the development dollar. The user should focus on the applications he foresees for the machine. The computer manufacturer should concentrate on the products required to accomplish these applications most efficiently and economically. When users are overawed by technology, they are, as someone has put it, like the stereo enthusiast who, wild over woofers, intrigued by intermodulation, tantalized by tweeters, and delirious over decibels, hates music.

The Fourth Computer Decade—1980 to 1989

The book's final chapter will give a more complete picture of what we can expect in the later eighties. Generally there should be a peaking of the mainframe business. It will grow, but much more slowly than the mini- and microcomputer areas; in fact, the market will see a blurring of the distinction between mainframes, minis, and micros.

Microcomputers appeared in the mid seventies, and their development paralleled that of the minis, till in the eighties they have become a driving industry force. At first, the micro was a limited, special-purpose device aimed at specific functions and with limited peripheral and software capability. The uses were similar to those of the early minis; in fact, micros replaced minis in many process and industrial control applications. However, by adding peripheral connections and enriching the software, the micro has become at home in the small-business world and also in the distributed-processing world.

As minis have moved up to encroach on the mainframes, micros have captured market territory previously the province of minis. The distinction between mainframe, mini, and micro has become blurred.

The micro vendors are typified by Texas Instruments, Motorola, National Semiconductor, Tandy, and Apple. The micro-based small-business computer is a natural offshoot. Micros appeared in this market in several ways. The first route is via companies who incorporate their own micro or build a system around someone else's micro and market via the traditional sales channels. The second route is typified by Tandy and Apple. Their micros started out as home or hobby computers, used primarily by technically bent engineers or professionals. With added capabilities, however, these machines began to find their way into small business, sold through the retail store—the same channel used for the hobby computer.

The major influence of the micro in the distributed-processing world has been via the growth of the intelligent terminal (or its more sophisticated big brother, the brilliant terminal). A simple cathode-ray-tube (CRT) terminal can be enhanced by microcomputer intelligence, or expanded into a cluster of terminal work stations replete with disk storage and printing capabilities. This now becomes an intelligent or brilliant terminal subsystem or satellite, similar to the mini-based satellite.

The general-manager framework carries over to the fourth decade of computer use, causing more emphasis on solid business practice and tighter control over computer and related expenditures. MIS departments are being scrutinized as closely as other operating departments within a company. The computer itself is being treated like other major capital expenditures, coming under stringent analysis regarding return on investment and cash flow.

There is a more formal planning by both the vendor and the customer. A comprehensive, quantitative data base of information about user buying profiles is now available, as is a qualitative data base on application areas, system trends, and future use patterns. The planning cycle now emanates more from user needs and requirements than from technology and product considerations. Users dictate the "what" of MIS while vendors supply the "how." This is exactly as it should be. The key justification criteria are becoming ease of use and total user benefit, rather than degree of sophistication. The computer designer works more and more under the constraint of "elegance in simplicity," providing advanced computing equipment and keeping the complexity transparent to the user.

Users no longer want to replace equipment just to have the most modern computer. They want to make sure they can change equipment without losing productivity, without unnecessary cost, and with commensurate benefits.

COMPUTER USE BY INDUSTRY

Figure 6.1 breaks down installed computer value by industry segment. The total of $79 billion of installed value in the United States comes from an extrapolation of International Data Corporation's 1982 year-end statistics, while the industry split is derived from a study by Quantum Sciences. The figure includes both mainframes and minicomputers.

More computers are installed in manufacturing companies than in other industries. This holds true for both discrete or assembly-type manufacturing (automobiles, electronics) and process manufacturing (food processing, chemicals, or petroleum).

Over $23 billion (30 percent of the total) is invested in computers in manufacturing. Banking and finance is the second-ranking industry while federal government, insurance, and business services (computer service centers, certified public accountants, research firms, lawyers, and personnel services) are next in volume of installed equipment. The federal government, which accounted for as much as 70 percent of the computer value in the early sixties, now represents only 9 percent. Education and health care are fast-growing segments.

We will now take a look at some types of computer applications, both basic and advanced, to gain a better perspective on the use of computers within various industry segments.

Manufacturing

The basic business applications are the same in both the discrete and the process type of manufacturing. Accounting, order processing, purchasing, and inventory applications are computerized in most manufacturing companies. Inventory status reports, sales analyses, and cost reports are commonplace documents to the management of manufacturing companies. In more advanced applications, forecasted sales volume is used as prime input into other subsystems—production scheduling, for example, to plan and control the entire production process. An increasing use is made of numerical control applications or CAM (computer-aided manufacturing) to control, for example, the drilling or milling of a machine part. In design automation, an engineer designs a part or product with the aid of a computer that tells how the part will react under stress and other conditions. This is called CAD (computer-aided design).

In the process, or continuous-flow, type of manufacturing, process-control computers are used to control the flow of the product or process automatically. Mix formulation is used to aid petroleum-refining, food-processing, or other areas where an optimum blend of raw material is processed to form the finished product while meeting certain cost and other constraints. For example, percentages of different octanes are constraints in petroleum, and nutritional and vitamin content are constraints in food processing. This complex process is materially aided by the computer. Simulation and revenue models are other examples of advanced manufacturing applications.

Business and Personnel Services

The business and personnel services category covers a broad range of companies. It includes computer service centers, consulting firms, certified public accountants, credit agencies, personnel companies, and the like. The applications in this industry segment cover a wide spectrum, ranging from basic service bureau applications such as payroll and order processing to the preparation of tax returns, accounting, and the maintenance of client records (in the case of service companies).

Industry Segment	Computer Value	Market Share	Basic Applications	Advanced Applications
Discrete Manufacturing	$14.9	18.9%	• accounting • order processing • purchasing • inventory control	• forecasting • numerical control • production scheduling • design automation
Process Manufacturing	$ 8.9	11.3%	• accounting • order processing • purchasing • inventory control	• mix formulation • process control • simulation • revenue models
Banking and Finance	$ 8.2	10.4%	• demand deposit accounting • check processing • proof and transit operations • cost control	• online savings • centralized file system • portfolio analysis • cash flow analysis
Federal Government	$ 7.3	9.2%	• accounting and administration • tax reporting and auditing • order processing • census analysis	• information retrieval • intelligence • command and control • pollution control
Insurance	$ 6.9	8.7%	• premium accounting • customer billing • external reports • reserve calculation	• actuarial analysis • investment analysis • policy approval • cash flow analysis
Business and Personnel Service	$ 6.1	7.7%	• service bureau functions • tax preparation • accounting • client records	• econometric models • time sharing • engineering analysis • data base
Education	$ 4.7	6.0%	• attendance accounting • grading and scoring • school administration • alumni records	• student scheduling • computer-aided instructions • library cataloging • student counseling
Utilities	$ 4.6	5.8%	• customer billing • accounting • meter reading • inventory control	• rate analysis • line and generator loading • operational simulation • financial models
State and Local Government	$ 4.3	5.5%	• utility billing • tax recordkeeping • payroll • school administration	• traffic analysis • budget preparation • police identification • city planning
Retail	$ 3.2	4.0%	• customer billing • sales analysis • accounting • inventory reporting	• point of sale automation • sales forecasting • merchandising • cash flow analysis

Fig. 6.1   Use of computers by industry

Industry Segment	Computer Value	Market Share	Basic Applications	Advanced Applications
Transportation	$ 2.9	3.7%	• rate calculation • vehicle maintenance • cost analysis • accounting	• traffic pattern analysis • automatic rating • tariff analysis • reservation systems
Health Care	$ 2.0	2.5%	• patient billing • inventory accounting • health care statistics • patient history	• lab/operation scheduling • nurses' station automation • intensive care • preliminary diagnosis
Distribution	$ 1.8	2.3%	• order processing • inventory control • purchasing • warehouse control	• vehicle scheduling • merchandising • forecasting • store site selection
Printing and Publishing	$ 1.2	1.5%	• circulation • classified ads • accounting • payroll	• automatic typesetting • home finder • media analysis • page layout
Other	$ 2.0	2.5%		
TOTAL	$79.0	100.0%		

Fig. 6.1   Use of computers by industry (continued)

The advanced applications include complex econometric input-output models, on-line processing and time sharing, computer-aided engineering design performed by architects, and various central data-base applications such as legal and medical information retrieval.

Banking and Finance

Banks and financial institutions are major users of computers. Much of their work centers around paper, an area where data processing finds its greatest utility. Checks with magnetic-ink characters are sorted by individual and bank before demand-deposit or savings-account records are updated. Proof and transit and other accounting and cost-control operations are common computer applications in banks.

On-line teller systems have been implemented by many banks. Centralized file systems combine savings, checking, personal loan, and mortgage files for an individual into a single integrated file. Banks and financial institutions also use computer-aided techniques such as portfolio analysis and cash-flow analysis to invest and control the funds essential for efficient operation. Automatic cash dispensers have come upon the scene, while bank-at-home services are being extended. Electronic funds-transfer applications are increasing and services extended to where individuals can debit or credit their accounts instantaneously via a money card over a communication line.

Federal Government

The use of computers in the federal government is a microcosm of their use in the rest of the business community. The federal government operates manufacturing plants, financial institutions, service operations, hospitals, education facilities, transportation, distribution outlets, and the like. Basic applications include accounting and administration, processing and auditing tax returns, maintaining and analyzing census data, and order processing and billing for the services the government performs for individuals and businesses.

The government uses advanced applications such as information retrieval for various functions of intelligence work, for command and control systems for the armed services, as well as for analyzing a variety of data—for example, demographic and ecological data to help curb the spread of pollution.

Education

Educational use of computer applications has expanded. Machines handle the attendance, grading, and scoring of students, as well as other administrative functions of a school. Other computer applications include student scheduling, a serious problem in large schools with a varied curriculum. Time-sharing networks allow access to computing power by students and faculty throughout the university. Electronic mail and message switching connect departments. Computers maintain indexes and cross-indexes to enable students and teachers to make better use of school library facilities. Computer-aided instruction also is a growing field. In addition, computers are being used to combine student records and personal data in order to correlate interests and suggest courses of study and career paths that the student might not have considered. Microcomputers have become almost commonplace in elementary schools.

Insurance

The insurance industry was an early user of computer equipment to simplify the handling of administrative paperwork. The volume and repetition of activities such as the calculation of customer premiums or the billing of policyholders make them ideal computer applications. In addition, computers produce a variety of external reports and handle statistical jobs such as calculating insurance reserves. The advanced applications move the computer into calculating actuarial statistics, approving policies, analyzing historical patterns, and predicting future actions on projected probabilities. In addition, the computer is being used in investment and cash-flow analysis: two areas vital to insurance company operations.

Utilities

The utilities industry includes the gas and electric companies as well as communications services, the teletype and telephone companies. With the volume of customers and variety of available services, the computer made early inroads into the basic applications of customer billing and accounting, as well as meter reading and inventory control for the variety of products and supplies handled by the utility companies. Advanced applications center around analysis of rate structures and facility scheduling and loading. In addition, simulation and financial models are used to determine the impact of population growth and other ecological factors on power and service demands.

State and Local Government

The applications in state and local governments range from the basics of utility billing, city and state payrolls, tax records, and school administration, to the advanced applications of analyzing traffic patterns and assigning traffic lights accordingly, budget preparation and administration, and as an aid in city planning. In addition, some cities and states have police systems that maintain data banks on criminals, suspected criminals, stolen cars, and the like, to improve law enforcement.

Distribution

The major function of a distributor is to maintain the flow of merchandise from manufacturer to retailer, and computers have aided materially in this process. Computers are used extensively for order processing, inventory control, purchasing, and warehouse control. Computers also aid in vehicle and load scheduling and in forecasting and merchandising, where the computer aids in spotting fast- and slow-moving items and in projecting the probable success of new items. Advanced systems can facilitate the development of ethnic and cultural models, which when combined with traffic patterns and competitive factors can aid in the selection of successful store and sales outlet sites.

Transportation

Transportation includes motor carriers (trucks and auto leasing) as well as the airlines, ship lines, and railroads. Basic applications center on cost analysis and accounting, calculating tariff rates from rather complex formulas and regulations, and handling vehicle maintenance by projecting repair schedules based on historical patterns. Advanced applications include the complex reservation systems developed by the airlines and sophisticated analysis of traffic patterns to optimize routing and scheduling. In addition, computers are being used to analyze, update, and maintain tariff tables, and to automatically calculate bills on the basis of individual loads, routes, and local conditions.

Health Care

Computers are becoming commonplace in the administrative functions of a hospital, performing jobs such as patient billing and inventory control of medical instruments and facilities, and also producing health care statistics and maintaining patient histories. Computers are beginning to cater to the more exciting advanced applications. Computers are scheduling lab tests and operations and scanning patient symptoms for preliminary diagnosis. Gradually the computer is being used to reduce the administrative load on nurses, giving them more time for other important nursing functions. In addition, the hospitals are using computers to monitor patients in intensive care wards, employing the principle of process control more familiar in process manufacturing. The CAT scanner that x-rays patients for tumors is an advanced use of computer-aided diagnosis.

Retail

Retailing, a slow industry to computerize, is now moving more rapidly. Computers handle the basic paperwork procedures of customer billing, sales analysis, inventory reporting, and the other accounting functions within a retailing environment. Some retailers have moved into the more advanced applications of sales forecasting and merchandising, where a computer can be used to spot trends in item movement and discern the impact of advertising and special promotions. Retailers are turning to source-data automation—the point-of-sale device that records the movement of goods from the store on machine-readable media can then be used directly as basis for reordering, inventory control, sales analysis, and profitability accounting. Cash-flow analysis is another example of the use of computers in an advanced application category.

Printing and Publishing

In the printing and publishing industry, computers are used to automate newspaper and magazine circulation as well as to bill for advertising and other services. In addition, accounting functions and payroll are commonplace computer applications. At many installations computers directly feed typesetting machines to produce hyphenated and justified print copy. This approach can be extended so that the computer composes an entire page layout. Computers also can be used to determine the optimum advertising space for maximizing revenue without reducing reader acceptance. Another application is maintaining a history of classified ads. For example, a subscriber could receive a listing of houses for sale in a particular price range, location, and size.

Miscellaneous Use

The above represent the major uses of computer systems by the major industries. Other uses fall across industry lines or are hard to classify because they are just developing or because of their uniqueness. For example, an English firm has introduced the concept called Viewdata, now called Videotex—the ability to provide interactive TV capabilities in the home. Individual subscribers can browse through information data bases for purposes such as ordering goods, making travel arrangements, checking selected weather and news, or obtaining the latest stock prices. Videotex can also be employed in business environments along with videoconferencing and electronic mail.

Another unusual example is that of the Club of Rome, who believe that the world's problems have become too complex and interrelated for resolution by the human mind. The Club therefore commissioned a systems analysis group at the Massachusetts Institute of Technology to program the world's problems and their interactions into a computer. The thesis of the study is that modern technology has made the world a single, extremely complex system with all its elements interdependent. No problem within that system—political, economic, or technological—can be solved by analyzing that problem alone. The MIT group was asked to express the many problems of the world mathematically so that their interactions could be described by mathematical equations. Then a computer analyzed the equations. The five prime variables are world population, capital investment in industry, capital investment in food production, the world inventory of natural resources, and the level of man's interference with nature (notably by pollution). The interactions and feedback influences of these variables on one another were described by the group in some forty complex equations, which were then analyzed by the computer model.

Other examples of exotic computer uses are writing music and poetry and interpreting the origin of various versions of the Bible. Not so exotic is the analysis of garbage via a computer model to determine the characteristics of the population that jettisoned it.

DEFINITION OF COMPUTER TECHNOLOGY

Technology as defined here covers a broader spectrum of products and services than it usually connotes. Technology covers not only the hardware or physical elements, such as central processors, magnetic storage units, and input-output equipment, but also the wide variety of software, application aids, and support services. Figure 6.2 divides computer technology into four elements: hardware, systems software, application software, and support services. The last is viewed as tying together the other three. For purposes of definition, the *hardware* element represents the things you can

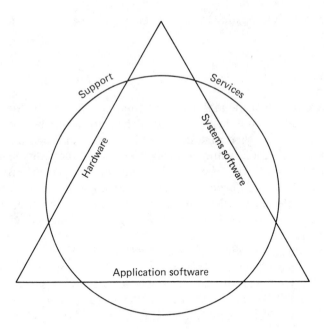

Fig. 6.2   Computer technology

see, touch, and feel, such as a central processor, a printer, or a CRT terminal. These devices are built from a variety of electronic and mechanical parts. I categorize *systems software* as the programs written for a specific computer to aid programmers and operators of that computer. *Application software* refers to the programs that the user programmers write to accomplish a specific application, such as inventory control, payroll, or production scheduling. In so doing, they utilize the software written for the specific computer. Hardware and software are really meaningless unless they can be utilized for the implementation of applications. Thus the three elements of the triangle are required before computer power becomes more than an academic exercise. *Support services* provide the people power, consulting and educating services, and a whole array of service facilities ranging from the renting of computer time to the subcontracting of a company's total data processing job. Thus the definition of computer technology covers the four major elements in Figure 6.2. I will now categorize the subelements that comprise each of the major elements. This is not an easy undertaking; however, I have checked the classification scheme by reviewing several data processing product catalogs and composite product listings; although some products and services combine two or more categories, the classification holds up.

HARDWARE ELEMENTS

Figure 6.3 lists the hardware elements, beginning with six general classes of hardware.

   Desk calculators accept keyboard input, and they have the ability to store a moderate-size program to process the input mathematically and print out the results

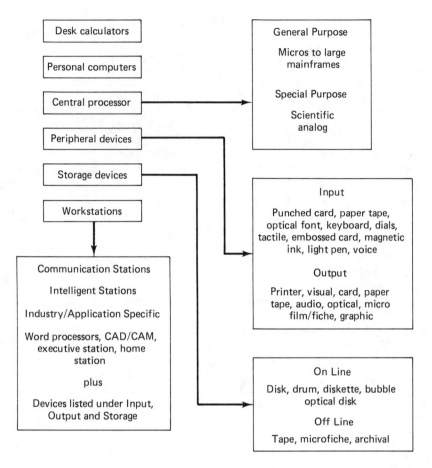

Fig. 6.3 Hardware elements

on a serial printer or a paper tape (like that found in adding machines). Hewlett Packard is a leader in the development of desk calculators.

Personal computers, as typified by the offerings of IBM, Hewlett Packard, Apple, Tandy/Radio Shack, and the myriad of Japanese models, having started as hobby or home computers, have now found their way into business environments. They are used in small businesses or to do specific jobs in a larger company where the main computer is backlogged with applications. The typical personal has a keyboard, display screen, printer, and a small amount of disk storage and is used in a one-on-one situation (a single user).

The remaining four hardware elements—central processors, peripheral devices, terminal devices, and source data-collection devices—are significant technological underpinnings of MIS and will be treated in more depth.

Figure 6.4 is a schematic of the four basic hardware components. In the center of the illustration is the central processor; it has the necessary control, arithmetic, and memory components to integrate and tie together the other hardware compo-

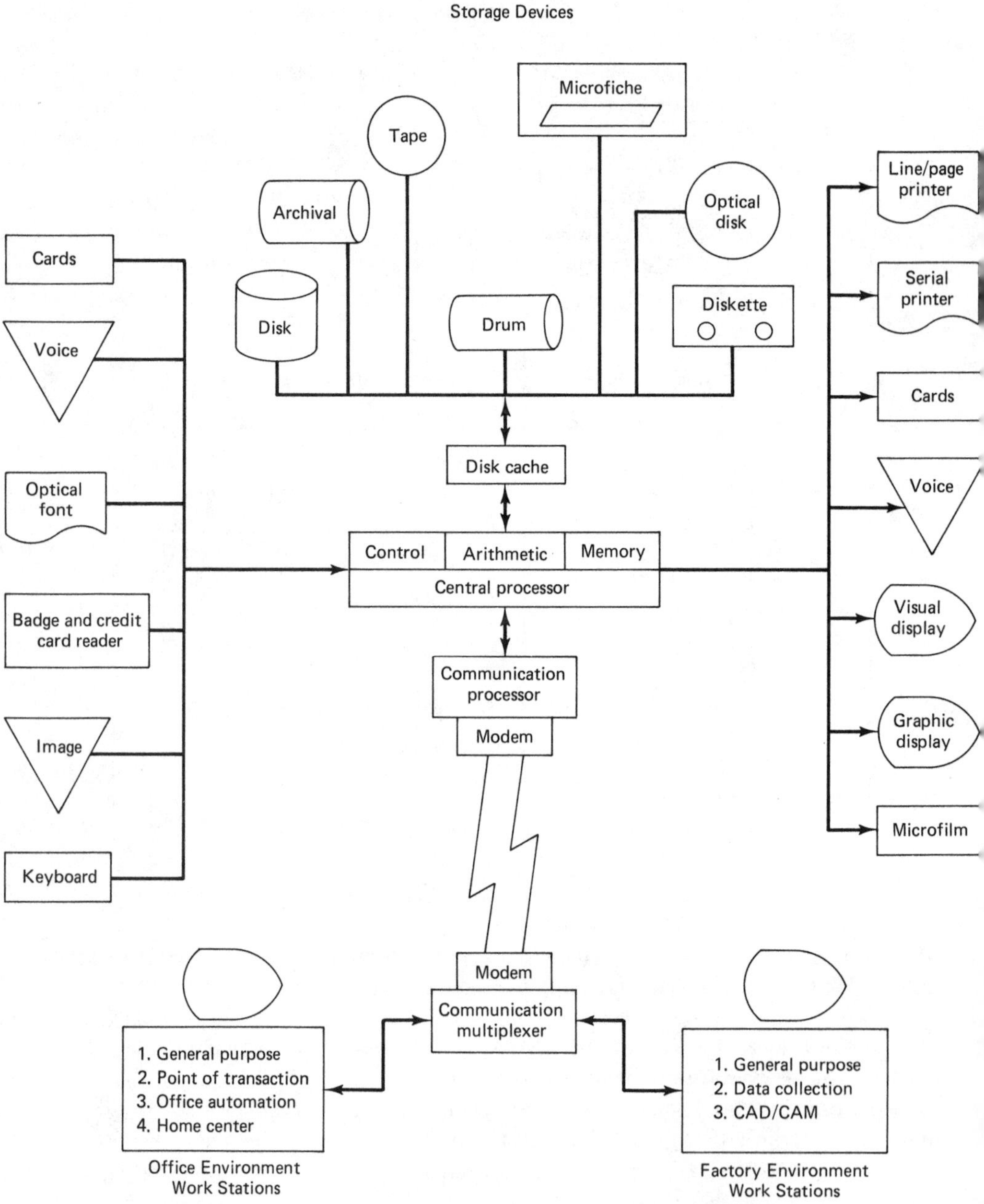

Storage Devices

Microfiche

Tape

Line/page
printer

Archival

Optical
disk

Serial
printer

Cards

Diskette

Disk

Drum

Cards

Voice

Optical
font

Voice

Control | Arithmetic | Memory

Visual
display

Badge and credit
card reader

Central processor

Communication
processor

Image

Modem

Graphic
display

Keyboard

Microfilm

Modem

Communication
multiplexer

1. General purpose
2. Point of transaction
3. Office automation
4. Home center

1. General purpose
2. Data collection
3. CAD/CAM

Office Environment
Work Stations

Factory Environment
Work Stations

Fig. 6.4   Computer hardware components

nents. Input devices are shown on the upper left, output devices on the upper right, and storage in the upper center. Remote devices are characterized into two classes of work stations, one class fitting the office environment and the other the factory environment.

Communications hardware is illustrated in the lower-middle and lower-right portions of the figure. The communication interface to the central processor is shown, as well as the modems (modulator/demodulator) on each end of the communication line that connects the remote site to the computer site (a telephone line or satellite). The communication multiplexor collects the data from a variety of terminal devices and prepares it for transmission over the communication line. Communications was covered more extensively in Chapter 5. The various hardware elements now will be described in more detail.

Central Processors

We have described "general-purpose" computers as ranging from micros selling for $2000 or less to huge mainframes in the multimillion-dollar range. The supercomputer high end includes systems selling for over $10 million with speeds of 500 *Mips* (millions of instructions per second). Figure 6.3 shows a breakdown of central processors into general-purpose and special-purpose.

Special-purpose processors include the wide range of scientific processors that have fast internal speed and floating-point scientific units which enable them to handle high-precision mathematical calculations. Analog devices are utilized primarily in process-control applications where it is necessary to measure temperature or viscosity and to take predetermined action based on the recordings. Continuous-process manufacturers, such as chemical, petroleum, or food processors, utilize analog or process-control computers to regulate production operations. They are also dedicated application-specific, special-purpose processors that are directed at a specific job such as typesetting or numerical control. These devices are usually special versions of scientific or analog processors. They may have special micro-coded instructions or hard-wired logic that enables them to do the specialized application more efficiently than a generalized processor.

Peripheral Devices

As stated, peripheral devices comprise the equipment necessary to provide the input and output to the users of MIS. Punched cards, for so many years the symbol of computers, are gradually disappearing from the scene. The keyboard/visual display (cathode ray tube or CRT) has become the workhorse for feeding data to today's computer systems. In addition, optical and magnetic fonts can be interpreted and transferred to electronic medium without human intervention. The most relevant example of *magnetic font* is the magnetic characters found on bank checks. Examples of *optical font* are the bar codes on grocery items that are sensed by optical readers at supermarkets and the optics on a price tag that are scanned by light pens at a retail store. The interpretation of a limited voice vocabulary is used in some instances, but it is not a prevalent input medium. Also appearing on the scene are image readers which can scan an entire page of data, including pictures, and convert it to electronic medium. Dial and embossed-card input is characterized by factory data collection devices, where the worker places his ID card in a special reader and moves dial settings or depresses buttons to record the job item and quantity of work he has completed. The automatic cash-dispensing machines in banks are activated in a manner similar to the factory data collection device.

The major output device is still the printed copy—either a serial printer, which prints a character at a time (typewriter), or a line printer, which has a drum or chain that can print an entire line at one time. Nonimpact printing, where a photoelectric process is used rather than the physical contact of a print drum or print stylus against paper, is increasing in popularity. This allows upwards of 18,000 lines of high-quality print per minute. Laser printers provide letter-quality high-speed printing. Card output has declined to a point where cards are used only as a form of returnable media, such as a punched-card invoice where the returned payment can be read back into the system for accounts receivable reconciliation. (However, this can be accomplished as well by printing optical font on the invoice.) Visual output devices, such as cathode ray tubes, are increasing rapidly, as are graphic devices that can produce visual graphs on a cathode ray tube or hard-copy graphic output on a plotter. Color has been added to many graphic devices. Also in use are audio devices where a prerecorded message can be selected under computer control and played back to the inquirer.

Computer-output microfilm (COM) devices are growing in number. In an MIS, a good deal of historical information may be required for audit purposes or infrequent information retrieval. If the volume of this type of data is high, it may be economical to put it on microfilm, which is a cheaper storage medium than magnetic-storage devices, such as tape or disk. COM devices have the ability to transform data from magnetic media to microfilm. Some people still resist the use of microfilm records, as they envision darkened rooms with large microfilm viewers and clerks poring over the film in endless search. The equipment today is much improved.

The key question is whether one prefers hard copy or film; many prefer the former, as it doesn't require a mechanical reader to retrieve data. However, cost is still a factor, and companies have shown significant savings in using microfilm, particularly with the rising cost of paper. In addition, there are advantages in space saving, ability to retrieve, and reduced computer printing cost, since product COM is considerably faster than a conventional printer.

Microfiche is replacing roll film as the most expedient microfilm storage medium. Microfiche are strips of microfilm in various sizes; a quite popular kind is $4'' \times 6''$ and is used, for example, to store copies of journals and periodicals. One $4'' \times 6''$ microfiche can store a 112-page journal. They can be indexed and information printed across the top that can be read without a microfiche reader. The strips are easy to manipulate, retrieve, reproduce, and disseminate. Thus, COM devices are becoming an adjunct to large central data-base systems, and though they do not provide on-line storage, microfilm records can be quite efficient and cost effective for storing archival data.

Storage Devices

Since, in MIS, record storage access often is the limited or gating factor in response time, special high-speed buffers called *disk cache* are used to balance the high speed of the central processor with the relatively slow speed of disk rotation.

Main memory is the only true random-access device, for every piece of data can be obtained in exactly the same time—there is no minimum or maximum. However, main memory is expensive and has limited capacity. It has an access time rated in nanoseconds (billionths of a second). *Drum storage*, used only in rare cases, offers more capacity at lower cost per character, but with much higher access time than main memory. *Diskettes* look like 45-rpm phonograph records and for this reason are called *floppies*. They can hold up to a million or so bytes of information, have slow access time, and are used as inexpensive storage for small microcomputer systems or for limited auxilliary removable media in some larger installations. *Disk* is the principal medium for storing the bulk of today's MIS files. Although its average access time is much higher than that of either drum or main memory, it is fast enough to satisfy the majority of demands for data file access. *Tape* is still the workhorse of many computer systems, but its slow average access time (astronomical when compared to main memory or even disk) limits its use to batch operations and the storage of historical and back-up data. *Archival storage devices* using magnetic cartridges are employed for files requiring capacity in the multibillion range but only moderate access time such as several seconds.

Because of the need for rapid access to data files in MIS approaches, the on-line storage device is the crucial storage medium. Disk technology has provided the foundation for storing multibillions of characters of information. Disk technology relies on a technique of recording magnetic spots on a disk surface. Data is represented on the disk surface by the presence or absence of magnetic spots on ferrous oxide surfaces running sequentially along concentric circles (tracks). Each character or group of characters has a unique address, so that the information can be transferred into the computer for processing. Each disk surface has its own recording head. The head can either read information from the disk into computer memory or write from computer memory onto the disk. The head moves mechanically across the disk surface, which is continually rotating.

Disk technology has been and continues to be improved mainly through higher-density recording techniques and increased speed of head positioning and disk rotation. This combination of increased density, accelerated head positioning, and faster disk rotation continues to give disks more capacity and lower access time. However, these are essentially mechanical techniques that have their theoretical and practical limitation limits. Many feel that eventually the new nonmechanical techniques will drive these mechanical devices into the dinosaur age. These new techniques employ elements such as RAM (random-access memory) or magnetic-domain (or bubble) devices; however, there remains considerable concern regarding the practicality of bubble storage. Whether the reader understands the technology or not, the important thing is that the resultant storage devices can provide trillions of characters of information with high-speed access and eventually at much lower cost per character than today's storage devices. The ideal storage device has the speed of main memory, the capacity of archival storage devices, and the cost of tape. The new RAM and bubble storage devices hold the possibility at least of approaching this objective.

Computer-output microfilm (COM) has already been explained under output devices and can be used for hierarchical or archival storage.

Of increasing interest is the video or optical disk as a potential new storage medium. An optical disk is in reality a piece of plastic in which is embedded a strip of thin film such as aluminum foil. A laser writes the information on the disk by burning small holes in the foil. These are the same disks that are used for storing movies for home use. A major drawback in the use of video disks for business information storage is that you can only write information on the disk; you cannot erase it. But video disks are becoming so cheap that this factor may lose its relevance.

Office-Environment Work Station

The key workhorse in today's information systems is the intelligent work station. This device enables the power of MIS to expand to remote sites, to offices and factories throughout a company's operating network. The work station combines features of the devices just covered—central processors, input, output, storage, and communications. In its basic form, a work station is an input/output device. In its advanced form, it is an information satellite, processing data in its own right and communicating to a remote larger host system when necessary.

I have divided work stations into those used broadly in an office environment and those used broadly in a factory environment. The list of both office-environment and factory-environment work stations starts with a general-purpose station. This is the most prevalent type; it has no special equipment but uses a combination of CRT terminals, output printers, disk storage, and a central processor (usually a mini or a micro) to accomplish routine data processing functions and to communicate with other computers in the network. The system is usually similar whether in the office or factory; however, the factory system might have to be environmentalized for operation in an area where there is greater temperature and physical volatility. I have broadened the term point-of-sale (POS) work stations to *point-of-transaction*, because the concept of recording and acting upon a transaction at the time it is made has increased in scope beyond the department store and grocery store. Point-of-transaction work stations include automatic cash dispensers and automatic branch banks where all types of credit and debit transactions are processed on-line. The evolution of credit and money cards and inter-industry linkages (e.g., banks, retailers, companies) is facilitating the emergence of electronic funds transfer and the cashless society. Also included in point-of-transaction stations are airline and travel agency operations, nurses' stations in hospitals, and other industry uses where it makes sense to record and process transactions as they occur.

Office automation, built around word processing that records letters and documents in electronic form such that they can be stored, altered, combined, and communicated electronically, is another prime example of an information-system work station. The office word processor is expanding to include other office functions such as electronic filing and electronic scheduling, as well as integrating with other more conventional business data processing functions. In addition, teleconferencing and video conferencing have become available and can be considered part of the office automation process. This is truly one of the big growth areas in the information systems industry. The same devices used in other work stations are combined in the office automation work station with a letter-quality printer for producing the same or better quality of letter that currently comes from an executive secretary's typewriter.

Finally, home work stations are becoming more and more prevalent. Combining the devices and capabilities shown in Fig. 6.4, the homeowner is able to use his TV screen to request selected information from a growing list of sources provided by companies, some of which are still in the conception stage. In certain areas of the country, two-way TV interaction is possible, whereby viewers can give responses to questions, order merchandise and schedule vacations and business trips. Alvin Toffler, in his book *The Third Wave*, forecasts the electronic cottage where people will work at home, often in concert with other family members, while linked via a home work station to a variety of business and social enterprises. Thus, the work station located in an office, point-of-transaction, office-automation, or home environment represents one of the most pervasive trends in information-system technology.

Factory-Environment Work Station

The same type of evolution is taking place in the factory. Besides the general-purpose work station, a prominent device is the data collection station, which is really a point-of-transaction terminal. Units produced, time, and employee identification are recorded at completion points in the production process, and the data either is processed on the spot or communicated to a host computer. Sometimes sensor-activated devices are part of the data collection work station. As a product moves down a conveyor belt, for example, a sensing device records its passage. Even more sophisticated equipment can measure viscosity and temperature. This leads into another class of factory-environment work station.

Computer-aided manufacturing (CAM) involves computer feedback to control a production process. Thus, a sensor device continually checks temperature and viscosity of a process and activates additional processes that keep the recordings within the desired tolerance. If the processes involve the use of robots or devices with armlike movements and actions, the technology is called *robotics*. Robotics is really an extension of numerical control, a CAM activity which employs mathematical models to automatically control machine tools and other equipment.

Computer-aided design (CAD) enables an engineer, working at a special graphic terminal, to design a product or a piece of equipment or to lay out a manufacturing process. An example is in laying out the circuit connections on a computer chip (a quarter-inch square) which has the equivalent of 50,000 logic points or gates. It would be impossible to accomplish such a job without the use of computer-aided design. Modern computers have been anthropomorphized by being given the ability to read, write, have memory, and so on; however, critics have suggested that one human quality they don't have is the power to procreate. With CAD, the power to regenerate its own kind might be added.

SYSTEM AND APPLICATION SOFTWARE ELEMENTS

Figure 6.5 combines two sides of the triangle described in Fig. 6.2, systems software and application software. Application software is further subdivided into business and scientific. The major distinction between systems software and application software is that the former is tied directly to the computer and consists of aids to assist the programmer in translating a particular application into machine language. This class of software also includes aids to assist the computer operation group in scheduling and running the computer efficiently. Applications, on the other hand, are the end product, an order processing or inventory control system in productive operation on a computer. These applications utilize the system software, which in turn utilizes the computer hardware.

Systems Software

System software is divided into the groupings listed in Fig. 6.5. Languages such as COBOL (COmmon Business-Oriented Language) are used by the programmer to express the particular job to be accomplished. Languages are roughly divided into two classifications; (a) machine oriented or those closely tied to the unique characteristics of a particular computer or (b) higher level (i.e., COBOL), which are English-language oriented and standardized such that programs written in the language can be executed on different computers. Other higher-level languages include FORTRAN, BASIC, PL1, APL, Pascal, and Ada. These are all well-developed languages that have generalized attributes but in addition are suited to a specific purpose (e.g., FORTRAN for mathematical manipulation, BASIC for time-sharing application.)

Utility programs assist the programmer or operator in performing common functions, such as sorting, collating, and various audit and checking routines that aid in program preparation and testing.

Because of the incompatibilities within a manufacturer's own line of computers, as well as those found between manufacturers' lines, the need exists for conversion software to aid the transfer of data and programs from one computer system to another. These conversion software aids may be required in order to interchange

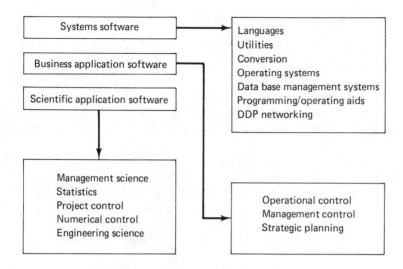

Fig. 6.5 Systems/application software elements

data files from one system to another or to replace one computer with another. The scope of the problem differs, depending on whether the former or the latter is the situation, but the nature of the job embodies similarities that can be materially helped by well-conceived conversion aids.

Operating systems are the internal monitors that reside in computer memory and direct and manage the execution of programs, some sequentially (monoprogramming) and some simultaneously (multiprogramming). Operating systems also help in the economical scheduling and allocating of computer resources in performing a specified job mix.

Data-base management systems (DBMS) software provides the capability of managing and controlling the integrated data base so important to MIS development. Included in the functions are the ability to organize, capture, update, and retrieve data from the various information files. Data-base software was treated in some depth in Chapter 4.

Programming-operating aids represent software techniques that enable the programmers and operators to accomplish their jobs in a more expeditious manner. Examples of this category are automatic flow-charting programs that can produce flow charts from written-application descriptions and automatic logging programs that can produce summaries of machine-time utilization. The former aids the programmer, the latter the operator.

With the growth of distributed data processing (DDP) and the need to tie remote sites together in a communications network, a class of software that I term DDP networking has become extremely important as a means of ensuring that the various systems tied to the network can communicate and cooperate. This was covered in Chapter 5.

Business Application Software

Computer vendors and a host of third-party software and system houses as well as consultants have realized there is a dollar to be made in supplying turnkey (or close to it) software offerings for specific user application requirements. If a particular application is general enough or if the solution can be generalized, it is possible that it can be used for a broad spectrum of customers. With the rising cost of systems analysts and programmers, package application software has become a very attractive business.

Packages are available in the three business-activity areas depicted in the Fig. 1.1 triangle. The most prevalent use, as might be imagined, is in the operational control area; there is less use in the management control area and even less in the strategic planning area. The reason is that the activities in the lower areas of the triangle are more understood, structured, and programmable. However, packages are available for production scheduling, sales forecasting, and even for financial and business modeling.

One must not yield too readily, however, to the appeal of packages. Companies in the same industry, although similar, are certainly not identical. Therefore, it behooves a prospective buyer of a package to check the fit between the application and his particular needs. He should ascertain also that the same features he requires in his system are present in the package—elements such as flexibility, ease of maintenance and alteration, controls, security, ease of use, and the like. Trouble can arise if the package requires customization to suit a particular environment and the necessary hooks and handles to alter specific portions are not present. It may prove easier and less expensive to build it from scratch.

Scientific Application Software

Although this class of software is classified separately, it has elements that are incorporated into both systems software and business application software. For example, business application areas, particularly strategic planning, utilize management science techniques and statistical routines. They are listed separately here because the industry treats them as such.

Management science software includes packages such as linear programming and general-purpose simulators that can be utilized as subprograms for major applications, such as inventory control, revenue modeling, and forecasting. Statistics are more finite techniques employing specialized mathematical functions, such as regression analysis and curve fitting, which can be used in both business and scientific applications.

Project control includes computer-based PERT (program evaluation and review technique) and CPM (critical-path method) techniques. These are well-recognized, rather standardized approaches to managing complex projects. Generalized computer systems have been developed to facilitate the implementation of these management aids.

Numerical control consists of generalized programs to produce tapes that automatically control a wide variety of machine tools. Packages called APT and ADAPT have been standardized and are available on a broad range of computers. Computerized NC systems have proven extremely beneficial to engineering departments of manufacturing companies.

The category of engineering science completes the list of scientific application software. This category includes such functions as stress and failure analysis, coordinate geometry programs, and programs designed to aid the civil engineering departments of larger companies. Also, packages are available in the area of computer-aided design (CAD), where complex designs can be visually described on special screens and then drawn on graphic plotters.

The fact that engineering science is better understood and more precise in its measurement facilitates the usefulness of scientific application software. Even though the scope of the application area is greater, the imprecise nature of operations in the business area accounts for the slower evolution of packaged application software.

SUPPORT SERVICES ELEMENTS

Support services are rapidly becoming predominant in the information processing industry. What has lagged is the people and support power for an effective merger of hardware and software in order to produce a viable management information system. Figure 6.6 breaks down support services into the categories of computer time, support, application services, and supplies.

Computer Time

Service centers have been considered by many as necessary only for the smaller companies who cannot afford or do not desire their own computer. However, the service center is a source of ancillary computer power of both a generalized and specialized nature. Computer users need extra capacity to handle peak loads and also as back-up facilities in case of prolonged down-time problems.

The on-line service center is becoming increasingly significant as a source of specialized assistance. A company may have 95 percent of its computer applications devoted to business use, with a 5 percent need for scientific use. It may prove wiser to utilize the facilities of an on-line service center for the engineering department rather than add the necessary facilities and support capability to implement the engineering applications in-house. Medium and large users are continuing to avail themselves of the specialized capability offered by on-line service centers.

Time sharing refers to the use of both the hardware and software of a third-party sharing service. Typically the use is of a scientific or professional nature, where an engineer or financial planner uses the statistical routines or modeling tools pro-

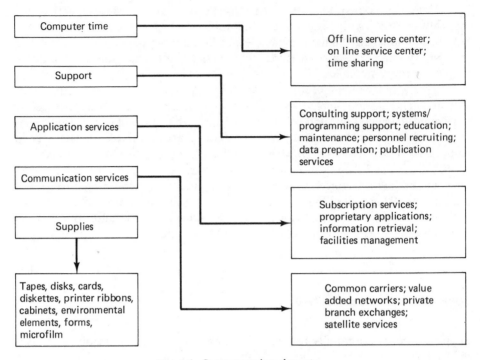

Fig. 6.6   Support services elements

vided by the service to solve a specific ad hoc problem. However, there are companies such as Control Data Corporation who provide an industry- or application-specific service; in CDC's case, an example is Plato, a computer-aided learning technique for educational institutions.

Support

A wide range of support functions are available to supplement or complement the user's own capabilities. They range from broad consulting help in the areas of MIS organization, long-range computer plans, and top-management MIS orientation to specific areas, such as providing temporary programming assistance or keypunch operators to reduce a backlog of customer transactions. The user can obtain assistance during every step of the application development cycle. The gradual evolution of the industry to the separate pricing of support services independent of hardware and software has been responsible for the proliferation of a wide variety of support services, some offered by sound companies with sound capabilities and others with less noteworthy attributes. In fact, the failure rate of support companies has increased dramatically in the past several years. It behooves prospective users to know what they need and to carefully assess the qualifications and claims of companies offering support assistance.

The list of support includes broad consulting, system, and programming support which can be employed during various phases of the application development cycle. Education is a critical item, and a company may develop the need to enroll key MIS and non-MIS personnel in various classes and seminars offered by companies specializing in educational programs, or it may require the services of a company to tailor a training program to its own particular requirements. The cost and efficacy of outside services should always be measured against the relevant in-house capability.

Computer maintenance, which is usually provided as part of the rental price, can be secured from a third party or separately negotiated with the manufacturer of the equipment if the hardware is purchased. This is true of third-party leases.

Personnel-recruiting services can be utilized to assist in the hiring of in-house system and programming capability. As mentioned earlier, data entry operators can be employed or work can be contracted out to handle peak data-preparation work loads. Finally, publication services, which include magazines, periodicals, books, special reports, surveys, competitive product information, researching services, and the like, can be utilized to complement training programs and provide necessary background information for making system and product decisions.

Application Services

Subscription services refer to companies who offer to implement specific application areas for subscribers of the service. The subscription service companies have concentrated on specific areas and have built up expertise in applying computer solutions to these problems. An example of this type of service is a system designed for handling the business applications of small-to-medium sized hospitals. Such a system produces customer bills and the required ancillary accounting reports from input furnished by the hospital's clerical staff. The service can either be off-line such that the input data is delivered to the subscription service company by manual means, or it can be on-line where each hospital has appropriate terminal and communication facilities.

Proprietary applications represent the development of application software described above that is designed to accomplish a particular function, such as sales forecasting, bill of material processing, or inventory control. A variety of packages are on the market today, ranging from basic payroll and accounting applications to advanced-production scheduling systems. As in the case of any support service, the user must carefully evaluate the package to ensure that it is designed properly, is operable, and can be used effectively in his environment.

Information retrieval services usually center on business areas where there is a need to access data from a common set of files. An example is the National Library of Medicine, which maintains an index of medical research documents cross referenced by several keys. Remote terminals can interrogate the files and obtain the listing and location of reference material pertinent to a specific inquiry. This type of service can be used by public libraries, financial institutions, educational institutions, legal firms, and general business firms. In the latter case, commercial data banks such as supplied by Standard & Poor and Dow Jones are providing useful data that is external to a company's data base.

Companies may not fall neatly into one of the support service categories listed, for many are engaged in a combination of two or more activities. Also, some companies are developing unique approaches by combining these services in different ways. For example, companies have been successful in offering a complete computer package to a prospective user. Such a company will contract for the entire computer system selection and implementation cycle, even running the computer at the user's site when the job is completed. The user states that he wants a system to accomplish order processing, inventory control, and production control; the subcontractor takes it from there. The service these companies offer is called *facilities management*.

Communication Services

With the strong trend toward distributed data processing, communicating data back and forth from remote sites to central host sites becomes a very important consideration. DDP was discussed more fully in Chapter 5. Suffice it to state here that users must carefully consider the evolving offerings of the Bell System along with the competing communication services from VANS (value-added networks) such as TE-LENET and TYMNET. In addition, PBXs (private branch exchanges) that serve to link intrafacility voice and digital data over a single in-house switching network are offered by independents such as ROLM and Northern Telecom. Coaxial cable and other forms of data highways are also used for local, in-plant communication. Finally, for large-volume data transmission, which might include teleconferencing or video conferencing, satellite transmission facilities are or will be offered by AT&T and by independents.

Supplies

Computer operations require a variety of supply items. Removable tapes, disk packs, and diskettes are required for interim storage of a company's data base, and more must be purchased as volume and activity increase and as older ones wear out. Punched cards, printer ribbons, and printer forms also must be procured, as well as microfilm or any other specific medium needed. Other items called for include cabinets for storing tapes, disk packs, cassettes, and other supplies, plus environmental elements required in the computer room, such as raised flooring, special cables, raceways, and shelving.

This completes the run-down of the technology required to power today's MIS. This is a broad and complex subject, with new and varied products still emerging with a rapidity found in no other industry. This section has presented a classification scheme for grouping and understanding the vast array of equipment available to MIS designers and implementors. While the focus of the book is on management rather than technical considerations, the latter cannot be overlooked.

SUMMARY

This book asserts that computer technology has not been the limiting factor in the development of management information systems. The computing power is available; the major challenge is management's ability to harness it.

Although technology is secondary in importance, its cost, complexity, and variety make it necessary for us to assess and evaluate properly the burgeoning list of devices being produced by a burgeoning list of companies in the hardware, software, and support-services business. After tracing the historical development of computers and information systems and discussing application uses across all industries, this chapter defined what is meant by technology and then proceeded to develop a framework or classification from which to view the total data processing industry. The thorough analysis and evaluation of these devices is the province of the MIS professionals within a company—or of consulting firms if the necessary internal expertise is not present. Top and operating management should certainly have a say in setting the criteria for the selection process and in assisting in any particular evaluations that are pertinent to their area of operation. The MIS personnel making the evaluation should also avail themselves of the legal department and procurement people within the company in writing up the contracts, establishing necessary acceptance tests, and, in general, ensuring that general procurement and business practices are followed. However, the major study and review of technical capabilities should be delegated to the MIS people.

This is the peek-under-the-hood chapter. While you don't have to know how a car operates or how to fix it in order to drive it, the workings of the machine are important criteria in its selection and subsequent employment.

CASE STUDIES

MARKET OUTLOOK FOR THE SEVENTIES*

I see future growth in demand for small computers coming from two very different types of business—the very large organization, which previously thought itself almost exclusively main frame, and the very small organization, which previously thought itself too small to own a computer.

The change in thinking in large organizations is particularly interesting. In the past the very existence of large computers encouraged users to think in terms of

---

*From "Market Outlook for the Seventies," by Heinz Nixdorf, *Computer Weekly International*, August 12, 1971. It is interesting to view Mr. Nixdorf's observations in light of what has happened. Nixdorf computers are today a strong force in the European market and have also been introduced into the U.S. market.

highly centralized units. However, the demand for rapid, accurate, and up-to-date information at operational level is causing companies to have a second look at their structures. Efficiency appears to demand a substantial measure of decentralization.

For centralization to work effectively man would have to live and work in units of 100,000 and more. In fact, he operates in groups of considerably less than 1000. Fortunately we now have computers that are small enough and cheap enough to service the needs of these smaller groups. If we add to this the capacity for the individual small computers to go on-line to a main frame computer, we begin to see computer networks capable of satisfying the demands for local operational information, and for centralized control and forecasting.

This move by large organizations toward the small computer is already well advanced in Europe, with banks, insurance companies, and retail and wholesale organizations installing increasing numbers of small computers. The basic common factor is that all these organizations have a large number of establishments or departments scattered over a very wide area, but each of necessity having to report to a central HQ.

We at Nixdorf are convinced that this move to decentralization, coupled with on-line capacity, is gathering momentum.

Playing a significant part in this type of situation will be the terminal which has itself been upgraded considerably. Intelligent terminals are now replacing their unsophisticated predecessors, or in some cases a small computer is used with on-line capabilities. The terminal market could possibly be one of the fastest growth sections of the computer industry and I expect this to more than double its size during the next two years. At the moment between 50 and 60 percent of small computers are purchased by the small-to-medium size business and 40 to 50 percent by the large organizations. However, as the larger companies realize the value of the small machines, these figures could change until the majority of these are purchased by large companies.

Just as the size of organizations using small computers is getting larger, so the size of companies able to benefit from the small computer is getting smaller. As wages and overheads rise throughout Europe, the number of employees required to justify the installation of a small business computer is becoming less. I used to say that every 21st employee should be a Nixdorf computer. I believe this should now be the 11th.

In the early days of computers, smaller businesses could not contemplate installing a computer because of their large size, their requirement for special air-conditioned rooms, and their high price. Miniaturization and other technological advances have made possible the small computer with a high capacity in a small volume that is suitable for in-office use. The same technological changes have brought the price within the reach of all but the very smallest companies.

In the immediate future, the small computer will be required to carry out much the same functions as at present, so the education will be in the use of computers not in the tasks.

During the next few years, I see the basic small computer duties remaining in the payroll, invoicing and stock control fields, because of the requirement for information at the source. I do not believe that in the near future computers will be used on any large scale to solve sophisticated business problems—managements will still have to manage.

However, there are areas that are emerging as possible big growth areas for tomorrow. Process control, for which the computer is ideally suited, is still only in its infancy as a computer market, but could develop very rapidly with the introduction of highly sophisticated technical processes. Here again a number of small low-cost computers are likely to be more cost-effective than one large, centralized main frame computer. We have 100 small computers controlling the manufacture of our own computers.

The other major growth area I see is teaching. In this field there is already a shortage of teachers, and as subjects become more complex and people remain at teaching establishments longer, this shortage is going to become more acute. This area could eventually become the major growth and development area, and in the not-too-distant future I can see manufacturers selling more teaching machines than either industrial or business types.

STUDY QUESTIONS

1. In light of what has happened in the small and minicomputer market, how prophetic was Mr. Nixdorf?

2. Do you think Mr. Nixdorf is correct in his assessment of the growth of small computers?

3. Do you think Mr. Nixdorf was right in predicting that more small computers would be purchased by large companies than by small companies?

4. What areas of growth other than process control and education, as mentioned by Mr. Nixdorf, do you think are the growth areas for computers?

5. What areas of growth not mentioned by Nixdorf have subsequently grown in significance?

FIELDING ELECTRONICS

Wallace Lott joined Fielding Electronics, a designer and manufacturer of semiconductor memory and processor chips for the computer industry, some six months ago as director of MIS. He was stunned to find that a company developing products in the forefront of technology would have internal computer systems that were (in Lott's words) hardly in the twentieth century. Though no one had expressed major concern with the information systems within Fielding, Lott felt that upgrading the hardware was one of his first priorities.

Lott was a graduate of MIT and had worked in their computer lab upon graduation. After a two-year period in which he concentrated on advanced simulation models, he became a salesman for Digital Equipment Corporation (DEC) and sold minicomputers and microcomputers on an OEM (original equipment manufacturer) basis to large engineering houses, who in turn would add software and applications for resell to end users. Lott was very successful at DEC, never needing home-office support, as he could provide his own technical expertise. He had a reputation of really knowing his product and what made it tick.

Lott's new company was running a large IBM 370 mainframe with a peripheral array whose age averaged eight years from time of first industry introduction. It was obvious to the new MIS director that Fielding was certainly not a leading-edge computer user; in fact it was at the trailing fringe.

His first major proposal to management was a plan to upgrade hardware. It called for a replacement of the mainframe with dual 32-bit, high-powered minis. The latest high-density disks would be added, even though Fielding could be a test site for them. Micro-based intelligent work stations would replace the current five- to ten-year-old CRT's that were controlled by the mainframe. Graphic terminals would gradually be installed in key executive locations and a communications network established so that an electronic mail feature could be added to the current word processing applications.

Lott's plan was greeted enthusiastically by the management of Fielding. They had always felt the existence of the "shoemaker's children" syndrome, and it was a bit embarrassing to show visiting customers their antiquated computer hardware. This was the major reason why Lott had been brought in. They were particularly excited about the machine-room model that an engineering design firm had developed for them. It featured a completely glass-enclosed computer room with model work stations and automated office modules. The telecommunications control center was particularly impressive, replete with screens, monitors, and switches. Each piece of equipment had its model number, capacity, and speed characteristics noted on a panel directly above it. There was no question that this installation, representing the state of the art in computer hardware, would be a showcase and give Fielding the hi-tech image they sought.

The installation went like clockwork; a PERT chart in the information system control room plotted every step along the way, and management could enter the room and ascertain the status via a specially conceived color code.

Nine months after the installation, Lott was summarily relieved of his duties and replaced by a senior MIS professional with fifteen years' experience in the field. The new director found a 24-month application backlog, a bevy of irate vendors who had been either not paid or paid erroneously, and a multitude of outraged internal users.

QUESTIONS

1. What went wrong with Lott's well-conceived plan?

2. What elements might Lott have overlooked or downplayed?

3. Was Lott the real problem, or was he a scapegoat?

4. What challenges face the new MIS director? What should be his strategy?

BIBLIOGRAPHY

"As Time Goes By," *Datamation* (Sept. 1982), 65–70.

Dertouzos, Michael L. and Joel Moses, Editors, *The Computer Age: A Twenty Year View.* Cambridge, MA: The MIT Press, 1979.

Goldstine, Herman H., *The Computer from Pascal to Von Neumann.* Princeton, NJ: Princeton University Press, 1972.

Husky, Velma R. and Harry D. Husky, "Lady Lovelace and Charles Babbage," *Annals of the History of Computing* (Oct. 1980), 299–329.

McLean, J., "The Computer Industry: The Moguls and the Mainframes," *Electronic News* (Jan. 25, 1982), 74–75.

Rogers, William, Think, *A Biography of the Watsons and IBM.* New York: Stein and Day, 1969.

Shorter, E., *The Historian and the Computer.* Englewood Cliffs, NJ: Prentice-Hall, Inc., 1971.

Stern, Nancy, "John Von Neumann's Influence on Electronic Digital Computer 1944–1946," *Annals of the History of Computing* (Oct. 1980), 34–62.

Thierauf, Robert J., *Data Processing for Business and Management.* New York: John Wiley, 1973.

Toffler, Alvin, *Future Shock.* New York: Random House, Inc., 1970.

Toffler, Alvin, *The Third Wave.* New York: William Morrow & Co. Inc., 1980.

Wiener, Norbert, *The Human Use of Human Beings: Cybernetics and Society.* Garden City, NY: Doubleday Anchor, 1954.

Chapter 7

The Application Development Cycle

This chapter describes the application development cycle, including the analysis, synthesis, and implementation phases. Emphasis is given to determining a meaningful user-oriented application specification, assessing and managing the level of risk in the project, and determining the return on investment. The so-called structured techniques also are discussed.

Referring to the organization chart of Figs. 2.6 and 2.7, this chapter focuses on those functions listed under Development—very important functions indeed for the future success of MIS. The discussion will also cover some of the technical support areas.

The chapter's outline follows the life-cycle steps described in Fig. 7.1. The inner ring divides the cycle into three general phases. These are then broken into seven areas (middle ring), which in turn are further categorized by the outer ring. After a brief definition of each phase, we consider the concept of an application business plan that documents and controls the cycle. Then a detailed analysis of each phase begins.

Certain areas of phases are developed more than others. The feasibility area is heavily emphasized through a discussion of return on investment, techniques assessing the marginal value of information, and a technique for analyzing and managing the risk of large application development projects. The section on feasibility concludes by describing a four-criterion method for determining the priority of application development. The resource utilization area is also emphasized, and a technique is described for analyzing and evaluating various application software resources re-

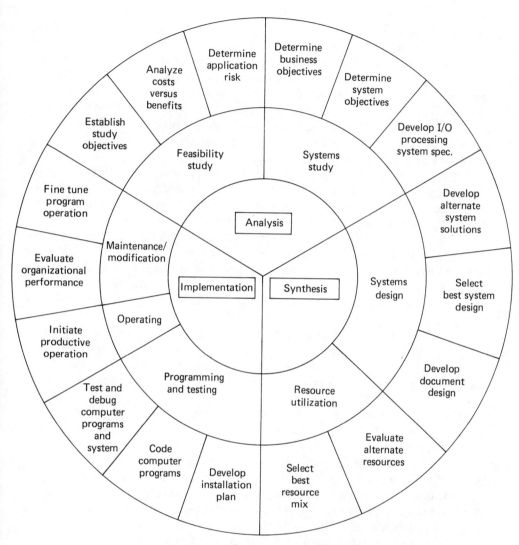

Fig. 7.1   Application development cycle

quired for the job. Because of the high cost of in-house development, outside procurement becomes a distinct possibility. In the implementation phase, the importance
of developing standards is discussed.

APPLICATION DEVELOPMENT CYCLE

Chapter 1 briefly described the steps that an application must go through to become
operable on a computer. Once the business and information model is developed, the
subsystems identified, and the implementation priority determined, each application

must be thoroughly planned, documented, programmed, tested, and put into productive computer operation.

Figure 7.1 illustrates the application development cycle. The hub of the wheel indicates that there are three general phases in this process: (a) analysis, (b) synthesis, and (c) implementation. Analysis is defined as the separation of anything into its constituent parts or elements. Synthesis, the opposite of analysis, begins to combine and build the parts or elements into a whole. The *analysis phase* dissects business operations to show up weaknesses and areas where information analysis can improve the planning and control of operations. The *synthesis phase* combines these elements in such a way as to improve the original operation.

The *implementation phase* is the proof of the pudding. Here the synthesis (or improved solution) is actually designed, programmed, and put into operation. The conclusion of this phase is the maintenance and modification of operational applications to ensure that they remain free of errors and discrepancies.

A further breakdown of the development cycle indicates that the analysis phase consists of two subphases: feasibility study and systems study. The *feasibility study* begins with the establishment of objectives, including the time and cost of the study, selection of the people who will conduct it, and the general manner in which it will be conducted. The feasibility study asks: Does this application offer sufficient benefits to a company to warrant further investigation? An effective *systems study* requires a considerable investment in time and money; it should be undertaken only if a preliminary study indicates that the proposed application presents a feasible solution to the problem. Further study may indicate that the application is not justified, but a company should be reasonably sure that it is before embarking on a comprehensive systems study.

The systems study begins with an analysis of overall business objectives and focuses on the information and control system, which enables a company to plan and schedule operations better in order to produce the product at the lowest possible cost and still satisfy customer demand. The total information system will be broken down into progressively smaller and smaller units of study until the focus is on meaningful and manageable subsystems. The input, output, and processing steps of these subsystems will be carefully analyzed to form the foundation for the synthesis phase of the application development cycle.

The synthesis phase consists of the resource utilization and system design subphases. The *resource utilization* subphase explores various alternatives for providing the resources necessary to accomplish the job. These alternatives range from using a company's own system and programming personnel, and its current computer if there is available capacity, to employing outside assistance in the form of systems help, software help, computer time, or time-sharing service.

The *systems study* answers the question of *what* is being done and compares that to what should be done. *Systems design* is concerned with *how* it is being done and compares that with how it should be done. In systems design, the detail produced during the systems study is used to develop alternate solutions that will better achieve the defined business and system objectives.

The implementation phase includes developing the *installation plan*, which outlines the resources necessary to prepare for running the application. The installation plan and schedule determine the specific availability dates of the necessary resources. The implementation phase includes the *programming*, *operating*, and *maintenance-modification* subphases. The implementation staff, after selection and training, transforms the systems design specification into progressively greater and greater detail, thus preparing the system for computer processing.

The resultant programs are tested both individually and as an information system and finally put into productive operation. The productive programs are then reviewed to determine if they meet the system objectives and, therefore, the business objectives. The resultant system improvements and benefits are measured against those that were projected.

The implementation phase does not end at this point but includes the important maintenance-modification subphase. The overall operational performance must be evaluated as a preliminary step to fine-tuning the running applications. It is inevitable that operational errors and program discrepancies will occur with time; a plan must be instituted for their resolution and correction. With the fine tuning accomplished, both short- and long-range plans for future growth are refined.

In reality, the phases of analysis, synthesis, and implementation are never-ending cycles. As soon as initial computer applications are put into productive operation, additional ones are tackled. The operational applications must be periodically reviewed and updated to run more efficiently and to adapt to changing business conditions and needs.

APPLICATION BUSINESS PLAN

A growing number of companies that have a mature and comprehensive planning process are using the concept of a product business plan. For each major product or project undertaken, a planning guide is utilized to ensure that all the elements needed for the success of the program are included and properly reflected. I feel that this concept can and should be carried over to the planning of major application subsystems within MIS and, indeed, to the entire MIS development process. I call this the application business plan. All too often the planning approach to MIS is a fragmented one. Different individuals and different groups get together and frequently accomplish effective work, but their efforts are not coordinated and their overall plan is not set down and documented in an official document. This is the purpose of an application business plan—to provide a vehicle for stating the pertinent agreements and rationale under which the activity must proceed. The application business plan must be a live document that is continually updated and modified. If a new system analyst or operating manager enters the project, the application business plan is the first document he or she should read in order to gain pertinent background.

Figure 7.2 presents an outline of the contents of an application business plan. The first section covers the rationale of the particular program—the purpose, objectives, goals, and similar factors—and the connection with the other portions of the management information system. The second section covers the definition and characteristics of the application. An individual not familiar with the application can obtain a concise but definitive explanation by reading this section. The next section covers the feasibility of the application. Whatever feasibility criteria a company employs, whether cost/benefit analysis or return on investment, the criteria and financial data are recorded in this section.

The remaining sections cover more detailed information about the application, the design and specification, the schedule and implementation plan, and, finally, the implementation status and review section. Thus the application business plan is an on-going document that covers the life cycle of the application from feasibility, justification, and design to implementation, schedule, and productive operation. A company must insist that no major program be authorized without a business plan.

An additional point is the possibility of dovetailing the application business plan concept with the company's program or project management organization.

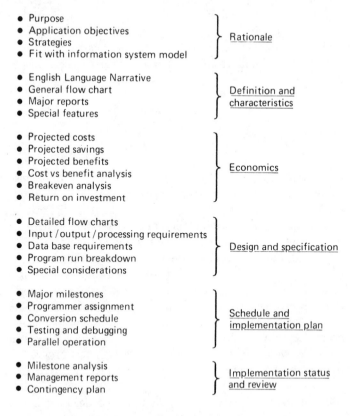

Fig. 7.2   Application business plan

Many companies have a program management office that assigns program managers to major projects. Although they do not control the departments responsible for implementing the project, they are responsible as catalysts and coordinators to see that the project is completed on schedule and as specified. It is possible that a program manager may be assigned to one of the advisory groups. It then becomes his job to schedule the meetings, see that the written plan is prepared, the schedules monitored, and action taken to remain on schedule. Many firms have not as yet considered major MIS subsystems as candidates for program management. The contention presented here is that perhaps they should. More systems have failed because of lack of management direction and leadership than for any other reason. The application business plan and the employment of program management are powerful techniques for ensuring the success of a management information system.

We turn now to a more detailed look at the various subphases. Subphases at the beginning of the cycle will be discussed more thoroughly than the others because of their management significance.

FEASIBILITY

Feasibility is a significant phase of the application development cycle. Many companies have launched major programs and moved well along in a dedicated productive effort when someone raised the question: We're making good progress, but are we working on the right problem? This is the purpose of the feasibility phase—to develop a set of selection criteria, a selection procedure, and an effective decision-making organization such that a company can be certain that it is working on the right problem and in the right sequence. The feasibility phase is a vital underpinning of MIS. Too often the selection of applications has been left to MIS people or has been rubber-stamped by management without real study or analysis.

Figure 7.3 is read from the inside out; thus the inner ring is broken into categories by the middle ring, while the outer ring gives examples of elements in the middle rings. The figure indicates that there are three general feasibility considerations: (a) technical, (b) economic, and (c) operational. It is important that management carefully consider all three, in addition to establishing their relative weight and significance. The technical considerations are directed at the question of whether the necessary hardware, software, and application tools are available or will be available when required by the particular applications under study. Often there is a risk or probability factor, because one or several of the technical elements may be future items promised by a certain date but not yet available. In this event, management must consider the reliability of vendor claims, whether the particular item is on the critical path, and what insurance if any can be established in case of late delivery. Of course, the risks increase greatly when several key items are in the future category.

Certain hardware items are required, such as input-output devices, communication capabilities, and bulk magnetic-storage devices. Software items, such as database management, operating systems, and special languages, as well as application

Fig. 7.3   Application feasibility criteria

packages and management science techniques, may be MIS requirements. Each of the required items must be carefully evaluated to ascertain its relevance to MIS development. The higher the dependence on sophisticated and/or technical items yet to be field-tested, the higher the risk factor in selecting a particular application for development. Special attention wil be given to risk assessment later.

A look at the economic and operational feasibility will further qualify application feasibility. Economic considerations represent fundamental feasibility criteria. If a company cannot improve its profit picture or return on investment in the short or long run, then it should not be considering MIS. In looking at the economics of MIS, one must consider its cost compared to the savings that MIS can accrue and/or the added benefits derived from the system. The cost categories of MIS operation will be covered in the next chapter under the headings of "MIS Budgets" and "Charge-Out Systems."

A *saving* is a definite MIS operating-cost reduction caused by the introduction of the particular application. It could be the reduction of operating costs or the reduction of clerical personnel as the computer system absorbs the routine administrative functions and increases the efficiency, for example, of data entry operation. More often than not, the introduction of MIS, although not without some clerical cost savings, will result in an overall cost increase because of the need for added computing capacity. Companies have found that computerization pays off not in reduced costs but in more meaningful and more timely information.

Turning now to the type of benefits that can be expected from a computer program, we can distinguish two general categories—tangible and intangible. A tangible benefit is one that can be accurately measured and that can be directly related to the introduction of an application. An example is a cost reduction where work formerly accomplished on overtime has been eliminated because of an improved production scheduling system. An example of an intangible benefit is an improvement in customer service brought on by a more responsive order-processing system. Although it is often clear that the improvement is a result of the application system, it is difficult to place a monetary value on the effect this has on overall company profitability. There are degrees of tangibility in system benefits. Certainly the benefit of improved company image as a result of the automated nature of an application is less tangible a factor than the benefit of improved customer service, although both benefits fall into the intangible category.

In assembling the final feasibility study, the time dimension—when the benefits will occur—is important. If the study encompasses the entire information system of a company, it is clear that such a development will take a rather lengthy period to implement. Some type of phase-in plan must be instituted, which means that the benefits will come gradually, and not all will be apparent during the first year of installation. The feasibility study return-on-investment analysis should reflect this fact.

Placing a dollar value on anticipated computer benefits is a difficult task. An example may illustrate the type of analysis that can be used for this purpose. Many companies have inventory problems that result in a major overstocking of certain items and understocking of others. The key consideration in inventory control is maintaining a balanced inventory that provides the required level of customer service. If asked how much reduction can be accomplished by automating the inventory control operation, most business managers would say "Plenty." This, however, is hardly a quantified statement of fact. One might look at other companies with similar operations that have computer-based inventory control systems to determine what reductions they have obtained. Another way is to use a computer system to analyze past history of demand and prior levels of inventory. Through a process of simulation (which uses mathematical inventory decision rules), the system can indicate what levels of inventory would have been required in order to meet the desired level of customer service. Comparing these simulated levels with actual levels gives a company a good idea of potential inventory reduction.

Although the simulation procedure described gives a solid indication of what is possible, it still may not be completely convincing. Another approach is to work backward, utilizing a breakeven analysis. After accumulating the projected computer costs, a calculation of the amount of inventory reduction necessary to cover these costs can be ascertained. Maintaining inventory results in carrying such costs as taxes, insurance, investment on the capital, spoilage, obsolescence, and space. These costs usually amount to about 15 percent of the inventory value, not including interest rate on investment, which has been extremely high in recent years. The latter should be added to the carrying charge, depending on the particular company's borrowing rate. If the total system costs (machine, operating, and system costs) are $60,000 per year, it can be calculated that an inventory reduction of $400,000 is necessary to offset these costs (15% × $400,000 = $60,000). Management now can ask how likely it is that an automated inventory control system can reduce inventory to that extent. Note that the inventory reduction needed will be even less when the interest-rate charge is added to the carrying cost. This type of breakeven approach can be used in assessing benefits in other operating areas as well.

An often-overlooked element of feasibility is *operational feasibility*. A particular application may be technically and economically feasible but fail to produce the forecasted benefits because a company is not able to get it to work. This is often perplexing to MIS management, who cannot understand why a well-conceived and designed system cannot be successfully utilized by the operating departments. There are several reasons for this situation. Some of the problems are motivational and psychological in nature and can be resolved by proper training and indoctrination. Some, however, are serious enough at the outset to warrant placing a lower priority on a particular application area until the problem is resolved. An example is the development of a sales report that shows profitability of sales by item and product line. If a salesman is compensated the same whether he sells item A or item B, the report will be cumbersome and of little value. In another case, a decentralized sales administration function is computerized as part of an MIS concept. Where local sales branches once processed orders and billed customers directly, these activities are now accomplished centrally. The new system is designed and installed with minimal local participation or involvement. As a result, the branches utilize tactics that serve to circumvent the system. The new system develops a billing backlog, customers become irate, management becomes disillusioned, and the system eventually fails. In these two cases, it may be wise to assign a lower system priority until specific policies are changed and tested. If this is not done, the computer and MIS will bear the blame for the failure, whether they deserve it or not.

It is necessary to assess management, nonmanagement, and general operational considerations as indicated in Fig. 7.3. The major focus of the application must be ascertained and, the resulting impact on top, middle, and operating management carefully analyzed. For example, a system may be built on a rather revolutionary approach to production scheduling. This factor obviously has a direct impact on the production scheduling supervisor and the production manager. If the production manager is a former production worker who has worked his way to his current position, is very conservative, and has shown himself antagonistic toward computerized production scheduling systems, this situation obviously represents a negative operational feasibility consideration. It must either be dealt with and resolved or else recognized as a strong factor in establishing a lower priority for the production scheduling subsystem. To a lesser extent this is true for nonmanagement personnel as well. A positive attitude and an acceptance of the system on the part of management can be reflected downward to the people who must implement the system. Frequently, the development of MIS can impose greater demands on clerical personnel, in the form of their learning new ways of doing business, assuming duties that add to their total work load, or both. These demands are important considerations in operational feasibility.

The "general" category under operational feasibility is a most significant one and must not be overlooked. Stories of customer reaction and the rigors of converting to a new billing system are legion. Most of us have received notices apologizing for dunning us for bills we have long paid, or for the myriad of other problems encountered because the company was converting to a new computer system. This situation is obviously a consideration in operational feasibility. An example of a vendor consideration is in the development of an inventory control system. If an automatic reordering system requires the delivery of a greater number of smaller orders with less lead time, the vendor must be conditioned to respond to this new policy, particularly if the items in question are in short supply. Similarly, the potential impact of MIS on regulatory external agencies must be considered. For example, if the system is designed to provide magnetic-tape audit trails, this procedure should be reviewed with the company's auditors and the Internal Revenue authorities. Thus it is important to consider carefully the three elements of feasibility described in Fig. 7.3. A proper blending, analysis, and weighing of the technical, economic, and operational elements will ensure that the correct priority is placed on application subsystems within an MIS and that a company is indeed working on the right problem.

RETURN-ON-INVESTMENT ANALYSIS

Another way to view MIS feasibility is to measure the overall impact on return on investment. The assumption is that if a computer is a beneficial tool, it will increase the profits of a company and/or reduce investment and thereby have an effect on improving return on investment. Although a simple return-on-investment (ROI) analysis may seem so basic as to be naive to the businessman, it is not that common to the MIS side of the house. The ROI concept is briefly mentioned here to reinforce its significance to MIS projects, many of which have been immune even to the most basic of business measurement tools. Profitability and return on investment are the two key yardsticks of measuring business performance. Figure 7.4 is a simplified schematic of a return-on-investment analysis. The top portion is a profit-and-loss statement for the company, starting with sales on the first line, subtracting cost of sales to arrive at net earnings before taxes, and then subtracting taxes (a 46 percent rate is assumed) to arrive at net earnings after taxes. Cost of sales consists of variable costs (labor, material, etc.), fixed costs (depreciation, rent, equipment cost, etc.), and

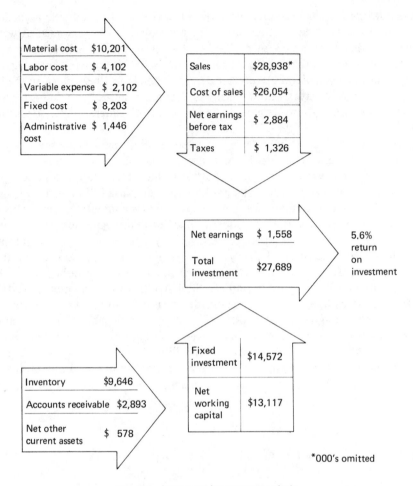

Fig. 7.4   Return-on-investment analysis

administrative costs (legal, personnel, accounting, etc.). Thus the $1,588,000 is the company profit for the year and forms the numerator of the return-on-investment equation.

The investment or denominator of the equation consists of fixed investment (money tied up in machinery and buildings) and net working capital, made up of current inventory, accounts receivable, and other current assets. The ratio of net earnings to total investment is equal to the company's rate of return on investment. ROI is really what a company is trying to improve, as it is the true measure of how well it is using the stockholders' money. If a computer can have an appreciable effect on improving this rate of return, then it is most certainly a desirable investment. For illustrative purposes, assume that Fig. 7.4 represents the company's ROI at the moment when it is evaluating the possibility of a computer. The figures exclude the last three zeros, so that the company in question is netting $1.5 million on a $27 million investment and has an ROI of 5.6 percent. This is very low for a manufacturer.

The ROI analysis can further determine whether you are working on the right problem or not. For example, a 1 percent improvement in material cost can add $102,000 to profit, whereas a 1 percent improvement in labor cost adds only $41,000. The reason is obvious, for material constitutes a greater portion of the total variable product cost. Consequently, everything being equal, it would seem wiser from an economic point of view to focus an MIS on improving material costs (e.g., a purchasing system that could take advantage of quantity discounts or a production control system that could reduce material variances and scrap loss). A simple calculation shows that a decrease of material costs of 3 percent through improved purchasing or production control can improve the company's ROI from 5.6 to 6.2 percent.

Another area of real payoff on the investment side is that of inventory. Almost 75 percent of the net working capital consists of inventory. A computerized inventory control system that could better control and balance inventories would have a significant impact on ROI. A projected 20 percent inventory reduction would amount to $1.9 million. In addition, the reduction in inventory reduces the inventory carrying costs. This reduction in carrying costs (assume a conservative 15 percent) reduces variable costs by $285,000 and adds to the yearly profit. The effect of these changes is to increase ROI from 5.6 to 6.6 percent.

These are merely examples of what an ROI analysis can indicate. It is not important to argue whether an inventory control application can reduce material costs 1, 3, or 5 percent or to discuss the specific impact it can have on inventory investment; it obviously depends on the particular situation. The point here is the desirability of looking at MIS as an integral part of the business operation, as an element in increasing profit, reducing investment, and improving ROI.

DISCOUNTED CASH FLOW

Another approach to ROI takes into account that the development of a major new system requires a long-term commitment by a company. The costs incurred and the benefits realized should be related to one another in such a way as to take account of the time periods in which each is realized.

The discounted-cash-flow method provides such an approach because it recognizes the time value of money: dollars spent or earned in earlier years are of greater value to the company than dollars earned or spent in later years. This is so because those same dollars could be invested elsewhere in the company to produce a profitable return.

Figures 7.5 and 7.6 illustrate the costs and savings from an MIS investment by a company. The same investment principles apply as well to a company replacing an existing computer, upgrading capability, or adding a new application.

Figure 7.7 indicates that over the four-year period $797,000 of net positive savings are realized from the investment. Figure 7.8 indicates a net positive savings of $242,000, using tangible savings only.

The ROI (return-on-investment) technique provides a better measurement for management because it translates the dollar into a common percentage format. This

Cost		Year of Installation			
	0	1	2	3	4
Initial systems and programming	66,000	20,000			
File conversion	3,000	3,000			
Parallel operation		4,000			
Other	1,000	1,000			
Total One-time Costs	70,000	28,000			
Hardware rental		62,000	70,000	75,000	75,000
Personal costs		90,000	100,000	105,000	115,000
Supplies and services	12,000	22,000	30,000	30,000	35,000
Other	1,000	1,000			
Total Recurring Costs	13,000	175,000	200,000	210,000	225,000
Total Cost	83,000	203,000	200,000	210,000	225,000

Fig. 7.5   Cost summary (in dollars)

Savings		Year of Installation			
	0	1	2	3	4
Reduction in current data processing costs		50,000	110,000	115,000	125,000
Clerical costs outside MIS		10,000	20,000	30,000	50,000
Inventory reduction (carrying cost)		40,000	125,000	150,000	160,000
Overtime reduction		5,000	20,000	22,000	32,000
Production variances			5,000	40,000	50,000
Other		1,000	1,000	1,000	1,000
Total tangible savings		106,000	281,000	358,000	418,000
Profit on sales (increased customer service)		5,000	50,000	100,000	100,000
Improved sales analysis			100,000	100,000	100,000
Increased management control					
More meaningful data					
Other					
Total intangible savings		5,000	150,000	200,000	200,000
Total savings		111,000	431,000	558,000	618,000

Fig. 7.6   Savings summary (in dollars)

is accomplished by use of financial tables that discount both the positive and negative flows until they equal one another. In the above examples, the ROI is 97.8 percent based on measuring full savings, and 37.6 percent when measured on tangible savings only. This return can now be related to the company's cost of borrowing or other investment yardsticks.

	Year of Installation					
	0	*1*	*2*	*3*	*4*	*Total*
Costs	83	203	200	210	225	921
Savings		106	431	558	618	1718
Net savings	(83)	(97)	231	348	393	797

Fig. 7.7   Net cash flows from computer investment (in $ thousands)

	Year of Installation					
	0	*1*	*2*	*3*	*4*	*Total*
Costs	83	203	200	210	225	921
Savings		106	281	358	418	1163
Net savings	(83)	(97)	81	148	193	242

Fig. 7.8   Net cash flows from computer investment—tangible savings only (in $ thousands)

MARGINAL VALUE OF INFORMATION

Marginal value (or *marginal utility*) represents the value (utility) to a buyer of each additional (marginal) unit of a product. It defines the price the end user or consumer is willing to pay for each additional unit of a product. The greater the quality the user already has, the less, supposedly, he is willing to pay for an additional unit. The law of supply and demand takes effect, and when the supply reaches a certain point (the saturation point), then demand, theoretically, becomes zero. The supplier must then wait to replace the item as it depreciates or becomes obsolete, or he must develop an innovative or attractively priced new item that eventually induces the buyer to buy it. An example is a suit of clothes. The typical businessman wears a suit to work five days a week. He may own three or four suits, but as he buys his fourth or fifth, the marginal value is reduced significantly. He can wear only one per day, and, if he is content with his first five, the sixth offers him little satisfaction. Obvious psychological factors affect this situation (many men for one reason or another own 20 or 30 suits or more), but the preceding analysis holds for the average businessman and explains the marginal-value concept.

Let us see if this concept can be applied to information produced by a management information system. Is there a marginal value? What is the point at which the value becomes zero? Some would say that, in the case of information, not only is there a marginal value, there is also a negative value. A condition exists in some companies that might be called "information glut": the organization seems to be choking with information. Report and analyses have proliferated, partly because of the ease and speed of today's high-speed printout systems. The company may not have made a report utilization survey or study for years. Reports are added on top of reports, and no effort is made to streamline, combine, or eliminate. While formal reevaluation and reassessment may be common practices for the external products the company produces, they are not practiced in the case of computer products (printed reports). The development of MIS should serve as a catalyst to trigger the much-needed appraisal of current information outputs. The system should encourage the management-by-exception concept as opposed to management by the ton (referring to mounds of paper spewed out by computer systems).

Although I do not believe the marginal value of information can be determined as precisely as it can be for other economic goods, the general concept does hold and, at a minimum, should serve as a design guide for a management information system. In some situations the marginal value of information can be determined fairly accurately, whereas in others it is difficult, if not impossible to determine. The value of information should always be a prime consideration in system design, even in the latter case.

A fairly clear-cut example is the value of calculating automatic reorder points and economic order quantities, as mentioned previously. Simulation (later confirmed by actual operation) can illustrate the specific monetary value expressed in lower inventory levels and improved customer service. If the inventory control system can reduce inventory by $200,000, then the value of the information generated by the system that accomplishes it is worth somewhere around $30,000 (15%, the carrying cost, × $200,000). Let us pursue this subject a step further. A basic ingredient of an effective inventory control system is a sales forecasting subsystem. Suppose that the current inventory control system utilizes forecasting technique A, whereas forecasting technique B is conceded to be statistically superior. It may well be that the forecast error has minimum leverage on the savings that can accrue from an inventory control system. Simulation may indicate that a forecasting system that is 20 percent more accurate has only a 3 percent influence on inventory levels. If there is a sizable system and programming cost in implementing the new forecasting technique, it may more than offset the value of the information. In this case, the marginal value of information is negative; the cost of acquiring the information is greater than the resultant benefit.

Another example is the use of information in a strategic planning subsystem. Here the marginal value is difficult to assess. Often the cost of the information is quite exact, particularly if the information is obtained from an outside agency. A market survey may be directed at answering questions, such as what are the user's criteria for changing vendors, for replacing their current product, or for adding another vendor's product. Assume that such a survey, because of its competitive implications, can be conducted only by an outside agency and that its price is $20,000. How can one assess the marginal value of this information?

If this information is part of the market analysis preparatory to designing a new product line, it is obvious that the stakes are quite high. But the strategic planning group has already assembled an extensive and comprehensive data base, one reflecting the future marketplace for the company's products. What is the marginal value of additional information? Is it greater than $20,000? This is a most difficult question to answer. One might begin by asking a counterquestion: what action might be taken as a result of the information? Assume, for example, there exists a question as to the impact of adding a specific and costly feature to a product, and assume further that the incorporation of the feature would result in a $200,000 development cost. If the survey will indicate without a doubt whether such a development is feasible, one might argue that it is worth $20,000 to save $200,000. However, the survey may not be conclusive and may only improve the probabilities of making the correct decision. Then management must weigh the costs and probabilities of improved product development and profit as an outgrowth of the additional data. It may be that similar surveys have reduced the risks in decision making such that the additional information is indeed marginal in value.

In conclusion, although there is no clear-cut method of assessing the marginal value of information, the need to do so is important. The value of some information can be accurately determined and weighed against the costs necessary to produce it, whereas the marginal value of other information is difficult to assess. This fact should not preclude the analysis of marginal value; it is certainly more desirable than following the supposition that all information has value. The consequences of the latter concept are often "information glut" and the development not of a management information system but of a management proliferation system.

RISK ASSESSMENT

Professor Warren McFarlan of the Harvard Business School has described a straightforward, easy-to-understand, effective technique for assessing the degree of risk in projects that may be undertaken by a company. This technique has been successfully used by numerous companies and is fully described in a case study called "The Dallas Tire Corporation" (fictitious name for a real company). This technique can be used to assess risks over a range of projects that affect the MIS department. The use illustrated here is in application development, an area where the major part of the MIS budget is expended.

There are some compelling reasons for assessing the risks in projects. First, an assessment helps you better understand the projects being implemented. An overall idea of its scope and size, its interaction with other projects, and its importance to the company can be better ascertained. Risk assessment helps you compare one project to another, enabling the ranking of projects on a risk scale. This is an important factor in deciding to move ahead on a project. Most business-oriented managers opt for a balanced portfolio of risks; that is, they will undertake a high-risk, high-payoff project if they have several lower-risk projects that will come to fruition while they are working on the high-risk one. The balanced-portfolio concept sustains management support and tempers the potential of failure of the high-risk project. Probably the most important reason for risk assessment is that it facilitates more efficient management of projects and assignment of personnel to various projects. A high-risk project demands resources and techniques different from the low-risk projects. For example, it would seem prudent to assign your best project manager to the high-risk project. If the high risk is caused by technical considerations, that person should have a good understanding of the project's technical dimension. Stricter control and higher management visibility would be given the high-risk project, with comprehensive reviews and audits scheduled at selected intervals. On the other hand, the low-risk projects can be assigned and managed routinely.

The risk-assessment technique utilized divides risk into three categories: (1) size, (2) structure, and (3) technology. In the size category we analyze a project in terms of projected man-years, dollar costs, elapsed time, and other indicators that measure its overall scope. The longer the time span, the more likely it is that the business environment will change during the project's life and compound the timing problem. Projects that have a longer time horizon and require more man-years are higher-risk than the smaller projects.

A high-structure project is one for which the company has the required expertise—one that has been done before, is familiar to the company, and is straightforward with few if any design options. A low-structure project is one that requires substantial judgment and perspective, presents many options, and calls for considerable flexibility. In terms of the company activity triangle of Fig. 1.1, where applications are grouped into three categories of operation control, management control, and strategic planning, applications are less structured as you proceed up the triangle.

The technology risk is related to the company's technological experience and expertise. While a particular technology may be proven in the industry, it is high-risk if it has not yet been applied by the particular company. Projects involving several new hardware devices, such as graphic terminals or a new type of disk storage, warrant high technology risk. When new software is also required, the risk can be compounded, because experience has shown that it is less risky to apply new software to proven hardware or to apply existing software to new hardware. The users' knowledge and experience, though not normally considered in the technology-risk category, should be included in the assessment.

The next step is to develop a list of weighted questions in each risk category. The selection and the comparative weighting of these questions are subjective elements, but subjectivity eventually becomes a factor in any technique of this type. The real benefit is to force a critical definition and assessment of risk, and to measure all projects with this same yardstick. Consistency of analysis is one of the key attributes of a tool such as risk assessment.

Figure 7.9 includes sample questions used in the Dallas Tire Comany case. I have selected six questions from each of the three risk categories. Each question has a weight, as do the various answers. The question weight is multiplied by the answer weight to obtain the score. Thus in the size-risk category, if the total systems and programming manhours were projected to be over 30,000, the score would be 20.

A. *Questionnaire Scoring Sheet—Size*

1. Total systems and programming man-hours

Weight
(5)

Weight

( ) 100 to 3,000   1
( ) 3,000 to 15,000   2
( ) 15,000 to 30,000   3
( ) Over 30,000   4

2. What is the estimate in calendar time?

(4)

( ) 12 months or less   1
( ) 13 months to 24 months   2
( ) Over 24 months   3

3. Length of economic payback:

(2)

( ) Less than 12 months   1
( ) 12 to 24 months   2
( ) Over 24 months   3

4. By whom will the work be performed?

(2)

( ) Mostly by on-site personnel (MIS and/or outside)   1
( ) Significant portions by on-site and off-site personnel   2
( ) Mostly by off-site personnel (MIS and/or outside)   3

5. Number of departments (other than MIS) involved with the system:

(4)

( ) One   1
( ) Two   2
( ) Three or more   3

6. With how many existing MIS systems must the new system interface?

(3)

( ) None   1
( ) One   1
( ) Two   2
( ) More than two   3

B. *Questionnaire Scoring Sheet—Structure*

1. The system may best be described as:

Weight
(1)

( ) Totally new system   3
( ) Replacement of an existing manual system   2
( ) Replacement of an existing automated system   1

2. If a replacement system is proposed, what percent of existing functions is replaced on a one-to-one basis?

(5)

( ) 0–25   3
( ) 25–50   2
( ) 50–100   1

Fig. 7.9   Risk assessment

3. What is the severity of procedural changes by the proposed system?   (5)

    ( ) Low   1
    ( ) Medium   2
    ( ) High   3

4. Proposed methods and/or procedures: (2)

    ( ) First of kind for data processing   3
    ( ) First of kind for user   3
    ( ) Breakthrough required for user acceptance   3
    ( ) Breakthrough required for data processing implementation   3
    ( ) None of the above   0

5. What degree of flexibility and judgment can be exercised by the   (1)
   system's architect in the area of systems outputs?

    ( ) 0 to 33%   Very little   1
    ( ) 34 to 66%   Average   2
    ( ) 67 to 100%   Very high   3

6. How committed is upper-level user management to the system?   (5)

    ( ) Somewhat reluctant or unknown   3
    ( ) Adequate   2
    ( ) Extremely enthusiastic   1

Fig. 7.9   Risk assessment (continued)

The absolute value is the minimum and maximum score for the total questions used in each risk category. The score in this case doesn't add up, since only a portion of the questions are given. In this instance project X is a low-risk project, scoring low in all three risk categories; Y falls in the 50th percentile but is high-risk compared to X because of high size and structure risk. The crucial point is that this approach allows you to measure project X against project Y, and, if you decide to implement either or both, it points out the type of project management that should be employed.

    A tabulation of the total question set for two sample projects (X and Y) is as follows:

		Project X		Project Y	
Category	Absolute	Category Value	Percentile	Category Value	Percentile
Size	26–83	33	12	72	81
Structure	21–158	39	13	92	52
Technology	21–258	45	10	65	18
Average Percentile			12		50

C. *Questionnaire Scoring Sheet — Technology*

Weight

1. Is additional hardware required? (1)

( )	None	0
( )	CPU	1
( )	Peripheral and/or additional storage to mainframe	1
( )	Terminals	2
( )	Mini or micro	3

2. Which of the above hardware is new to your organization? (3)

( )	None	0
( )	CPU	1
( )	Peripheral and/or additional storage	2
( )	Terminals	2
( )	Mini or micro	3

3. Is special nonstandard hardware required? (5)

( )	None	0
( )	CPU	3
( )	Peripheral and/or additional storage	3
( )	Terminals	3
( )	Mini or micro	3

4. Is the system software (nonoperating system) new to the MIS project team? (5)

( )	Programming language	3
( )	Data base	3
( )	Data communications	3
( )	Other — specify	3

5. How knowledgeable is the user in the area of MIS? (5)

( )	First exposure	3
( )	Previous exposure but limited knowledge	2
( )	High degree of capability	1

6. How knowledgeable is the MIS team in the proposed application area? (5)

( )	Limited	3
( )	Understands concept but no experience	2
( )	Has been involved in prior implementation efforts	1

Fig. 7.9   Risk assessment (continued)

PRIORITY ANALYSIS IN SELECTION OF INFORMATION SYSTEMS

This section concludes the important area of application feasibility by tieing together the return-on-investment and risk-assessment techniques just covered. Such a vehicle for establishing application development priorities is considered crucial.

Return on Investment

This criterion is probably the most tangible and measurable of the four to be used. The accepted technique for measuring ROI is discounted cash flow, which in essence follows the principle that near-term dollars are worth more than longer-term dollars because of the interest value of money. The table below is based on the company's accepted rate of return. If the company's acceptable rate of return is 30 percent before tax, then an ROI of 30 percent scores 10 points; 45 percent, 15; and 60 percent or above, 20. On the down side an ROI of 15 percent scores 5 points. Point scores are interpolated between these benchmark points.

Weight	ROI
20	Acceptable rate + 100%
15	Acceptable rate + 50%
10	Acceptable rate of return
5	Acceptable rate − 50%

Risk

This criterion is based on the relative risk of the application's working and being implemented on time and within budget. As mentioned earlier, three elements of risk are evaluated: (1) size, (2) structure, and (3) technology. This criterion is inverted in that if the risk is high, the particular weight is low, and vice versa. Size is a measurement of the man-years and development dollars. Structure is a measure of the degree of flexibility and how well known the application in question is—the higher the degree of flexibility, the greater the risk. Technology reflects the extent to which a particular application requires new hardware and software or techniques never before used or tested. The table below assigns the risk weight on the basis of the three elements.

Risk Elements	Weight
All three factors high	0
Two factors high	5
One factor high	10
All factors low	20

Impact

This factor measures the degree of intangible benefit emanating from successful completion of the application. While subjective in nature, the intangibles can be quite significant and have a major impact on company operation. Intangibles range from improved customer service to enhanced employee morale.

The following matrix indicates a method for assigning the ten-point weight of this element.

| | Significance | |
Benefits	Moderate	High
Short Term	4	10
Long Term	1	7

Demand

This criterion reflects the demand for the application within the organization. It is a measure of who wants it specifically and the extent of the demand. The following matrix seeks to assign the ten weight points to the application.

Weight	Demanded by
10	Three or more top managers
7	The president or key executive
4	Six or more key middle managers
1	A single sponsor

Sample Use of Priority Analysis

The table below illustrates the use of application priority for a particular company. It is obvious that it takes a good deal of subjective judgment to assign weights to the various factors; nonetheless, the method offers a systematic and consistent approach for beginning to understand which applications should be computerized next and why.

| | | Factors | | | |
Application	ROI	Risk	Impact	Demand	Totals
Billing/ordering consolidation	18	10	7	8	43
Product-line reporting	14	13	8	5	40
Sales forecasting	12	14	7	6	39
Sales/customer analysis	9	18	5	4	36
Job production scheduling	13	6	6	6	31
Financial modeling	8	8	6	4	26
Factory data collection	5	9	3	4	21
Truck loading/routing	4	11	3	2	20

THE SYSTEMS STUDY

As indicated in Fig. 7.1, the systems study focuses on the determination of basic business objectives, the establishment of system objectives based on the business objectives, and the development of an input-output processing system specification for the application being implemented.

Figure 7.10 presents a more detailed schematic of the systems study phase. The starting point is the marketplace in which the company competes. Although it is not the responsibility of the systems study group to develop the overall business objectives from the nature of the marketplace, the group must be aware of the development and the policies at this level. Beginning at such a high level may seem presumptuous, but it is essential if the study is geared to improving company operations.

The process outlined here is a microcosm of the long-range MIS plan methodology covered in Chapter 2. As the MIS LRP must be in concert with the overall corporate business plan, so the new major application systems must be tested against the corporate strategy and objectives of the particular business processes affected by the application in question.

Definitions of terms, business objectives, external and internal strategies, and business system objectives are in order at this time.

Business Objectives

Business objectives state the reason the company is in business. A direct parallel is the job description of an individual, which explains the purpose and nature of his

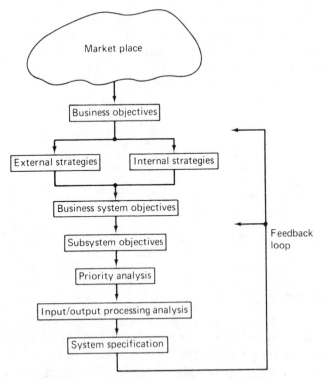

Fig. 7.10   The systems study

job and the objectives he is to accomplish. For a business, the broadest category usually is to maximize revenue, keep costs down, improve profit, and increase rate of return on investment. These goals normally are quantified by specific dollar figures.

Business Strategies

Of more significance to the systems study group are the specific external and internal business strategies evolving from the business objectives.

External strategies are related to the marketing function and state the way the company plans to attain the necessary sales revenue from the marketplace in which it competes. The external marketing strategies generally revolve around the answers to three basic questions:

1. With whom do I want to do business?
2. What should I sell them?
3. Why should they buy from me?

The answers will lead to strategies such as extending the geographical boundaries of the marketing area, concentrating a homogeneous product line in a specific marketing area, expanding product offerings to provide a full line, expanding sales 15 percent per year, and so on. These external objectives have considerable influence on the system study group.

Internal strategies concern those functions related to turning out the product or service offered to the marketplace. These strategies are built around the central focus of providing the product and/or service that meets the external marketing strategies and yet utilizes the company's resources in such a way as to minimize the costs, thus attaining the company's profit and return-on-investment goals. These internal strategies affect the basic production, purchasing, inventory, quality control, accounting, personnel, and engineering and research functions of a company. As a rule, specific internal strategies have great bearing on the system study group. A strategy might be to level production because of the scarcity of skilled labor or to achieve a 98 percent quality control standard because of the costly impact of product failure to a customer. Another internal strategy might be to institute a standard cost program to control production costs and establish a better basis for pricing. The system study must be aware of these internal strategies, the probabilities of each occurring, and their expected time frame.

The combination of the external and internal strategies is the necessary "front end" of establishing business system objectives. It is true that objectives can be established independently of this type of analysis, and many reasons can be presented for so doing. For example, it is apparent that some companies have ill-defined or undefined overall strategies. The decision then becomes one of waiting until the strategies are determined or of assisting in the establishment of the strategies before embarking on the system study. This is a trade-off that a company must face, realizing that a system that is inconsistent with overall company objectives can prove quite detrimental. It is possible to assume on one's own what strategies the company should have and to build a system from there, but doing so can be risky. This is one of the underlying and hidden reasons that a system study takes so long; often it is not the fault of the system study team but the result of management's inability to agree on basic business strategies. System people, in their zeal to begin, may tend to avoid the major overriding issues in an effort to bypass what they consider top-management red tape. The system group can take this attitude, but in many cases it is like building a house on quicksand. It is better to face the issues, convince management that it must reach decisions, and begin the system study on solid ground.

Business System Objectives

The next term requiring a definition is *business system objectives*. An information system is defined as the paperwork complex that parallels the physical operations of a company. As explained in Chapter 1, an information system is not the physical operation itself, although the two go hand-in-hand. For example, a manufactured product is produced by fabricating and assembling various raw materials, piece parts, and assemblies at various work centers. The physical process of bringing together the necessary materials and machines to produce a product is an example of a physical operating system. On the other hand, the process that produces a production schedule telling the foreman what materials and what machines are needed to produce a specified number of products by a specified time is defined as an *information system*. It is the paperwork system that controls the operating system.

Subsystem Objectives

In analyzing a company's operations, it will be obvious that the overall information system can be broken down into a hierarchy of subsystems, and the subsystems in turn into other subsystems. The starting point of the system study should be an analysis of the hierarchy of business processes that exists within the company being studied. Such an analysis will enable a clearer definition and statement of system and subsystem objectives.

Priority Analysis

After the definition of the system and subsystem objectives, it becomes apparent that the achievement of the entire range of objectives is a gargantuan task and that some type of phasing or priority analysis must be undertaken. The feasibility study should have established some framework for determining priorities. The system study by now should enable the system group to present various alternatives to management for its evaluation. The establishment of priorities is a management, and not a system, prerogative.

Input-Output Processing Analysis

Once study priorities have been established, detailed data comprising the input, output, and processing requirements of each subsystem are gathered, categorized, and analyzed.

System Specification

The final result or output of the systems study is a system specification. System specs should be developed along the same lines as engineering specs for a specific piece of equipment. The clearer and less ambiguous the spec, the more realistic the proposed computer solution will be. If, for example, the spec omits a requirement to handle a volume up to 20 percent greater by the time the system is installed, the computer configuration will be underestimated, thereby posing a serious problem at the time of installation. The specification, thoroughly understood and with the key measurement criteria (response time, output reports, report content, etc.) signed off by the ultimate users of the system, is the critical output of the systems study.

The development of the systems module concept with its feedback/control loop has been described in Chapter 1. Figure 7.10 includes a series of feedback loops. Feedback is extremely important at this stage, because discrepancies not now identified and dealt with can lead to major problems and rework later on, either in the implementation cycle or in actual operation. In many instances, system designers construct a simple prototype or breadboard of the system in order to provide a high level of feedback at an early stage.

The Structured Techniques

A set of methods that have evolved over the past ten to fifteen years, the *structured techniques*, have become more or less the accepted ways to develop application programs. It is appropriate to discuss these techniques here as they are subdivided into structured analysis (the subject we have just discussed), structured design, and structured programming (subjects to be discussed as we move through the development cycle). Like any new branch of accepted wisdom, the techniques stem from basic and sound practices that have been followed for years by professionals, many of whom feel there is now a fancy name for what they have been practicing all along.

Structured analysis applies to the systems study subphase and involves the use of tools that define and document users' requirements in a way that they can understand. The output of structured analysis is the system specification. An overall principle of the structured techniques is the top-down concept. It recognizes that systems are developed for users and that the first step is to determine user information requirements and to reflect these in sample reports and response-time projections. The structured approach analyzes systems as one analyzes a company organization chart, in a hierarchical fashion, where subfunctions are combined logically under other subfunctions and eventually become major functions that combine under a single executive or single systems entity. The structured approach mandates looking at the major functions or top boxes first before delving into the subfunctions.

Structured design is built on the divide-and-conquer concept of breaking down a problem into tightly defined, clearly understood subsystems or modules. If the top modules are defined well and in such a way that they are self-contained entities with minimal module coupling or interconnection, then the underlying modules become relatively easy to design and implement. Too often, design proceeds quickly into the detail of lower-level modules, which then all have to be reworked if there is a change in one of the upper modules. Top-down design and modularization make structured analysis and design the accepted way to develop both systems and applications software.

A brief description and illustration of several of the key tools of the structured techniques will complete this section. The tools described are:

- Data flow diagram
- Data dictionary
- Structured English statement
- Output report layout
- Hierarchical design organization

Figure 7.11 indicates a typical structured data flow diagram. It depicts physical entities (e.g., store and warehouse), data stores (customer and inventory file), and process boxes (edit and verify order). The objective of the process illustrated is to accept an order from a store and eventually deliver the goods ordered back to the store.

The first process is to edit the particular order form and verify that the proper ordering procedures have been followed. The customer data store (file) is then interrogated to ascertain if the particular store's credit is within specified limits. Once this has been determined, the order is screened against the inventory data store (file) for inventory availability. If the items are in stock, the quantities are extended based on price, weight, and so on and an order form is produced. This is the authorization for the warehouse to pick and load the order on a truck or whatever and deliver the goods to the store that originated the order.

This simple, first-level flow diagram does not include processes such as billing the store for goods ordered and collecting the payment. However, these and other processes can be added and described in greater detail in order to eventually flow the total process.

The data flow diagram is a straightforward way to describe the processes of a system—what is going on and the major outputs. Formerly, flow charts with fixed symbols (usually a dozen or so) representing different types of processes and computer resources were used to describe an application. The data flow diagram is simpler, more flexible, and easier for a user to follow and understand. Figures 7.12 and 7.13 are adjuncts to the data flow diagram, describing the contents of each data file (the data dictionary) used by the application and stating in a shorthand sort of English the steps in each process.

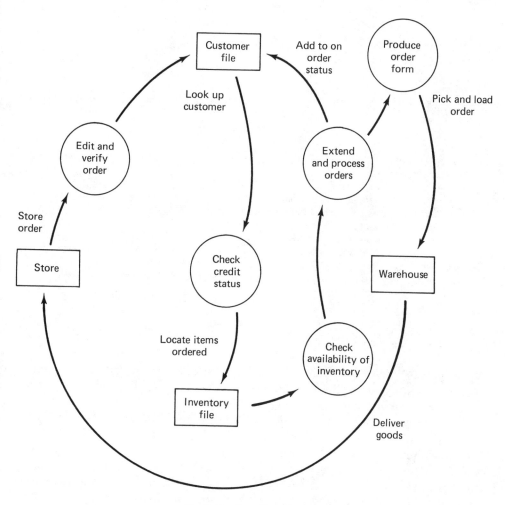

Fig. 7.11 Data flow diagram

Very important in the system specification are the output reports, as these are the user-visible portions of the application. It is essential to carefully review these documents with users. (Figure 7.14 illustrates an inventory report and a billing form.) The result of systems analysis is a user-oriented specification, and one of the keys to successful development is to obtain a user sign-off on the specification. This will involve a careful analysis of the output reports as well as an agreement on the response time of on-line transactions and the turnaround time on batch or periodic reports.

Figure 7.15 is a hierarchical diagram used in the design phase. The application is broken down into a process organization showing the various systems modules (processes) and the components of each. This is an excellent technique for ensuring that the total job is understood and divided into logical entities that fit together to comprise the process of the next higher order.

CUSTOMER ORDER =	*INVENTORY ITEM =*
• Customer name	• Item name
• Account number	• Item number
• Address	• On-hand balance
• Credit rating	• On order
• On order	• Item price
• Balance owed	• Item weight

Fig. 7.12   Data dictionary

Credit Checking Process
1. Check credit category of account
    (a) if A, process order routinely
    (b) if B, ensure that amount ordered plus on order does not exceed amount indicated
    (c) if C, send to sales administration for review before processing.
2. Check accounts receivable balance
    (a) if less than 30 days, process routinely
    (b) if greater than 60 days, but less than 120 days, process but print reminder to sales administration
    (c) if greater than 120 days, kick out for sales administration review before processing.

Fig. 7.13   Structured English statement

Systems Design

Figure 7.1 indicates that the systems design phase is directed at developing alternate solutions, exploring the various designs, and then selecting, developing, and documenting the one that appears best.

The design phase begins with the hierarchical chart illustrated in Fig. 7.15. The particular application is broken down into specific functions—those of lower order building to create those of upper orders. Structured design requires these functions to be self-contained, such that they can be defined and then coded with the knowledge that they will fit into the total structure. The design phase is the bridge, translating the system spec into a language and structure that can be turned over to programmers for writing the particular machine instructions. Systems design is peeling back the onion, dividing each module into progressively finer and finer modules. Each module is defined, bounded, and given its proper place in the hierarchy.

The interface points between modules are very important. To maintain the focus of structured design, these interfaces or couplings should be minimized and simplified. The more complicated they become, the more difficult it becomes to test and make changes. The highest level of data being transferred from one module to another can be noted on the hierarchical chart. For example, if module A processes a record—that is, it takes the items ordered by a particular customer and sums the quantity, price, and weight—and passes the totals to module B, this is the connection or coupling point and should be so noted on the hierarchical chart. The design phase also includes the expression of each hierarchical module in a pseudo code similar to that of Fig. 7.13. This then becomes the link between the systems design and the actual writing of machine instructions.

Inventory Action Report

Inventory action report | Date _____

Item no.	Description	On hand	On order	Total available	Projected demand	Reorder point	Economic order quantity

Inventory action report | Date _____

item no.	On hand	This order	Amount short	% available	Action code	Substitute item no.

Billing Form

Store copy

| Store address | | | | | | Store # | Order # | Date _____ |

Item description	Item retail	Unit retail	Item number	Quantity	Discount unit and allowance cost	% gross margin

Fig. 7.14 Output report layouts

231

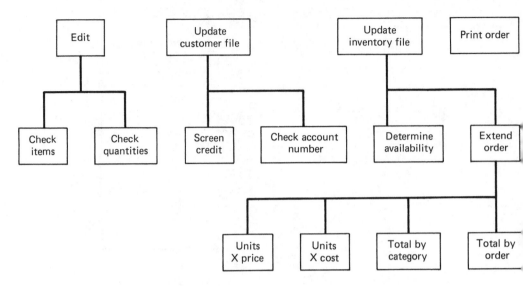

Fig. 7.15 Hierarchical design organization

A term used quite often as part of the structured techniques is the *walkthrough*. Walkthroughs are review points that take place at periodic intervals throughout the development cycle. They are a way of pulling coders or designers away from the detail for a time in order to stand back, make a review of progress, and ensure that what they are doing is on track and in line with the original specifications. The purpose of a walkthrough in the design phase is to look for errors, flaws, weaknesses, omissions, and ambiguities in the design prior to commencing the coding. The later an error is found, the more embedded it becomes and the more difficult it is to correct. Walkthroughs are not the formal, management type of reviews that also are part of the development cycle; they are more informal, local, and working-level oriented. In the case of a design walkthrough, the designers would step through the modules of one trunk of the hierarchical chart. The group may consist of two or three designers, with the person who developed the specification also sitting in. The logic of the module plus the coupling points between modules would be checked and tested for logic and continuity. Walkthroughs should be conducted frequently at logical breakpoints in the design.

Resource Utilization

Up to this point we have not considered hardware or software configurations, except in very broad terms to supply costs for calculating return on investment during the feasibility phase. At this juncture, the objective is to verify the ROI or cost/ benefit analysis, since we have a better handle on system objectives and the components of the system itself as a result of completing the analysis phase.

During the feasibility phase, we had to guesstimate the hardware and software resources necessary to accomplish the application. The systems study has helped confirm the guesstimates, and the resource utilization phase should enable us to pinpoint the hardware (central processor, disk storage, terminals, printers, etc.) necessary to accomplish the job as well as the systems software and supporting services. With the advent of distributed data processing, as described in Chapter 5, the job of resource selection is a bit more difficult. Systems have more options open to them, such as mini- or microcomputers, shared data bases, and remote work stations. All these elements must be analyzed to come up with the final configuration.

At this point, a good hard look at the resources necessary to complete the design and implementation of the application is in order. If this application has been considered in the long-range plan, we should have already incorporated the necessary hardware, software, and people resources into an operating budget. However, things have a way of changing, so it is important to review the various options. The first consideration is doing the application in-house. If ample application designers and programmers are available, this of course is a straightforward solution. More often than not, however, there exists a heavy backlog of application development, and people resources will be tight.

An alternative approach is to see whether an available application package will do the entire job or at least serve as a framework for it. Packages are becoming a more viable alternative to in-house development; potential package solutions should be investigated thoroughly to determine if they will do the job or if it will take more work to tailor and specialize than to begin from scratch. One advantage in following the sequence outlined in this development cycle is that, at this stage, you will have completed the systems study and have a good idea of just what the package must accomplish.

Another outside resource that should be carefully analyzed is time-sharing services. Time-sharing companies have developed hardware and software systems aimed at specific areas of operation that may be extremely critical to MIS. For example, some time-sharing services are focused on scientific or management science applications. It may be possible to satisfy a good portion of the engineering and research department's system needs by utilizing such a service. A terminal can be placed in the engineering department. The central computer has access to a library of scientific subroutines, regression analysis, coordinate geometry, stress analysis, and the like, allowing the engineer to enter variable data pertinent to the products being designed. He then calls forth subroutines from the time-sharing service company's scientific library to solve his particular problems.

Also available are a variety of support arrangements ranging from part-time programmers to "facilities management" firms. The latter will undertake to bid on any job or system requirement. This area may involve (a) basic consultation on a specific subsystem or (b) full responsibility for the resources (including the computer itself) necessary to accomplish a major system. For example, a company might subcontract the development and implementation of its entire market system to a facilities management firm.

The proliferation of hardware, software, and service companies presents a challenging dilemma for the MIS manager. Available to him are a wide variety of alternatives for obtaining computer power. Although there are opportunities for selecting a source or a combination of sources that can get him where he wants to be in a faster and more economical manner, he must be careful to base his decisions on an analytical evaluation of the alternatives. There is significant risk in contracting the wrong job to the wrong service company.

OBJECTIVE SELECTION TECHNIQUES

Whether a company is acquiring a new computer system, systems or application software, outside consulting/contracting services, or any combination thereof, an objective method of evaluating competitive offerings is essential. The method need not be highly sophisticated or statistically based to be effective. Often a simple technique of deciding what the decision criteria are and then rating the potential vendors against them will do very nicely. The important thing is to know the job well enough to determine which criteria are important and which irrelevant. A good systems study should lay the groundwork for determining these criteria.

A basic method, for example, of selecting a potential application package would have the following steps. This technique can be used to evaluate different options, including hardware selection.

1. Determining decision criteria
2. Establishing relative importance of criteria
3. Rate each package (vendor) on how well it fulfills these criteria.

1. Determining Decision Criteria.

The decision criteria emanate from the basic system specifications. It is somewhat like selecting an individual for a particular job opening: the first step is to have a thorough understanding of the job. Decision criteria usually can be separated into two categories: (1) the necessary criteria, which must be met before further consideration is given, and (2) the desirable criteria, which, though not essential, are considered extremely important in the evaluation. The necessary criteria should be selected carefully, because a hasty selection may arbitrarily eliminate a package at this stage. Examples of necessary criteria are as follows:

Necessary Criteria	Package A	Package B	Package C	Package D
Accomplishes at least 75 percent of job	x	x	x	x
Has been successfully installed	x	x	x	
Is easily modifiable	x	x	x	x
Vendor can provide adequate support	x		x	x

In this instance, all four packages are deemed suitable for the job, but package D has not yet been installed. Since the company does not want to be a pioneer in an application area vital to its operation, it eliminates package D. All four purport to be easily modifiable, but the vendor of package B is evaluated as not having the necessary support personnel to assist in modifying it. This is considered very important to the company and therefore package B is eliminated, leaving packages A and C as potential candidates for the job.

Next we turn to available criteria upon which to rate the remaining packages. Since we have not placed any relative weight on the mandatory criteria, we want to include them as well in our rating. Figure 7.16 lists a set of desirable criteria under the categories of functionality, support, and cost.

2. Establishing Relative Importance of Criteria.

Figure 7.17 indicates a weighting of the various criteria. This obviously will be a function of a company's situation, its level of resources, and the expertise of its personnel. For example, if a company plans to do the customization of the package in-house and there is ample expertise, little weight would be placed on a vendor's ability to customize the package. In this instance a weight of 50 has been placed on functionality, 30 on support, and 20 on cost. The individual items within each category are likewise dependent on the company's capabilities. The items shown here are merely a checklist to ensure that all cost elements are considered. Cost obviously is the most readily quantifiable of the criteria; if not properly addressed, however, it can be quite illusive.

3. Vendor Rating.

Figure 7.18 adds the rating score given to each vendor on each of the decision criteria. In this example a rating scale of 1 to 10 is used. As one goes through an evaluation of this type, it becomes obvious that a good number of value judgments must be made. However, the method provides a consistent framework for evaluating those elements for which objective methods exist and for pointing out those areas where more subjective evaluation is required. This allows the decision maker to subdivide the problem into individual elements, thereby separating those that can be resolved by objective means and from those that require more subjective methods.

In the example used here, package A is superior, offsetting the greater ability of B to train, consult, and assist in tailoring the package as well as the lower cost of B. As mentioned, other factors must be included in the selection, such as the company's ability to tailor the package itself if package A requires it.

Methods are available to qualify your ratings, if the degree of uncertainty or risk in your evaluation warrants their use and if time permits. To begin with, this may be the logical time to consider an outside consultant. If the company has a solid awareness of the job to be done and has established its own decision criteria using the described decision framework, a consultant may prove very useful. A consultant may possess the necessary knowledge and contacts with companies using competitive products so that he can present a reasonable and fairly accurate competitive ap-

General Category	Desirable Criteria	Value	Package A		Package B	
			Score	Wgt.	Score	Wgt.
Functionality	Ability to meet specs					
	Ease of use					
	Ease of tailoring					
	Source code available					
	Audit controls					
	Documentation					
	Maintenance/update plan					
	Subtotal					
Support	Education/training					
	Routine consulting					
	Advanced consulting					
	Assistance in tailoring					
	Responsiveness					
	Proximity					
	Vendor relationship					
	Subtotal					
Cost	Program license fee					
	Installation charge					
	Maintenance fee					
	Customizing charges					
	Training fees					
	Subtotal					
	Grand Total					

Fig. 7.16

praisal. At the same time, the company's internal staff may want to proceed with its own independent evaluation.

Such an independent evaluation would include a careful review of the available literature and presentations made by the prospective vendor. It might also involve a formal issuance of the specifications, requesting interested vendors to submit a proposal indicating how their product would meet them. Reference accounts are certainly valuable in assessing how the product has performed in other environments. This approach must be used judiciously, as every situation is to some degree unique. Probably the most valid evaluation, although costly to conduct and not always feasible, is a benchmark test. The company develops test input to drive the application system. The vendor then makes whatever arrangements are necessary to demonstrate his application, using the prescribed input data. The company can then measure response time, adequacy of output, and system performance for those vendors who are

General Category	Desirable Criteria	Value	Package A		Package B	
			Score	Wgt.	Score	Wgt.
<u>50</u> Functionality	Ability to meet specs	20				
	Ease of use	10				
	Ease of tailoring	5				
	Source code available	2				
	Audit controls	3				
	Documentation	5				
	Maintenance/update plan	5				
	Subtotal	50				
<u>30</u> Support	Education/training	10				
	Routine consulting	10				
	Advanced consulting	2				
	Assistance in tailoring	2				
	Responsiveness	2				
	Proximity	2				
	Vendor relationship	2				
	Subtotal	30				
<u>20</u> Cost	Program license fee					
	Installation charge					
	Maintenance fee					
	Customizing charges					
	Training fees					
	Subtotal	20				
	Grand Total	100				

Fig. 7.17

capable of running the benchmark. While this looks to be the most objective measure of them all, it does place demands on the company to develop a comprehensive set of test data that is representative of the projected workload, and it may penalize a vendor who has a highly functional package but limited resources to conduct the demonstration.

IMPLEMENTATION

Figure 7.1 lists the major functions performed during the implementation phase of a management information system. If the implementation involves a major addition of hardware, site preparation work is required. Otherwise, implementation involves the individual programming, testing, and operational running of programs that consti-

General Category	Desirable Criteria	Value	Package A Score	Package A Wgt.	Package B Score	Package B Wgt.
50 Functionality	Ability to meet specs	20	8	160	5	100
	Ease of use	10	8	160	5	100
	Ease of tailoring	5	10	50	6	30
	Source code available	2	10	20	10	20
	Audit controls	3	6	18	4	12
	Documentation	5	8	40	4	20
	Maintenance/update plan	5	8	40	4	20
	Subtotal	50		488		302
30 Support	Education/training	10	8	80	10	100
	Routine consulting	10	8	80	10	100
	Advanced consulting	2	6	12	10	20
	Assistance in tailoring	2	6	12	8	16
	Responsiveness	2	6	12	8	16
	Proximity	2	10	20	8	16
	Vendor relationship	2	10	20	10	20
	Subtotal	30		236		288
20 Cost	Program license fee					
	Installation charge					
	Maintenance fee					
	Customizing charges					
	Training fees					
	Subtotal	20	8	160	10	200
	Grand Total	100		884		790

Fig. 7.18

tute the application subsystems that in turn are part of the MIS. The maintenance and modification phase covers the continued modification, correction, and updating of operational computer programs. It reflects the fact that continued productive running of computer applications, as well as the inevitable changes in business conditions, will necessitate periodic changes and alterations. This important maintenance and modification activity must be anticipated and planned for in advance.

Not much more will be said of the actual coding of applications. It is the detailed and rather painstaking task of translating the documented design into computer instructions. A particular computer language is selected on the basis of internal standards and the nature of the application. The structured walkthrough is pertinent in the coding phase. Particularly in coding, it is easy to get wrapped up in detail, so that periodic reviews by all members of the team are important to ensure the coding is moving along in line with the original systems analysis and design.

One organizational concept that has become popular is the *chief programmer team*, an adaptation of the division-of-labor concept. Rather than have every programmer do his or her own coding, documenting, and general administrative work, a chief programmer is made responsible for most of the programming and all of the critical sections. He or she directs the effort of a group whose members are assigned the other supportive duties. The chief programmer and his support team have been compared to a head surgeon leading a surgical team or a pilot heading up a flight team. This division and specialization of duties is said to produce better and faster results.

Testing is a vital part of the implementation phase. The structured techniques also include structured or top-down testing. The key is to test the top modules first to see that they are logical and work before testing their components. This enables dealing with end products and end users—and, since they are the system's final beneficiaries, this is critical. If there is a flaw in an end report, it is certainly better to detect it in the beginning and in a top module rather than in a lower module and have to change all the intermediate modules. In order to test in this manner, dummy routines or what are called *stub modules* must be created to produce output from the lower modules before they are coded so that the higher-order modules can be tested. Individual module or program testing must be supplemented by full systems testing. It cannot be assumed that, because the modules test out individually, they will also test as a system. Systems people have been trying to avoid this trap for decades.

Fred Brooks, a prominent software developer, refers in his book *The Mythical Man Month* to a "9 times" principle. It is observed, much to the chagrin of professional programmers from large corporations, that small so-called garage shops or personal computer programmers can seemingly turn out working programs in a fraction of the time it takes the big shops. In reality, however, as Brooks points out, the programs they develop can be classified as 1 times programs. To fully document, develop controls, build in error checks, and test a program takes 3 times, and to document, test, and so on as part of a total system takes 9 times. The garage-shop program does a specific job for a specific environment. In a large corporation's MIS development, however, applications must be integrated and run in a complex-data-base, distributed-data-processing environment. This is demanding of time, skill, and effort. Whether the figure is 3 times, 6 times, or 9 times, the point is valid that there is a difference between what developers call a "productized" application and a garage shop ad hoc application.

THE MAINTENANCE/MODIFICATION PHASE

Maintenance/modification is the last phase of the application development cycle. Often this vital phase is not properly considered in MIS development. With the pressure of getting the application installed and in operation, the use of short-cuts, temporary patches in programs, and a variety of expedients is inevitable.

During the implementation phase, the programmers and systems analysts accumulate a list of changes they know should be instituted. These have been deferred because they do not affect the day-to-day running of the application and can be added later—for example, checking features that increase the accuracy of the input and output but do not necessarily prevent the job from running to completion. Besides the internal list of desirable changes and modifications, there are external lists. The users of the system will point out what they think are errors and inconsistencies in the computer reports they receive. Though some such problems may be resolved by additional discussion and clarification, some remedies no doubt will have to be incorporated into the system.

Furthermore, it is inevitable that undetected errors will appear later, as volume running produces unique combinations of transactions and conditions that were not foreseen and therefore not tested.

A prudent course of action is to undergo a period of introspective evaluation before moving on to other applications. This will ensure that there is a solid foundation on which to base further additions and extensions. Thus the first activity of the maintenance and modification subphase is *evaluation*. The evaluation sets the stage for the second activity, called *fine tuning*, when the problems uncovered in the evaluation are analyzed and resolved.

After the evaluation, the first order of business is to establish priorities among the problem areas. Errors in applications such as payroll or commission payments, which involve monetary payments to employees, represent high-priority items. On the other hand, inconsistencies in a quarterly report that do not involve monetary payment are low-priority items. In these examples it is relatively easy to determine priorities; in practice there will be situations that require considerable judgment before a realistic priority can be established.

It is important to distinguish between two categories of computer problems. The first represents problems that are definite errors and have to be corrected in time. This class of problem falls under the category of *maintenance*. The other category is called *modification*. Modification requests do not represent actual errors but rather alterations or changes that will improve the effectiveness of an application. For example, it might be as simple as a buyer wanting to see the sequence of columns reversed on a particular report for greater clarity, or it may be the addition of a maximum/minimum field to an inventory status report. Although these are desirable changes, they are not errors as such. Most of these modifications are a result of the lack of communication between the systems analyst and the operating department during the design of the application.

Another cause is that the operating personnel begin to see additional benefits, once they receive computerized reports on a regular basis. The MIS department should have a procedure for handling the maintenance and modification problems, because these can get out of hand easily and cause a great deal of user dissatisfaction.

Another important consideration is the development of the proper organization to routinely handle systems changes. One must recognize that there is a basic conflict in assigning people to the maintenance function. For the most part, systems designers are creative individuals who are looking for increased systems challenges. They are anxious to work on the advanced or more sophisticated application areas. Therefore, they do not look with favor on reworking and refining applications that are already in operation. A paradox exists, for though the maintenance work may not be the most desirable activity, it requires a highly experienced and skilled programmer or systems analyst. The analyst must be able to interpret and understand a program that he was not involved in and that often is not completely documented. It becomes a demanding logical exercise to trace through the problem, find the error, correct it, and test it against a variety of conditions. In addition, it is necessary to ensure that the correction resolves the error but does not cause additional problems in other parts of the program.

For these reasons, many companies establish a separate maintenance section distinct from the new application section. They staff the group with competent junior personnel who can benefit from this experience and can see an opportunity to display abilities in the logic and diagnostic area. It is an excellent training ground for broader systems work.

Whether it be assigned to a separate group or the same group that originally designed and programmed the application, the importance of a sound maintenance and modification program to fine-tune programs cannot be overstressed. The MIS department must counter the tendency to move on to new application areas prematurely. System errors have a way of proliferating unless they are caught and corrected early.

Throughout the development cycle, it should be apparent that the establishment of standard procedures and protocols is an important element in the process. It is worth mentioning the role of standards at this point.

MIS STANDARDS

We shall not discuss here in detail the myriad of standards that comprise a well-run MIS department. Rather, a few general remarks are in order as well as a listing of areas where standards can be of benefit. A bit of a conflict exists in that the complexity and need for integration demand at least a minimal level of standardization, while at the same time the nature of analysts and programmers makes them somewhat reactive to standards, particularly if standards are overly confining and restrictive. The degree of discipline and detail depends on the nature of the operation, but a good philosophy to follow is to incorporate only that level necessary for communications and efficiency of operation—standards for standards sake are counterproductive and can cause a rigid, bureaucratic environment that is not conducive to good morale and productivity.

There are areas where standards are mandatory and areas where they may be desirable but not crucial to operations. An example of the former is a communications protocol. *Protocol* can be defined as the rules or conventions governing the format and transmission of message exchanges between computer and terminal devices. If applications must be linked within a communications network, it is essential that they are designed with a common protocol. Another example is utilizing a data dictionary in an integrated-data-base environment. The major concept of a data-base system is that a variety of applications utilize a common data. In order to accomplish this (and there are big advantages when you do) adherence to a common definition of data elements is essential. Another area where strict standards should be followed is in change control, whether the changes are in systems software or application software. If changes are not properly documented, tested, and implemented, chaos can occur, particularly since other applications are dependent on the changes. Also, subsequent changes are built on previous ones, thus compounding the problem.

Standards are crucial but not mandatory in areas such as project management, management reports, and organizational matters. While proven techniques can be suggested, it may be better to allow flexibility in these areas, so that a standard that is foreign to those using it need not be imposed when a similar, more familiar one will accomplish the objective.

Here is a sample list of areas where standards (or what in certain areas would be called procedures) might prove very useful:

Definition of a structured methodology for the planning, development, and implementation of new applications with variation for maintenance or small projects
Project request and selection procedures
Project control system
Systems and programming documentation standards
Programming standards
Application internal control guidelines
Production program change controls
Production scheduling and control procedures
Hardware operating standards
Operations documentation standards
Personnel and equipment performance standards
Production problem/incident reporting
Computer security program
Management reports
- systems project requests and backlog (month, trend)
- project status and performance reports and department summary
- production schedule performance (month, trend)
- equipment usage and performance (month, trend)
- manpower utilization and forecast
- budget/expense
- terminal access security violations (month, trend)
- long-range goals/objectives performance history

SUMMARY

This chapter focused on the application development cycle, with Fig. 7.1 depicting its analysis, synthesis, and implementation phases. Top and middle management are directly involved (or should be) in the analysis phase. The major contributors to the synthesis and implementation phases are MIS management and system personnel, although there still must be a strong management direction and involvement. Since management is most concerned with the feasibility and systems study, a greater proportion of the chapter was devoted to these functions.

Systems feasibility is a most important starting point of MIS development. The various feasibility criteria were presented. Technical and economic feasibility have received greater attention than operational feasibility. The last criterion recognizes that every company has a special character, philosophy, and way of conducting business. A management information system must fit into this environment. If major organizational changes are planned in conjunction with MIS implementation, they must be carefully analyzed and reflected in the overall schedule. Inadequate attention to operational feasibility considerations has been a major cause of MIS failure.

Return-on-investment analysis, a discussion of the marginal value of information, and risk assessment added further background to the economic-feasibility considerations. The words *management* and *business* were emphasized. Management has been remiss in not applying to MIS the same basic business procedures and measurements found successful in other areas of their operation. The rather mysterious and esoteric aura of MIS, in many cases, has made it immune to business scrutiny. The time has come for applying business perspective to MIS operation, and the tools and techniques described represent excellent vehicles for accomplishing this end.

CASE STUDIES

WOODMAN PRODUCTS INC.

Bob Washington of Woodman Products Inc. must determine the relative feasibility of three application development projects, ranking them in order of priority. The first application is converting the current remote batch order-processing application to an on-line system. It is a far-reaching application that requires a major rewrite of the current system. Intelligent terminals are required that will have access to both a remote data base and a central data base as needed. This application will break new ground for the company. The annual net savings (after additional data processing costs are subtracted) in clerical and administrative personnel is conservatively estimated at $225,000 per year, with a one-time computer and development cost of

$400,000. Besides the cost savings, management sees significant intangible benefits in the form of improved customer service. It is estimated that it will take 18 months for the on-line system to be operational.

The second application is a financial modeling system requested expressly by the company's president. The costs to implement are estimated at $100,000, including the purchase of a software modeling package, the purchase of a color graphics terminal, and the development cost. The benefits are very difficult to measure, but the president is emphatic that the application will enable him and his staff to keep abreast of competitive trends and to assess a variety of product and market strategies in light of these trends. Washington is a bit concerned that the president was oversold at a recent decision-support-system seminar conducted by their computer vendor, but he knows that once the president makes up his mind, he is difficult to dissuade. Also, Washington has heard of the success that some companies have had with this modeling package.

The third application involves marketing and has been requested by the five marketing managers of Woodman Products as well as by the product planners. There is common agreement that while the marketing data base is a good one for processing transactions (some 10,000 per day) and serving as a base for billing customers, it has been far from satisfactory for giving the various marketing departments the reports they need on product movement by product line, by salesman, by territory, and by various marketing divisions. Some reports do originate from the system, but they are inflexible and often require manual calculations and formatting to be of value. Furthermore, the reports are not up to date when received. This application requires a redefinition of the data base and the acquisition of an end user-report writer and inquiry facility. Because of the complexity of the transaction data base, a program is needed that will periodically strip summary data from the file to form a simpler management file. Once accomplished, the new file system will be readily accessible by the marketing and product managers in the format they desire. The cost of implementation is estimated at $20,000. The benefits are intangible, but there is common agreement that with the increase in volume and multiplicity of product lines, continued use of the old system is unworkable. Lack of information about product lines can result in emphasizing a line that is losing money while ignoring others that are growing in size and profitability. One market manager estimated the worth to him of a comprehensive product-reporting system at $100,000 per year.

QUESTIONS

1. What criteria should Bob Washington use in determining the feasibility of these applications?

2. How should he rank the priority of these applications and why?

3. What are the constraints in pursuing these application developments?

4. How would you tell the president his application came out third and you didn't have the budget for all three (if this was the result of your feasibility study)?

5. How important is technical risk in the feasibility and priority analysis?

BROWN MANUFACTURING COMPANY

Paul Foster is a system analyst for the Brown Manufacturing Company, manufacturer of a wide range of paper products. Foster has been with the company for two years, serving in the MIS department. Prior to this job, he was a programmer and system engineer for a prominent computer manufacturer. He was considered an intelligent, hard-working individual with creative ideas. There was no question that he was a most competent system analyst.

Foster's major system job was to install a statistical forecasting system to aid the sales, inventory, and production departments. His primary focus was to enable the company's procurement department to base ordering policy on an exponential smoothing type of forecasting, which formed the basis of automatic calculation of reorder points, economical order quantities, and quantity discount analysis. The system would automatically produce a purchase order that needed only the buyer's initials before release to the vendor. Foster incorporated several new ideas in the forecasting and ordering algorithms. He used an advanced seasonality analyzer and also was able to include the effect of known external events such as special promotions and holidays. He was quite proud of the system he had developed and was determined to see its successful implementation. He was sure it would materially aid the Brown Company by better balancing inventory, reducing ordering costs, and eliminating expensive stockouts.

At the outset of the implementation phase, Foster conducted a special seminar for the procurement department. He brought in a leading expert on exponential smoothing from a consulting company. Although the session was quite technical in nature, he detected an enthusiastic response from several of the buyers. He thought they were quite impressed with the degree of sophistication in the system they were installing. Foster followed up the seminar with individual discussions with two of the buyers who appeared rather passive to the new system. He had an additional briefing session prior to productive running. A disturbing element to Foster was the fact that, although he tried, he could never make contact with A. L. Metcalfe, director of purchasing. Metcalfe was a busy man and was either on the road or tied up when Foster held his seminars and briefing sessions. He did speak to Metcalfe briefly during the implementation phase and was assured of the director's endorsement of the system.

Foster was somewhat concerned that his system was a little difficult to comprehend because of the nuances that he had incorporated. However, he was convinced that the techniques were well conceived, had been proven at several companies in other industries, and would work at the Brown Company. He felt that the significant benefits produced by the sophisticated system were well worth the risk. The forecasting and ordering system would put Brown in the leadership position in its industry; the system would be superior to any system then in use.

The system was installed on schedule. A conversion seminar was held prior to installation in order to explain the different forms and operating procedures employed by the new system. Several instructional sessions had to be cancelled in order to maintain the schedule and cut-over schedule that had been established. A post-installation audit was conducted three months after the system was put into operation. The audit indicated that only two of the ten buyers were utilizing the order forms emanating from the system. The majority had reverted back to the old method of utilizing a manual system for ordering. They used the computer printout on weekly movement to post and update their manual records but chose to ignore the ordering methods. Most buyers were utilizing the same techniques they had used in the past but were comparing their decisions with the computer's suggested ordering strategy. However, when there were significant differences, they followed the techniques that they knew.

QUESTIONS

1. How did Paul Foster handle the situation? What should he have done differently?

2. Was the Brown operating culture ready for Foster's system?

3. How do you rate Metcalfe's role in the situation? Is he typical of purchasing directors?

4. What should Foster do now?

BIBLIOGRAPHY

Brooks, F., *The Mythical Man-Month*. Reading, MA: Addison-Wesley, 1975.

Couger, J. D., M. A. Colter and R. W. Knapp, *Advanced System Development and Feasibility Techniques*. New York: John Wiley, 1982.

DeMarco, T., *Structured Analysis and System Specification*. Englewood Cliffs, NJ: Prentice-Hall, Inc., 1979.

Honeywell Information Systems, "Business Information System Analysis and Design." Minneapolis, MN: Honeywell, Inc. (1968).

Keen, J. S., *Managing Systems Development*. New York: John Wiley, 1981.

Lucas, Jr., H. C., *Why Information Systems Fail*. New York: Columbia University Press, 1975.

McFarlan, F. W., "Portfolio Approach to Information Systems," *Harvard Business Review* (1981), 142–150.

McFarlan, F. W. and R. L. Nolan, Editors, *The Information Systems Handbook*. Homewood, IL: Dow Jones–Irwin, 1975.

McFarlan, F. W., R. L. Nolan and D. P. Norton, *Information Systems Administration*. New York: Holt, Rinehart & Winston, 1973.

The President and Fellows of Harvard College, "Dallas Tire Corporation, Harvard Business School Case Study," Boston, MA: Intercollegiate Clearing House, (1979).

Yourdon, Edward, *Managing the Structured Techniques, 2nd ed.* Englewood Cliffs, NJ: Prentice-Hall, Inc., 1979.

Yourdon, E., *Techniques of Program Structure and Design*. Englewood Cliffs, NJ: Prentice-Hall, Inc., 1975.

Chapter 8

Managing and Controlling
the MIS Function

This and the preceding chapter are companions in that they deal with the MIS function, specifically its planning and control. Chapter 7 described the life cycle of application development. This chapter covers the tools to manage and control the life cycle. Referring to Fig. 2.7, this chapter will discuss functions under the organizational headings of operations and technical support, such as capacity planning, data security, and MIS audits, also functions under the organizational heading of administrative services, such as MIS budgeting and cost charge-out systems. The first subject covered will be project management. While project management is used extensively for application development projects, the principles apply to operations activities such as expanding a facility, converting to a new hardware system, or installing a communications network.

PROJECT MANAGEMENT

Management should carefully establish time and cost parameters of MIS development. MIS development, if not properly controlled, can get out of hand and can run a good deal longer than necessary, eating up huge sums of money. Although management must be cautious not to apply overly restrictive time barriers for the effort, the overall project must be bounded by a time frame. The MIS group should feel that it can ask for an extension, if necessary, but should work under the pressure of meeting a deadline. Periodic status reports can indicate to management if the study group is working under undue time constraints.

Though broad in scope, MIS development is a discrete project, and, as such, should be controlled by some type of project management technique. Whether the technique be a simple time-based event (Gantt) chart or a more sophisticated PERT system, the need for control is present.

Two techniques will be discussed here: (1) PERT, and (2) design process review, which has been successfully used by the MIS department within a large electronic company for many years.

PERT

PERT (program evaluation and review technique) is in widespread use today, princi-pally because of its sponsorship by the U.S. Department of Defense. Most companies that have used PERT find it a most practical and useful tool. However, its popularity has given rise to tongue-in-cheek tales, such as the following:

> When the Pharaohs of Egypt were building their pyramids, operating man-agement was already on the scene and firmly entrenched. In fact, although it is not generally known, a worker on one such project, having just pulled a block of stone seven miles across the desert in the wrong direction, suggested a better system. He called it PERT—Pyramid Erection and Routing Technique. It is recorded that his supervisor had him flogged to death on the spot.

A prerequisite to using PERT is dividing the overall project into its basic com-ponents. For example, if the overall project is hanging a picture, the basic compo-nents or activities of the project might be: (1) procure hammer, (2) procure nails, (3) position picture, (4) hammer nails, and so on. The PERT system organizes these project components into a meaningful network showing the appropriate relationship of one to another.

This network of activity relationships is probably the most familiar aspect of PERT. The PERT network is a diagram representing the plan for achieving some goal. It has two basic components: events and activities. An *event* is a point in time in which something is completed or at which some new situation arises; for example, an event might be the completion of a study or the delivery of a computer. An *activity*, on the other hand, is the effort applied to produce an event; for example, it might be the work of the study group or the manufacture and shipment of the computer. By show-ing the events necessary to complete a project and the various activities leading up to each event, the PERT network portrays the overall schedule of a project. The PERT network, by depicting the interrelation of events, highlights the events that must be completed before other activities can be initiated. Thus, the PERT network serves two important purposes. First, it outlines an entire project; second, it establishes a schedule for that project.

An example of a simple PERT network to depict the project of hanging a picture is shown in Fig. 8.1.

Figure 8.2 is a general PERT network outlining the MIS feasibility study phase. Keep in mind that this is the schedule for only the broad study and feasibility phase. Similar PERT charts would have to be constructed for the design and implementation phases. It indicates the start point at time D (decision to conduct an MIS study). The various activities and the estimated time each will take in relation to the starting point are indicated. As can be seen, the general management guidelines for the study will be established and reviewed (Event 5) two months from the start date (time periods are in months and fraction of months). The presentation to management (Event 14) will be completed in eight months. The interim events and scheduled completion dates are indicated.

The purpose here is not to give a complete picture of how PERT works. A variety of reports and review forms are used. In addition, the completion dates are sometimes stated as (1) most likely, (2) most optimistic, and (3) most pessimistic. These three points are then mathematically averaged to statistically determine the odds of completing a project on time. In addition, critical paths are calculated indicating those events that are necessary for other activities to begin. These critical paths become evident when the entire PERT network of events and activities is completed. Computer programs exist which can develop, process, and update PERT networks, turning out computer reports indicating progress against plan.

PERT can also be used to accumulate costs, measured at each event point. The major expense of application development is normally the salaries and overhead for analysts and programmers, so that a simple compilation of people-months can provide 80 percent of the project cost. However, MIS projects involving major costs other than people can entail a more detailed accumulation of cost data against specific event compilation. No matter what project management technique is used, a balance of the need for project detail versus the effort of tracking cost and time data

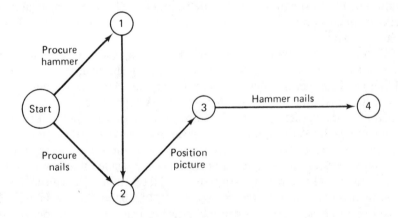

Fig. 8.1

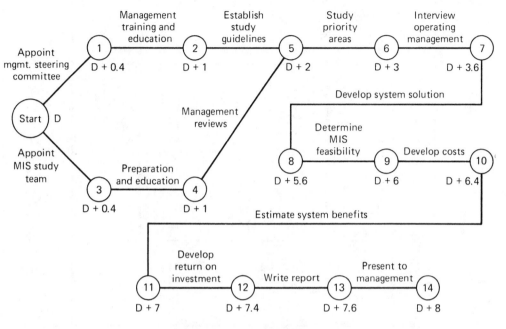

Fig. 8.2 PERT Chart of feasibility study

must be reached. The level of detail and project complexity will determine whether an automated system is desirable.

An effective technique, whether using PERT or another method, is the employment of a visual project control room. A control room showing key event goals, dates, and responsible persons can have a major motivational impact on the project. Used properly, the room becomes a central location for team meetings, team assignments, and project review. The very existence of the room gives the project importance, and the visual indication of responsible parties applies boss and peer pressure to keep an individual's part of the project on schedule. Also it impresses top management that the team is serious and committed to the major projects.

DESIGN PROCESS CONTROL

It should be apparent that no single MIS planning and control technique can be said to be clearly superior to another. As with any management tool, the results depend on management's use of the tool and on the environment in which it is used. Figure 8.3 illustrates a project control technique, developed by John C. Field, that has been successfully employed by the Large Information Systems Division of Honeywell Information Systems. It is called Design Process Control and divides a project into eleven Systems Development Phases. The general tasks covered by each phase are described while the user-shared responsibilities are also defined. I think the latter is

Management Reviews	◁ 1	◁ 2 \ 3	◁ 4	◁ 5	◁ 6	◁ 7	◁ 8 \ 9	◁ 10	◁ 11
Project Checkpoints	1 – Project selection and authorization	2 – Completion of preliminary study 3 – Completion of projection plan	4 – Completion of systems analysis	5 – Completion of systems design	6 – Completion of program design 7 – Completion of programming and program testing		8 – Completion of system test 9 – Completion of parallel test	10 – Implementation completion	11 – Post-implementation audit
System Development Phases	Project initiation	Preliminary study	System analysis	System design	Programming		Testing	Implementation	Post-implementation audit
General Tasks	– Define objectives – Authorize preliminary study – Establish study review date	– Define project scope – Define skills required – Recommend future action – Develop plan – Develop cost estimate – Develop Hardware Software Assumptions – Commit resources for analysis – Perform cost analysis – Commit functional specification	– Data gathering – Define functions – Analyze input and output requirements – Develop alternatives – Select best alternative – Update plan – Update cost analysis – Review Hardware Software Assumptions	– System flow chart – Design outputs – Design inputs – Define files – Processing spec. – System controls – Conversion rqmt's – Design input forms – Commit Hardware Software Requirements – Finalize cost analysis	– Define program logic – Develop test plan – Production run plan – Conversion plan – Complete coding – Complete program checkout		– Complete system test – Complete parallel test – Review: parallel test results production run plan contingency plan – Finalize program documentation – Finalize operation documentation	– Review: problems in user area problems in computer operations – Identify required changes – Verify system operational	– Review performance against: target dates cost estimates benefits projected – Review system operation – Identify required improvements – Decide action to be taken
User shared Responsibility	– Define objectives – State anticipated benefits – Cost savings	– Establish total user commitment – Define desired system character – Define information requirements – Provide user operation cost estimates – Assignment of personnel to task – Benefit measurement criteria	– Support analysis tasks – Update objectives, benefits, cost savings	– Define user procedures – Define system controls – Approve design freeze – Define training requirements	– Review, revise, approve display elements – Organize for testing		– Support analyst in review of plans and results – Train user personnel in the use of the system – Produce user operational documentation	– Formal system acceptance – Identify problems in user area	– User reactions – Measure system results against original requirements and anticipated benefits

Fig. 8.3 Design process control

particularly important and often not properly emphasized in systems development. Project checkpoints are indicated by the triangles numbered from 1 to 11. These are the reporting and measurement points as the project progresses.

Particular note shall be given to the tasks listed under User-shared Responsibility. It is easy to make the error of thinking only of tasks performed within the MIS group and neglecting the important activities that are part of the user interface. At the outset the tasks include the user's participation in defining objectives and benefits; in the middle portion of the project they include approval of the design freeze and definition of training requirements; at the project's conclusion, user reactions to the system are carefully assessed.

The Project Status Report (Fig. 8.4) is a straightforward and simple reporting form which can be issued at intervals in accordance with particular needs and operational style. The report centers on actual results against plan based on the eleven project checkpoints. Both the Design Process Review form and the Project Status Report allow for six management reviews, scheduled at strategic junctures. This, then, is an easy-to-understand and effective project control tool that does not overburden the developers with so-called "project control overkill." It has been used quite effectively by Honeywell's Large Information Systems Division in Phoenix.

BENEFITS OF PROJECT MANAGEMENT

We have looked at two project control approaches that can assist management during MIS development. The benefits of such approaches may be summarized as follows:

1. Forces systematic thinking.

A computer is a systematic and logical entity. Sometimes the planning effort that goes into installing one, however, is not very systematic and logical. Project control institutes the use of efficient planning habits and a continuing awareness of the elements that go into a computer installation. It makes one ask: "What must I do to complete the job?" It assures that various factors are not deferred or completely ignored in the lengthy time period that precedes the installation. Too often a supervisor or manager will commence work on a particular project without ever sitting down and looking at the overall job to be accomplished. In an attempt to move ahead quickly, the initial planning considerations often are overlooked. This almost always results in needless retracking and duplication of effort at latter stages of the schedule.

2. Establishes more realistic schedule.

A schedule should always be based on the work to be done and the manpower available to complete it. A contrived schedule based only on the earliest possible delivery date has been a major cause of installation disappointment. A schedule should be built forward, not backward. Project control enables a company to develop a realistic schedule based on the resources available to it—or it can indicate what additional resources are necessary to meet a required date. Establishing a degree of realism and

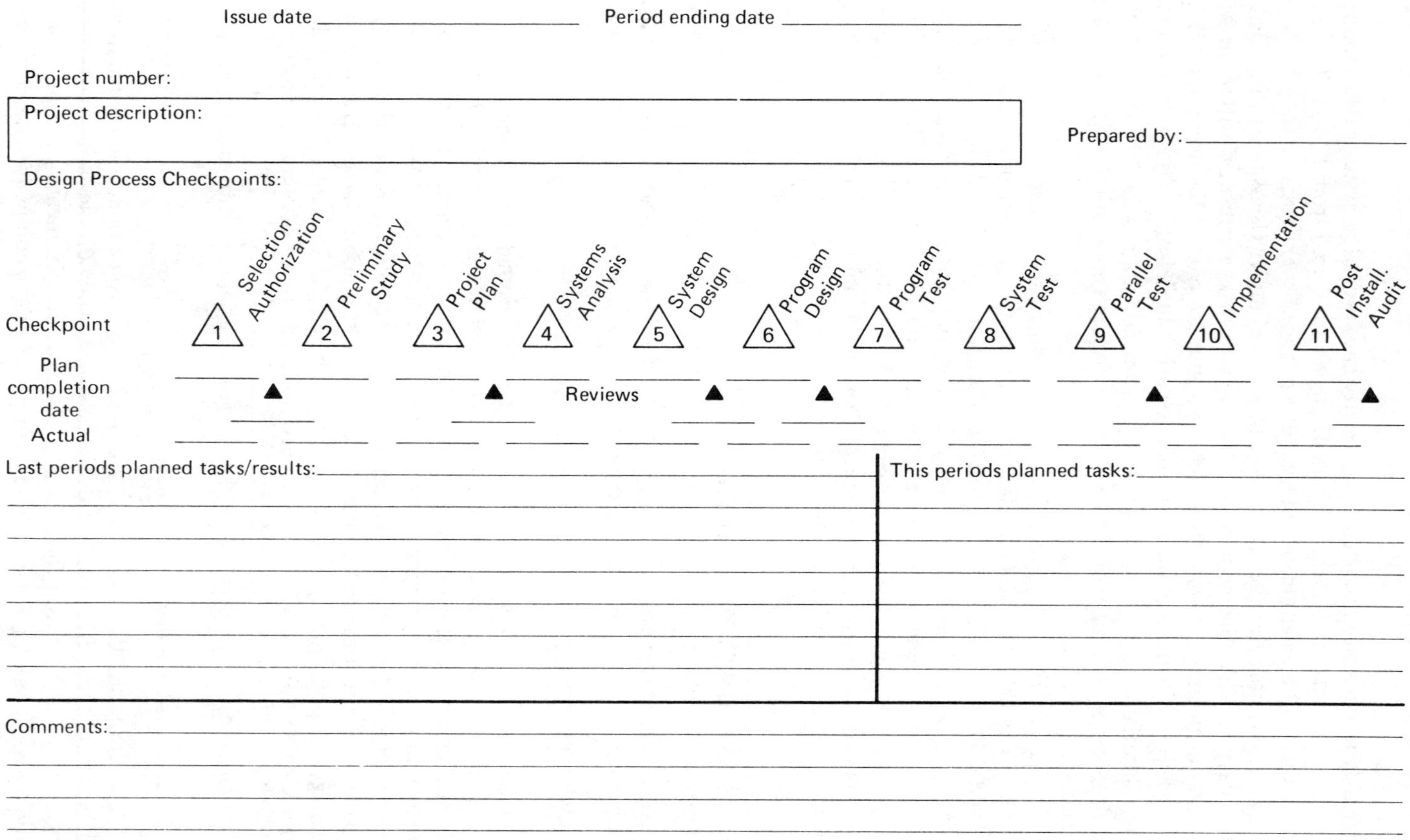

Fig. 8.4 Project status report

Project number: _____

Issue date _____ Period ending date _____

Project description: _____

Prepared by: _____

Design Process Checkpoints:

Checkpoint	1 Selection Authorization	2 Preliminary Study	3 Project Plan	4 Systems Analysis	5 System Design	6 Program Design	7 Program Test	8 System Test	9 Parallel Test	10 Implementation	11 Post Install Audit
Plan completion date											
Actual											

Reviews

Last periods planned tasks/results: _____

This periods planned tasks: _____

Comments: _____

254

developing the schedule are essential to the successful completion of that schedule. The effectiveness of a working force in accomplishing an overall job can be reduced materially if the target dates established have no relation to reality. In very short order all semblance of a schedule and any type of organization are lost.

3. Provides base for estimating manpower needs.

Project control allows a company to measure adequately its manpower needs; for example, the schedule may indicate that an important deadline will be missed if the current staff of programmers is not augmented by new hiring. Project control allows the company to see immediately that either more programmers are needed or the projected target date will have to be extended. It establishes the important but often overlooked relationship between personnel resources and time in completing a job.

4. Measures programmer productivity.

The question of measuring programmer productivity is frequently avoided. Computer programming is a relatively new field, and work measurement for programmers always has seemed a very nebulous subject. However, if utilized properly, project control can serve to evaluate programming productivity and can point out ways to increase productivity by comparing performance and passing on useful procedures and techniques of the different programming groups. By requiring programmers to account for their time, project control instills a discipline and an awareness on their part of how effectively their time is utilized. It lends a sense of urgency in making progress on a particular application. Caution must be exercised by the manager who reviews the application status report—he must realize that the quality of a program is as much a criterion as the time to write it. Although the effectiveness of a particular program is never determined fully until it is completely checked out and timed, an experienced manager should be able to ascertain the quality of the work. Project control is not intended to place a straightjacket on a programming force. Its primary aim is not to force the following of a rigid reporting and evaluating procedure. Rather, it is designed to give some indication of the amount of effort it takes to accomplish a job and, in a broad sense, to enable the measuring of one job against the other.

5. Provides historical record.

There is a continuing need in the computer field to develop statistical or historical data that can be used to refine future schedules and plans. The advancements in cost accounting systems have not been utilized fully in the expensive and time-consuming task of implementing a computer system. It is surprising that many companies do not know how long a particular job takes or the actual man-hours that are expended on the job. This is particularly important when the computer is operated as a service center, charging time to the particular departments using the facilities. The development of historical information is extremely important in order to continually refine the time and cost estimates of getting new applications on the air.

6. Indicates schedule progress.

One of the more important benefits derived from project control is the production of a schedule and the measurement of progress against that schedule at periodic intervals. Project control affords the means to develop the schedule, record actual time against the schedule, analyze the phases that are behind or ahead of schedule, and point out the action necessary to get back on schedule. The action taken as a result of the analysis is an important part of the overall technique. A good schedule not only establishes projected target dates but also has built-in flexibility or the means to get back on schedule in the event that a target date is missed. Project control enables the company to know when such action is necessary in order to meet the target date.

7. Anticipates problems.

Project control can make a valuable contribution to a company by helping it anticipate problems before they actually occur. Without a definite schedule, a manager is unaware of what actually is around the corner or what he should prepare for in order to meet the schedule. For example, if he looks ahead and sees that testing on volume test data will begin at a certain date, he knows that he must make preparations to produce the volume test data prior to that date.

8. Provides documentation and uniformity.

Inherent in project control is the type of systematic thinking that provides documentation and uniformity. Both are extremely important. The results of a computer installation normally are commensurate with the methods used to obtain them. Shoddy work habits produce shoddy results and cause a great deal of rework and wasted effort; documentation must be thorough and precise, and no back-of-envelope type of techniques can be tolerated. It is normal in the MIS area for companies to have programmer turnover during the installation effort. Where the documentation is poor, it is not uncommon for the new programmer to be forced to restart from the beginning. There can be no continuity of effort without effectively documenting the work being done.

Project control also aids in developing a degree of uniformity among various programmers or programming teams. It ensures that every programmer is working under the same ground rules. This facilitates movements between teams and communications within the computer group. The contribution of project control in the area of uniformity and documentation is extremely significant.

Requirements for Effective Project Management

Certain fundamental elements must be present in any project management technique; their absence represents the pitfalls of the technique. The following is a list of such requirements.

- *Competent leadership.* Managing a complex project that requires cross-functional integration, when most of the resources are not under his or her control, is a real challenge to the project manager. Communication skills as well as technical and operational skills are of prime importance. A forceful but nonetheless consensus type leadership is required.
- *Right composition of project team.* This is usually a trade-off of people qualified versus people available. The project manager must be practical, in that he can't demand all the top people for his project, yet he must know when there can be no compromise.
- *Proper assessment and sizing of the project.* The risk-assessment technique described in the preceding chapter is an important tool in this area. The objective of project management is to produce the right product on time and within cost constraints. It appears obvious that a thorough assessment of the project must be done to establish the proper perspective. Risk assessment is also important at repetitive points in the development cycle. At each stage it may be prudent to abort the project or delay it because the risk factors are just too high.
- *The specification is crucial.* Probably the single most significant reason why projects fail is lack of a meaningful, comprehensive specification that has been signed off by user and developer at the outset and then reviewed at specific points in the project. It has been found that the first questions top management asks about projects are "When will you finish?" and "What will it cost?" rather than "What will it do?"
- *The 99-percent-complete syndrome.* The measurement of progress against predetermined milestones is a matter of judgment. Projects tend to reach a stage of 90 to 99 percent complete, whereupon last percentage points become quite elusive. Project managers must be practical and present a balanced picture of progress throughout the project.
- *The proof of the pudding.* The proof is indeed in the tasting or in this case the testing. The original specification should include performance objectives as agreed to by the user, and tests should ensure that the performance standards are met. In the rush to accomplish the last 5 percent of the project, testing may be scaled down or eliminated. This can be disastrous.
- *The medium is the message.* Some project management techniques produce very elaborate reports and even a fancy control room with charts and visual symbols measuring project events. These should not be facades for good solid project management techniques. It is more important to spend time managing the project and to forego an excessive scaffolding of administrative work that can reassure one into a false sense of security.

NEED FOR CAPACITY PLANNING

As indicated previously, capacity planning is an outgrowth of the proliferation of computer applications during the stage 2 contagion period. The need to control the

rapid budget growth of MIS together with the transition to on-line applications necessitated a careful inward look at computer room operations.

Operation wasn't that difficult under a batch mode; jobs were scheduled one at
a time and processed on the computer as time allowed. The advent of multiprogramming and the ability to overlap several application runs added a bit of complexity but
still did not present a serious challenge. A software scheduler, using basic scheduling
algorithms, combined jobs in an efficient run sequence to take advantage of the
multiprocessing capabilities of a particular hardware system. Also, as response time
was not a key factor, there was added flexibility, because batch jobs could run on
second and third shifts; application output could be delivered to the user at the start
of the next day.

The growth of on-line systems and distributed data processing applications put
severe pressures on the scheduling algorithm. New and critical variables had to be
added to the formula. Users increased dramatically and required access to the machine within seconds. Customers could be lost and key areas of a business disrupted
as a result of overloaded computer systems. While the daily on-line workload was
being processed, new-application demand required machine time to test and debug.
On-line applications predominated, placing severe demands on prime-shift operations. Second and third shift could be used only to accomplish the declining volume
of batch applications.

Another extremely important element developed as a result of the growth of
on-line applications: the need for back-up in the event of a computer breakdown.
This need spawned the concept of dual systems and cross-barred peripherals. If one
system of a dual was down, the other one could take over its load, albeit the output or
response time would be degradated. Cross-barred peripherals had two input/output
lines connected to two central processors. Either processor could access either set of
peripherals. This, again, was to prevent system failure in the case of individual component failure.

Distributed processing has radically changed the concept of capacity planning
by offering alternatives that heretofore were not economically feasible. The work of
large mainframes can be offloaded to minis or micros, and central data bases can be
decentralized or shared with remote processing systems. These changes in system philosophy, together with the growth in volume as new applications were computerized
and transaction volumes on existing applications increased, placed a huge demand on
computer operations and the need for greater sophistication in capacity planning.

THE EFFECTIVENESS-VS.-EFFICIENCY ISSUE

There are competing views of company strategy in computer operations. In one view,
the major emphasis should be on effectiveness or customer service—that is, on producing results and adding new applications. Proponents conjecture that efficient machine operation is strictly secondary. They argue that an inordinate amount of time
devoted to saving a few minutes of machine time or avoiding the purchase of new disk

drives is counterproductive to the main goal of MIS, which is delivering information to management and their people. They also point out that hardware costs are dropping sharply, so that the price of redundancy or inefficiency is less each day.

Those geared to efficiency say that computer operations have gotten out of hand, that MIS operations managers have no idea what is going on inside their equipment. Multimillion-dollar mainframes are being utilized the same as their transistor predecessors; applications are not taking advantage of the revolutionary new features of fourth-generation hardware. Jobs are taking two and three times what they should if they were fine-tuned to better utilize the hardware on which they run. The efficiency proponents point out that hardware is being added promiscuously, with prior inefficiencies being merely passed through to the new gear. The answer thrown at any problem is bigger and faster equipment—solve problems with capacity overkill. The efficiency folks point to a day when added capacity won't help any more and operations will reach a point of no return. Ignoring or downplaying efficiency will inevitably lead to this type of cul-de-sac; it's either pay now or pay later.

The Experience of a Large Major Bank

Citibank faced this problem directly in a classic case of the efficiency-vs.-effectiveness issue. It has been widely written about in the *Harvard Business Review* and other publications and extensively covered in a series of case studies used by the Harvard Business School.

In the early 1970s Citibank faced a crisis in its operations group. This group was responsible for check processing, statement preparation, funds transfer, and in general all the bank's paperwork processing. This back-office group consisted of 8000 people when Senior Vice-President John Reed, at age 31 the youngest man in the bank's history to become a senior vice-president, took it over. The operating group was responsible for all the computer systems that processed the huge number of daily business transactions. For example, they sent out 30,000 check accounting statements per day and processing 7.5 million checks (a stack of 7.5 million checks would be as tall as a 66-story building).

The problem was that since 1962, the number of employees in the back office had risen an average of 18 percent per year while transactions had grown an average of 5 percent per year. Citibank had spent $1,983,000 in overtime in 1970. Task forces of clerks, secretaries, trainees, and junior officers would spend evenings and weekends to get the back room out of repeated holes. There were some 36,000 unresolved errors in customer accounts in the backlog. This was the situation in June 1970 when John Reed took over.

The approach he adopted to clean up the mess, and the results are well known. John Reed decided that the back room was really not a computer center, it was a factory. As a result, he brought in managers who had experience in production scheduling and control in an operation that featured high-speed, continuous-process production operation—the assembly line of the Ford Motor Company. Bob White and several other Ford managers brought to Citibank the Bob McNamara philosophy that budgets, measurements, and controls were the only way to run a production operation. A new type of organization was instituted, whereby each line of transactions was viewed as a product line and managed by a single individual. Quality control measures were established under a strict umbrella of top-down budgeting and target setting. Also, many manual operations were computerized. When this program was initiated, labor represented 90 percent of the total cost of the operation. It gradually was reduced to 75 percent as more and more jobs were converted to the computer.

The results of Reed's program were impressive. Head count was reduced 30 percent from 1970 to 1975 in the face of an inflationary trend; overtime was dramatically reduced as well as lost cash availability (lost interest on funds because of paperwork transfers). The following summary is taken directly from the case study:

FIRST NATIONAL CITY BANK OPERATING GROUP

Results

Year	Headcount		Overtime		Lost availability	
	Number of employees	Cumulative % decrease from 1970	$ (000)	Cumulative % decrease from 1970	$ (MMs)	% of potential
1970	7,975	—	1,983	—	56.4	4.0%
1971	6,610	17%	1,272	35%	32.8	2.0%
1972	5,870	26%	845	57%	26.5	1.8%
1973	5,528	30%	564	71%	14.2	0.5%

This program was not without its problems. First, the reaction to what old-timers called "The Ford Kids" was quite severe; turnover and morale problems were significant during this period. The following is a sample of comments from the case study recorded during the Reed/White transition era.

"My frustration is I wish there were more old-time bankers in there, and fewer systems and organization types. There is a huge loss of old guys I can turn to for help in getting things done, people who know banking. Maybe they should keep just a few. Some. A few cents a share might well be worth it."

"One of John Reed's magazine articles that came around *said something about people being replaceable, like machines.* That hurt. You lose solidarity."

"Somebody asked me once if I liked it that we were working in what Reed called a factory. That really struck home. So, maybe it is like a factory. *Why do they* have to *say* it?"

"I'll tell you why people didn't protest the change, or question their instructions. We were scared—afraid of losing our jobs if we didn't seem to understand automatically."

"The changes were accompanied by a great fear that people would get fired. Most lower managers and clerical workers felt management—that's AVP level and above—was highly insensitive to people."

In 1975 Citibank launched another program aimed at customizing service by reorganizing along market-segment lines. This would involve Citibank's early entry into the world of minicomputer and distributed data processing. Like the cost-reduction program of 1970–1975, the approach was bold and radical and was not without its negative as well as its positive ramifications. The basis for this new decentralized approach was noted by Richard J. Mattais, a senior vice-president of Citibank, in an article in the *Harvard Business Review* entitled "The New Back Office Focuses on Customer Service":

In taking our cue from the production management disciplines of manufacturing enterprises—a necessary first step, to be sure—we had tended to blur the difference in what a customer expects from a manufactured product as distinct from a service delivered. In gaining the control needed to achieve production efficiency, we had perforce homogenized the services that we processed. By imposing a kind of product uniformity on our processing, we had sacrificed what is the very essence of a financial transaction service: its uniqueness.

There was a second message in survey results. We were being told that another premise of service had been devalued: personal ministration to the customer. Obviously, we could not go back to the "preboom" era of lower volume and a slower pace. But, just as obviously, it was necessary to find a way to build in the kind of personal service that our customers were still finding in other banks—particularly, as the survey made clear, in smaller ones.

Bob White stated it this way in a document dated March 15, 1974:

We believe the importance of our contribution (efficiency) has been understood by top management, but because our approach has been counter to the conventional wisdom that says "you have to spend money to provide good service," and because it has had negative impact on the security of people, and because it has stretched some of the bank's heritage and bruised its culture, it has been misunderstood or unappreciated by the rest of the bank.

We believe we have built an infrastructure of management, processes, procedures, and systems that will continue to achieve optimum operational efficiency for the next five to seven years. This is a machine-intensive operation that will keep costs flat by being on the computer learning curve rather than on the labor-intensive 6-8% a year automatic cost increase curve.

We now want to change the thrust of our strategy to one of effectiveness in Institutional Service rather than efficiency in Operations. We have hired and trained the right people, developed the management disciplines and procedures to provide better support to the marketing groups. The key is to move away from our posture of planning and producing average products for an average customer.

Additionally, we would now like to provide increased employment security for our staff, to provide them with the atmosphere they need to help us positively implement the new systems and organization. Although few people have actually left the bank as a result of layoffs or firing, the continuing possibility has kept our staff tense and less receptive to change than if we had a full employment policy.

The Citibank experience is a classic case of the efficiency-vs.-effectiveness conflict. It is extreme in that one mode of operation was emphasized at almost the total expense of the other for a full five-year period. The message is that attention must be paid to both. No doubt effectiveness leads, because the starting point of any information system is the specification—what is to be accomplished—working on the right problem. However, efficiency, or *how* something is accomplished, becomes increasingly important, because a company obviously doesn't have unlimited resources to devote to the task.

CAPACITY PLANNING

The Institute for Software Engineering defines capacity planning as "that set of functions concerned with determining and monitoring the proper balance between the workload and the equipment configuration at a minimum cost consistent with throughput, response time and reliability objectives."

Technological and management changes have placed greater emphasis on this area. More often than not, computer center managers project future work from past work without really understanding present utilization or forecasted change in demand patterns. Programs written for a previous-generation machine may still be running in their original mode on the new-generation machine, when, for example, a change in disk access methods or memory utilization may halve the run time or better. Changes in corporate and systems strategy can make straight-line extrapolation completely misleading. In the Citibank case, for example, if computer capacity in 1975 was forecast from the previous five-year period, the whole thrust of decentralization and distributed data processing would have been overlooked. A colossal mismatch of resources and applications would have occurred.

Since it is unwise to proliferate inefficiencies, the first step in capacity planning is to determine the efficiency of existing operations. It makes little sense to order more hardware when there is a 30 percent waste of existing resources. Software modeling systems are available to evaluate current performance and predict future performance. They operate as shown in the diagram on page 263.

The first step is to develop a model of current computer operations. In order to do this, workload parameters are gathered and inputted. These parameters include the number of jobs and whether they are batch or on-line, the average number of transactions, the peak usage rates, number of accesses to storage devices, and so on. Some of these statistics can be determined by analyzing existing documentation; others can be provided by hardware or software monitors.

The specific hardware/software device or configuration is the other major input into model formulation. It is more difficult to develop these parameters from

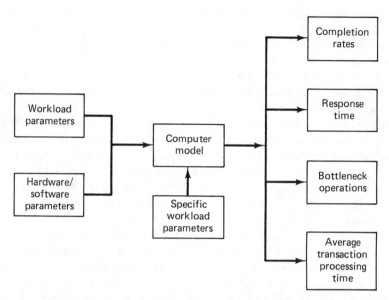

observation and analysis of documentation, and therefore accounting packages as well as hardware and software monitors are used in the process. Normally, four key measurement points are critical parameters: (1) central-processor utilization and response, (2) input/output performance relative to central-processor access, (3) channel time from central processor to direct-access storage area, (4) direct-access storage time to process a request.

From these sets of parameters, a software model is developed that can now analyze a variety of workload mixes to determine operational characteristics such as completion time of each job, arrival rate of jobs, response time of different transactions, bottleneck operations (e.g., storage access), and average time per transaction—a very critical element in computer operation. The model utilizes a series of mathematical equations that reflect the mix of jobs being tested. Once the model is tested using derived workload parameters, the model results can be compared to actual results to determine relative accuracy. Though not exact, a well-designed model can represent a reasonable approximation of the daily operation of a computer center. Once the model is verified, a variety of specific workloads can be inputted to determine what will happen under conditions of changed volume, changed job mix, or a change in transaction response time. For on-line systems, the number of terminals is obviously quite important as well as the amount of time required by operators between transactions or portions of transactions. The model will not only project the future but also point out inefficiencies in existing operations.

An insurance company, for example, was moving into a highly decentralized mode of operation. They wanted to know how many additional applications they could add to each remote facility before having to add capacity. The model in this case indicated the limit of the current configuration performing in its existing mode and also projected the amount of added capacity through additional processors, memory, storage devices, and terminals. Perhaps equally important, the model pointed out where file-access methods could be improved to add 30 percent to existing capacity without adding a single piece of equipment.

Another example is that of a financial institution where the transaction workload had just about doubled over the preceding two-year period, new applications were coming on-line, and the development staff required more test time for the development of new applications as well as for the updating and tuning of old ones. The model in this case indicated that utilization was not the problem, that peak loads were already outdistancing available capacity, and that customer service levels and on-line response time were already affected and would deteriorate with the added workload. The company ran several projected workloads through the model and concluded that by acquiring a new computer processor initially for development work and then adding storage capacity to the new processor to offload a specific portion of the production workload, they could handle projected peak loads.

A more complicated case arose in a steel company that had just acquired another steel company about half its size. The parent company was in the process of moving to a new modern computer facility that had ample room for expansion. Time-sharing applications, on-line data order processing, and manufacturing database applications took up most of the first-shift time, while the second and third shifts were used for batch jobs, mostly of an administrative and financial nature. On the other hand, the acquired company, whose general business was similar to the parent's, was literally bursting at the seams with round-the-clock operations in a facility that was already becoming physically overcrowded. The computer system had been acquired from a vendor different from that of the parent company; also the terminals and minicomputers employed were incompatible with the parent company's equipment.

The company decided to postpone the move into the new facility until it had an opportunity to model the recently acquired data processing workload. It discovered that the bottleneck operation was disk access and communication load. While the acquired company had planned a system upgrade (new processors, disks, and so on), it was found that reasonable capacity for the next nine to twelve months could be obtained by a change in disk-access methods, an upgrade in disk drives, and an upgrade to the front-end communications processor. This would hold the line until the consolidation of both systems into the new computer facility of the parent company could be effected.

Subsequent running of the model with a host of different options resulted in a decision to combine the time-sharing applications of both companies on a single system, convert the manufacturing systems to utilize a common set of programs on a dual-processor configuration, and combine the financial and administrative systems on a third system. Standard protocols would be used such that interaction between the manufacturing and administrative systems could be achieved, though the volume was low enough not to cause a major problem. This was not an easy consolidation and took two years rather than the originally estimated nine to twelve months, but the MIS executive agreed that without the ability to model both installations, this consolidation could not have been implemented.

These three examples just touch on the need for comprehensive capacity planning. The shoemaker's-children analogy is nowhere more appropriate than in the information systems business. So much attention has been given to providing computer power to help users, that a good hard inward look has been neglected. Software and hardware monitors and models have improved and, with the complexity and growth of information systems, they have become indispensable for economical deployment of hardware and software resources.

MIS BUDGETS

Caught up in the advanced technology of our times, it is easy to overlook the fact that all these items have a price tag and that, when the cost of people and facilities necessary to support the technology is added, a sizable budget is the result. A bit of a disclaimer is in order at the outset. It can be misleading to compare MIS budgets on an intercompany or interindustry basis. A basic problem is the definition of MIS; some companies include elements such as telephone service, data entry operation whether part of the user department or not, reprographics services, office automation, and so on, while other companies do not. We will use industry averages and spending patterns as guidelines and rules of thumb, but this semantic problem should be kept in mind.

Data Processing Costs

International Data Corporation projects the data processing costs for U.S. companies from a survey they make each year. Figure 8.5 indicates budgets by category for the year 1982. The statistics were compiled from 250 users, segmented by budget size and cross-checked with known industry parameters. The costs can be broken down into three general categories: hardware, personnel, and supplies and services.

Hardware Costs

Hardware costs include rental or lease payments and depreciation charges for equipment that is purchased. Also included are data entry, data communication equipment, and remote equipment as well as maintenance charges on all the hardware. Because of continued cost reduction as a result of microminiaturization, hardware costs as a percentage of total MIS costs have gone down over the years, though the absolute value is up. The reason for the latter is that companies are adding more and more applications. Management may argue that increased productivity from lower-priced hardware should offset this absolute-value increase, but this is a difficult issue to resolve.

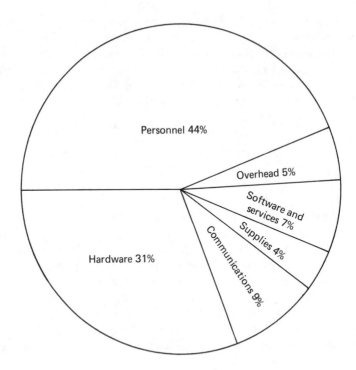

Fig. 8.5   EDP budgets

Personnel Costs

The largest element of data processing cost is the salaries and related salary support costs of the systems analysts, programmers, and operations staff who comprise the department. The overhead costs of 5 percent are predominantly salary related, so we can combine them with the personnel cost to get people-related expenses of 49 percent. Salary expense has shown a steady growth over the years.

The growth in personnel expense is a result of several factors. Inflationary pressures are at work here. Another factor is the increasing application workload that has been added to most computer systems, fueled by such developments as distributed data processing and data-base technology. Also, the application saturation level is relatively low in many industries. However, as in hardware, a key question is productivity. Advances in software development have not kept pace with hardware development. The developments of higher-level languages and improved data-base construction and flexibility have increased user productivity, but there is still a long way to go in the area of application development tools. On the management side, advances have been made in the planning and control of application development. People productivity should be a top priority in MIS departments.

Supplies and Services

This expense category includes business forms, tapes, and other media supplies. While a combination of exception reporting, integrated data files, and terminal screen interaction have been expected to reduce the heavy paper output of computer systems, this just hasn't happened. Supplies continue to rise and in 1982 were up 12 percent over 1981. Data communications costs, including communication-line costs, representing 9 percent of the 1981 budget, are up 30 percent over 1981. The increasing amount of communications is partially offset by the declining per-unit cost. Software/outside services, the remaining portion of the supplies and services expense, is another fast-growing element. This category includes software packages acquired from third parties, custom software and consulting, and time-sharing services.

International Data Corporation estimates total U.S. expenditure on data processing of $77.7 billion in 1982, up 17 percent over 1981. Data processing is taking a healthy portion of a company's revenue dollar, highlighting the importance of measuring and improving MIS productivity.

Method of Acquiring Computers

The methods of acquiring computer power are an increasingly important topic in an inflationary, high-interest-rate economy. Generally speaking, computer systems can be rented or purchased. There has been a definite trend toward purchase, tempered somewhat by the recent high interest rates. As users become more sophisticated and realize that a computer decision is really a three- to five-year commitment (or longer), they feel more secure in purchase. Other financial avenues are available, such as the third-party leasing company. The leasing company or agent procures machines from the manufacturer or in the open marketplace and leases them on the basis that the actual life of a computer is longer than the usual five years over which the manufacturer figures depreciation. A third-party leasor can offer equipment at a 10 to 20 percent reduction from purchase price and still earn money over the life of the machine.

With the advent of common or standard interfaces, a user can buy or lease equipment from several manufacturers or can lease some equipment from a third party while buying or leasing other equipment direct from the manufacturer. The multiple options available and the third-party participants make mixing and matching a common practice. Another force in the marketplace is the so-called *plug-compatibles*. These are third parties who concentrate on high-volume peripherals and central processors that can be added and plugged into another vendor's system. Since IBM has about 60 percent of the equipment installed, these plug-compatible vendors have concentrated on the IBM user base, though there are plug-compatibles for other mainframe equipment as well.

No attempt will be made to discuss in depth the variety of acquisition alternatives, but equipment selection and the financial options must be carefully analyzed. Discounted cash flow is usually an effective analytical tool to use.

Sales Volume and MIS Expenditure

Surveys made of computer installation have brought out the correlation of sales volume and expenditure for MIS. One of the first such surveys in the 1960s by McKinsey & Company found that expenditures average $5600 per million dollars of sales. A survey made by IDC in the late seventies indicates an expenditure of $7000 per million dollars of sales. With the expansion of MIS into other information areas, the figure is closer to $10,000 or 1 percent of sales (some companies spend as much as 3 percent).

By simple calculation, a company could take 1 percent of its sales volume and compare the result with its actual MIS expenditure. Remember, however, this is only a crude rule of thumb, as there are many other significant variables, among them that the 1 percent will vary with the particular industry, the size of the company, the company's position in the industry, and the definition of MIS. Also the level of application saturation is obviously crucial. At any rate, it is human nature to look for a short-cut, a simple yardstick, or a rule of thumb, and in this 1 percent figure we have such a device.

The ultimate measurement of the return on computer investment rests in the resultant savings and benefits. Companies may be wise in expending twice the industry average or half of it, depending on their internal situation. In the long run the formula is:

$$\frac{\text{savings and benefits}}{\text{computer investment}} = \underline{\quad\quad} \% \text{ ROI}$$

Companies should place the highest priority on an increased understanding of this equation.

CHARGE-OUT SYSTEMS

MIS budgets must be controlled by MIS management using the planning and control techniques described earlier. Charge-out systems whereby MIS costs are allocated to the using departments on some type of usage basis should not be considered a cost control tool. It may be thought so by the using departments, but not by the MIS department. The purpose of charge-out systems is usually one or several of the following:

1. *Indicate value added for product pricing.* For example, a manufacturing unit prices its product based on overhead costs as well as variable costs—MIS is considered part of the overhead.
2. *Facilitate economic trade-offs.* A department can compare the MIS cost to that of its current manual system, an outside service bureau, or the develop-

ment of its own system. The latter is becoming a more realistic option with the growth of the distributed data processing concept.

3. *Modify behavior.* If a department is being charged on a per-transaction basis, it can control its cost allocation by limiting the number of transactions.

4. *Educate users.* Users are more aware of MIS services and economic trade-offs when they understand the basis of cost allocations.

5. *Increase service orientation of MIS.* Charge-out systems emphasize the service concept of MIS—that its prime role is to serve its users (for a cost, of course).

Keep in mind some basic precepts when developing a charge-out system.

1. Charge on the basis of services rendered or output received, not of internal hardware or channel cycles used.

In an article, "Controlling the Costs of Data Services," in the *Harvard Business Review* Richard Nolan presented the following example of a charge-out system.

Data Processing Services Bill

Resource	USE	Charge per Unit	Total
Elapsed time on computer (minutes)	253,000	$0.04	$9,720
CPU (seconds)	2,430,000	0.0167	40,500
Kilobytes (1 K memory/minute)	14,515,000	0.0016	23,220
EXCP (I/O accesses)	105,000,000	0.0002	21,000
Total Due			$94,440

The user receiving this bill continually fought the system, claimed they were being charged too much, and, after long meetings with MIS management, failed to reach any common ground. It is obvious that the user did not understand what a kilobyte or an I/O access was and couldn't care less. While these measurements may be suitable to measure computer capacity, they are totally inadequate for allocating MIS costs to users. The allocation basis should be service oriented, such as report lines received, transactions processed, or inquiries handled.

2. Understand the company organization philosophy.

If the MIS department is a separately held subsidiary providing services, for example, to independent member banks or insurance agencies, this establishes one cost charge-out framework. The other extreme is a single-product, single-division company with a highly centralized organizational style. A carefully conceived charge-out system is essential for the former, while for the latter the need for a charge-out system is suspect. The degree of concern for charge-out systems increases in companies that have profit centers rather than cost centers.

3. Establish a fit with the company culture.

A general concern of this book is the importance of matching management control tools to the company culture. Charge-out systems can be viewed as complicated, burdensome, and useless exercises in companies that are not highly structured or disciplined and that follow the keep-it-simple dictate. Cost systems designed by technicians or accountants must be watched very carefully, lest superfluous detail creep in.

4. Establish goals and objectives at the outset.

No one charge-out system can satisfy all the objectives defined for the system. It is critical, however, to establish objectives in the beginning and the relative priority of each. These objectives have been referred to earlier. It should be decided, for example, whether a charge-out system is primarily to add value (costs) to products for pricing purposes or to motivate users to make the most economical use of information. An emphasis on one or the other will have major impact on the system's design criteria.

5. User involvement is essential.

The charge-out system should be jointly developed with users, utilizing the accounting department as an advisor. The charges must be viewed as fair by the user or the system will not work. User sign-off on a charge-out system is as important as the sign-off of an application system specification—or more so.

Gathering and Distributing Costs

These phases of a charge-out system are related but distinct. The company's chart of accounts or general ledger is usually the starting point for gathering the costs of MIS. However, depending on the particular system objectives, the chart of accounts may or may not satisfy the requirements. As a starter, costs should be gathered and organized by categories as depicted in Fig. 8.5. Costs are usually accumulated in the categories of direct and indirect. *Direct* costs in the case of MIS are those that are directly associated with MIS operations, such as hardware, personnel, supplies, and the like. *Indirect* costs are those that are allocated to the department on some sort of usage basis, such as facility charges (including heat, air conditioning, utility, etc.) and service charges (telephone, mail room, and the like).

In developing a chart of accounts, the developer must keep in mind the objectives and use of the information as well as the degree of difficulty in accumulating the costs. The work backlog in MIS is already large enough without adding a job- and time-reporting chore that is not well thought out. However, because the same cost data is used to control MIS operations, it may already be captured. Since Fig. 8.5 shows that 49 percent of MIS costs (44 percent personnel plus 5 percent overhead, which is salary related) are people costs, it is obviously quite important to get the necessary people breakdowns. The largest portion of these costs is, more often than not, application developers, which in turn is broken down into new-application development and maintenance of existing applications. Costs should be captured by these categories and by project and job identification. Operating costs are usually more difficult to capture by job, since operators are supporting a computer system that is executing many operations simultaneously. Indices such as those previously discussed are used to allocate operating costs to using departments.

The distribution or allocation of costs to the using departments is the second major step in charge-out systems. This usually involves separate billing or costing bases for the three major cost elements: (a) development, (b) maintenance, and (c) operations. *Development* costs for new applications are usually estimated at the onset of the job and agreed to by the requesting department. There are several concerns in this allocation. First, applications may serve several departments, so that the development cost must be shared. Second, actual development costs can exceed estimated costs, and the question arises as to direct charge-back of the overage versus treating it as overhead for eventual allocation to all departments. Prudent practice favors direct charge-back. Another question is the assignment of analysts and programmers to a particular development job. A department may be penalized if junior analysts work on the job rather than senior, experienced personnel. This leads to the possibility of several analyst/programmer rates depending upon expertise and experience. Whether this type of refinement is necessary depends on the particular situation, the overriding consideration being to keep the system as simple as possible yet consistent with the user's perception of what is fair.

The second category of cost, *maintenance*, emanates from user requests for improvements/enhancements as well as correction of system errors and efforts to make applications run more efficiently. The using department may hold still for the former type of charge-back but may be reluctant to absorb error correction or efficiency improvements. Compromises must be worked out.

The final category of cost, *operations*, can be the most demanding and difficult of all. Placing too heavy a recording or reporting burden on the users is also an issue here. The method used should be reflective of the work performed, easily understood by users, and easy to administer. Trade-offs and compromises will no doubt be necessary to balance these factors. For example, most on-line systems center around terminal (CRT) interaction. Since different types of transactions take varying amounts of input and output time, communication-line linkage, data-base access time, and so on, a system of charge-out based on the number and type of transactions would make sense. If there are only minimal differences in the time of different transactions, a single rate can suffice.

Another charge-out issue is that of a standard-cost system versus an actual-cost system. The advantage of the former is that charges are more consistent throughout the year, with less volatility and fewer surprises for users. If the standard is not accurate, however, a department can be hit late in the year with a large variance that can have an impact on budget performance.

Many MIS directors and consultants who have installed charge-out systems have concluded that the best charge-out system is no charge-out system. They feel that it can detract from the mainline responsibility of MIS and can lead, at best, to a great deal of confusion and at worst to severely strained user relationships. Furthermore, the advent of integrated data bases, distributed processing, office automation, and the like make viable charge-out systems even more difficult. However, there still exist good reasons for charge-out systems, and when charge-out is necessary, the principles discussed here should prove helpful.

DATA SECURITY AND PRIVACY*

The advent of distributing data processing, data bases, and the concept of information resource management, where data is viewed as a valuable and powerful resource, gives new importance to the subject of data security and data privacy. These are separate but related subjects. Data *security* is concerned with the physical protection of data from a host of inside and outside causes, ranging from accidents such as operator or program error, hardware failure, flood, and explosion to willful acts such as fraud and embezzlement. On the other hand, data *privacy* is concerned with ethical and moral protection of data and involves issues such as the right of a company or agency to accumulate data about individuals and groups, the purposes for which that data is used, and the rights of an individual or group to inspect and have access to the data gathered about them.

The issue of data security can be approached by categorizing and discussing four general types of physical encroachment: (1) fraud and theft, (2) systems errors, (3) maliciousness, and (4) accidents and disasters.

1. Fraud and Theft

This category includes events such as the one involving an insurance company, Equity Funding Corporation, where massive collusion resulted in the computerized development of false insurance policies to cover huge cash deficits, resulting from thefts by employees. This has been referred to in the literature as the billion-dollar bubble. A series of multimillion-dollar frauds have been traced to computer records and computer programs that access them. Many such losses, estimated to total in the billions, are unreported, but of those that are known, the average loss is in the $400,000 range as compared with $10,000 for bank robbery. The stakes are high in computer theft.

*This section builds on the work of Jerome Lobel of Honeywell Information Systems, a specialist in the field of data security and privacy.

The first requirement to prevent fraud and theft is to control the physical access to the computer room and the terminal work stations that access computer systems. In this regard environmental security is employed in the form of guards; sophisticated lock systems opened by plastic cards, picture ID, or in some cases fingerprints; vaults for media storage, intrusion alarms, and the like.

Security precautions of another kind prevent personnel who have access to the computer facility from committing fraud. This usually involves unique identification codes or passwords. To go a step further, certain user ID's or passwords are restricted to specific terminals and specific working hours or to specific applications or data files. This is an important precaution if ID's and passwords are stolen or given away without authority. A user access matrix may be developed as follows:

	Terminal 43	Terminal 44	Data File 1	Data File 2	Application A	Application B
User A	x		x		x	
User B		x		x		x
User C	x	x	x	x	x	x

Special procedures may have to be established for particularly vulnerable areas. In these cases, data is encrypted and irregular changes of code names and passwords are employed. The more sophisticated the techniques, the more resources such as people effort and hardware and software facilities are used. Therefore management must determine the scope and potential risk in each environment and situation and develop the security measures to match.

A common technique employed by auditors is that of splitting responsibility so that the system requires collusion of two or more people to commit a fraud—like the practice of requiring two signatures on checks greater than a specified amount.

A good checklist of controls that can reduce fraud and also help in controlling system errors and maliciousness is reproduced here.

*Controls that make it difficult to commit fraud with a computer**

1. Changes in master memory records such as payroll, inventory, and control accounts should be initiated by people other than those closely involved with the change. For example, information regarding personnel joining or leaving the company should be transmitted by personnel department representatives rather than foremen or timekeepers.
2. Changes to master records should be made, whenever possible, on a serially prenumbered document which is registered at the point of issue and again in data processing—which authorization for the change also should be checked.
3. Personnel who check and record the receipt and distribution of input, output, and traffic between program and machine steps should work independently of computer operating personnel. Furthermore, computer pro-

*Reprinted with permission from Alexander Grant & Co., Los Angeles, California.

gramming personnel should have nothing to do with actual operation of the computer.

4. Master records in data processing should be controlled by suitable batch totals, so that control accounts are maintained independently of the computer for each type of master data. In payroll, for instance, control accounts should be maintained for each type of deduction.

5. Concise records should be kept of file maintenance updating. The point of issue should be notified to confirm updating, and original notifications kept on file in data processing to back up all changes made.

6. Master data should be printed out periodically to check source data.

7. The data processing control group should have these records of movement of data:
   (a) Receipt from source
   (b) Issue to operations (computer)
   (c) Returned from operations (computer)
   (d) Returned to source
   (e) Output records and reports received from operations (computer)
   (f) Distribution of output records and reports

8. The records control group in data processing should have these input controls:
   (a) Document count
   (b) Control totals for hours, rates, dollars, units, quantities, serial numbers
   (c) Batch controls, including document counts and control totals
   (d) Batch summary controls—daily, weekly, or other cycle
   (e) System summary totals to control variety of document batches involving total system, such as payroll.

9. The records control group in data processing should have output controls such as:
   (a) Columnar totals
   (b) Hash totals, like totals of the order numbers in a batch, to determine that data is included
   (c) Record counts corresponding to the number of records involved in a transaction or an account balance, or total system balance
   (d) Cross footings to check columnar total
   (e) Limit checks, causing computer to reject listings of any data not within programmed limits
   (f) Check points during processing to provide means of locating errors quickly, and make it unnecessary to rerun an entire program when an error is discovered
   (g) Zero balance to prove accuracy of computations within a known total.

10. Parity check should be built into the computer. It assures that proper sequence of data is maintained.

11. All computer usage—especially overtime—should be preauthorized, in-

cluding operating instructions, programs to be used, reference files to be drawn from data processing library, and planned start and stop time of run.

12. Computer operators should maintain operating logs, including estimate vs. actual run time, and explanation of stoppage or interruption of run.

13. If practicable, no operator should be allowed to enter the computer room and operate the computer alone. A second operator should be present and both should initial the operating log.

14. A register of errors should be maintained, including computer printout of error, action taken, and record of manual intervention. If possible, a printout record of all manual intervention should be recorded.

15. Control totals should be checked by someone other than the computer operator. For double check, have the computer build up and check its own controls against input data. No output should leave data processing without passing through the records control group.

16. Magnetic tapes or disks should be kept in a library, and someone should be responsible for their safekeeping. He should:

    (a) Maintain a written record of each tape reel or disk with history of its use, including contents, periodic updating, run numbers, and number of passes. This should include the reference label and other information which positively identifies the reel or disk.

    (b) Link tape or disk usage with preauthorization of computer usage so that no tape or disk can be issued without proper preauthorization.

    (c) Use a trailer label with control totals of major items updated during processing. Records control group should maintain similar controls for comparison.

    (d) Not allow any reference tape or disk or master tape or disk to be overwritten during an amending or updating process. A new tape or an updated disk should be written, the older becoming the sire, the newer the son, and so on, maintaining generation identification.

    (e) For master tapes or disks of unusual importance, like a customer list, keep the supporting documents and a copy of the tape or disk in different locations for security.

    (f) Provide point-of-use protection for disks and tapes with a safe file.

17. Programs should include a register of all changes, showing dates, reference to specific program, and cross reference to other programs which might be affected by the change. No changes or new programs should be allowed in operation until they have been tested and authorized by the head of data processing.

18. Only one person should be responsible for an operation at any one time. Draw lines between the employees who authorize a transaction and produce the input, those who process the data, and those who use the output.

19. Rotate employees within the data processing group. This prevents an employee from so dominating one area of operations that losses from fraud or error are not detected.

2. System Errors

The second category of security intrusion is system errors. This includes errors caused by hardware, software (both systems software and applications software), and people. Systems errors can range from a computer failure that causes less than a minute down-time to situations involving millions of dollars. In one prominent instance, improperly placed decimal points on dividend checks actually caused the erroneous payment of some $15 million to surprised stockholders.

Hardware reliability should be a key criterion in selecting a computer system, keeping in mind that the system that never fails has not yet been built and may never be built. Therefore back-up must be provided in the form of redundant units, sometimes three or four (or more) deep in the case of electromechanical devices, which fail more often than electronic devices. Furthermore, restart and rerun procedures must be established so that in the event of a failure, for example, in hour 16 of a 17-hour run, the operation doesn't have to revert to hour 1 once the malfunction is fixed.

The use of proper audit controls, some of which were covered in the above list, can prevent serious consequences from software failure. Following sound application development procedures such as the structured techniques described in Chapter 7 will materially reduce systems errors. Particularly important is the testing and debugging of programs at both the individual program level and the system level. Also, program change control procedures are vital to error-free (or close to error-free) operation.

Personnel are probably the leading cause of system errors. Inept equipment operation can cause system problems and, if proper interapplication protection is not provided, can bring havoc to a system. Training is important, as well as ease-of-use features to reduce the expertise required of many new users desiring access to computer data bases.

3. Maliciousness

An example of maliciousness is the story of a retired civilian programmer in a government agency, who supposedly redressed his grievances in an ingenious way—setting a conditional decision path in a key program that would occur approximately a year after his retirement and would systematically destroy the master files and program tapes. There is a fine line between the terms, but maliciousness under other circumstances might be termed vandalism or even sabotage.

Today, maliciousness takes a variety of forms. Computer rooms have even been bombed or set afire by dissident groups, whose causes range from antigovernment to antiautomation. Modern day Luddites are destroying equipment as they destroyed textile equipment in the eighteenth century. The techniques of physical or environmental control described under fraud and theft are pertinent here but must be enhanced to counter potential intruders armed with modern weaponry and technical devices.

4. Accidents and Disasters

This category includes "natural" accidents and disasters, such as fire, flood, earthquake, power outage, and the like, as opposed to deliberately induced ones. There are two areas to discuss: how to minimize or avoid the occurrence of accidents and disasters, and what to do in the event of an occurrence.

In the avoidance area, important safeguards are adherence to fire protection principles including fire and smoke detectors, alarms, automatic power-off, generator or battery back-up power supplies, and environmental control through air vents, air conditioning, proper false floorings, and outside-wall windows. Proper precautions are needed also for safety and the avoidance of accidents due to electric shock, falling objects, and the like. MIS directors should fully utilize the services of corporate facility security and safety officers to provide safeguards in this area.

A visibly growing area of concern on the part of MIS directors is that of back-up and recovery once an accident occurs. Alan G. Merten and Dennis G. Severance in the June 1981 *MIS Quarterly* reported on a survey of 673 corporations. From the responses of MIS and non-MIS executives on the subject of coping with an unanticipated loss of their computer facility, they reached the following conclusions:

- Corporate management generally believes that its computer operations are much better prepared to meet a disaster than is actually the case.
- Although a certain amount of lip service is paid to disaster recovery, most EDP managers are not really uncomfortable with their level of preparedness because they believe that the probability of disaster is extremely low. In addition, given their present budgetary constraints, they have more pressing problems.
- Either consciously or unconsciously, most EDP managers who rely on "vendor support" for system recovery substantially overestimate the vendor's ability to provide assistance, and they underestimate the time required for, and the complexity involved in, recovery.
- Almost all attempts to establish intercompany back-up agreements have floundered on compatibility and capacity problems.
- Recovery plans, by and large, attempt to reestablish batch operations only, conceding that any recovery of lost telecommunication operations would be a much more difficult problem.

There are different approaches to disaster back-up, starting with a risk assessment estimating the potential losses from different types of disasters. From this base point, various options can be analyzed, ranging from the designation of a selected data-center facility of a corporation to back up another, to the employment of a Sungard center, a service that provides users with total back-up including the facility, computer equipment, media, and extensive communications facilities. Sungard disaster recovery and back-up centers are provided by Sun Information Services of Radnor, Pa. Other companies provide facility shells, with the user having to supply the necessary equipment. There are also corporations formed by a group of corporations that provide a shared back-up facility.

A number of issues are involved, such as the need to back up storage media as well as processing, peripheral, and terminal equipment. Companies with on-line storage in the multimillion- or billion-character range face a particularly demanding challenge. Regardless of the difficulties, disaster back-up is becoming an increasingly important matter, not only to the MIS executive but also to the corporate officers of a company.

Privacy

An issue that overrides the entire area of data security is privacy and individual rights. The advent of computers and the ability to build huge, readily accessible data banks has the inherent risk of violating individual rights, leading us toward a "big brother" society. Thus it is technically feasible to have in one location an individual's tax record, credit record, legal record, voting record, and so on. It is not difficult to see the use or misuse of such data by, say, government agencies. In a lighter sense, the proliferation of mailing lists and "junk mail" is a product of the computer era and many feel this is an invasion of privacy.

The Privacy Act of 1974, approved by Congress on December 31, 1974, will affect the data processing industry for years to come. Currently the Act applies to the public sector, but its implementation in the private sector is being discussed. Its basic contents are: (1) Congress finds that an individual can be directly affected by the collection, maintenance, use, and dissemination of personal information by federal agencies and that the right of privacy is a personal and fundamental right protected by the Constitution of the United States. (2) The increasing use of computer and sophisticated information technology has greatly increased the harm and potential harm to an individual. (3) The purpose of the Act is to provide safeguards against the personal invasion of privacy by federal agencies. (4) It provides that no agency will disclose any record to any person or another agency without the prior written consent of the individual to whom the record pertains. (5) Each individual has access to his own record. (6) Each agency will maintain only that information relevant and necessary to accomplish a purpose of the agency.

The Privacy Act stipulates civil remedies, fines, and criminal penalties for violating a person's privacy rights as indicated under the Act. It also establishes a Privacy Protection Study Commission to further study data banks, automated data processing programs, and information systems of government and regional and private organizations in order to determine the standards and procedures to protect information and recommend relevant courses of action to the President and Congress.

There is a growing concern over privacy in the private as well as the public sector of our country. Companies and institutions as well as public agencies can and do accumulate data on individuals and groups. A simple case is the exchange or selling of computerized mailing lists. An individual joins the Audubon Society and soon thereafter he is receiving requests for donations from a variety of ecological foundations. Individuals have already challenged the legal right of companies to mail unsolicited products to households. Of greater concern is the collection from several sources of data that can serve to affect an individual's credit standing even when the data is erroneous or obsolete. Should the individual be able to challenge and inspect his or her data file as the Privacy Act legislates? This is one of the provocative questions that surround the privacy issue.

Developing a Security Plan

We close this section on security and privacy with a listing of general steps in developing a more secure MIS operation.

1. Obtain executive participation
2. Appoint a systems security officer
3. Relieve "suspect" personnel immediately
4. Do not "bury" infractions
5. Organize a cooperative security effort

After a security officer is appointed as in step 2 above, the following are examples of a cooperative data security program:

1. Organize a security team
2. Prepare a system security plan
3. Provide special training (as required)
4. Implement security operating procedures
5. Design and implement test procedures
6. Document your system disaster recovery plan

We have just skimmed the surface of the data security problem, which is becoming an increasingly serious one as MIS expands to include large data bases and communication networks where data files are accessed from a host of terminal points. One concluding remark: it is essential to think of data security as an integral part of MIS development, not a "tack-on" after the system is implemented. Although this may seem obvious, experience indicates that it is worth pointing out.

MIS AUDITS AND ORGANIZATIONAL REVIEW

At periodic intervals, it may prove desirable to stand back and take a good hard look at overall MIS operation. Some form of review should be considered on at least a biennial basis. With so much at stake and with business becoming so dependent on

MIS, periodic audits should be viewed positively by the MIS director and corporate management.

Several recent MIS surveys have reached similar conclusions regarding the degree to which companies utilize outside and inside groups to evaluate computer operations. Less than 25 percent of companies with installed small and medium-scale computers conduct outside evaluations of their computer operation. In companies with large computers, one out of three conducts outside evaluations. Outside evaluation, then, is not the rule even with companies that are expanding upward of $20 to $30 million per year on MIS.

On the other hand, more companies subject computer operations to periodic inside evaluations. Two out of five small and medium-sized companies and three out of five large companies conduct internal evaluations. The surveys indicate that outside evaluations normally are conducted by consultants or auditing firms and inside evaluations by personnel outside the MIS department, usually representatives of the operating department or internal company auditors.

Inside vs. Outside Evaluation

There are pros and cons to the use of outside evaluation services for assessing the efficacy of computer operations. A company must determine if it has the necessary resources and capabilities to carry out its own evaluation and whether the internal evaluation will have the impact of an independent analysis of operations.

A prime consideration is cost. A special audit team formed by the Boeing Company to audit its computer operation included an experienced MIS manager, two people who were experienced in systems/programming work, an internal auditor, and a person with considerable accounting experience. After analyzing the job to be done, the five-man group estimated it would take 33 man-years for a complete review and evaluation of all computer systems, including a thorough and detailed analysis of programs. Such an effort can be justified when one considers that the possible reduction in running time of just a small percent can mean the saving of thousands of dollars for a company like Boeing, one of the largest users of MIS in the country. This estimate provides an idea of the upward boundary of an evaluation effort. It is obvious that the small computer user is not going to conduct such an analysis. In Boeing's case, the company decided to select an application area as a test case before making a final decision to undertake the complete study.

A Booz, Allen & Hamilton study of 108 leading manufacturers using computers points out that 62 percent of those firms employing regular audits confine them to the critical computer operations. The study also indicates the significant degree to which operating managers are involved in the audits. The operating managers usually serve as members of the committee that reviews and analyzes the results of the audit. It is obvious that the involvement of operating management or of people with no direct MIS experience depends on the objectives and level of the evaluation being conducted. The performance areas that are most studied will be reviewed later. The scope and selection of these areas can help determine who should conduct the evaluation and whether it can best be accomplished by inside or outside sources.

Unless the problems seem particularly severe and major directional and organizational changes are anticipated, the evaluation normally can be effectively handled by an inside group. The desirability of having a department evaluate its own performance is open to question. It provides the proper psychological climate for eventual resolution of the problem areas uncovered, but on the other hand it may not result in the most objective kind of appraisal. A compromise solution is to have a person in the MIS department assist with the evaluation, since someone with MIS experience is required at the detail level. However, the person selected should not have been directly involved in the application under scrutiny. It is wise to include one or more members of the department that is a major user of the system under study. That person need not be the manager or a supervisor of the department, but can be an assistant or administrative aide who reports to the manager. The head of the evaluation team should be a manager of an operating department. He probably will not be a full-time member of the team but will direct the activity, maintain the perspective of the study, and see that the objectives of the study are carried out.

An evaluation team consisting of combined MIS and operating personnel should be able to point out weaknesses in the system and recommend action to improve the situation.

PERFORMANCE AREAS

It is important to have a clear idea of the objectives of the evaluation before it starts. As an example, the audit team of the Boeing Company had the following general objectives:

1. Assure that computer systems fulfill their stated objectives.
2. Assure that computer systems meet requirements in a cost-effective manner.
3. Analyze all systems costs to see where costs can be reduced and capability extended.

Experience shows that when evaluations are made, companies cover the following performance areas:

1. New application and equipment planning
2. Project schedule punctuality
3. Standards and documentation
4. Systems errors and discrepancies
5. Report-deadlines promptness
6. Computer report usability
7. Overall use to management

8. Operating budget adherence
9. Computer department practices and procedures
10. Audit and systems control within applications
11. Machine-room efficiency
12. Programming efficiency

The list is by frequency of evaluation coverage. The rankings differ somewhat among small and large computer users. The first four areas are universal in their significance. Items 5, 6, and 7 are not as important to the larger companies, indicating those companies have overcome these discrepancies. However, items 8 and 11 receive higher priority from the larger users. This is not surprising, considering the dollar expenditures of the larger user on MIS.

PROBLEM AREAS

Besides considering the performance areas most often evaluated by computer users, it is significant to view the major problems uncovered by these evaluations. The following list indicates the results of an extensive survey directed to this question. The problems are listed in the order of their frequency of response.

1. Internal communications between MIS and management
2. Complex and time-consuming implementation of applications
3. Scheduling and priorities
4. Short- and long-range planning
5. Software performance
6. Equipment performance
7. Equipment down-time
8. Skilled personnel—shortage and turnover
9. Training

MANAGEMENT CHECKLIST

Figure 8.6 provides a convenient checklist of questions that a top executive might ask his MIS director and users of MIS services. It breaks down the questions into eight categories, starting with overall effectiveness (what is being done) and efficiency (how it is being done) and ending with management involvement. This is not aimed exclusively at MIS management, because the top executives of a company are equally or in some instances more responsible than MIS personnel for the state of MIS services. The message here is to open up communications between MIS management and the users. It may come as a brutal shock to MIS management to discover that the users' perception of service is quite at odds with that of the providers. The sooner this issue is on the table, the quicker the resolution.

HOW WELL IS MIS SERVING OUR COMPANY?

A. Effectiveness (What is being done?)
    1. What functions are computerized? Administrative applications (payroll, order   ☐
       processing), logistical applications (inventory control, scheduling), Strategic
       applications (planning models, simulation)
    2. Who sets priorities on application development?   ☐
    3. What are the feasibility criteria for new applications?   ☐
    4. What is the application backlog?   ☐
    5. How useful is the information coming from data processing applications?   ☐
    6. What new applications have been computerized in the past several years?   ☐
B. Efficiency (How is it being done?)
    1. What is the user satisfaction level?   ☐
    2. How timely and accurate is the information received?   ☐
    3. What is the ability to recover in cases of unforeseen delays and minor calamities?   ☐
    4. Are periodic equipment utilization studies conducted?   ☐
    5. Do users generally have a positive attitude toward MIS?   ☐
C. Financial Operation
    1. How much is being spent on MIS?   ☐
    2. How does this compare to industry averages?   ☐
    3. What has been the growth rate in MIS over the past several years?   ☐
    4. What is the split between hardware, software, supplies and services?   ☐
    5. What type of financial justification is there for MIS and MIS applications?   ☐
    6. Does your MIS department operate as a profit or cost center, charging for its services?   ☐
D. Organization
    1. To whom does the function report?   ☐
    2. Is MIS organization consistent with overall company organization? (i.e., centralized   ☐
       vs. decentralized)
    3. What is the pay rate, salary structure compared to the industry?   ☐
    4. Does MIS control clerical, word processing, office automation activities?   ☐
    5. How is the MIS overall operating milieu and morale?   ☐
    6. Are there training/education programs for MIS personnel?   ☐
    7. Are there good career opportunities and an exchange of personnel between MIS and   ☐
       other business operations?
E. Management Techniques Employed
    1. Does the MIS department use project control techniques to control application   ☐
       development?
    2. Are ROI or benefit/cost analyses employed?   ☐
    3. Does the MIS department have periodic audits or reviews?   ☐
    4. What type of evaluation technique is used for acquiring additional facilities?   ☐
    5. Is there a set of internal working standards and procedures?   ☐
F. Planning
    1. Is there a short-range MIS operational plan?   ☐
    2. Is there a long-range plan?   ☐
    3. Do the plans tie into the objectives/goals of the organization?   ☐
    4. Who reviews and authorizes the plan?   ☐
G. Technology and Status of MIS Function
    1. Is the equipment state-of-the-art?   ☐
    2. Does it have expansion potential without major conversion effort?   ☐
    3. Is it modular and open ended?   ☐
    4. Are industry standards/practices employed?   ☐
    5. Is the technology level consistent with company philosophy? (i.e., pioneer, innovator,   ☐
       or follower)

Fig. 8.6

H. Management Involvement
    1. Is there a Management Steering Committee?   ☐
    2. Are users involved in the design and implementation of systems?   ☐
    3. Are user education programs provided?   ☐
    4. What is the interaction level with MIS personnel?   ☐

Fig. 8.6 (continued)

SUMMARY

Chapter 2 introduced the concept of information resource management. The present chapter emphasized the management element. Six areas were presented, each representing an essential area where management skill and expertise must be exercised. These six areas were:

Project management
Capacity planning
MIS Budgets and charge-out systems
Data security and privacy
MIS audits and organizational review

Together with the preceding chapter, which stressed the application development cycle, return on investment, and risk assessment, the major MIS organizational responsibilities have been covered, and tools and techniques have been described that can help to manage these responsibilities. One can derive from this review that the scope of the MIS director's job is immense. Indeed it is, and it calls for the highest combination of managerial and technical skills.

CASE STUDIES

IMPLEMENTATION CONSIDERATIONS

The following conversation took place between a consultant and the MIS director of a large oil company.

Consultant: You've been head of the MIS department for five years now. You were in charge of the feasibility study, recommended your existing system, and managed the entire program since installation a little over a year ago. As you look back, what do you think your major problems have been?

MIS Director: My major problem has been the lack of communications with management. Somehow, despite everything, they don't seem to understand how to make the most effective use of MIS. We should have meetings where the basic problems are recognized, explored, and resolved, but for some reason we don't. I have a difficult time selling them my program.

Consultant: What would you say are your secondary problems?

MIS Director: Next in importance is the problem of hiring and keeping good system and programming people. Somewhat related is the problem of getting applications on the computer in a reasonable time frame. I have an existing application backlog that is over two years' work and growing.

Consultant: Do you use any type of project control techniques to schedule the implementation of applications?

MIS Director: We don't have a formal method. I can pretty well estimate from previous experience how long it's going to take. I can tell you at any one time how far along each application is and the estimated operational date. However, because business keeps changing and the information system changes along with it, the completion date is always highly problematical.

Consultant: Do you have historic records of the time and cost of computerizing the applications that are currently operational?

MIS Director: No, but I can tell you within reasonable limits what each application cost us.

Consultant: Do you supply management with any progress report or have meetings to discuss the status of your department?

MIS Director: We don't have regularly scheduled sessions. When we first began to prepare for the new system, we had scheduled meetings with my boss (the controller) and several of the key operating managers. However, I don't think that management could understand what was going on, and they didn't seem very motivated to find out. We met for a couple of months, but gradually the operating managers dropped out until it was just my boss and me. Since the two of us discuss problems on a day-to-day basis when any crisis arises, there didn't seem to be any need for a formal status review, so we dropped the regularly scheduled sessions.

Consultant: Do you think it is possible to utilize a project control method to plan and control a project like a computer installation?

MIS Director: To a certain extent, yes; but you must remember this type of operation is not like a production-line process. We are dealing with skilled personnel who are in great demand and who can leave you tomorrow for a better job if they react unfavorably to too rigid a control system. Also keep in mind that systems and programming work is still an art and not a science—as such, it is very difficult to establish a schedule in which one has a great degree of confidence.

STUDY QUESTIONS

1. How typical do you think the situation is?

2. What is your impression of the MIS Director?

3. Do you think the MIS Director is correct in his assessment of the situation?

4. What is the reason for poor communications and lack of management meetings?

5. What type of controls are needed? How would you go about instituting them?

THE PRIVACY ACT OF 1974

Be it enacted by the Senate and House of Representatives of the United States of America in Congress assembled, that this Act may be cited as the "Privacy Act of 1974."

Sec. 2
(a) The Congress finds that—
(1) the privacy of an individual is directly affected by the collection, maintenance, use, and dissemination of personal information by Federal agencies;
(2) the increasing use of computers and sophisticated information technology, while essential to the efficient operations of the Government, has greatly magnified the harm to individual privacy that can occur from any collection, maintenance, use, or dissemination of personal information;
(3) the opportunities for an individual to secure employment, insurance, and credit, and his right to due process, and other legal protections are endangered by the misuse of certain information systems;
(4) the right to privacy is a personal and fundamental right protected by the Constitution of the United States; and
(5) in order to protect the privacy of individuals identified in information systems maintained by Federal agencies, it is necessary and proper for the Congress to regulate the collection, maintenance, use, and dissemination of information by such agencies.

(b) The purpose of this Act is to provide certain safeguards for an individual against an invasion of personal privacy by requiring Federal agencies, except as otherwise provided by law, to—
(1) permit an individual to determine what records pertaining to him are collected, maintained, used, or disseminated by such agencies;
(2) permit an individual to prevent records pertaining to him obtained by such agencies for a particular purpose from being used or made available for another purpose without his consent;
(3) permit an individual to gain access to information pertaining to him in Federal agency records, to have a copy made of all or any portion thereof, and to correct or amend such records;
(4) collect, maintain, use, or disseminate any record of identifiable personal information in a manner that assures that such action is for a necessary and lawful purpose, that the information is current and accurate for its intended use, and that adequate safeguards are provided to prevent misuse of such information;

(5) permit exemptions from the requirements with respect to records provided in this Act only in those cases where there is an important public policy need for such exemption as has been determined by specific statutory authority; and

(6) be subject to civil suit for any damages which occur as a result of willful or intentional action which violates any individual's rights under this Act.

STUDY QUESTIONS

1. What are the underlying reasons for the Privacy Act?

2. Will the Act really protect individual rights to privacy? In what way?

3. Should the provisions of the Act be carried over to the private sector? What would it require?

4. What would be the costs and problems in implementing the law in the private sector?

5. What are the benefits, if any, for the company in implementing the provisions of the Privacy Act?

BIBLIOGRAPHY

American Institute of Certified Public Accountants, *The Auditor's Study and Evaluation of Internal Control in EDP Systems.* New York: AICPA, 1977.

Biggs, C. L., E. G. Birks and W. Atkins, *Managing the Systems Development Process.* Englewood Cliffs, NJ: Prentice-Hall, Inc., 1980.

Block, Victor, "How Secure Is Your Computer Room?" *Infosystems* (Sept. 1980), 38–52.

Canning, Richard G., "Quantitative Methods for Capacity Planning," *EDP Analyzer, 18,* 7 (July 1980).

Cash, Jr., James I., Andrew D. Bailey, Jr., and Andrew B. Whinston, "A Survey of Techniques for Auditing EDP-Based Systems," *The Accounting Review* (Oct. 1977), 813–829.

Institute of Internal Auditors, *Systems Auditability and Control (SAC) Study.* Palo Alto, CA: Stanford Research Institute, 1978.

Kelley, Albert J., Editor, *New Dimensions of Project Management.* Lexington, MA: D. C. Heath, 1982.

Maciariello, Joseph, *Program Management Control Systems.* New York: John Wiley, 1978.

Matteis, Richard J., "The New Back Office Focuses on Customer Service," *Harvard Business Review* (1979), 146–159.

Miller, Arthur R., *The Assault on Privacy.* Ann Arbor, MI: The University of Michigan Press, 1971.

Murray, John P., "Retrofitting the Data Center," *Computerworld* (1982).

Nolan, R. L., "Controlling the Cost of Data Services," *Harvard Business Review* (1977), 114–124.

Nolan, R. L., "Effects of Chargeout on User/Manager Attitudes," *Comm. ACM 20*, 3 (1977), 177–185.

The President and Fellows of Harvard College, "First National City Bank Operating Group, Harvard Business School Case Study," Boston, MA: Intercollegiate Clearing House, (1975).

The President and Fellows of Harvard College, "Project Paradise, Harvard Business School Case Study," Boston, MA: Intercollegiate Clearing House, (1975).

The Effect of MIS
on Management
and the Management Process

Chapters 9 and 10 are companion chapters focusing on the important topic of user management. Chapter 9 explores the effect MIS is having or will have on non-MIS management, and Chapter 10 considers the involvement level of management in MIS. If MIS is destined to play such an important role in company operation—if indeed information is a valuable resource as established in Chapter 2—then it behooves management to seek the proper MIS involvement level.

Chapter 1 described the different levels of management and delineated the principal job requirements and responsibilities of top, middle, and operating management. The reason for this breakdown into levels is to avoid lumping together all of management when we consider the impact of MIS. In this chapter we present two opposing views of the impact of MIS on management—one stressing the major influence of MIS, the other denying such influence. These positions will establish the framework, or at least the poles, of the subsequent discussion, in which the impact of MIS on each level of management will be explored. It will be apparent that the role of MIS varies considerably at the three levels, and herein rests a good deal of the MIS confusion. An important discussion of MIS-aided decision making will follow. The concept of the electronically-aided executive will be explored as well as the growth of decision support systems. Thus this chapter is devoted to one of the key premises of the book—that MIS, to be truly effective, must have an impact on middle and upper levels of management.

SECOND- VERSUS THIRD-WAVE THINKING

Alvin Toffler, in his provocative book *The Third Wave*, categorizes the development of a society into three waves. During the first wave, the agricultural age from 8000 B.C. to 1700 A.D., the majority of people worked the earth as farmers, living primarily off what they produced and trading or purchasing the few items they didn't produce or make themselves. The second wave, the industrial age, changed all that with the introduction of different forms of energy and machinery. The second wave initiated the type of thinking that I will use as one pole in discussing the impact of MIS on management. The second wave brought with it bureaucracy and the hierarchical management style that still predominates: standardization, specialization, and synchronization; concentration, maximization, and centralization. Order, discipline, and assembly-line mentality are the foundation of the second wave.

The third wave, beginning about 1950, is built around four clusters of industries that Toffler thinks will be the backbone of what he calls the new technosphere: (1) *Electronics and computers* (the focus of this book). (2) *Space industries.* Toffler projects that we can accomplish things in space not possible on earth. For example, with no gravity in space, there is no need for containers nor is there any problem in handling highly poisonous or reactive substances. TRW has identified 400 alloys we cannot manufacture on earth because of gravity. (3) *The oceans* will become the source of much-needed food, of minerals (silver, gold, zinc, copper), and of phosphate ores for land-based agriculture. We will have the aquavillage under the oceans and the floating factory in space. (4) *The biological industry.* Toffler feels this area could be the most important of all. Metal-hungry microbes will mine valuable trace metals from ocean water while genetic engineering will be employed to develop people, for example, with cowlike stomachs to digest grass and hay, thus alleviating the food shortage. We will use bacteria to turn sunlight into electromechanical energy and use microorganisms to eliminate the need for oil in plastics, paint, and so on. The cloning of mice and the test-tube conception of babies are actual examples of what is to follow.

The technosphere will be blended with the *infosphere*, which will have an equally profound effect on society. Information in the new infosphere will be demassified with the advent of more local newspapers, regional newscasts, the additional selectivity of cable TV and its myriad of channels, and personalized computer-based information for business use. Toffler sees a shift away from second-wave temporal rhythms of working a prescribed shift to a more flexible, individually tailored work pattern and style. The epitome of this trend is the previously mentioned electronic cottage, where because of home computers and terminal links to corporate and other data bases, activity can again center on the home as it did in the agriculture or first wave. The words are flexibility, diversity, and personalization with the accent on flexible working hours, individually customized compensation packages, participative management, matrix management, and the like. Figure 9.1 illustrates the changes brought on by the third wave.

Toffler suggests that second-wave leaders today are like passengers on the *Titanic* squabbling for deck chairs, the dying order trying to hold onto their position

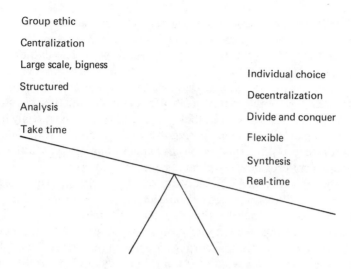

Group ethic

Centralization

Large scale, bigness

                                    Individual choice

Structured

                                    Decentralization

Analysis

                                    Divide and conquer

Take time

                                    Flexible

                                    Synthesis

                                    Real-time

Fig. 9.1   Shift in third-wave thinking

and power while their world sinks under them. In another vein he remarks that no corporate president would run a large company with a table of organization first sketched by the quill pen of some eighteenth-century ancestor whose sole managerial experience consisted of running a farm, as was the case with our Constitution. Our institutions were designed in a pre-Marx, pre-Darwin, pre-Freud, and pre-Einstein era, and before the airplane, automobile, factory, computer, nuclear bomb, and birth control pill.

TWO VIEWPOINTS ON THE IMPACT OF MIS

We are ready now to compare second- and third-wave thinking about MIS impact on (1) higher-level management decision making, (2) higher-level management information style, (3) company organization, and (4) overall job structure and content. This will set the framework for the discussion that follows.

Second-wave managers feel business will be run much as in the past. They see the prime role of middle management as motivating and directing the workers under them to achieve prescribed goals. Second-wavers feel that the computer can do little to aid in this process. They observe also that for over 20 years now the seers have been claiming that computers will replace managers, and little if any headway has been made. The responsibilities of top management are to plan the long-range activities of the firm and to ensure that the necessary resources are available to reach long-term revenue and profit objectives. With this longer-range outlook, the idea of a top executive needing to have instantaneous real-time data on current operations and to be hooked on-line to the computer represents faddism rather than the result of a careful business cost/benefit analysis. The on-line, real-time executive is a business anachronism. Though the top executive may tell the board he will earn $36,000,000 for the firm this year, he does not tell them he will earn $100,000 each of 360 days.

Supporting the on-line, real-time case is the highly acclaimed and still quoted article by Harold J. Leavitt and Thomas L. Whisler, "Management in the 1980's," which appeared in 1958 in the *Harvard Business Review.* The two professors projected an on-line management world in which middle management would be eroded as top managers with information models and an information elite corps at their side would plot the strategy of the company. These strategies would then be translated into structured decision rules and actions that could be implemented directly by machines and operating personnel, thus eliminating the need for middle-level management. I think it is accurate to say that this just hasn't happened and there is little evidence of a middle-management erosion during the remainder of the 80's.

Second-wavers still believe in a centralized, hierarchical form of organization. They point to the failures of matrix management, where an individual has two or more bosses, and suggest that this runs counter to the natural order of things where one works for a single boss who in turn reports to a single boss. MIS, they conclude, is a central service provided to the corporation and should be run centrally. As MIS users, they want to prescribe what they want, but they don't want to be involved in developing applications and running computer centers. That's for the professionals. The second-wave managers state, let me do what I do best, running business operations, and let the MIS people do what they do best, providing the technical leadership for keeping the technology under control.

Second-wave managers feel that information technology will have an impact on their job but not a major one. They take more of a defensive than an offensive role. They feel they should have a fundamental understanding so that MIS people cannot pull the wool over their eyes and not charge them an extraordinary amount for mediocre services. They are aware of the growth in MIS budgets and are concerned that the charge-out of these costs will impact their ability to meet department expense goals and affect their yearly bonuses. Thus the position is a reactive rather than a proactive one. The key is that they are not convinced that MIS will have a significant influence in the way they conduct their business.

Third-wave managers, the other extreme, feel MIS can have a major influence on their decision making. They see an evolving innovative and highly individualistic management style being abetted by personalized executive decision support systems. They see computerized decision models to which they will supply parameters in the form of "what if" questions, with the model spilling out the results of various options, thus enabling the executive to select from among them while adding the subjective and intuitive elements that only he or she can. The third-waver envisions the ability to personally browse through a data base for specific performance data and projections of future performance based on a variety of selective factors.

The third-wave manager is an on-line executive in that his style is consistent with the personal use of an executive terminal. He sees office automation in the broad sense not only as a help to his secretary in typing memos and reports and communicating them electronically to predefined distribution lists, but also as a personal productivity tool. He is the electronically aided executive who runs a nearly paperless office because his correspondence, departmental instructions, meeting schedules, and the like are computer produced through the use of electronic filing and communication systems.

He believes in a team management style in conjunction with MIS. His company has organized around market segments or niches, wherein products and markets have been pinpointed and selected because of the company's particular expertise and desire to penetrate and dominate. No longer does competing across the board make sense. The successful companies are those that specialize in growing and profitable segments and subsegments of a specific marketplace. Third-wave management views decentralization as essential in achieving the necessary entrepreneurial thrust and motivation. This means the manager must control as much of the information flow and support for his department as it logically makes sense to control. Highly defined and distinct market segments make this a viable approach. The third-waver believes in carrying into the business world the political viewpoint that the government that governs best, governs least.

Finally, the third-wave manager feels MIS will have a major impact on his future job, probably more than any other single force in his company or in society. He senses that if a manager does not recognize this, he will probably be obsolete in five years. With this in mind, it behooves the executive to be heavily involved in MIS projects that affect his operation. Not only will he become involved when asked to, he will be taking greater leadership in directing the MIS efforts. He sees the impact on his job not just in the operation and control areas but in the strategic area as well. The future third-wave manager will be an on-line executive tapping his personal as well as the company data base for information. He will need to have this capability to compete against companies whose executives operate in this mode.

Perhaps I will be accused of buying Toffler's third-wave concept and setting up a straw-man second-wave manager. While I find a great deal of merit in what Toffler says, I don't see a great deal of evidence for some of his conclusions, and certainly there is no indication of even a broad time frame in which this will all happen. Therefore, I see merit in hanging onto the so-called hierarchical ways, particularly if they work, until the new-wave directions are better known and proven. There is a good deal of wisdom in the logic of second-wave managers as stated in the above scenario, and it will be some time before the *Titanic* sinks, if indeed it does. Every manager must act as a change agent, understanding the trends of society, the culture of his company, and his own proclivities and then metering third-wave thinking and techniques into his or her world. With this framework, let us take a look at the relative impact of MIS on the various levels of management.

EFFECT OF MIS ON TOP MANAGEMENT

Before speculating on what future influence MIS might have on management, let us take a look at the situation as it appears today. Figure 9.2, which is based on several computer surveys and verified by my own experience, indicates that MIS has had less

	Decision making process	Job content	Job numbers
Top management	Moderate influence	Scant change	No influence
Middle management	Moderate plus to major influence	Moderate plus change	Scant influence
Operating management	Major influence	Major change	Moderate influence

Fig. 9.2   Effect of MIS on management

impact at the top management level than at the middle or operating management level. MIS has had moderate influence on the decision-making process, little impact on job content, and no influence on reducing or increasing the number of top managers required. The major responsibilities of top management involve long- and short-range planning, resource and capacity analysis, setting of profit and budget goals, and, in general, establishing the business objectives of the company. There is a heavy planning content as opposed to a heavy control content at the lower management levels. Information systems have been more effective in the control than in the planning area. However, the harbingers of potentially significant changes in this area are leading-edge executives such as the president of Northwest Industries, described later in this chapter. A look back at Chapter 1 and Fig. 1.4, which summarizes the job content of the different management levels, illustrates why this is so. Control functions tend to be more structured, more programmable, more straightforward, and, therefore, more receptive to automated information systems.

The decision-making process consists of the following six elements:

1. Identify areas of improvement.

This involves either the uncovering of a new opportunity that will produce increased revenue and profit for the company or the resolution of a problem that has been detracting from profitability. The introduction of a new product is an example of a new opportunity area, while a competitive price weakness in a particular product market segment is an example of a problem area.

2. Analyze these areas.

There are a host of potential solutions to improve the areas that are identified. This step in decision making analyzes the situation in more depth in order to develop the scope and range of possible solutions and to give priority to the solutions in accordance with predetermined criteria, such as resource availability and time to resolve. In the preceding example, the introduction of a new product could be focused on filling a gap in the existing product line or could open up an entirely new market. Possible alternatives to the competitive price weakness could be the development of new pricing contracts or a heightened merchandising program that stresses specific product features and advantages.

3. Develop alternate solutions.

Each of the potential solutions must now be developed. The specifications of each solution are identified so that they may be evaluated in the next step. If a new product is to be introduced, its characteristics must be determined, specific market targets for the new product described, and the necessary marketing support, training, and sales plans developed.

4. Evaluate alternate solutions.

This step involves projecting the potential profitability and company impact of each of the alternatives. Although there are many quantitative factors in the analysis, many factors will be qualitative in nature and will involve an analysis and weighing of relative risk. For example, the introduction of a new product may be two to three years away, such that the marketplace at the time of product introduction is the significant element. This may be difficult to predict in a rapidly changing industry.

5. Make the decision.

This involves the selection of the course of action that best matches the company's short- and long-range goals. It is obviously the culmination of the decision-making process.

6. Implement the decision.

Although carried out after the decision is made, implementation considerations must be a strong element in the decision. In some instances, a pilot or test model is necessary to validate the final decision. Thus the implementation effort serves as a feedback loop to the decision-making process.

In reviewing several studies on this subject and through my own personal contact with executives of medium and large companies utilizing computers, I view the impact of MIS and computers on top-management decision making as illustrated in Fig. 9.3. Since top management does not regularly receive computer printout directly, the effect of MIS on decision making is scant. However, this is not to say that their decisions have not been influenced by MIS through the intercession of middle management and that they won't be further influenced in the future.

Although computerized performance reports may indicate areas of improvement, these areas are usually pertinent to a specific operational entity. For example, reports may show that production variances of material and labor are reaching alarming proportions or that the order backlog is growing because of inability to fill orders from inventory. The areas for improvement are generally not of the scope that require top-management decision. Similarly, the areas of improvement that represent new opportunities (as opposed to problem resolution) do not come from computer-

	Top management	Middle management
Identify areas of improvement	Scant	Moderate
Analyze these areas	Scant	Moderate
Develop alternate solutions	Scant	Moderate
Evaluate alternate solutions	Scant	Moderate/Heavy
Make decision	None	None
Implement the decision	Not applicable	Heavy

Fig. 9.3 Effect of MIS on the decision-making process

ized reports. New opportunities evolve from a variety of sources, including staff-planning departments, executive committee meetings, "brainstorming" sessions, attendance at seminars and trade shows, outside consultants, and just recently from strategic and financial computer modeling.

The steps most influenced by computer systems are the development and evaluation of alternate solutions. The degree "moderate" does not indicate that the majority of companies are utilizing computers for this purpose; it indicates that a good number (probably around 50 percent) represent the leading edge in the use of techniques such as simulation that are required to develop and evaluate solutions to problems. Although a few top managers utilize these techniques directly and review computer output, most often the middle managers and/or staff departments act as the information middlemen between the computer and top management.

I have encountered few situations where the computer analysis provided the final decision on an issue that was the exclusive province of top management. The writers who state that computers are making decisions for top management usually are referring to operating decisions that happen to be made by top management. These decisions should rightfully be delegated to middle management and even to operating management. Important elements that are subjective or nonquantifiable in nature bear heavily on decisions of this type. Therefore, although the computer may have accomplished a good deal of the analysis and testing of alternatives, the final decision was not tied directly to the automated information system. Automated management information systems can make decisions on lot sizes and length of production runs, but they as yet are not utilized to any major degree in making final decisions on the introduction of a new product, the site of a new warehouse, or the need for an additional factory. Decision support systems, which are becoming more prevalent and which show great promise in upgrading the "scants" to at least "moderate" and in some cases "heavy," will be discussed later in the chapter.

MIS plays a prominent role in the implementation of decisions once made. For example, the entire introduction cycle of a product from initial design to its availability in the marketplace is materially aided by automated information systems. Indeed, the overall schedule and resource allocation for the new product can be controlled by a computerized PERT or critical-path system.

REASONS FOR LIMITED MIS IMPACT ON TOP-MANAGEMENT DECISION MAKING

There are some basic reasons for the relatively limited effect of MIS on decision making to date. They are presented here as an indication of what areas must be further studied and what obstacles overcome to increase the successful employment of MIS in decision making.

Unstructured Nature of Data

Chapter 1 (see Fig. 1.6) discusses the business dimension of data. It indicates that the data required by top management is unstructured, nonprogrammed, future oriented, inexact, and external. Such data is the most difficult to acquire, update, and process, and therefore not many computerized systems exist in this area. Another factor restricting the development of MIS for top management is the lack of definite cause-and-effect relationships of data. An example is a sales forecast for a new item that is planned by a company in a future period. In order to project a reasonable forecast, the company must know such factors as the market in which the product will compete, the market saturation for the particular product, and the impact on existing products in the line. Whether the most reasonable forecast is an extrapolation of how similar items have behaved in the past or a competitive share of market analysis, is open to question. The basis selected is obviously quite crucial to the forecast. Even if the necessary data is available—for example, past sales history by item—there may be no proven or logical basis by which to show the effect on sales of the introduction of a new item. There are many other examples where mangement decisions must be made in the absence of quantified cause-and-effect relationship of data. This is not to say that these relationships will never be known. However, the problem of obtaining the type of data required for top-management decisions when combined with the questionable decision rules of how to analyze the data meaningfully presents a formidable obstacle for computerized information systems directed at the strategic planning area.

Limited Use of Management Science Techniques

Although in many cases these types of methods have been used with a good deal of success in aiding top-management decision making, the companies that utilize management science are still in the minority. Assuming that the proper technique has been selected for tackling a particular problem, there are still some major barriers to overcome. A communication gap exists between management and the operation research analyst who is responsible for preparing the set of linear equations if, for example, the problem is one that can be handled by linear programming. Management is skeptical of making a decision based on a set of ill-understood equations, and often the OR specialist is incapable of explaining in management terms just what the mathematical processing will accomplish. Furthermore, if a manager realizes that the data used as input to the model does not have a high degree of accuracy, he is suspicious of the results. Although the only alternative may be a complete "seat of the pants" decision, the manager somehow feels more secure doing so than depending on the model. At least it is cheaper, he rationalizes. What he fails to realize is that, although perhaps neither the OR solution nor the "seat of the pants" solution will prove accurate, the odds on the OR solution (if the technique is properly used) are a good deal better.

The Element of Intuition

Many top managers feel that good strategic decisions are made more by intuition than by a quantitative analysis of the available data. They do not ignore the data completely but believe that there is a strong intuitive factor, particularly when little or no data is available. It has been observed that the higher a man is in the organization, the more incomplete is that data on which he bases decisions and the more he relies on something called intuition, hunches, or instinct. We may be putting too much faith in machines and data, in the logical decision maker versus the so-called nonlogical decision maker. Studies suggest that some managers have more "precognitive" ability than others and that this ability gives them a better batting average in making decisions intuitively as opposed to logically. A particular study involved dividing 25 chief executives into two classes on the basis of their proven performance based on profitability. The tests included things like matching a series of numbers (0–9) printed out randomly by a computer. An average score is 10 percent. The successful executives outscored the nonperformers in 22 out of 27 tests. Statistically the chances of this happening by accident are fewer than 5 in 1,000.

This study does not claim to define the role of intuition in decision making, but it does raise some interesting questions. If there is such a thing as intuitive ability and if the ability can be tested, to what degree should the intuitive decision be valued in contrast to the logical decision based on advanced management science techniques? Granting that the logical decision is the preferable one when the data is known and quantifiable, what degree of data reliability is the breakeven point where the logical decision becomes the preferred one? One need not answer these questions to realize that management is well aware of the somewhat illusive quality called intuition or precognitive power. Many have extended the thesis and used it as a rationale for ignoring quantitative and logical approaches to management decision making.

Other Factors Limiting MIS Decision Making

Effective tools are still lacking to define problems. Data processing developments have not focused on the area of problems definition. Despite the advances in hardware and software, there have not been major advances in basic systems methodology. We talk about the "systems approach" to solving problems, but we really haven't made significant advances in the tools for defining the problem to be solved. For example, how does one go about analyzing the determinants of profitability so that the resultant formula can be modeled on a computer? This is not a trivial job when one has to consider both the short and long range. It seems obvious that before a computer can help, the problem must be defined and the cause-and-effect relationships determined.

The "bottoms-up" approach has predominated. Computers have been put to work on those things that are best understood, easily structured, and which require little management involvement. While it is true that there is a necessary application foundation for management information systems in the basic operational areas, it doesn't necessarily follow that an MIS will spring forth as a by-product of the data gathered at the lower levels. The bottoms-up applications often are fragmented and are not built around an integrated data base required for management control and strategic planning applications. The findings are that a "tops-down" approach or at least a simultaneous tops-down and bottoms-up approach is required at the outset to ensure that the necessary framework and plans are established to evolve an MIS.

Business conditions are always changing. Many well-intentioned MIS designers have discovered that dramatic changes in business strategy coupled with changes in top management personnel as well as organizational structure have muddled the systems approach they had planned. While computer systems handling the operational functions such as order processing and inventory control remain relatively stable in times of organizational change, management systems are geared to individual management temperament and style and can be impacted dramatically by personnel changes at the top.

The management/systems gap still exists. Information systems that impact management require a greater degree of interaction and involvement between the systems function and the management function. Coming from different worlds with different backgrounds and different motivation, this contact has often resulted in confrontation rather than communication. Systems personnel often are enamored more by the purity and sophistication of the approach than the satisfaction of seeing a less sophisticated approach succeed. Although it is lessening, this management/systems gap is still a major cause of the slow evolution of systems aimed at improving the management decision-making process.

MIS requires long-range planning. Because it is so sensitive to organizational and business strategy changes, the MIS planning focus must be longer range than has been the case for more conventional information systems. Effective long-range planning is never easy, particularly in the data processing field where technological change has seen many computer installations go through four generations of hardware in less than ten years. Most computer shops have been preoccupied with hardware and software planning without the proper focus on the most important planning area of them all—systems planning, or what you want the computer to be doing for management three to five years out.

Business-oriented systems people are scarce. Finally, one of the most significant reasons why computers have not impacted management to a greater degree has been the lack of systems analysts who are business trained and/or have a basic business perspective. This is one of the principal reasons for the management/systems gap referred to above. Because hardware and software developments have been rapid and for the most part have simplified the interface of the data processing professional to the computer system, the systems analyst hopefully may be able to spend more time dealing with the management users of the system.

MIS-AIDED DECISION MAKING

Despite the problems referred to above, a growing number of companies are making effective use of MIS in aiding the decision-making process. A prominent paper company has developed a computerized model of their timber and wood products division to aid them in gaining the most efficient use of timber land and site location for new plywood plants. The model consists of 8000 equations and 15,000 variables. A major chemical company uses a computer model to simulate an industry segment and the company's potential for a share of market and profitability. A glass company has a corporate financial model that allows executives to test the impact of ideas and strategies on future profitability and to determine the needs for funds and physical resources. Other examples described in business periodicals and trade publications indicate where companies, in addition to simulation, have utilized computer risk analysis, gaining an integrated picture of the key factors involved in implementing a new policy, and determining the probabilities of each event's occurring on time and the composite odds for success. Another area is sensitivity analysis or the measurement of the effect of the variation of individual factors on the final result (for example, in certain instances the leverage of an individual factor is high—a 5 percent increase in sales may trigger a 30 percent increase in inventory and may have a major impact on the overall result of a program, whereas in another case a 50 percent fluctuation in one element has minimal effect on the final outcome).

A large oil company is using what may be the largest and most complex corporate financial model yet developed. The computerized model takes into account the production, transportation, manufacturing, and marketing operations of the company. It is significant that the working version required thirteen man-years to complete and an additional ten man-years to familiarize management with the operation of the model, to solicit comments and suggestions for improvement, and to incorporate some of the suggestions into the model. It is rather interesting to note that it took almost as much time to get the model into effect as to build and implement it in the first place. This highlights the need to reduce the skepticism that managers have toward sophisticated computerized decision-making aids. This type of model puts pertinent information into an analytical framework that aids the management decision-making process. The following benefits are ascribed to the model.

- Makes an accurate forecast (within 1 percent) of net income for one year.
- Prepares short-term profit plans and long-range (ten-year) projections.
- Provides preplanning information in budget preparation.
- Calculates variances between budgeted and actual results.
- Triggers revised forecasts if not proceeding in accordance with plan.
- Acts as early warning system for monitoring activities and signaling necessary reactive plans.
- Indicates effect on income and cash flow by following alternate investment strategies.
- Assists in planning the addition of new facilities and a host of special studies.
- Accomplishes all the preceding items with great speed (for example, the computer processing time to simulate one year of operation is 14 seconds).

The developer of this corporate model feels that it is the first step in building a management information system. There may be disagreement on that point, for (1) the model obviously depends on data fed into it by other information systems within the company, therefore the model cannot be the first step; (2) if the model is the first step, then there will be few management information systems, because few companies possess the capability or will invest the monetary resources necessary to develop a model of the scope described. However, there is little doubt that if MIS is going to have a major impact on the strategic planning process of top management, the corporate financial model of the type described is a key element.

Although the effect of computerized information systems on top management has been relatively limited, their use is rising. There is no question that advanced information systems can materially aid the six-step decision process described previously. A basic example will illustrate the point. Over 32,000 stocks are listed on the various stock exchanges. The job of the investment counselor is to develop a stock portfolio that best meets the requirements of his client. A computerized information system can materially aid in this process (in fact, such systems are in use at several investment firms). A three-stage system development plan produces the required portfolio. The first stage is the determination of what characteristics or indices are pertinent to evaluating stocks. An analysis of this area introduces such elements as price/earnings ratio, dividend record, and price performance during recessions. Those elements that are considered pertinent to predicting future value are captured and put in machine-readable format. A system to update and keep current the data that is collated must not be overlooked.

The second stage involves the categorization of the stocks based on a predetermined classification scheme. Thus the stocks are ranked according to such categories as high yield, growth, and volatility, categories that are pertinent to the requirements of investors. It is obvious that a good deal of professional judgment and expertise is needed to establish the key stock indicators in stage one and the classification scheme in stage two.

Stage three involves the categorization of the investor based on a predetermined classification scheme. The salient elements of such a categorization include current and anticipated income level, current cash position, investment objectives, and so on. There may be some seemingly intangible but necessary personal criteria: for example, the stocks must be in certain industries and the companies must not be doing work for the military defense effort. These criteria must be considered beforehand so that the necessary information is contained within the system to make this classification possible.

With the completion of the three developmental stages, the resulting model is now able to aid the decision-making process of the investment counselor in selecting a portfolio individually suited to his client. The model permits the counselor to develop a wider range of alternative solutions and to test them out under a wider variety of circumstances. The computerized system widens the scope of potential stocks and minimizes quick and premature decisions, which are often resorted to because the counselor lacks the time or the knowledge and which are unfavorable to his client.

The example illustrated here aids steps 3 and 4 in the decision-making process (Fig. 9.3). There are many parallels in the use of this type of approach to business operation. A direct parallel is an investment decision when many alternative choices are available. Market models and revenue models are extensions of this technique. It is obvious that the type of information analysis does not give the complete answer and thus allow the decision to be made by the computer system. Certain subjective, external factors must also be reflected quantitatively or, if this is not possible, qualitatively. However, the development of this programmed type of analysis in an ever-expanding variety of business operations will give the manager more time to explore the intangible subtleties of problem solving and thus reach better man-machine-based decisions.

MAKING DECISIONS UNDER CONDITIONS OF UNCERTAINTY

The preceding discussion has assumed a "black-and-white" world; that is, either something is known or it is not. In actual business operation, however, obviously there are certain risks or probabilities that a certain course of action will be successful. The technique of risk analysis is called *decision theory* and is being linked to a computer system in a growing but still selective circle of companies. A basic example of the technique and its benefits to decision making may help qualify its future use.

The problem to be solved by the use of decision theory is the evaluation of prospects for the purchase of a high-value durable goods item that entails a good deal of presale effort. The selection of prospects that hold greatest profit potential is of prime significance in order to focus a limited sales force on an expanding marketplace.

In analyzing the situation, the following questions must be tackled one at a time and an economic evaluation made of each.

What is the payoff or profit potential of each prospect?
What are the costs involved in bidding for the account?
What are the odds on getting the account?

The profit potential is based on the revenue that can be expected over a five-year period. A five-year period is selected because a customer can be expected to contribute add-on business after the initial sale. If installation is not anticipated before twelve months, the profit potential must reflect this factor. For example, a multidivision company expecting to sign a contract for one machine ($110,000 revenue) to be installed in twelve months with two similar machines to be installed two years after the first would have a five-year revenue potential of $880,000 ($110,000 × 4 + $220,000 × 2). The revenue potential must then be viewed in light of its profit contribution (based on the company's accounting methods) and must be discounted in light of the fact that revenue does not all accrue the first year. The resultant discounted contribution margin for the above sale might be $170,000.

What presale effort must be expended in an attempt to sign the account? This figure covers the cost of special engineering, system analysis, special training courses, demonstration programs, proposal preparation, and other support needed to bid for the business. For example, if an elaborate proposal, plus considerable special engineering, is required, the costs might be as follows:

2 engineers for 2 months (4 man-months × $5000)	$20,000
1 illustrator/designer for 3 months ($2500/man/month)	7,500
Supplies and proposal material	1,500
	$29,000

The next step is the determination of the betting odds or the probability that the sale can be closed. This is a rather subjective evaluation, but an analysis of competitive factors, plus past experience, can be used to establish the odds. The result is stated in terms of a percentage probability.

To see how decision theory works, assume that there are two prospects and that it is desired to rank them according to priority, for it is not possible to expend a major sales effort on each. The decision table on page 304 indicates that prospect B holds the greater profit potential. It brings this out by comparing the expected monetary value of the two accounts. Prospect A has higher potential but with less probability of realizing it and with a greater selling expense. If prospect A is signed, a profit return of $170,000 will result, whereas a loss of $29,000 will be incurred if the prospect is lost. If prospect B is signed, a profit return of $90,000 will result, whereas a loss of $6,000 will be incurred if the prospect is lost. The expected monetary value of B is $32,400 as compared to $10,800 for A. These figures are obtained by multiplying the probability of getting the sale (20 percent in the case of A) times the profit if the sale is

DECISION TABLE STATEMENT OF PROBLEMS

Account A (the account described above)   *Account B*

Revenue potential	$880,000	$560,000
Profit potential	170,000	90,000
Sales cost	− 29,000	− 6,000
Net profit potential	$141,000	$ 84,000

Alternatives	Bid on Prospect A	Probability	Bid on Prospect B	Probability
Get the sale	+ $170,000	20%	+ $90,000	40%
Lose the sale	− 29,000	80%	− 6,000	60%
Expected monetary value	+ 10,800		+ 32,400	

made ($170,000) and subtracting the amount obtained by multiplying the probability of losing the sale (80 percent) times the sales cost or loss if the sale is lost ($29,000).

Decision theory is a systematic method of facilitating decision making under conditions of uncertainty. The example used here has but a few variables and there are only two alternate courses of action. As the variables and alternatives are multiplied severalfold, as is the case in most business decisions, the need for techniques such as decision theory becomes more apparent.

Decision theory analyzes the factors underlying a decision and allows the decision maker to quantify the major parts of the probelm so that he is free to concentrate on those factors that cannot be readily quantified. The human mind has a difficult time handling multidimensional problems. Decision theory divides a problem into its logical parts, analyzes each part separately, and then puts the parts back together in their proper prospective in order to reach a decision. Decision theory follows the philosophy of "divide and conquer"—that is, divide a problem into its logical components, analyze and quantify each component, and thereby conquer the overall problem.

Thus the examples of computer-aided portfolio analysis and of choosing between sales prospects by use of decision theory illustrate in a simplified manner the way information systems are impacting top-management decision making.

THE MANAGEMENT PROCESS

Figure 9.4 is an abbreviated illustration of the management process as described by R. Alec MacKenzie ("The Management Process in 3-D," *Harvard Business Review,* November/December). Although this article was published in 1969, I feel the basic management process has not changed a great deal and that MacKenzie's analysis of the management process remains quite valid today. I am most impressed with the framework that MacKenzie has developed; and as I compared it with my own man-

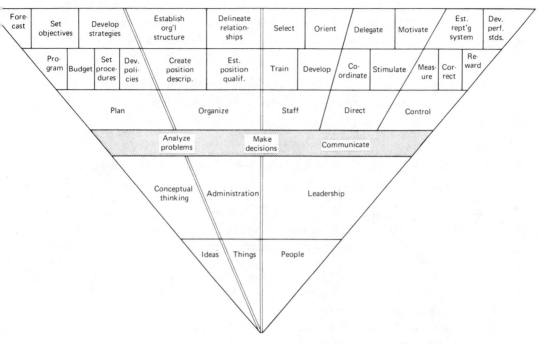

Fig. 9.4   The management process

agement role and those above and below me, I realized how much thought went into what appears to be a rather simple schematic. My purpose here is to explain the elements of the manager's job in enough depth to ascertain the effect that a management information system can have in helping the manager carry out his job responsibilities.

Figure 9.4 indicates that the manager basically deals with three elements—*ideas*, *things*, and *people*. These elements are reflected in the *tasks of conceptual thinking*, where one formulates new business ideas and opportunities, *administration*, where the details of the management process are handled, and *leadership*, where people are motivated to accomplish business objectives. The functions of *analyzing problems*, where facts are gathered and alternate solutions are evaluated (much like the steps in decision making discussed earlier), *making decisions*, and *communicating* the decisions to the people who must implement them are termed *continuous functions*, for they occur repeatedly throughout the management process rather than sequentially.

The *sequential functions* consist of *plan*, where a course of action is selected, *organize*, where the work is arranged for accomplishing the plan, *staff*, or the selection and allocation of the work to the people who will perform it, *direct*, the commencement of purposeful action on the work at hand, and *control*, where the plan is carried out and satisfactorily completed.

The activities indicate what constitutes the five sequential functions of the management process. In order to develop a *plan*, one must *forecast* or determine the effect on future sales, costs, or profit; *set objectives*, the end results; and *develop strategies* on how to achieve the end results. One must *program* or establish a priority and sequence of the strategy, *budget* or allocate resources, *set procedures* or arrive at standardized methods, and, finally, *develop policies* ensuring that rules and regulations exist to govern significant recurring matters.

An example might serve to bring the plan function into perspective. My experience as a planning manager in developing a product business plan follows the seven listed activities. In planning the introduction of a new item, a forecast of the future marketplace and impact of the product in the market are important starting points. Then objectives, such as desired market share and revenue and profit goals, are established. The strategies of how to achieve these goals involve statements such as the following: we will go after new markets, we will offer the lowest-price products, we will offer the best-quality product, or any combination thereof. The programming involved is to indicate what products with what features will be offered first and why. The budget for the project must be established at this point, and it must be consistent with what it will take to carry out the objectives and strategies, and yet it must not affect on-going programs to any great degree. The procedures and policies begin to blend into the *organize* function because they involve statements stating, for example, that PERT will be used as a project control technique with monthly status reports prepared for top management.

The organize function is more straightforward and, following the example above, includes *establishing the organizational structure* for the production of the new product. If the product is to be produced by the existing line organization, this point will be determined, or it may be that a new operational unit is organized to design and produce the new product. If a new organization is set up, top management must *delineate relationships* between the new and the existing structure and define communication and liaison points. The *creation of position descriptions* and the *establishment of position qualifications* will indicate whether the plan can be carried out by the existing organization or whether additional people with specifically required skills are needed.

This leads into the *staff* function, where the qualified people for the required positions are *selected*, *oriented* to the plan objectives, strategies, policies, and so on, *trained* in the necessary tasks to be performed, and *developed* to the extent of making them feel a part of the company and the project on which they are working.

The *direct* function involves the steps that are normally associated with "getting things done through people." These steps include *delegating* or assigning responsibility and accountability, *motivating* to persuade and inspire, *coordinating* to ensure that the efforts of one group are consistent with the efforts of others, and *stimulating change* when differences occur, conflicts arise, and it is necessary to resolve these differences before proceeding with the task.

The *control* function completes the cycle and involves the *establishment of a reporting system* that is consistent with the total reporting structure but that reflects pertinent milestones and progress against a schedule, the *development of performance standards*, to set the conditions that will determine if the job is properly completed, a technique to *measure results* to ascertain if the desired quality was attained and the extent of variance from the goal or standard, the taking of *corrective action* to get the task back on schedule and up to standard when deviations occur, and, finally, to *reward*, whether by praise or remuneration for the accomplishment of the job and the meeting of goals.

Having analyzed the management process, it is appropriate to assess the relative impact of management information systems on the various functions and then to overlay the categorization of top, middle, and operating management that was developed in Chapter 1 to get a clearer idea of how MIS can be expected to influence management.

I feel that MIS can be expected to influence the five sequential functions in the next five to ten years in accordance with the following percentages:

Plan	40%
Organize	30%
Staff	50%
Direct	10%
Control	90%

It has been shown that the plan function can be materially influenced by MIS; the 40 percent reflects this. MIS will not have a great deal of influence on the organize function, although job and skills inventories will assist in the process. The computerized skills and job inventories can materially assist the staff function, but I still feel that a strong qualitative element will remain. The direct function is people and motivation oriented, and I see little if any impact of MIS in this area. The big area for MIS is in the control function; here, more experience in analyzing business operations and in experimenting with programmed decision rules will bring more functions under automatic programmed control.

It is obvious that the categorization of management into three levels is an oversimplification, because the nature of the work within the same category differs greatly and no definite line separates the top from the middle and the middle from operating management.

For example, a job of managing a group of forecasters whose job it is to project the sales, shipments, returns, and so on, differs dramatically, depending on the nature of the product. If the product is a stable one that is influenced by competitive and other external factors to only a minor extent, the job of forecasting is much more receptive to computerization than if the product is highly unstable and subject to external forces. Similarly, a job shop manufacturer dealing in one-of-a-kind specials has a different problem than a repetitive, assembly-line operation. In order to ascertain the impact of MIS on a management job, the percentage of time devoted to the five functions described can serve as a general indication. For example, Fig. 9.5 indicates an MIS quotient of 41 percent for top management, 58 percent for middle management, and 70.5 percent for operating management. Again, this figure is a gross oversimplification; it indicates only a relative evaluation, not an exact one. This ap-

	Percent Susceptible to Computerization	Top Management		Top Management		Operating Management	
		Percent of Job devoted to	Weighted Value	Percent of Job devoted to	Weighted Value	Percent of Job devoted to	Weighted Value
Plan	40%	70%	28.0%	20%	12.0%	5%	2.0%
Organize	30	10	3.0	10	3.0	5	1.5
Staff	50	10	5.0	10	5.0	5	2.5
Direct	10	5	.5	20	2.0	15	1.5
Control	90	5	4.5	40	36.0	70	63.0
Computerization Quotient			41.0%		58.0%		70.5%

Fig. 9.5 Computerization quotient

proach has many subjective factors, but I think the exercise is a good one. The message to be gleaned is that before assessing the future impact of MIS on management, we need to know exactly what functions management people perform and what responsibilities they have. The computerization quotient is a thought process that does that.

THE ELECTRONICALLY AIDED EXECUTIVE

We have divided management activities into three general categories: (1) administrative, (2) leadership, and (3) conceptual thinking. The first and second categories can be aided by electronic means as an extension of office automation, the third by executive decision support systems. We now discuss these areas.

The first application in automating the office is usually word processing, and this is no surprise. Typewriting has been with us for decades, and word processing, which provides functions such as automatic paragraph insertion, simplified editing, spelling verification, and the like, is a natural extension. Also there is a fairly well-defined cost/benefit resulting from either pooling the typing or increasing the productivity of typists. However, there is potentially a bigger payoff in automating the office—and that centers on automating the managers as well as the secretaries. As much as 30 percent of a manager's job can be spent on administrative matters, such as letters, memos, reports, expense accounts, meetings, travel, and telephone calls. If electronics can reduce the time it takes to carry out these administrative duties, it is obvious that more time can be spent on the conceptual-thinking portion of the job, where the real payoff is.

Figure 9.6 builds in stages the accoutrements of the electronically aided executive. The terminal device can be used either directly by the executive or by a secretary or aide. The first stage is to be able to write letters and memos and store them on electronic media. The terminal can be a typewriter, a dictating device linked to a telephone line, or even, in the future, voice messages electronically interpreted directly

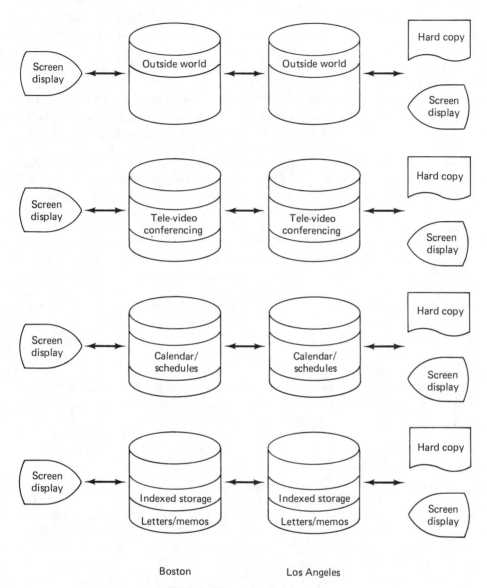

Boston   Los Angeles

Fig. 9.6   Electronic administration

into electronic storage, thus bypassing the typing or keying by an intermediate. Because of communications lines and networks, the origination point can be any site where a communication linkage exists. Thus the executive is freed from his office. He can initiate a memo or a letter from his home, at the airport, or in his hotel room. The inputted data is transmitted to his personal file, where it can be accessed by his secretary for further processing or can be sent directly to individuals at various destination points. Figure 9.6 shows that the executive's office is in Boston, where he is communicating to executives in Los Angeles. He sends a memo to the electronic file of a Los Angeles executive, who can receive it either on a terminal screen or on a hard-copy printer.

Letters and reports are maintained in indexed storage for retrieval at a later date. The key element is a proper indexing system, usually involving cross-indexing so that the executive can retrieve, for example, the Jones letter, or the letter on chemical waste, or the letter he wrote last Wednesday. The file can include graphic material and even digitized pictures and illustrations. Thus the executive begins to build an electronic file system that can be accessed directly via a communication link.

The next stage of automating the executive is the addition of personal calendar and schedule processing. A personal time calendar is maintained on the file with meetings, appointments, and the like noted. The executive's subordinates, peers, and superiors do the same. It is akin to a schedule board in a sales office; in this case, however, the schedule board is electronic and can be changed or updated on-line from the home, the airport, or the hotel room. Reminders, memory joggers, and the like can be part of the file. It works this way. You want to call a meeting of the plant steering committee on July 8 from 1 to 3 P.M. The personal files of those on the steering committee are checked for availability, the appropriate meeting room for the size of the steering committee group selected and reserved, and a list of the preparatory materials necessary for the meeting indicated. Once scheduled, the personal calendars of each of the participants would be so reserved.

At this point a particular management style and work ethic come into play. A workaholic executive can have a field day with this type of system. He has an idea at 3 A.M. and has orders in Jones' file when Jones arrives at 8:30 A.M. that day. He can easily stay in the act while traveling or on vacation. This can be both positive and negative. The real benefit, as always, comes from judicious use of the new media. When one realizes how long it takes to personally contact six people (telephone call, executive out of town, secretary at lunch, and so on), the productivity benefits of this type of communication are evident.

Stage 3 of Figure 9.6 adds teleconferencing and video conferencing to the electronically aided executive's array of tools. Many companies now have teleconferencing rooms for "many-to-many" communication to and from remote locations. A meeting is convened in Boston, but there are neck microphones and an audio link so that voices can travel to and from the Los Angeles area where the other half of the meeting attendees reside. Charts and other visual exhibits can be transmitted and displayed when necessary to clarify a point. Also access to electronic files can be made. Though this form of communication may not be as effective as face-to-face, it saves so much time and cost that it becomes a viable substitute in many instances.

Currently, freeze-frame television pictures are also being employed to give a video impression to the conference. It is likely that satellite transmission will make continuous videoconferencing a cost-effective medium. Whether tele- or videoconferencing, it is apparent that productivity of executives can be increased dramatically by the reduction of travel and the ability to hold meetings without the delay of travel.

The final stage of Fig. 9.6 adds the outside world to the electronic file. This extends the effectiveness of the system, since, for example, market data bases or competitive market-share statistics from data service companies can be accessed. The executive can also add his personal file to the media, thus maintaining his bank accounts, assets, stock records, reminders of birthdays, physical exams, and the like. This is an alternate to having his own personal computer in the home. He would be the only one to have the password for access to this portion of the file.

It is interesting to speculate on the ramifications of this mode of operation, aside from the obvious productivity improvements and the impact on work style, motivation, and the work ethic. Currently the office is the locus for the executive. He spends perhaps the majority of his working hours there. He writes, phones, meets people, reads, looks up things in his files, and so on. But if the scenario described here comes to pass, the locus can change to wherever there is terminal access—and this could almost be anywhere. We not only have the paperless office, we have the office-less office. We have removed the geographical boundaries of where business can be conducted and begin to see why Toffler's electronic-cottage concept may not be far-fetched.

EXECUTIVE DECISION SUPPORT SYSTEMS

This type of electronic support for executives differs from the management-science type of aids described earlier but retains certain of their elements. The executive decision support systems (EDSS) are geared for an individual executive or a group of executives. These systems may link to the integrated data base of the company but for the most part they involve a separate personal data file, part of which can be stripped from the main file or created apart from the main file, but geared to the needs of the individual executive. Professor John Rockart of MIT has devoted a good deal of time to studying and analyzing such systems. The best way to explain the concept is to use a case from a research study conducted by the Center for Information System Research, which Professor Rockart directs.

Northwest Industries*

Ben W. Heineman, President and CEO of Northwest Industries, decided in 1976 that he needed an executive information system to aid him in planning, projecting, and monitoring the progress of his nine major divisions. Heineman was, and is, a great believer in the advantages of "not being the captive of any particular source of information." He felt a great need to analyze various aspects of the business himself, but saw little opportunity for this without a computer-based system that would reduce data handling chores.

An experimental support system was at first designed to allow executives to retrieve more than 70 predefined reports and to perform limited analyses such as compound-growth calculations, variance analysis, and trend projections. In January of 1977 the six top executives were given access to this system. By February,

*From research paper that later appeared in John F. Rockart and Michael E. Treacy, "The CEO Goes On-Line," *Harvard Business Review*, January/February 1982.

Mr. Heineman had stretched the limits of its analytic capabilities and was demanding more.

The additional capabilities came in the form of a new access and analysis language called EXPRESS. EXPRESS includes not only simple file-handling and data-aggregation facilities but also much more extensive capabilities which facilitate extensive modeling and statistical analyses of data series.

To complement this access facility, Northwest Industries has continually expanded its "Executive Data Base" to currently include:

1. 350 financial and operational data items of actual, budgeted, forecast, and planned monthly results for each operating company for the past eight years.
2. 45 economic and key-ratio time series.
3. Several externally subscribed data bases, including Standard & Poor's Compustat and DRI services.

Northwest Industries' system is truly a corporate-level executive support system. It is now used by almost all managers and executives in the corporate office to perform their monitoring and analytical functions. The corporate controller's department, the planning department, and the top line executives all use the data base independently to service their particular information needs. As a result, the data base is more all-inclusive and extensive than any other we have seen to date. It is constantly growing as new data items and series are added by various managers as they are found to be of use.

The driving force behind the system, and its most significant user, is Heineman. Use of the system is an everyday thing for him, a natural part of the job. He programs using the EXPRESS language and a full ten-finger typing approach to the terminal keyboard. He believes that the knowledge he can bring to the analytic process from his viewpoint makes personal analysis preferable, in many situations, to handing assignments to staff personnel. What is more, instant access to the data base, to try out a thought he might have, is very useful. For this reason, terminals are present at home and available during vacations.

Supporting Heineman and others in their development and use of the data base is an information systems group whose capabilities and tasks are quite unlike those of the data processing personnel found in the operating divisions of most companies. The corporate I/S personnel rarely design or program any reporting systems. Rather they function as "coaches" to the various managers at the corporate level. Their primary function is the training of the users, not the provision of service. They aid in helping a user determine whether the data he needs is already available, and whether any additional data needed can be obtained. They further assist by getting the data into the data base, coaching the users in access methods, and helping the users to understand what sort of analytic routines are best fitted to the particular types of analyses which are desired. Only for major "modelling" applications do they take part in the system design and programming process.

As pointed out in the research paper, EDSS requires a different approach or at least a modification of the approach used in more conventional MIS development. First, the concept requires an interested executive who really sees benefit in pursuing this type of system. He is usually a reflective type who is willing to spend time and sees the payoff in analyzing the critical success factors for him and his company. The EDSS executive will be demanding but understanding of the weaknesses as well as the strengths of the systems that support him. He will realize that the system has to be more regimented and disciplined than he may be accustomed to and cannot possess infinite flexibility. He will be willing to make trade-offs and compromises, sometimes settling for what he thinks fulfils 80 percent of his needs rather than wait another year to get the 100 percent.

Second, EDSS requires a user-oriented data base and a user-oriented data-base language. Many of the data bases and data-base languages purport to be user friendly, but their "user" is the professional whose background has made him or her familiar with computers and information systems. The executive is a different breed and needs an executive-friendly system—and this doesn't mean typewriters or highly structured languages. The executive interface features simple function keys and, if a language is needed, it is English or pseudo English. Heineman's willingness to type is a rarity among executives.

Another requirement of an EDSS is MIS people with consultant skills. These consultants must bridge the gap between the technical world and the world of the executive. They must view the executive as a valued client and work with him or her in order to understand and be able to express the executive's information needs. They must assist him in translating these needs into a system that the executive can use directly, if that is his style, or use through an aide or accountant. This calls for skills of listening, probing, analyzing, and conceptualizing. It means understanding the elements of the business and the executives who run it.

Finally, the focus of EDSS is on effectiveness as opposed to efficiency. MIS applications aimed at performing repetitive operational tasks must have a high degree of efficiency. Since they are executed often, they must avoid elements such as data storage redundancy and excessive hardware and software overhead. Executives do not operate their EDSS's around the clock; in fact the usage is sporadic and may even be on a weekly rather than a daily or hourly basis. For this reason, the system should be optimized around effectiveness. It is perfectly permissible to waste a bit of file storage (EDSS files are not large anyway) or a bit of operating overhead in order to make the system available and easy to use for the executive. Availability and ease of use are the system design criteria. The once-a-week use may have greater payoff than the around-the-clock use of an operational control system.

This, then, is the concept of the executive decision support system. The electronic office aids referred to earlier go hand-in-hand with EDSS. The former allow greater productivity in administrative duties, thus freeing up the executive to do the job he is being paid to do—conceptual thinking.

EFFECT OF AN MIS ON OPERATING MANAGEMENT

Figures 9.2 and 9.5 indicate that the impact of MIS on operating management is far greater than the impact on top and middle management in all three listed categories. This is true because the operating manager's job is directed more at the control functions, which Fig. 9.5 shows are highly receptive to computerization. This discussion will focus on the nature of the change in job content caused by computerization, which is the reason for predicating the need for fewer operating managers to accomplish the same amount of work. An analogy to automated factory machinery will be used to illustrate the changes in job content occurring because of computerized management information systems.

There are lessons to learn by analyzing the accelerating trend toward numerically controlled machines. In numerical control, or CAM (computer-aided manufacturing), a machine such as a drill press or lathe is controlled by a computer. The software program in the computer (usually a micro) generates the necessary impulses to control the drilling of a hole in a specific spot in a piece of metal. The reason that the process is called *numerical control* is that the movements of the drill and the work to be drilled are controlled by numbers representing the shape of the desired finished part. It is more accurately called *symbolic control*, because the actual machining process is described by symbols, some of which happen to be numbers.

Figure 9.7 represents a schematic of the process. Ⓐ and Ⓑ in the schematic will be explained later.

It is interesting to analyze the ramifications of numerical control. It can be considered an evolutionary stage in automation in which the machine assumes a job previously performed by man. In this instance, the machine usually can accomplish the work more economically and accurately than man. Before the advent of the drill press, the worker drilled holes in metal by hammering a boringlike device of prescribed size through the metal. Later he used a hand drill with an adjustable bit. Then he used a drill press to position the work piece under the drill and pressed a button to lower the drill through the work piece. These evolutionary drilling developments removed the physical portion of the job from the worker and reduced his direct contact with the machine. The advent of numerical control removes him still further from the machine, indeed almost all the way. However, one should not overlook the continuing human involvement; the significance is that it occurs at a different part of the work cycle and the type of involvement has been changed markedly.

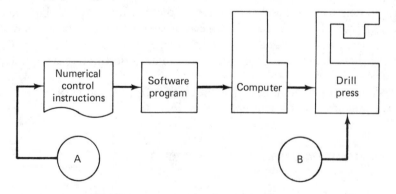

Fig. 9.7   Numerical control of machine tools

It is appropriate now to discuss the job of the operating manager in an information system, keeping in mind the parallel to the effect of numerical control on the drill
press operator. Figure 1.2 indicates that the manager of inventory control reports to
the vice-president of production. The inventory control manager has reporting to
him two assistant managers, who in turn have buyers reporting to them. The buyer
controls a number of inventory items and supervises a clerical staff that prepares
stock requisitions and purchase orders. For illustrative purposes, we shall analyze the
effect of a computerized inventory control system on the job content of the buyers
and assistant managers. Although it may be stretching things to call a buyer a manager, he is in effect because he supervises a group of people and manages the procurement and stock control of a group of inventory items. The buyer is an example of an
operating manager.

Operating management has an initial advantage because it has been dealing in
symbols for quite some time. The assistant inventory manager or buyer looks at an
inventory status report, sees that there are 25 gauges in inventory, and orders 50 more
even though he has not seen a fuel gauge in some time or perhaps ever. The buyer is
dealing in a symbolic world. There is no earthshaking revelation. Of more significance is the level of symbolism being employed—to what extent the buyer uses symbols to control his operation.

A computer system that merely records the status of inventory for the buyer is
one level. Here it is using internal reported information. But when the computer automatically produces a purchase order or schedules a new lot of an item when it
reaches a predetermined minimum, then we have another level. Here it is using internal processed information and using it in a most meaningful manner. Figure 9.8 represents a schematic of this process. (Again, Ⓐ and Ⓑ in the schematic will be
explained later.) The automatic inventory system changes the character of the buyer's
job just as numerical control changes the character of the worker's job. It dictates
that the buyer shift to a new symbolic plane.

First, what effect does an operating-type management information system of
the type discussed have on the number of operating managers involved? It is apparent

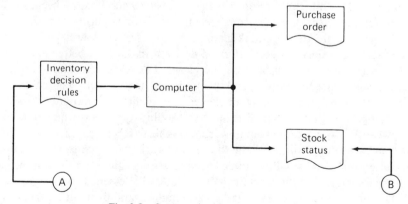

Fig. 9.8   Computerized inventory control

that it can reduce the number of buyers and assistant managers required for a specific function. Fortunately, because of the shortage of both skilled machinists and skilled managers, and because of the growth of industry in general, reduction does not present a problem. Buyers still will be required, but automated information systems have extended their reach to the point that perhaps two will be needed where five are needed now; thus the computer has not replaced operating management, it has reduced the number involved. The management-by-exception principle is being followed. A machinist is still needed to handle exceptions and to determine when the symbolic control system has gone awry. Similarly, the buyer or assistant manager is needed to handle exceptions where the computer system cannot handle the situation with preprogrammed logic.

Second, what effect does an automated information system have on the job content of the machinist and the buyer? In addition to the exception control they must exercise, both must play a significant role in developing the symbolic systems that control the operations. Their input is needed, but at a different stage in the operation cycle, more toward the front end. In Figs. 9.7 and 9.8, the contact point with the system is now Ⓐ rather than Ⓑ. (Point Ⓑ is now resorted to only on an exception basis.)

This example shows that the closed-loop type of operation represented by CAM can be applied in the business arena as well. Norbert Wiener called it cybernetics, where servomechanisms with automatic feedback loops control both simple and complex processes as found in advanced robotics. This is the reason for the high computerization quotient for operations management shown in Fig. 9.5.

SUMMARY

There is no question that computers and MIS have had impact on management and will have progressively more. Existing systems have influenced lower levels of management, particularly operating management. The effect on middle management is growing rapidly, while that on top management is also accelerating because of management science, electronic aids, and executive decision support systems.

A review of the decision-making process indicates that key steps in the process can be materially aided by computerized decision making. A better understanding and quantification of external data, accelerated development and acceptance of management-science techniques, and the proper distinction between qualitative logical facts and intuition are important elements in facilitating computer-assisted decision making. The type of change in job content illustrated by the numerical-control analogy can be expected to creep upward to higher levels of management. Whether tomorrow's executive will be of the "keyed-in" variety is open to speculation. The information middleman will continue to play a strong role, even though the gap between the manager and the machine will be materially lessened.

The ability of computers to gather, accumulate, and turn out information rapidly and effectively from their data bases has produced a syndrome called "information glut." The manager may be getting more information than he wants; in particular, electronic aids may make it too easy to send letters across the country or to schedule meetings. A statement made fifteen years ago by an automotive company president is appropriate here if we simply update the technology to that described in this chapter:

> We think that the jet aircraft with its high-speed comfort has made our life easier. Instead, we now find we spend more time traveling—not less. We go greater distances, but in doing so may accomplish less.
>
> Thirty years ago, a trip to London or Frankfurt was carefully planned. It was not an easy trip and, therefore, was made only after proper preparations. Today, the trip is so quick, so easy, that we tend to do it without planning. . . .
>
> As a result, we often come back without accomplishment; and because the trip was so easy and so quick, we are less disappointed when it is not productive. Many times a thoughtful letter or an intelligent and well-prepared telephone conversation could have accomplished more.
>
> Before the arrival of the electrostatic copies we thought carefully about the distribution of documents. A great deal of work was necessary to make extra copies and, as a result, only those who really could use the data were given copies. Today, we push a button and 20 copies come out in an instant. . . .
>
> My greatest problem is not lack of information, but rather a surplus of it. There is no surplus of what I need to know, but there is a surplus of what others think I should know. We must return to concise and economical communications.

CASE STUDIES

ROSS TOGS DEPARTMENT STORES

A prominent Midwest department store chain, Ross Togs, has employed operations research to help it consolidate its warehousing activities. The chain formerly supplied its retail outlets from three warehouses in the greater Chicago area. A series of changing conditions led management to consider that one warehouse could do the job in a more economical fashion and still maintain the desired delivery cycle.

An initial consideration was the addition of dock facilities necessary to handle the increased truck traffic. The additional facilities could be planned realistically if three factors were known—the number of trucks, their arrival time, and the time to service each truck. Economic considerations also were involved. The trucks were leased, so waiting time had a definite cost associated with it. However, additional dock facilities, while cutting down waiting time, necessitated a considerable monetary investment. The problem of cost factors in economic conflict with each other and the waiting-line principle is a classic case for the application of queuing theory. Here's the way the company went about solving the problem.

A study analyzed the existing traffic flow at the three warehouses, and the results were projected to that expected at a single warehouse. The study involved a sample seven-week period in the spring. The effect of seasonal variations was projected from the basic data, using historical company records. It was discovered that the number of trucks increased only 5 percent during the Christmas rush but the number of pieces handled increased 50 percent. In addition, truck servicing time was found to vary within certain bounds, depending on factors such as size of truck and type of merchandise. A service-time pattern was found to be a combination of a fixed time interval and a variable time interval dependent on the number of pieces being handled.

While the number of truck arrivals had certain patterns and frequencies (for example, an average of 105 trucks arrived in the morning, while 65 arrived in the afternoon), there was a chance relationship that precluded a simple arithmetic solution. A new wrinkle was added to the classical queuing-theory solution—the use of the "Monte Carlo" method. (The name Monte Carlo implies the presence of chance.) Using the frequency distributions produced by the studies as boundaries, the Monte Carlo technique randomly selected a time of arrival and a service time for each of the arriving trucks. This is where the power of the computer comes into play. The computer simulates a day's operation by totaling the waiting time and length of queue of each truck serviced that day. The computer runs through a full year's operation using random numbers to simulate actual conditions while assuming a varying number of docks. These iterations are repeated to the point where computer output indicates to management the trade-offs of waiting time and investment in new dock facilities. This then forms the basis for the most economical solution to the problem.

QUESTIONS

1. Do you think management would be convinced that computerized simulation and the Monte Carlo method helped them resolve the dock problem? Are there any potential pitfalls in the logic?

2. Can you see other opportunities for this type of approach to assist a company in decision making?

3. Compare this dock-and-truck model with a financial model that a company might employ. In which are there more variables and more assumptions?

4. Why aren't these types of approaches more prevalent in business?

PERSONAL COMPUTER POLICY

TO: Purchasers of Personal Computers
FROM: R. J. Desmond,
            Director of MIS
SUBJECT: POLICY ON PERSONAL COMPUTERS

It is realized that many of you are being attracted to the purchase of a personal computer for business reasons. This letter in no way should be interpreted as a negative statement or an attempt to strictly control your use of personal computers. Rather, it is intended to assist you in making the right decision. The MIS department stands ready to help you in training and education in their use.

You must first determine whether your primary needs are for home or personal use, or for business use at the office. If the former is the case, the company is offering interest-free loans and a 15% discount on the Apple or TRS 80 models. You can get the details from your purchasing group. If your primary use is business and your department head has approved, we also recommend Apple or TRS, but you may want to buy another brand. You should buy directly from a local computer store and make the arrangements yourself. Our advice is that you select the applications you wish to accomplish first and then buy the computer that has those applications. We suggest that you plan to do no programming yourself and select a standard model that has a standard configuration and standard peripherals. Do not get into exotic input and output devices or special features.

Your use of the personal computer should be strictly on a stand-alone basis. You should not plan to use telecommunications or to tap a company or external data base. This will get you into unnecessary complications and begin to take more time and effort than the potential benefits would warrant. In other words, the criteria for acquiring a personal computer should be a specific application that is freestanding and that involves no programming. An example of this is VISICALC, which is a software package that enables you to use a personal computer as you would an electronic spread sheet. It is good for budgets, profit projections, and the like.

You should expect to pay from $3,000 to $6,000 for analytical use, $6,000 to $10,000 for accounting use, and $6,000 to $15,000 for data processing use.

The MIS department is running a series of seminars on personal computing. The sessions are six hours in length, the first series running from 12:00 to 1:00 P.M. over a three-week period and the second series from 5:00 P.M. to 6:00 P.M., also over a three-week period. You can also pick up a series of documents especially prepared by the MIS department which will acquaint you with personal computer applications and configurations.

I hope this brief policy provides perspective on the use of personal computers within the company. They are not for everyone, and your specific need and particular operating style will dictate whether a personal computer can help you in performing your job. Your MIS department is prepared to help you in this determination.

R. J. Desmond
Director of MIS

QUESTIONS

1. What do you think of the general approach taken by Desmond?

2. Do you think the approach is too broad or too restrictive?

3. Is this a reactive or proactive position statement?

4. If you received this policy statement, would you be encouraged to purchase a personal computer?

5. What follow-on activities or actions would be appropriate?

BIBLIOGRAPHY

Alter, S., *Decision Support Systems: Current Practice and Continuing Challenges*. Reading, MA: Addison-Wesley, 1980.

Barcomb, David, *Office Automation: A Survey of Tools and Techniques*. Bedford, MA: Digital Press, 1981.

Keen, P. and M. S. Morton, *Decision Support Systems*. Reading, MA: Addison-Wesley, 1978.

Leavitt, Harold J. and Thomas L. Whisler, "Management in the 1980's," *Harvard Business Review* (1958), 41–48.

Mason, R. O. and E. B. Swanson, Editors, *Measurement for Management Decision*. Reading, MA: Addison-Wesley, 1981.

Poppel, Harvey L., "Who Needs the Office of the Future?" *Harvard Business Review* (Nov./Dec. 1982), 146–155.

Rockart, John F. and Michael E. Treacy, "The CEO Goes On-Line," *Harvard Business Review* (Jan./Feb. 1982), 82–88.

Rockart, John F. and Michael E. Treacy, *Executive Information Support Systems*, W.P. 1167-80. Cambridge, MA: Center for Information Systems Research, Sloan (MIT), 1981.

Tapscott, Don, *Office Automation: A User Driven Method*. New York: Plenum Press, 1982.

Toffler, Alvin, *The Third Wave*. New York: Morrow, 1980.

Chapter 10

Management Involvement and Influence in MIS

The preceding chapter discussed the impact of computers and MIS on management. The conclusion was that although the impact varied, MIS affected all levels of management to some degree. The trend most definitely is that MIS will have an accelerating influence on management. The typical manager's job has not shown a revolutionary change up to now, but most would agree that computer-powered MIS provides enough potential to affect his job and the business environment surrounding his job materially. It is time for the manager to become more involved and to gain a comprehensive understanding of MIS and related activities. No longer do managers feel that computer applications and system development are activities that can be delegated exclusively to the technical people who are expert in these areas. They do not argue *whether* they need exposure and involvement; the issue now is *what kind of* involvement.

Two major issues will be discussed in this chapter. The first is the level of involvement required of management. As we shall see, this depends on such factors as the particular level of management, the immediacy of the impact of MIS, and the degree of companywide computerization. The level of involvement is also closely related to the computerization quotient discussed in Chapter 9. Once the role is recognized, the second issue is how the manager proceeds to gain the necessary training, education, and practical MIS experience.

MANAGEMENT'S ROLE IN SYSTEM DEVELOPMENT

Figure 10.1 establishes the framework for discussing the involvement required of different levels of management. The middle triangle is similar to that used in Chapter 1 to describe the various vertical stages of system and subsystem development. Reading from bottom to top, it lists seven major elements in putting an information system in operation. It starts with the overall business objective and goals and then proceeds to a definition of external and internal business and product strategies required to meet these general goals. These elements were described more completely in Chapter 7. The integrated system specification establishing the overall MIS framework leads into the design criteria for the integrated system. The former describes the *what* of MIS, the latter *how* it is to be accomplished. The cycle next proceeds through individual subsystems specification and design and, finally, to the programming and operation of each application area selected for implementation.

The inverted triangle on the left of Fig. 10.1 comes from Chapter 1 and illustrates the three levels of management: top management setting the overall company goals and strategies, middle management interpreting the goals and strategies and planning their implementation, and operating management actually carrying out and performing the work to implement the plan. The MIS management on the right of Fig. 10.1 is a microcosm of general management in that top management within MIS develops the overall goals and objectives in the same way that the top management of the total company does for the company. The various system analysts and project leaders are the middle managers of MIS who interpret MIS top-management policy and take charge of pertinent subelements or subsystems. Programming and operating management make certain that the individual computer programs are consistent with the established system specifications and that, once programmed and tested, they are operated in accordance with predetermined procedures.

Figure 10.1 establishes the relative management-involvement levels and the interface points between general management and MIS management. It indicates that the top management is concerned with the first three system development elements. Overlapping exists in the involvement of different levels of management, as can be seen from the chart.

Middle management is concerned with the establishment of external-internal strategies through subsystem specification, while operating management's involvement in the various systems elements can be seen on the right of Fig. 10.1. The interface points between general and MIS management are through the common system elements with which each is concerned.

Figures 10.2 and 10.3 define general management and MIS management's involvement in MIS by particular management level. It becomes clear, in viewing the respective roles, that there are common areas of concern. It is necessary for both sides to come together and mutually discuss these areas. Unilateral resolution of particular system problems has been a major cause of system failure. This point is particularly true of MIS, where the interaction of middle and top management levels is extremely important. Conventional system approaches, which attack lower-level

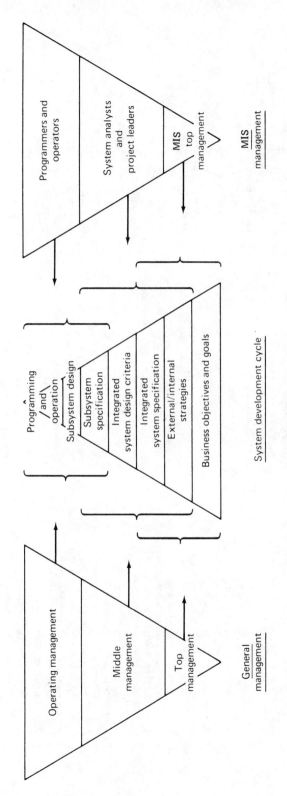

Fig. 10.1 Management's role in system development

323

Top management

-- Concern with business objectives; explain what is essential for EDP; ensure an understanding; monitor to see that the understanding and awareness are present.

-- Ensure that external/internal strategies are understood, e.g., production scheduling system must take into account the level employment of skilled workers; all application areas must take into account the financial and capital requirements; applications must be built on the assumption that business conditions will change.

-- Participate in establishing and reviewing integrated system spec; this is overall game plan — the framework or road map — and is very important. Should have opportunity to review any major system changes.

-- Participate in establishing over — all schedule. Review major milestones and project status.

Middle management

-- Awareness and participation in establishment of external/internal strategies. Middle management is cognizant of the effect of these polices on actual operations.

-- Participate in development of the overall integrates system spec.

-- Representation on steering committee. Involvement in the subsystems that affect the manager's department or affects those departments with whom he interfaces.

-- Obtain proper people involvement by setting the proper example. Middle management is not concerned with specific system design but the issues discussed and reviewed at steering committee meetings will impact design.

-- Assign analysts within a particular area or at least provide contact point, an individual who can speak for the department or has perspective to know when middle management should be called in to approve a major issue.

Operating management

-- Develop and produce procedure manuals. Train people in use of system. Make necessary preparations for the conversion and transition period. Should be on call to handle detailed questions or respond to specific issues

-- Help establish psychological atmosphere for acceptance and co-operation of operating people involved. Develop outlook that emphasizes that system benefits will offset the effort of change and transaction.

-- Explain where the individual parts or roles of operating people fit into total MIS picture. Maintain positive motivation.

-- Ensure that system operates according to specification — feed back any discrepancies or problems.

Fig. 10.2 General management involvement in MIS

MIS top management

- Aware of over-all company business goals, **MIS** goals and the relation of the two.

- Aware of company strategies as they affect the overall system planning and **MIS** design.

- Major participant along with general management in setting specifications, schedules and milestones for **MIS**. Must take leadership role and ensure proper level of management involvement.

- Complete responsibility for the design of the overall integrated system (**MIS** and integrated system are used synonomously in this context). The selection of the particular computer system with the required input/output and storage devices rests with **MIS** top management.

- Must be knowledgeable in **MIS** state of the art — what other users are doing, what computer manufacturers, software houses and service companies are doing.

MIS middle management
(System analysts and project leaders)

- Work with **MIS** top management and general management counterparts to aid in the development of the integrated system spec.

- Project leaders are responsible for developing individual subsystem specs in conjenction with key management of the affected departments. Must ensure that spec is what using department wants and sees as its requirements.

- Responsible for subsystem design. Design must satisfy specifications. Must review and seek resolution of and spec change or on major trade off decision.

- Work with programmers to effect adequate translation of system design into coded programs.

MIS operating management
(Programmers and operators)

- Develop individual programs consistent with subsystem specs.

- Check out and fully test resulting programs.

- Review questionable areas with system analysts and project leaders.

- Establish operating procedures for productive execution of programs.

- Execute and monitor productive programs in daily operation.

- Develop detailed conversion and cutover plan for new applications.

- Provide feed back loop to system designers for incorporation of new features in subsequent re-writes and modification of applications.

Fig. 10.3 MIS management involvement in MIS

subsystems on a department basis while underplaying the integration aspects of systems, require interaction at the operating management level only. MIS, with its emphasis on integration and automatic decision making, requires interaction at the middle and top management levels.

ISSUES OF IMPORTANCE TO MIS PROFESSIONALS

The Society for Information Management (SIM) (of which I am a charter member) is comprised of the top information executives in their respective companies. It also includes MIS consultants, representatives of professional agencies, and MIS educators. Thus the group consists of individuals who represent a high level of MIS experience and know-how. In 1981 the members were surveyed on the MIS issues of most concern to them. Figure 10.4 lists the top eighteen responses in priority ranking.

The top issues for the most part are nontechnical in nature. Long-range planning (the subject of Chapter 2) leads the list. Note that effectiveness, issue 2, has a high priority, while efficiency is not even on the list. The information resource management concept (treated in Chapter 2) is issue 3. Distributed data processing (covered in Chapter 5) involves issues 4, 6, and 7, while issue 5 (discussed in Chapter 9) is directly related to management users. It is encouraging that importance is given to MIS ethics, issue 8. Education of non-MIS managers is issue 9 (and will be covered in this chapter). The issue of employee training and career paths completes the top ten.

The significant thing about the list is that each of the top ten issues, possibly excepting items 8 and 10, requires heavy user involvement to be successful. The SIM has recognized the importance of user involvement, and each of its annual meetings

		Mean Response on 1–6 Scale
1.	MIS long-range planning and integration	5.13
2.	Gauging MIS effectiveness	5.07
3.	The developing role of the information resource manager	4.82
4.	Impact of communications on MIS	4.53
5.	Decision support systems	4.48
6.	Office-of-the-future management	4.42
7.	Centralization vs. decentralization of MIS functions	4.31
8.	MIS ethics	4.04
9.	Education of non-MIS management	4.02
10.	Employee training and career paths	3.95
11.	Problems in maintaining information privacy	3.92
12.	Management science and the MIS environment	3.90
13.	Problems of maintaining data security	3.87
14.	Impact of software engineering on MIS	3.80
15.	Providing end users with own development tools	3.77
16.	Employee job satisfaction	3.70
17.	Professional recruitment	3.25
18.	Impact of personal computers	2.97

Fig. 10.4 Importance of issues to SIM members

has included a panel of user executives, often the top executive of a company. Its membership has dictated a focus shift from the technical to the management.

A similar type of survey was conducted by MIT's Robert Alloway and Judith Quillard in 1981 as they interviewed both user and MIS management on the subject of what is critical to MIS success. They grouped the replies into four general priority categories and found close agreement between the user and MIS groups. The first order of priority is to improve MIS's responsiveness to user needs (interestingly enough, users and MIS people agree that they meet efficiency-oriented criteria for success better than effectiveness-oriented criteria). The second priority for success involves a grouping of responses including development of better communications with managerial users, the training of users in general MIS, and the acquisition of user-oriented system analysts who understand user operations. The third priority involves MIS strategic planning and allocation of resources, while the fourth includes a series of issues, among them being the improvement of user attitudes, improved quality and timeliness of MIS reports, and reliability of hardware and software.

The SIM and MIT surveys have a common thread that establishes the rationale for this chapter: the user's perception of MIS service is probably the number-one critical success factor of the MIS director. In order to improve this perception, user involvement is paramount. We turn now to a discussion of management involvement, specifically what level is necessary and how it is obtained.

ESTABLISHING THE PROPER INVOLVEMENT LEVEL

As in learning any new skill, there are several ways to acquire the necessary MIS knowledge. The first is to learn by doing, by participating in the actual system and/or programming activity during some part of the implementation. This, of course, can either be full-time or part-time participation. For classification purposes, I have chosen to divide the participation method into (a) direct and (b) indirect, depending on the level of participation. Another method of acquiring computer knowledge is by formal training or education. In reality, knowledge is usually acquired by a combination of (a) direct participation, (b) indirect participation, and (c) education. Since many of today's managers attended college when computer courses were not well developed, the education has to be acquired after college. Let us look at each of the three methods.

DIRECT MIS PARTICIPATION

Looking at the MIS picture from an operating-department point of view, we list several assignments where one can acquire computer and system know-how.

- As an in-department system analyst.
- As an out-department system analyst.

- As part of a special task force.

In the first instance, the department whose activities are being computerized assigns an individual(s) to devote full time to the effort. This person works as the in-department system analyst, analyzing and defining the department's information needs, assisting in developing the system spec, the design of the system, and the necessary preparatory work before turning the application over to the programmers. This is an excellent way to become involved in the computer project. The individual learns about computers and systems by practical experience while, at the same time, he represents the interests of his department. He usually remains organizationally in his current department but has a dotted-line relationship to the MIS department. He works full time on the project and produces periodic status reports for his department's management. Often, after a period of time, the system analyst becomes so interested in computer systems that he requests transfer to the MIS department. This is a healthy situation, for there is a shortage of good system analysts, and experience in general company business operations is excellent background. The MIS staff that has business-based system analysts generally is more responsive to operating needs and is better able to bridge the user-system designer gap that exists.

The out-department system analyst operates in a similar manner, except that the individual is transferred from his current department to the MIS department. This move may be required for budgetary reasons or for control purposes. The man is on loan to the MIS department but is responsible for reflecting the interests of the department from which he transferred. This situation has some advantage over the in-department setup, but the risk is that the individual loses the user orientation that is so important to good system work.

Finally, a member(s) of the operating department may be placed on a special task force that is established to computerize a specified application area. The participation can be part time or full time, the latter being preferable if the budget exists for it. The individual, who may be a manager if the participation is part time, does not act in the role of a system analyst but rather in the role of a fact finder, system reviewer, sounding board, control point, or whatever you wish to call it. Again he represents the using department and works with the system analyst to provide him with the necessary background information about the department's operations and requirements.

It is obvious that in each of the three cases mentioned, some type of formal training should supplement the practical experience. However, the major focus is on learning by doing, by working with experienced system analysts and MIS personnel in actual implementation of an application.

INDIRECT MIS PARTICIPATION

There are other ways to become involved in MIS without the full-time or direct participation just described. The following represent assignments that can indirectly involve people in the MIS process:

- Steering committee
- Department coordinator
- System spec developer

These are more passive approaches, but they can still be quite effective in providing proper operating-department involvement. The steering committee is a group establshed at the outset to act as a higher-level management review board. The group normally meets weekly, or less frequently, to go over progress, review the key problem areas, and recommend solutions. It controls people and budgets and can recommend that additional resources be utilized if the program is behind schedule. It then has the authority to assign the additional people. Weekly review meetings are commonly supplemented by periodic tutorial sessions to equip the committee with the knowledge to assess progress more accurately.

The department coordinator continues to work full time on his assigned tasks within the operating department. However, he is assigned the role of coordinator to the systems group working in an applications area that affects his department. He is available to answer any questions or, if he cannot answer the questions directly, to set up sessions with pertinent people in the department. This approach is more passive and relies on the ability of the full-time system analysts to ask the right questions.

The system spec developer is also a part-time participant who works with the MIS staff through the development of the system spec. He signs off on the spec for his department. Since the spec specifies the objectives and purpose of the application, as well as the detailed input, output, and storage requirements, a sign-off at this stage is an important consideration. However, the risk remains that the implementation may proceed counter to the spec in certain areas or that subsequent system design may force system spec trade-offs. If the individual is available only up to system spec sign-off, too much reliance may be placed on the MIS staff.

EDUCATION AND TRAINING

MIS education has become a vital concern to the profession. It is important both inside the MIS department and to MIS users. While this chapter focuses on users, a word is in order for the MIS group. Population researchers tell us there wll be fewer college graduates in the years ahead, yet the demand for systems analysts and programmers continues to increase rapidly. The responsibility of the MIS director is to establish educational programs that satisfy both the need for an increasing cadre of trained system analysts, whether they are assigned to MIS or to user departments, and the need for intelligent involvement of the user community. This section will present a broad review of MIS educational facilities.

Education facilities include the following classes, each of which will be discussed in turn.

Schools
Secondary schools

Colleges
Business schools
Graduate schools
Internal on-site company training
MIS department
Computer vendor
Consultants
Private educational institutions
External training
MIS professional societies
MIS educational agencies
Seminars and business meetings
University continuing education programs
Self-study courses

MIS Education in Schools

There has been some confusion concerning the teaching of computers in schools, from the elementary and high schools to the business colleges and postgraduate universities. Confusion arises because of the role the computer plays, first, in a business and scientific sense and, second, in the daily lives of each of us. It has come on the scene so quickly that educators as well as businessmen are not quite sure of the computer's place in society. Only recently has the computer been viewed as opening up an entirely new functional area of business operation called information technology or information science or MIS. The earlier attitude toward computers established a computer fundamentals course, usually within the accounting department, and then treated computers as an adjunct to other functional course areas. This attitude has changed to the point where today, for example, the school of business administration at the University of Minnesota offers a program that grants a master's degree or doctorate in management information systems. The school has also established an MIS Research Center to focus research efforts in this area of study. The course is aimed at providing both (a) a knowledge of the management process and the functional areas of business and (b) a knowledge of computer technology hardware, software, and programming, plus its application to the analysis, design, and administration of management information systems.

An analogy might help bring computer education into better focus. A student learns a foreign language in school for several reasons. First, like most educational processes, it is an intellectual logical exercise that stretches the mind and forces the student to think of the subject as a series of grammatical rules and relationships. Second, learning a language can help a student achieve a better understanding of the history and the economic, social, and political workings of a particular country or culture. Finally, a foreign-language skill can provide the necessary preparation for a career as a translator or interpreter, or for one in the field of international business.

I see the teaching of computers in preparatory schools, and in many colleges as well, as being primarily in the mind-stretching capacity. Most students will not be computer system analysts or programmers in the future, just as most will not be biologists or physicists. Computer programming is an excellent mental discipline that forces the individual to think logically and rationally and to focus on solving a specific problem. Furthermore, it can be an enjoyable educational experience and an educational motivator to many students. In addition, it should be noted that the basic computer programming courses given in secondary schools, particularly those schools with terminals that can communicate with a remote computer, also aid in the understanding of information processing and data communication in general. The students gain an awareness that data, like voices, can be transmitted over telephone lines and that the computer at the other end will act in accordance with prescribed rules.

With computers and information systems affecting so much of our daily life, a basic understanding of what they do and how they work is a necessary ingredient in what has come to be called computer literacy.

Computer usage and education are growing in liberal arts colleges. Since colleges do begin to specialize students for particular jobs, there is more reason for teaching computers as a skill to be utilized in business or science. John G. Kemeny, father of the Dartmouth computer system, developer of a specialized language that facilitates direct communication with the computer, and former president of the college, has stated, "Learning to use a high-speed computer should be an essential part of a liberal education." He goes on to state:

> Not only will this give Dartmouth alumni an idea of the multitude of problems computers can be asked to solve and how to ask the right questions, but as lawyers, businessmen, doctors, engineers, they will also have a sophisticated understanding of how to use social science data in creative ways. The result of this special approach is not to use a computer instead of a teacher or a book to give students information and to answer student questions. Instead, students must learn to teach the computer, by programming it to sort stored information in useful ways.

It is significant that Harvard College, a bastion of liberal arts education, as part of its new core curriculum and as a prerequisite for graduation requires the learning of a computer language.

Business and graduate schools present a different problem, because here students are trained for business and professional specialization. A distinction must be made between training (a) the student who plans to be a specialist in data processing and (b) the student who plans to pursue a general business career, specializing in a field other than data processing. Figure 10.5 illustrates the span of curriculum—at the top, those courses of study suited for the specialist, and at the bottom, those geared for the generalist. Depending on the type of program and professional focus, courses can be selected from the top or the bottom half. My view is that the more the twain meet—that is, the greater the extension of the technical specialist into the gen-

Basic Technology
Hardware/software/programming languages
Computer Operations
Terminal use/debugging/machine-room operation
Basic Technical Concepts
Batch, on-line, time-sharing, networking
System Development Cycle
System analysis and design
MIS Managerial Techniques
Project management, risk assessment, planning
User Interface Languages
Terminal access; nonstructured, English-like language
Conceptual Framework
Stages theory, information as a resource
Key MIS Application Concepts
Integrated data base, distributed processing
Pivotal Managerial/Organizational Issues
Decision support systems, centralization/decentralization
Societal/Individual Issues
Privacy, ethics, computer literacy

MIS
Technical

General, or User
Business Manager

Fig. 10.5   Relative education priority

eral manager area and of the general manager into the technical area—the more effective will be the interaction level of the two groups in a real-life business setting.

Though change is occurring at the leading MIS universities, there is still a tendency to emphasize the technical subjects at the expense of the managerial ones. A major reason has been that many of the instructors and professors are themselves technically oriented and have an unbalanced view of the technical versus general business aspects of computer training; they stress the former. This situation is accentuated by the fact that they are most familiar and comfortable with the technical. Furthermore, the technical aspects are easier to teach. The gap exists because the older faculty, who are more experienced in general business requirements, did not learn computers in school and did not encounter them much in their business careers. They have handed over computer training to the computer specialists and now suffer the same communication and interface problem that exists between the general manager and the MIS specialist within a company. I have taught a variety of computer courses in several business colleges and I realize the instructor's tendency to teach what he is comfortable with, which usually means shying away from subject matter of the type at the bottom of Fig. 10.5. A fundamental programming course in FORTRAN, COBOL, or BASIC, or the use of a terminal is more specific and straightforward, besides being easier to teach.

Internal On-Site Company Training

Since many business managers went to business schools before computers were properly brought into the curriculum, today's management needs training. It is also apparent that those managers who did receive MIS training need continual refreshing and updating. A common method of obtaining this training is for a company to conduct its own on-site education program tailored around its individual requirements. The larger, more experienced users of MIS may have a training department for this purpose. In most firms it is a by-product responsibility of the MIS department. Training is so important that it is beneficial to establish a training group or possibly a training steering committee consisting of non-MIS as well as MIS people. Doing so makes sense, because the majority of the people being trained are not part of the MIS department.

Most companies look to the MIS department as the primary source of educators. Although it is quite possible that talent of this type exists within the department, the company must guard against too technical a focus. As has been illustrated, the general manager requires more than a basic hardware and software course. Other sources of on-site training are computer vendors and consultants. The major computer vendors have been in the education business for many years and have the talent and the course material to assume a good deal of the training burden for a company. However, like the business schools, they, too, have specialized more in technical training, and their basic system and computer management courses may not be geared properly. Most vendors will tailor a course or an entire educational program for a particular company. The computer vendor has the advantage of having a full set of instructional aids, complete course outlines, and educational documentation, all of which is extremely important. However, a company should carefully review the course objectives, course content, and instructors to ensure that the course is suitable for its own requirements.

Consultants and private educational institutions can provide the same type of services offered by the computer vendor. These two sources usually have the advantage of not gearing the education around a specific piece of hardware, as might be the case with the computer vendor. However, normally they do not possess the experience or course documentation of the vendor. These courses can be given on company time, in the evening, or a combination of both day and evening sessions can be utilized. It is important to state clearly the objectives and background expected for each course and to have a group with roughly the same background and interests in the sessions. Management's enthusiasm for computers can diminish quickly if they attend technical sessions with highly technical people. If the company resorts to the use of consultants or private educational institutions, course objectives and capabilities should be thoroughly evaluated before a contract is signed.

External Training

A wider variety of course offerings and educational opportunities exist if the company is willing to go outside for its training. Professional societies, such as the American Management Association, or MIS groups such as Association for Computing Machinery (ACM) and many others, either present courses on a variety of MIS subjects or can help organize and arrange outside training sessions. MIS educational agencies can be utilized for training outside the company just as for internal training.

The outside courses offer the opportunity for managers and personnel to mix with their counterparts from other companies, to exchange ideas, and broaden their appreciation for MIS. Most of the sessions put on by these agencies are well constructed and tested and clearly state the objectives and purpose. Many are aimed at management-level people. However, a caution is in order, because some courses are not what they look like on paper. It is wise to spend time in evaluating the offerings before signing up. Several telephone calls to prior attendees in a position similar to your own might help qualify the particular session. It is also desirable to discuss the seminar content with someone from the company's own MIS department to qualify it further.

In addition to the paid courses discussed above, there are good opportunities to attend seminars and business meetings devoted to specific MIS subjects. Special-interest groups on either an industry or functional basis (sales, finance, etc.) are adding computers and MIS as subjects at their regular business meetings or holding periodic seminars on these subjects. These sessions offer excellent opportunities to further one's MIS education and have the added benefit that the people attending are in the same line of work and have similar MIS background.

Most universities have credit and noncredit courses as part of their continuing education program in computer and computer-related subjects. These courses are presented in the evening and can offer an attractive method of acquiring MIS background. Again, one should be aware of what he is getting into, and a call to previous students or to the instructor himself is often a good idea.

Finally, the executive should not rely completely on organized classroom study. Outside reading of books and periodicals should be used to supplement the formal training. A subscription to one of the MIS journals may prove a good investment, or the occasional reading of a management-based computer book. Firms such as Deltak, a division of Prentice-Hall, have a library of video tapes that can be utilized along with packaged documentation as self-study programs. The programs range from basic systems concepts to data base and distributed data processing.

SURVEYS FOCUSING ON THE INVOLVEMENT OF MANAGEMENT IN MIS

I would now like to review the findings of several comprehensive surveys that were conducted in the seventies, leading to the analysis of a survey on the involvement of management in MIS that I conducted in conjunction with the Harvard Business School in 1978 and 1981.

Corporate Presidents

Thomas P. Ference of Columbia University and Myron Uretsky of New York University ("Computers in Management: Some Insights Into the State of the Revolution," *Management Datamatics*, January 1976) reported on a survey of 76 corporate presidents in the United States. The subject was the relationship of computers to top management, specifically the role played in solving ill-structured problems and in the formulation of strategy. They pointed out that in the early sixties, management writers thought computers would evolve to a point where they would influence management problem solving and decision making with the development of sophisticated operations research methods, simulation procedures, and the like. Their general conclusion was that the survey data didn't prove the prediction wrong, but the data did indicate that it hadn't yet been fulfilled. The method they used was a fixed-choice questionnaire mailed to the 76 top executives with a personal contact validation of 10 percent of the respondents. Here are the key conclusions of the survey:

- The corporation is not being managed by computers; the computer is not seen as an essential resource for the manager.
- The computer revolution insofar as higher-level management functions are concerned is far from accomplished.
- The president's involvement with the firm's computer is general rather than specific, custodial rather than operational. While presidents are involved in the approval of budgets and capital expenditures and in the general evaluation of performance, they are removed from the operations of the system and are not themselves users.
- The low level of importance assigned to informal contacts with computer personnel indicates the continuing lack of integration of EDP personnel into the ongoing management activities of the firm.
- The computer plays a minimal role in the decision-making activities of top management.
- Only 20 percent saw any likelihood that executives would be "tied in" to the computer and to office terminals in the near future.
- Despite the preceding points, the general attitude of presidents toward the computer effort was almost uniformly positive; it was just that nothing thus far in their experience had caused them to focus more on the computer as part of their day-to-day activities.

Middle Management

Professor Art Guthrie of Simon Fraser University in Burnaby, British Columbia ("Attitudes of the User-Managers Toward Management Information Systems," *Management Informatics*, Noordhoff International Publishing, Leyden, The Netherlands, Vol. 3 No. 5, October 1974), surveyed 1991 middle managers from organizations in Canada. He attempted to develop the same thesis as Ference and Uretsky, showing that the results of Management Information Systems have fallen short of expectations and that the use of computers in managerial decision making has not yet reached an advanced level.

Guthrie had three hypotheses which he wished to test by the questionnaire that he mailed to the Canadian middle-management group.

1. Managers do not perceive a strong need for MIS such that it would prompt their active participation in the development. I think this is an interesting point in that Guthrie believes a felt need is a necessary condition for organizational change of the type that MIS brings to a company.
2. MIS development will reduce the need satisfaction in their management positions. Reducing job need satisfaction would be expressed by a resentment or fear of the encroachment of computers into the manager's job function and a concern that computers and MIS will affect their working environment, take decision power away, and possibly undercut the manager's personal worth and position within the company.
3. Familiarity and successful experience with MIS will correlate with positive attitudes and vice versa. Although this seems like a truism, Guthrie felt it was worth pursuing.

The findings for the most part validated hypothesis 1. The felt need for MIS is low, and in general the user managers cannot be expected to give information system development significant time and effort. Hypothesis 2 was not validated; the findings showed that the managers felt MIS would have a somewhat positive effect on their job satisfaction; there were pockets of negative attitudes but no mass resistance to MIS or managerial apprehension or fear. Hypothesis 3 was partially validated in that the findings supported that positive MIS experience correlates with positive MIS attitude, but development experience (participation) does not correlate with positive MIS attitude.

Guthrie also had each manager complete a data sheet about his background, length of service with the company, job function, and so on. Here are some additional findings:

- Newer employees perceive a stronger need for MIS and more positive expected effects from MIS than managers with longer service with the company.
- Both MIS need and MIS expected effects are affected positively by recent management training programs.
- Those top managers that were surveyed scored lower than middle managers in both MIS need and MIS expected effects.
- A strong underlying feeling was a concern about information deluge or information overload. Managers were troubled not by too little information, but by too much information.

Guthrie's survey, in my estimation, paints a rather bland or indifferent attitude on the part of management toward the use of computers. Managers feel little need for MIS and computers; it would appear they are skeptical about the influence MIS could have on their job functions. This indifference was not the result of any negative influence that MIS might have; rather it was the absence of any positive influence.

Harvard Program for Management Development

In conjunction with the Harvard Business School, I developed a questionnaire which was presented to the Program for Management Development (PMD), an intensive thirteen-week course for middle managers. I conducted the survey twice, once in 1978 and again in 1981, and it is interesting to compare the change in three years as well as the changes from the Ference/Uretsky and Guthrie studies.

First, let us look at the composition of the group. The PMD is a program to which companies send their top middle managers—the high achievers and promotable young managers whom they expect to play a dominant role in the company. There were roughly 100 in each group, mostly from medium to large companies. The companies in the surveys range from $2 million in sales to $50 billion, with the median around $450 million. I feel the 1978 and 1981 groups are similar in makeup and represent comparable samples. The average age of the 1981 group is 36 compared with 37 in 1978. Of the 1981 group, 88 percent have college degrees compared with 83 percent in 1978; 42 percent in 1981 have advanced degrees versus 39 percent in 1978. The industry split is consistent with the economy in general, with about 40 percent in manufacturing industries, 15 percent in finance and insurance, and the rest distributed over retailing, transportation, government, and education. The results in general are more favorable than either of the other two surveys in assessing the view that managers have of MIS, and the changes between the 1978 and 1981 groups also show a dramatic shift.

Recalling the split in MIS applications illustrated in Fig. 1.1, the following was their response to the impact of MIS on the various categories of business functions.

BUSINESS FUNCTION IMPACT

	% Positive	
	1978	*1981*
Operational control	88%	94%
Management control	67%	72%
Strategic planning	44%	60%

In each case there is a marked increase in positive response. While the high percentages might be expected in operational control and management control, the 60 percent of 1981 managers who think MIS has had a positive influence in strategic application areas is higher than one might speculate.

The next set of questions focused on computer expenditures and whether their companies were getting an economic return from their investment.

COMPUTER EXPENDITURES

	1978	*1981*
Positive return on investment	59%	84%
Concerning the level of expenditure we should:		
Spend more	21%	32%
Spend less	13%	9%

While this is obviously only a subjective response, since most companies do not have a way of measuring return on MIS investment (at least for the total MIS department), it is surprising to see the significant increase in managers who think the return has been positive. Until fairly recently, there has been a skepticism surrounding the budgets of MIS groups. Managers have seen budgets continuously grow, sometimes by 30 percent per year or more, without what they feel are commensurate returns. The survey results show a marked increase in those who thought their company should be spending more rather than less. The other answer was that they were spending just about what they should be. This question obviously needs further qualification, because the rate of expenditure should be determined by the ROI of additional spending, and I would imagine most managers would make an MIS investment if the return was there and the risk in achieving it was reasonable. However, it does indicate a subjective vote of confidence for MIS and a more aggressive view toward what it can do for a company.

The next series of questions centered on the specific involvement of managers in MIS. This is a key area; a hypothesis might be that their improved view of MIS is a result of greater personnel participation in the MIS process and in the use of MIS output.

SPECIFIC INVOLVEMENT

	1978	1981
See MIS output daily or weekly	76%	73%
Contact with MIS personnel weekly	47%	36%
Involvement with computer projects		
greater than once a year	56%	59%
Personally use on-line terminal		
Now	42%	50%
3 to 5 years	50%	73%

The first two questions show a slight downward involvement level from 1978 to 1981. An explanation of the drop in MIS personnel contact might be that the managers are doing their own thing (refer to increased terminal usage) and not calling on the MIS personnel as much. This is speculation, since I did not ask the question. Managers are getting involved in MIS projects only slightly more in 1981 than 1978, but still a full 40 percent do not get involved more than once a year. The surprising statistic to me is the significant increase in on-line terminal usage, with half of the group using them in the conduct of their business and 73 percent feeling they will be using them on a routine basis (that was the way the question was worded) in 3 to 5 years. The proof of the pudding in this case is the using, and these 36-year-old managers are doing just that. This statistic should be hailed by terminal-device manufacturers.

A set of questions probed the manager's educational background and knowledge level as a possible reason for the change in involvement levels.

The percentages are viewed from the negative side to stress the fact that the majority (less in 1981) of these young managers had scant or no MIS education in

EDUCATIONAL/TRAINING LEVEL

	1978	1981
Scant or no MIS education in school	77%	66%
Scant or no MIS knowledge	50%	43%
No attendance at MIS courses/seminars during last 2 years	76%	59%

school. MIS literacy, recalling the high percentage of graduate degrees, may still be a way off. It is interesting to speculate what would be the involvement level, use of on-line terminals, and so on with a group that has had comprehensive MIS education. About half in each year feel they have scant or no MIS knowledge, though the 1981 group is a bit more knowledgeable. Despite the lack of MIS education in school and the so-so knowledge level, 76 percent in 1978 and 59 percent in 1981 have not attended an MIS course or seminar in the last two years. There is still work to be done in this area. Although it cannot be concluded from the statistics, there is a strong suggestion of a correlation of education/knowledge and a manager's view and use of MIS.

The final questions focused on their feeling of the future influence of MIS on their jobs.

FUTURE MIS INFLUENCE

	1978	1981
Extensive impact on your job in next 3 to 5 years	43%	63%
Cause elimination of your job	1%	
Computers now doing the things they were touted to do		86%

The 20-point jump in the manager's feeling of MIS impact on their job is quite significant in my mind. This is a major shift from the attitudes expressed in surveys conducted in the mid-seventies. Since only one brave soul in 1978 thought his job could be eliminated by MIS, I substituted a question in the 1981 survey and was surprised to see that a full 86 percent feel that the computer and MIS have lived up to expectations.

To summarize this survey, I see a distinct change in the three-year period. Although influences other than MIS-related ones may have been felt during this interval, I feel the major ones are in the progress that MIS has made. Inflation has intensified as a factor to be dealt with, deregulation has changed the makeup of several key industries, and the business economy has in general been more volatile. All these elements must be considered as part of a manager's response to the MIS questionnaire. Yet, to my mind, there is evidence of a turnaround in users' attitudes toward MIS—a departure from the conclusion in the Ference/Uretsky survey that the computer revolution, as far as high-level management functions are concerned, is far from accomplished. If these PMD managers represent tomorrow's top managers (and there is every indication that they do), the change in view in three short years can signal that the revolution is either here or close at hand.

INCREASING THE EFFECTIVENESS
OF MIS

If computers are capable of helping the strategic decision-making process and if this has been proven in the so-called leading edge of corporation management, what can we learn from this experience? I will conclude here by summarizing approaches which I feel will alleviate some of the above conditions and assist the manager in the effective use of the computer in the performance of his job and as an aid in decision making. These points have been made elsewhere in the book; they are repeated here to conclude this section and for emphasis.

Motivate Management

Guthrie makes the point that management must feel a need for MIS in order to be motivated to participate in its development. He also states that we don't have to fight fear or insecurity on the part of managers. Managers do not see computers replacing them or usurping their prerogatives, although some remain unconvinced of the rule of MIS in their managerial sphere.

Effort must be made to motivate management on the favorable impact MIS can make. The best way appears to be by demonstrating successful results. If there are none within the company, then get representatives of successful users to discuss their experience with members of your management. Another method is the development of a small test situation where a specified analytical report is produced for management, indicating the type of assistance that is available. This would serve to pique management's appetite and avoid the discouragement of the long gestation period that accompanies most MIS.

MIS personnel must turn into effective salesmen, but caution must be exercised not to oversell or prematurely sell. Develop and present realistic proposals that make sense and don't go too far too fast. Management participation and involvement are the objectives; evidence supports the need to convince them why they should want MIS.

Involve Management

Evidence shows that those companies with successful MIS have had a higher level of management involvement. How does one obtain this involvement? The prime requisite is to motivate management based on what they can expect to gain from the system. Once this is accomplished, the management steering committee is a good vehicle. Many studies have proven the effectiveness of this approach, one such study indicating that a successful MIS is impossible without a steering group. It is not necessary to have a formal, complex hierarchy of steering groups, but a small carefully selected team of management and MIS professionals to overview the development of specific management systems can prove quite beneficial.

Joint system development between user departments and MIS groups can break down communication barriers and foster management involvement. I was impressed by the system developed by Campbell Taggart (described in *Business Week*): at this large baking company in Texas a communication-linked cost control and profit-and-loss system was actually designed by the president.

I am familiar with an on-line inventory system within Honeywell where progress had come to a complete standstill until system analysts were transferred to the line manufacturing groups and the director of manufacturing assumed personal responsibility for the system. This system is regarded as one of the best of its kind in the industry; hundreds of visitors come to Boston each year to view and discuss the system with its designers.

Establish Consistent Performance and Work Criteria for MIS

MIS should be measured by the same criteria that are used throughout the business. If the organization utilizes MBO (management by objective) or has a particular "results" orientation, those same principles should be applied to MIS. The same return on investment or profit standards should be applied. Cost accounting reports and other management reports should be incorporated for MIS as they are for other areas of the operation. As the MIS department begins to adopt the procedures of the company, so should the individuals. Accounting for time spent on jobs and efforts to measure productivity should be incorporated. More and more, the MIS department's mode of operation should be consistent with the rest of the organization. The procedures should be applied fairly and uniformly to avoid a counterreaction from the MIS people. These measures should be instituted in such a way that the individuals regard them as an aid in better managing their time and activity and not as a bridle to their innovation and creativity.

Consider the Basic Computer Feasibility Criteria

It is important not to attack the wrong management problems and attempt to computerize an activity that just isn't a feasible MIS application. Although they may not be familiar with the detailed costs of implementing and operating a computer application, management people do sense when the benefits obtained are not commensurate with the costs. There are seven computer-feasibility criteria, most of which, I feel, are necessary to constitute a payoff from computerization. They are (1) high volume of transactions, (2) repetitive nature of transactions, (3) reasonable degree of mathematical processing, (4) quick turnaround time, (5) accuracy and validity of data, (6) common source documents, and (7) well-understood processing logic. I believe these criteria apply to management-oriented applications as well. One-time functions that involve a good deal of programming and data gathering are not feasible applications to tackle. It is better to explain this to management at the outset than continue to pursue a "will-o'-the-wisp" application with marginal return at best.

Credibility will be established, paving the way for acceptance of management applications with real payoffs.

Maintain Simplicity

I have always liked the phrase "elegance in simplicity" and am convinced that the most effective computer applications are those that are straightforward, easy to understand, and easy to operate. Systems analysts will have better success working with management if they talk about simplifying the analysis or the data that the manager must review. Guthrie warned of the information-overload syndrome. Business operations have grown in volume and complexity; a good system man can help cut through this complexity, eliminate the extraneous, combine two reports into one, eliminate other data completely. We still kill too many fleas with elephant hammers.

In my visits to computer shops and in discussions with managers, I often wonder whatever happened to the management-by-exception principle. No wonder paper costs have risen; our high-speed printers and copying machines turn it out by the ton—and no relief in sight. I am firmly convinced that MIS can favorably impact management if we can show them how to streamline and simplify the decision process and the underlying data that supports the decision. I like the comment appended by a professor to a very long letter sent to a colleague, "I would have written a shorter letter, but I didn't have the time." It takes effort to be concise and meaningful—but we should make that effort. Business, government, and life, in general, have become complex enough—we should employ our profession to simplify rather than add to the complexity and confusion. Thus, a plea at this stage for elegance in simplicity.

"Systems perspective" is another phrase I like. It implies ability to make tradeoffs which favor practicality, pragmatism, and workability over scientific purity and sophistication. I favor a "systems poetic license" that permits compromises in order to shield the complexity from the user while recognizing the law of diminishing returns when greater accuracy or greater detail doesn't add to the effectiveness of problem resolution.

Train Systems/Business Analysts

Obviously a necessary prerequisite to accomplishing any job is competent people. So it is with MIS. More and more, the major qualification of successful systems people is a solid business perspective. The technical side of the job is important—the *how* something gets done—but the *what* is even more important. It is the *what* dimension that MIS people have in common with non-MIS managers; this should be the springboard for closer cooperation and communication.

To develop systems that aid management, we need a new breed of systems people who are business-oriented first and MIS-oriented second. Schools and universities must help in the training process; I have long felt that institutions stress the technical side of computers and give inadequate attention to the relationship of information to the management process and how computers influence this process.

This new breed has been called "Renaissance People" by Dean Donald C. Carroll. He points out that information technologists who don't understand management problems often err by developing elegant solutions to nonproblems. The "Renaissance People" would combine technical expertise with the management function and organization. Dean Carroll indicates that the Wharton School of Business has developed a new curriculum that recognizes this need.

We must recognize that the control of business and business decisions is not in the hands of specialists; it is in the hands of business generalists. The MIS professional must fully comprehend this basic truth and direct his intellect and expertise toward aiding the generalist in making better decisions—remembering that the decisions and the manner in which they are made are the province of management.

One of the healthiest situations has been the interchange of people within the MIS and operating areas of a company. It makes good sense to staff the MIS department with personnel from operating departments who show an aptitude and an interest for system work. Similarly, system analysts should receive a tour of duty outside of MIS, in order to appreciate the problems of the actual business world and understand the difficulties of putting an advanced new system into productive operation.

It is important that this rotation of people not be a way of dumping the marginal performers within a department. Management should recognize the long-term benefit of transferring proven performers in key support departments like MIS. Many companies have filled key MIS management positions with individuals with records of success in operating departments who possess a system outlook but lack direct computer experience. Transfer of people from MIS to key operating department positions should also be encouraged. This is certainly one way, and a good one, of alleviating the difference in motivation and aspiration referred to earlier.

Whenever possible, MIS and operating personnel should be assimilated in everyday business activities. At conferences, work sessions, or business get-togethers, the groups should be encouraged to work together, to take every opportunity to discuss and explore things together. If possible, MIS people and operating people should travel together, engage in social activities together, and develop an awareness of each other's standpoint on business matters. Most people are prone to stay with employees of their own department and to discuss matters with people of similar background. This situation does nothing to facilitate the understanding and resolution of problems; it merely reinforces one's predetermined judgment on the matter. Another opportunity to work together is on special projects that require interdisciplinary participation. Mutual confidence and respect are built up when a task is accomplished by such a group.

A THREE-PHASED MANAGEMENT-INVOLVEMENT PROGRAM

To conclude this chapter, I present an approach to obtaining management involvement in an area that is of prime interest to management. A phasing approach geared to the timing and appetite of the particular executive, it is a takeoff on John Rockart's critical-success-factor concept discussed in Chapter 2 and has a bit of his executive decision support system described in the preceding chapter. It starts with an education process that has been emphasized in this chapter. The approach is based on an actual situation involving a senior executive in a plant in which I worked.

Management Operating Style

An interesting scenario of the manager is presented by Henry Mintzberg in his provocative *Harvard Business Review* article, "Folklore and Fact." He classifies as a myth the picture of a manager as a reflective, regulated, scientific professional whose decisions are supported by MIS. Rather, the facts show the manager as working at a relentless pace, his activities characterized by brevity, variety, and discontinuity; he is strongly oriented to action while disliking reflective activities. He further points out that managers favor verbal soft, externally based information rather than the aggregated information provided by an MIS. Mintzberg states as his main theme "that the pressures of his job drive the manager to be superficial in his actions—to overload himself with work, encourage interruptions, respond quickly to every stimulus, seek the tangible and avoid the abstract, make decisions in small increments, and do everything abruptly."

My experience supports this characterization. The successful managers I have observed are often poor managers of time; they will prolong an hour meeting into a full day if they sense its importance while stacking up people who are waiting for the next meeting to commence. Recent studies indicate that a congressman spends only eleven minutes alone during a typical eleven-hour working day. Though possibly a little extreme, a similar pattern can be found in the successful businessman. This affords precious little time for reflective activity. Furthermore, managers operate in real time when the boss is concerned; they will completely revamp an entire week's schedule if they sense the new subject is the boss's hot button. Whether believable or acceptable, the evidence shows this is the way of business life.

User Involvement in Decision Support Systems

A study reported by Stephen Alter in the *Management Information System Quarterly* focused on the prevailing wisdom concerning systems implementation: "Implementation will be most successful if the potential users really want the new system and if they participate actively in its development." The author obtained data from 56 case studies of decision support systems in use within organizations. The data was gathered by conducting structured interviews with both implementers and users of each organization.

The results show that in 31 of the 56 systems, users did not initiate the system, and in 38 of the 56, the user did not participate actively in its development. Only 12 of the systems were consistent with the prevailing wisdom of having both user initiation and user participation. While it is surprising that more systems did not follow the accepted techniques for implementation success, the study definitely supported the prevailing wisdom. There were more problems with systems where users had low participation and low initiation; conversely the more successful systems were those that users initiated and in which they participated.

Two general hypotheses have been presented. The first is that the operating mode of many successful managers runs counter to the image of a thoughtful, reflective decision maker. The second is that user initiation and involvement are necessary ingredients in the design and implementation of a successful system. A conflict arises when one tries to build on these hypotheses. Management involvement is essential; yet the very style and characteristics of top managers suggest an aversion to MIS and computer-based systems.

An Approach to Involve Management

The starting point is to thoroughly assess top management. Too often, systems managers give little or no thought to the management part of MIS and concentrate on the areas where they are comfortable—on the computer, on the system, and on the technology. As a starter, it is important to determine to what extent the top-management customers for MIS fit the management prototype that has been described. Quite possibly management might be the Renaissance type, the reflective, analytical problem solver type, in which case the job should prove a good deal easier. However, it is predicted that more often than not, management will fall into the defined pattern.

Having carefully assessed the management audience within the company, the following strategy is proposed. It requires human relations skills and strategic and tactical planning in order to succeed.

A basic premise is that today's non-Renaissance manager lacks a meaningful understanding of the workings of information systems and computers, particularly as pertains to the elements of software, data base, and interactive computer communication via terminals. Furthermore, this lack of understanding bothers the manager. Viewed from the positive side, the manager would consider such knowledge as a management asset, particularly if he could use it to his advantage in his business milieu.

The techniques employed to impart this knowledge have not met with success to date, a major reason being inadequate attention to the management operating style described earlier. The distinction between education and training is important. Education refers to learning of an academic nature where ideas, theories, and technical knowledge are presented, usually in a classroom setting. Training has an on-the-job orientation where specific skills are imparted to help the individual improve his or her specific job function; it is practical and immediately relevant. Management is more attuned to training than to education, and the approach proposed here has a training focus.

The training target is the key operating executive of the organization. The concept is to develop a strong training relationship between the MIS manager and this key operating executive. The theory is that success in training the key executive in the use of an on-line terminal that supports his specific job functions, will have a tops-down impact on the entire organization. The MIS director should oversee and play a principal role in the training. The side benefit of establishing a strong working personal relationship with the top operating executive can prove to be as important as the objective at hand. Research shows that, historically, this relationship has not been a strong or effective one.

The Three-Phase Plan

The next element is to develop a specific plan. An assessment of the MIS director's skills and the information-processing capabilities of the company are necessary underpinnings. Look to a three-phase plan. Initially ask the manager for an hour a week (any hour suited to his schedule) for the initiation of his personal training program. Explain its purpose and objectives. The first stage is to jointly develop a simple program using BASIC or some other elementary interactive language that is available and can be run on a terminal. Any of a number of programs can be used, such as one that produces a report on selected common stocks held by the executive. The input for file preparation is the number of shares and cost per share of each stock. Then the current market price per share is keyed in, while the program generates percentage gain or loss of each stock and its performance against the Dow Jones average or some other stock index. This is a good training example because it is personal, and the executive can quickly envision how the program can be enhanced to produce more useful analysis. The analogy to the business situation is quickly made. So much for phase one. Success will depend on the logical step-by-step explanation of the carefully preplanned programming exercise. It must be oriented to the executive's level and, above all, must not be shrouded in technical detail.

The second phase involves a review of the executive's individual goals or objectives. These are vital to him because they normally determine his compensation package for the year. The intent here is to strike directly at the area which has the manager's highest priority. The goals will include quantifiable measurements such as dollar profit, dollar sales, production volume, product margins, and expense levels. Also included are specific event goals such as releases or first ships of specified products or specific milestones for new-product plans and specifications. In addition, the executive will have facility goals such as completing a plant extension, initiating a new production line, or opening a new sales office. Finally, there will be people goals, such as maintaining a specified employee count, turnover rate, or EEO (minority) percentage.

The objective during this second phase is to establish the key indicators or measurements for these top-level executive goals and to develop an information retrieval system so that the executive can ask the computer via his terminal for an updated status for any given time period. One can immediately conclude that this will require a degree of systems work, but if kept simple, it should not be a major effort. The real benefit comes from a joint analysis of how the executive's goals are measured and the best way to gather the data in order to measure the goals. The measurement data usually comes as a by-product of other computerized systems and can be incorporated manually, thus avoiding the effort and time of linking ongoing systems to the executive's data base. Though the computer is being used only in a reporting mode during this phase, it serves to focus on the key indicators and measurements of the organization. This phase is a starting point for top-management involvement and a springboard into phase three.

Before entering phase three, it is possible to enhance and add applications to phase two to make that phase more meaningful. The same terminal can be used as a word processor and/or electronic mail medium by the executive's secretary, if the company has sufficient capability and experience in this area. Another possibility is the use of the terminal as a time and meeting scheduler, similar to what was described in the preceding chapter in the discussion of the electronic executive.

Phase three is when the executive begins to see the meaning of MIS—as a top-management decision-making aid. Still focusing on his personal goals and objectives, he is now able to ask "what if" questions. If his objective is a specified profit margin and he is the plant manager, he may want to know the year-end profit rate based on current product margins, overhead rates, and the latest volume forecast. He may then want to project year-end results based on reducing the overhead rate, increasing the product margin, increasing the volume, or some combination thereof. This moves the executive into the simulation and decision support arena. This phase will require closer working relationships and involvement than the other two, but by this time the required management motivation should be established. This phase will take longer to implement because of the systems work that is required; however, the pressure and priority to complete will be present. The brevity of discussion here should in no way understate the effort that is needed in this phase. It is no mean task, and the burden will be on the MIS manager. But if he has done his job well to this point, he will have convinced top management of the worth and benefit of MIS and the need for the required resources to move ahead.

Benefit of the Program

This, then, is the three-phase executive MIS program. There is risk in such a program. If it falters in midstream, there can be a reverse impact, a worsening computer and MIS image in the eyes of the executive, and—more damaging—a deterioration in the relationship between the MIS manager and the executive. However, the potential benefits of such an approach are far reaching and well worth the risk. A Renaissance operating manager will have been created, and in the process a Renaissance MIS director as well. The thrust of MIS will be focused in the real payoff area—the strategic, decision-making arena. In establishing the framework to do so, the goals and objectives passed down to middle management levels will become a part of the analysis and measurement system and emphasize the value of the tops-down philosophy. If I had my choice of having the chief operating executive motivated and involved in MIS versus the entire middle management team, I think I would opt for the former. The approach postulated here will heavily involve the operating executive and the MIS director, but I feel it will prove to be invaluable to both.

The characteristics of the manager developed earlier may seem antithetical to this approach. However, by establishing the motivation of acquiring more knowledge and more on-the-job application of that knowledge, and by avoiding the formality of the classroom and the embarrassment of displaying one's lack of knowledge in public, this approach can prove very beneficial for the executive. The idea of his controlling the training environment, proceeding at his pace on his turf, should provide the necessary executive motivation. The number one caveat of this approach for the MIS director is: Don't be a technocrat; be a businessman first and a technician second. This approach is geared to the top operating manager; knowing the boss and his style of operation may well be the greatest challenge faced by the MIS director. It could be the most important and most rewarding as well.

SUMMARY

This chapter has been concerned with the level of involvement and influence that management should have if a company plans to implement a management information system. The role of general management, as well as the role of MIS management, has been discussed because MIS involves the proper interaction of the two groups. Once the level of involvement is established (and this factor depends on the relative position of a manager within the company), the next issue is the various methods of obtaining the necessary involvement and MIS awareness. Direct and indirect MIS participation were discussed, the former involving full-time interaction with the MIS department, the latter a part-time but crucial role in directing and guiding the system development activity.

Management education and training were emphasized as a means of developing MIS involvement, for education is a cornerstone of understanding any new activity. Three paths were explored, including schools and universities, internal on-site company training, and external off-site company training.

The chapter concluded by reviewing several surveys on the impact of computers on management. Steps were presented which, if followed by general management and MIS management, should improve the situation and move MIS and the computer more into the management realm. Finally, a technique was reviewed, a plan to form a partnership between the MIS director and the top operation executive of the company. Based on his key performance indicators, a system is developed to aid in their measurement and attainment. Chapters 9 and 10 form a most important portion of the book. Unless management understands the potential impact of MIS and then takes the necessary steps to become properly involved, management information systems will remain the myth they have been to many companies.

CASE STUDIES

RUTGERS ELECTRONICS

The following conversation takes place in the office of the vice-president of Marketing of a medium-sized electronics company. MM (Modern Manager) in the dialogue below represents the VP of Marketing while TT (Technical Type) represents the director of MIS.

MM: Let's review the situation briefly to put the problem in perspective. It was a year ago today that I told you I wanted a cathode ray tube display in my office. We're in the electronics business, and I think we should be in the forefront of the people using our products. I indicated I wanted to be able to make inquiries of our customer file to find out the current status of customers, shipments, on order and the like. I asked you when you thought you could have this set up for me and you said six months. Is that correct?

TT: I would have to say that your recollection is basically correct, but I think there are some real mitigating circumstances underlying the problem.

MM: Before you get into that, let me continue for a minute. The terminal was not installed in six months as you indicated but three months later than that. The terminal was hooked up and could communicate with a local time-sharing company computer and also with an educational institution in the area, but it didn't communicate with our own data base. You indicated we could be ready on a week-to-week basis, but the fact of the matter is that another three months has passed and I still don't have any results. It's quite embarrassing to have people come into the office, ask about the CRT and what I can do with it. Frankly, I usually tell them what I wanted to do with it, and try to mix the tenses so they don't realize it's what I'd like to do and not what I can do. I usually have to make some kind of excuse if they ask me to demonstrate it.

TT: What you say is true and I apologize for the lack of results, but I would like to review the circumstances. You remember when we started out with this project, I told you the terminal itself was the simplest part of our problem—like the iceberg analogy, 10 percent is visible above the surface (that's the terminal), while 90 percent is below the surface (that's the customer data base and communications software that provides the data to the terminal). Frankly, we've had one heck of a time developing the customer data base. That's where the problem lies. We had a tape file, and we've had to go to disk to facilitate on-line inquiry. We've also had problems keeping the file current and incorporating the information you wanted as well as the information desired by other parts of the organization.

MM: Are you saying that my demands have been given low priority?

TT: Not exactly, but I think you would agree that the first thing we must do is bill our customers accurately for the products and services they get from us, and then setting up the accounts receivable so that we get the cash.

MM: That may be so, but it seems we should be able to do that type of thing with no trouble at all. When can I use my terminal the way you and I talked about it?

TT: I want to be frank with you because I'm well aware of your impatience and disappointment—I assure you I share your feelings. It's still difficult, despite our experience, to predict when we can have the system operable. You know our business has been growing and changing very rapidly and the minute we think we've got the situation under control, something else breaks that impacts the system—a new sales division is added, or we add a new product line and so on. I've discussed the matter with my systems people, and I think we can reasonably promise you that your CRT can be hooked on-line three months from today.

MM: If that's the situation, take the device out of my office. It's stupid to pay for a machine I'm not using. It's an expensive office play toy when you get nothing from it. This time you tell me when you're ready to go; I've lost confidence that we'll ever make it.

STUDY QUESTIONS

1. Do you think this situation is typical?

2. Do you feel TT's explanation of the delay is reasonable?

3. Do you think MM bears some of the blame for the problem?

4. How do you think TT should have handled the situation from the outset?

5. What should be TT's plan of action now?

6. Does MM really need the terminal, or is it just an office toy?

MIDEASTERN ELECTRIC

A large utility with over two million customers, Mideastern has been using computers for over fifteen years. A conservative approach to computers and organization has resulted in the situation where the president has become upset with the lack of progress in MIS. Upon his return from an advanced computer seminar, he asked his staff assistant to make a quick assessment of their use of computers in relation to other utilities doing about the same volume of business.

The report, which the assistant indicated was only a cursory treatment in view of the six-week deadline the president had placed on its completion, centered on the lack of imagination and rather prosaic approach that the current MIS staff had taken. It was true that customer billing was running smoothly, but the computer offered management minimal help in areas such as power loading or in improving cost effectiveness; in other words, the company was paying over a million dollars per year in computer hardware costs alone, but was reaping very few benefits in the management area. The report was most direct, hard-hitting, and very critical of most of the computer operations. While it didn't single out current MIS management, the conclusions were tantamount to a severe indictment.

The MIS director was a long-term Mideastern employee having been with the company for 22 years. He ran the tape-oriented system when Mideastern started with data processing and slowly evolved into his current position over the period of time that the company was going through three generations of computer hardware.

On the basis of the report and his own intuitive feeling, the president had decided on a change in MIS management. He wanted the current staff assistant to the vice-president of engineering, Bill Vosbury, to take over the job. The staff assistant had been with Mideastern 15 years, was involved in a variety of management jobs, most of them important line functions, and always performed these functions most effectively. He had a record of achievement and was also a technically competent individual, not afraid to tackle new jobs which weren't exactly in his area of expertise. He knew very little about computers, particularly about running a large-scale MIS department. He had a bachelor's and master's degree in electrical engineering, so that he knew the basic principles of computers and the electronics that powered them.

Vosbury had given a great deal of thought to the president's insistence that he take the job; however, because of the importance of the job and the fact that it was different from any other job Vosbury had held, the president left the final decision to Vosbury. Vosbury had two days before his meeting with the president. The president would expect his decision on taking the job as well as his initial feelings on the approach to be taken to improve Mideastern's data processing function. Vosbury was spending considerable time mulling over what he would say to the president; he knew it was an important crossroad in his career.

STUDY QUESTIONS

1. Is Vosbury qualified for the job?

2. Did the president act with intelligence on the basis of the report by his assistant?

3. What should Vosbury do if he accepts the job?

4. What should be the role of the old MIS director in the new organization?

5. How long do you think it will be before Vosbury gets results?

6. Does Mideastern have management involvement?

DELCON APPAREL

Bob Harris, systems manager for Delcon Apparel, had tried every technique he could think of to get Burt Rutherford interested in the system they were installing in his department. Rutherford had been negative on computers from the start and was quite upset when one of the first major applications selected was computerized inventory control, an operation which had a major impact on how Rutherford's department performed.

Harris had met with Rutherford at the outset of the system design and had asked for Rutherford's opinion on the system requirements as he saw them. Rutherford promised to get back to Harris, but never did. Next, Harris scheduled a three-day management overview and personally invited Rutherford to attend. Again a promise, but Rutherford declined the day before the session because of a pressing meeting. Rutherford received copies of the monthly status reports on the inventory control application, but Harris felt certain Rutherford never looked at them.

The application was scheduled to go into production in two weeks. Harris carefully considered what his next move should be.

STUDY QUESTIONS

1. Did Harris do all he could in the situation?

2. What do you think of Rutherford's actions?

3. Do you think it's wise to go ahead with the system introduction?

4. Are there any other ways to get Rutherford involved in the system? Is it really necessary to do so?

BIBLIOGRAPHY

Alloway, Robert M. and Judith A. Quillard, "Poll: Users Opens Agree on Criteria for Success," *Computerworld* (July 6, 1981).

Alter, Stephen, "Development Pattern for Decision Support Systems," *Management Information System Quarterly* (Sept. 1978).

Davis, Gordon B., "The Knowledge and Skill Requirements for the Doctorate in MIS," *Proceedings of the First International Conference on Information Systems* (Dec. 8–10, 1980), Philadelphia, PA.

Ference, T. P. and M. Uretsky, *Computers in Management: Some Insights Into the State of the Revolution*, New York: New York University, 1974.

Guthrie, A., *A Survey of Canadian Middle Managers' Attitudes Towards Management Information Systems*. Ottawa, Ontario, Canada: Carleton University, 1972.

Hoffer, Jeffrey, Alan G. Merten, and John F. Rockart, "Teaching the Current or Future General Managers: A Critical Function for the MIS Faculty," *Proceedings of the First International Conference on Information Systems* (Dec. 8–10, 1980), Philadelphia, PA.

Mintzberg, Henry, "Folklore and Fact," *Harvard Business Review* (1975).

Nunamaker, Jr., Jay F., Daniel J. Couger, and Gordon B. Davis, "Information Systems Curriculum Recommendations for the 80's: Undergraduate and Graduate Programs," *Communications of the ACM* (Nov. 1982).

Chapter 11

The Future of MIS
and Information
Resource Management

Chapter 6 touched on the major MIS trends through four decades. This chapter will explore more of the trends and changes that can be expected and the manner in which users over the next decade will be utilizing the increased capabilities of tomorrow's computers. Many of the specific subjects to be discussed have been mentioned throughout the book. They will be summarized here and placed in perspective.

The general trends that make up the four computer generations of the past and the fifth generation just beginning to develop will be discussed. Particular attention will be given to the personal computer and computers in the home. Finally, we will take a look at some of the sociological and psychological considerations that are becoming increasingly relevant in the growing age of automation and computers.

THE FUTURE OF DATA PROCESSING

This section will summarize the major technological and developmental trends that underlie the impressive growth of computer systems over the last three decades, and will take a look at the next decade.

Data processing (DP) has been viewed historically as a series of generations with specific developments characterizing each. The first two generations were easy to define, the departure point being the replacement of vacuum tubes by transistors as the principal electronic element. However, the dividing line between subsequent generations has blurred as a kaleidoscope of emerging technologies and products reached the marketplace. The approach used here is to first describe what I term "environmental development rings," the elements that are necessary to a functioning data processing system. I will then use these rings as a base point to trace the major developments over the last thirty or so years. In so doing, I will group the commercial life of DP into five eras, beginning with what I call the iron age of computers. I will spend a bit more time describing the elements of the fifth era, which is just emerging.

Environmental Development Rings

Figure 11.1 indicates by a series of concentric rings the elements necessary for a successful information system. It begins with the raw technology at the center and fans out to include society, the outermost ring. A brief definition of each element follows.

An example of *technology* is the development of LSI (large-scale integration), a process which enables the fabrication and integration of logic elements on a silicon die called a chip, maybe a quarter of an inch square. The level of integration varies, but the state of the art in LSI is currently the ability to place the equivalent of 100,000 transistors on a chip.

Architecture refers to the way we put together the technology, such as using LSI to produce microprocessors, which are used over a vast spectrum from powering small home calculators to controlling specific functions like input, output, and communications within a large-scale computing complex.

The design concept of early mainframes was to place all the logic of the system into a single central processor, but today's concept is to reduce complexity by separating logical elements into micro-driven subprocessors. Architecture represents the way

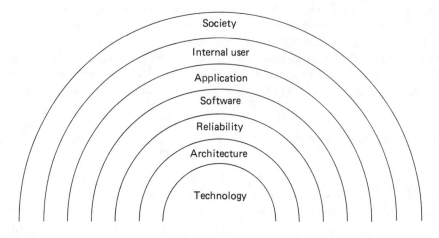

Fig. 11.1 Environmental development rings

the system looks to users; an analogy is a prefabricated house where the floors, ceilings, and walls might be made of the same elements, but the way they are put together, the architecture, makes all the difference.

The *reliability* ring is often underemphasized but is quite important. Reliability, availability, and maintainability are essential ingredients to effective and productive operation of a computer system. An information system, particularly an on-line one, cannot tolerate down-time and must approximate 100 percent availability.

Reliability is usually achieved by a combination of the technology and architecture rings (hardware) and the software ring. The distributed-data-processing and transaction-oriented system trends depend on high reliability.

Software (the languages and operating systems) is needed to harness today's computer power and has been emphasized throughout the book. Historically, this element has lagged technology and architecture, though it has been said for years that the three should be developed as an entity.

The *application* is what the computer actually does, be it inventory control, maintaining patients' bills in a hospital, or scheduling school classes. The reader should be aware of the wide range of computer applications, as described in the various chapters.

The *internal user* environmental ring includes the management and non-management end users of the information system within a company. This book has focused primarily on the management users.

Society represents the outside environment, covering (1) the economic forces such as inflation, competition, the energy situation, and so on, (2) the government forces such as laws and taxes, and information demands, and (3) personal forces such as privacy, environment, and individual rights and expectations.

All seven elements are essential to an effective system; their evolution will be discussed in relation to the DP life cycle spanning five eras.

Traditionally, DP has been a technology-driven industry. The planning emphasis has taken an inside-out approach, when it should be the other way around, from the outside in. The main emphasis should not be whether or not the product will work, but what kind of work it will do; the criterion should be, not the ability to do something, but the advisability of doing it; the concentration should be not on how something is done but on what is done.

I don't prescribe that it has to be exclusively outside-in; obviously there have been some significant, useful achievements made by technologists without outside direction; however, there have been equally significant failures and huge wastes of funds working on the wrong problems. The inside-out approach often succeeds the first time, but repeated success from the same source does not occur.

Five Eras of Data Processing

Figure 11.2 lists five generations or eras (named perhaps a bit grandiosely), beginning with the iron age when the major emphasis was on hardware or "iron" and continuing through to the fifth generation, which begins in 1983, and whose general

Era	Time Period	Technology	Architecture	Reliability	Software	Application	User Impact
Iron Age	1951–1958	Vacuum tube	Mono-programming	Brute force	Simple monitor	Administrative	Accountants
Age of Expectation	1959–1963	Transistor	I/O overlap	On-site support	Multi-function monitor	Mainstream	Controllers
Age of Proliferation	1964–1974	Integrated circuit	Multi-programming	Self-logging	Operating system	Communications	Technocrats
The Renaissance	1975–1982	MSI/LSI	Firmware, virtual system	Self-diagnosis	Interactive	Data base, networking	Middle management
Golden Age	1983–	VLSI and gallium arsenide	Minis, micros, and terminals	Fail-soft and never-fail operation	Integrated transaction processing	Distributed processing	End user and strategic management

Fig. 11.2 Historical computer eras

direction we are able to discern based on the evolutionary environmental development rings of the past.

Iron Age

This period covers the 1951–1958 time span when the vacuum tube was the main electronic element. The hardware architecture was geared to handling one sequential operation after another. There were limited reliability aids centering on basic diagnostics, such as I/O exercises which tested input-output devices during a preventative maintenance cycle. Brute-force maintenance was the rule, field service engineering kept machines running by concentrated repair and attention. Computers employed rudimentary software with simple monitors which loaded one program at a time into memory.

The application focus was strictly on the administrative functions. In the user environment, the early computers were viewed as an extension of the accounting function, and there was little if any management involvement outside the data processing operation itself; the controller was interested, but that was all. A good deal of apprehension and doubt accompanied the installation or thought of installation. Enough said about this era; it was the beginning, and few could forecast the dramatic growth of this fledgling industry thirty years hence.

Age of Expectation

This era ushered in the transistor, which replaced the vacuum tube; it was a marvelous development. Computers decreased in size, power required, maintenance required, and, most important, in cost. Where the computer had been considered a device for large companies, now smaller firms could afford them. (Not that they needed them in all cases.) Not only did the transistor offer faster circuits and therefore more processing power, but the architecture allowed the overlapping of the relatively slow input and output devices by a technique of "buffering," thus providing significantly increased throughput.

Reliability aids were improved, with test and diagnostic routines enhanced to test more areas of potential hardware weaknesses. Larger sites had on-site maintenance, carrying forward the concept of brute force from the first generation. While the internal software monitors were not advanced enough at this stage to be called operating systems, they could accomplish several functions at a time; thus the monitor could be processing a payroll while printing invoices or reading transaction cards for later input into another application. The assembly language of the first generation had given way to COBOL (*CO*mmon *B*usiness *O*riented *L*anguage) as well as FORTRAN (*For*mula *Tran*slation) for mathematical programming.

The predominant application type was still administrative, but there were increasing examples of mainstream applications such as production scheduling or inventory control. Application packages, preprogrammed routines developed by the computer manufacturer, were first introduced on a broad scale in this period.

The user environment found management enamored by these new devices and anxious to install and experiment; they were important as status symbols. Cost effectiveness was a secondary concern during this time frame. Organizationally the computer resided in the controller's department; he was the one who established application priorities.

Proliferation

During the proliferation period, companies really got on the bandwagon and began installing computers wherever there seemed even a remote requirement. The technology during the time span of 1964–1974 was the integrated circuit, which continued the more-power-per-dollar trend that the transistor introduced. This was the era of the family concept in architecture. Machines were designed that had little brothers and big sisters such that a company could start small and upgrade to the next higher model. In addition, a company could have smaller satellite computers in division plants and offices that were compatible with the larger central computer at the corporate headquarters.

During the era of proliferation, nationwide field engineering groups provided service in remote as well as major cities. Techniques were developed which monitored performance and recorded failures. These self-logging devices were significant aids to system performance and preventive maintenance.

Operating systems came into their own during this period; this facilitated multiprogramming. Communication processing grew, and most medium and large companies had at least several terminals that transmitted data back and forth from remote sites. Mainstream applications accounted for about as much computing time as administrative applications, and some companies were beginning to integrate the mainstream and administrative functions to form the beginnings of MIS, though the design of this new approach was in the hands of the DP personnel or "technocrats." Management was just beginning to awake to the potential of the computer, but not to the extent where they took leadership and became heavily involved in MIS development. The advent of the operating system made computer operations much more complex than they were under the simpler monitors and supervisors. Simplicity and ease of operation were unrealized objectives with manufacturers, and the job of understanding, evaluating, selecting, and implementing these systems was the bailiwick of the technocrat. This period was accompanied by a proliferation of devices, particularly in the terminal and communications areas. Technical skill was a requirement, if only to read and understand the literature and to analyze the claims of vendors for their newly developed products, most of which were still on the drawing board.

The overriding mood during this period was one of optimism and enthusiasm; computers, it seemed, could solve most any paperwork problem. Indeed, every company had to have a computer; it was the age of proliferation.

The Renaissance

Communications, networking, and the integrated data base are the cornerstones of the Renaissance era, the period in which the real potential of information systems begins to be unleashed. Medium and large-scale integration, which provide more electronic elements per square inch than the integrated circuit of the previous generation, are the principle technologies along with metallic oxide semiconductor (MOS) memory, which replaced conventional core memory. The architecture is built around firmware that allows subdividing functions into small modular processors, each specialized for a particular job. The concept of the virtual system, as already described, is a feature of fourth-era architecture.

The requirements for high-up-time systems dictated the use of on-line diagnostics as maintenance aids—no longer could a system be down because a field engineer had to diagnose an error or a potential error. Test and diagnostic routines become a part of the operating system, called into operation routinely and without shutting down the entire system. This period also saw the extension of self-logging and self-diagnostic routines whereby potential failures can be spotted and fixed before they occur.

The software is still built around the sophisticated and complex interactive operating system, which has now been structured to handle the growing load of communication, interactive, and associated applications. The concept of management information systems comes on strong during this period and begins to have an impact on middle management. Applications are built around an integrated data base. Inquiry languages allow access to pertinent data files by both DP and non-DP types, the language being constructed such that the users can deal directly with the system without going through intermediaries. Enlightened business awareness of data processing and a cost/benefit consciousness characterize this time frame.

Golden Age

This era, beginning in 1983, is in reality an evolutionary step from the fourth era. While there are and will be technological breakthroughs in basic computer circuitry, the major gains will come more from architecture, software, and application. The economies of scale and the continuing of large-scale integration should permit central processing power to show a significant performance/cost increase, consistent with past generations. Architecture will take advantage of the micro- and miniprocessor to surround the central processor, itself comprised of multi-minis with small, powerful subprocessors, specialized to do specific functions quickly, efficiently, and cost effectively. Gradually the micros will replace the minis in more situations. Also the employment of user-oriented terminal work stations will grow.

Graceful degradation of the type described as part of the Multics system in Chapter 5 will be a major reliability mode. If, for example, one memory unit is malfunctioning, the other three units will pick up the slack and the system will continue to operate, albeit in a slightly slowed-down mode. Completely redundant system components will ensure in essence 100 percent up-time.

Software will feature extensions of inquiry and data-base-oriented languages, making it even easier for non-MIS personnel to communicate with the integrated data base. Applications will feature transaction processing, all integrated so as to trigger immediate action throughout the organization, and communications, with more companies exchanging data and developing industrywide methods of computer interfaces. Finally information systems will have as significant an impact on top and strategic management levels as they have on operating and middle management levels today. Managers will communicate with the computer much as they now use the telephone. End-user languages geared to the different classes of professional users will make this feasible.

We now take a closer look at the environmental development rings of the fifth era. As can be seen, many of the developments had their genesis in the fourth era and some even in the third. This is not surprising, for as computer vendors and users alike have developed a greater sense of business perspective toward this rapidly changing technology, it has become obvious that evolutionary growth without traumatic transition and conversion between generations of equipment is an important criterion. Figure 11.3 indicates the key areas of development during the fifth era.

KEY DEVELOPMENT AREAS

Technology

As previously stated, greater densities of electronic elements will be utilized on silicon chips; mass-production techniques will make these chips extremely inexpensive and therefore their use will spread as processors, input/output controllers, memory, and firmware. The eventual successor to silicon chips might well be chips made from a compound of gallium and arsenide that promise circuit speeds two to five times greater. In addition, gallium arsenide doesn't overheat and for a given circuit speed consumes only 1/100th of the power required by silicon. The ultrafast so-called Josephson junctions must be cooled to near absolute zero. The latter is required only for ultra-fast circuits and will evolve more slowly than gallium arsenide.

Optical disks, with extremely high density as a result of laser-beam technology, will become a mass-storage medium. They have the advantage of storing both digital and pictorial data, but once written on, the impression becomes permanent. However, optical disks are well suited for historical records.

The grocery front-end checkout counter utilizes a laser reader to interpret the bars of the universal product code that was developed by the food industry. Optical readers are being used in retailing and banking operations. These optical/laser readers will cause a proliferation in point-of-sale devices. Associated with this trend is the development of the electronic funds-transfer system made possible by the use of a money card or credit card which can be optically read.

Technology
- VLSI
- Gallium arsenide
- Optical disks
- Point-of-sale optics
  (OCR and laser readers)
- Voice input/output
- Flat-screen display technology and
  color graphics
- Data-transmission enhancements

Architecture
- Virtual machine extensions
- Mini/microprocessor
- Distributed data processing
- Firmware extensions
- Data orientation/security

Reliability
- Fault logging
- Self-diagnosis
- On-line testing
- Graceful degradation
- Replace in lieu of repair

Software
- Efficient multirunning
- Design modularity/simplicity
  (ease of use)
- Enhanced data-base management
- Management inquiry languages
- Conversion/expansion emphasis

Application
- Management information systems
- Mainstream functions
- Distributed data processing
- Transaction processing
- Decision support systems
- Office automation
- CAD/CAM and robotics
- Personal computers
- Home information and
  control systems

User impact
- Results orientation
- Aid in decision making
- Integration/unification
- Reduced application gestation
- Information as a resource
- Cost/performance

Society
- Increased regulation
- Security/privacy issue
- Rise of the knowledge worker
- Socially useful as a criterion

Fig. 11.3   Fifth-era environmental development

In conjunction with the above, the punched card is now all but extinct, having been replaced as the principal computer input medium by direct on-line data entry. Keyboards or transaction terminals will transmit data directly to the computer, which will react immediately to verify the input and affect the particular transaction in real time. Voice synthesis will be used both for input and output such that verbal commands can be recognized by the system, while synthesized voice messages will emanate from the system.

On the output side, flat or plasma screens will begin to replace cathode ray tubes as the principal output device. Plasma screens improve registration and allow graphic and pictorial matter to be displayed; for example, executives will be able to see, graphically, product or profit movement projected over a five-year long-range plan period based on alternative assumptions. Design graphics will also be available, with the use of color increasing in both design and business graphics.

The cost of communicating digital data will fall as volume picks up and private companies such as Satellite Business Systems and Microwave Communications, Inc., enter the picture. Satellite and packet switching will make data communications more efficient and will support the increasing growth of networking systems. Packet switching technology is developing as a result of the need for rapid response time, high reliability, low error rate, dynamic allocation of capacity, and the ability to charge in relation to traffic volume. Packet switching breaks down messages into packets, which are then sent over communication lines. Fiber optics, utilizing optical or glass fibers produced from silicon and upon which light beams (from light-emitting diodes or lasers) can travel simultaneously in both directions, will begin to replace copper both in telephone lines and coaxial cable.

Architecture

The virtual machine concept of the fourth era will mature in the fifth era. The objective of a networking system is to have each user interact with the computer system as if he were the only one using it—and this remains so despite the number of users. In order to do this in an economical manner, the concept of the virtual machine will have to rapidly load and unload programs from fast "backing storage" and be able to access hierarchical storage devices in a microsecond time frame.

As mentioned, the mini- and microprocessor will be utilized for specific functions. The mode of architecture will follow a divide-and-conquer objective; that is, in order to make operational the growing complexity and variety of functions that must be performed by fifth-generation computers, the concept of subprocessors, each performing a specified portion of the task, will emerge. By dividing up the job and delegating it to mini- or microprocessors, the complexity is overcome and viable networking systems become possible. This is really the basic premise of distributed data processing (described in Chapter 5), where functions are delegated to remote units based on usage patterns and on overall economy.

The firmware-oriented machine is cost-effective and flexible. It affords the opportunity of suboptimization of languages (e.g., ALGOL, COBOL, FORTRAN, PL/I), operating systems (e.g., pushdown stacks, table handling, and priority queuing—all essential for effective multirunning systems), emulation of other machines, and the possibility of application packages or at least some portion of them. However, a prerequisite is that the process to be incorporated within the firmware (usually etched chips) be well enough known so that it is not subject to frequent change. Firmware lies somewhere between software and hardware; it is not as flexible and easy to change as software, but it is not hard-wired or as permanent as hardware. Figure 11.4 indicates how increasingly complex functions can be performed by firmware from the micro-function level to the application package level. However, the accomplishment of an application like a payroll would not appear to meet the criterion of infrequent change; thus application firmware may prove illusive even in the fifth computer era.

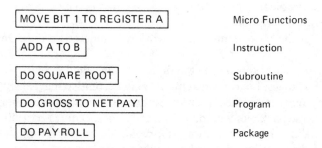

Fig. 11.4 The firmware concept

Figure 11.5 illustrates the fifth-generation architecture which separates data from instruction through the use of an intermediate "data descriptor." This type of architecture facilitates the application of the virtual machine concept to data and increases data security by applying a ring number or security code to each piece of data.

Reliability

It has become increasingly expensive from a maintenance standpoint to keep communications-oriented systems operable, particularly since many require 24-hour-per-day up-time. Because maintenance is a labor-intensive activity, the cost has risen with the rise in wage rates and has not followed the downward curve of electronic circuits, where mass-production techniques have reduced labor requirements dramatically. The key to fifth-generation reliability is ensuring high up-time through the use of fault logging, self-diagnosis, and on-line test and diagnostics (T&Ds) while controlling costs. T&Ds will become integral parts of the operating system, periodically being called upon to automatically test the entire system, check logs and counters, and print out or display instructions if manual intervention is required, or automati-

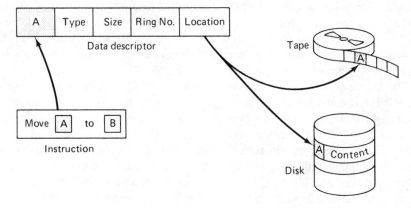

Fig. 11.5 Data orientation

cally fixing the problem if it is under machine control. The test routines will cover central processors, peripherals, and terminals, as well as the communication lines themselves. Thus the entire computer network will undergo periodic and regular on-line testing.

In order to control costs, the repair of packages and circuits will give way to replacement. Packages, boards, and circuits may become so inexpensive that it could be more economical to replace a circuit rather than expend the labor to repair it; furthermore, these packages would be replaced on a scheduled basis like light bulbs, often in the coactive mode where the user would do the replacing based on simple cookbook-style instructions rather than calling in a maintenance engineer.

The concept of graceful degradation or fail-soft capability will become an important attribute of future transaction-oriented systems. This concept means that if a machine failure occurs, back-up circuitry can keep the system operational. In certain cases, cost factors will make it more practical to switch off the failing circuit and simulate it via other circuits while the failure is repaired. The point is that even though there is a system malfunction, the redundant or simulated circuit takes over until the failed unit is fixed or replaced. The system may be slowed for a period of time, but it continues to operate, and the system degradation is usually not noticed by the users. This is the meaning of a soft failure.

Software

Multirunning, a combination of multiprogramming and multiprocessing, will continue to become more efficient. Operating systems often have more impact on throughput rates and turn around time than the internal speed of the circuitry. Operating systems will be designed more flexibly and simply, utilizing the mini- and microprocessor and firmware architecture concepts. By dividing up the functions while embedding many in firmware, efficiency will be greatly improved.

The data-base systems of the fourth era will be further enhanced to produce the highly interactive data files required for distributed data processing. They will utilize virtual machine concepts and hierarchical file structures to economically store huge data files required by the growing number of data-base users. The concept of shared files, which are integrated for use locally or in concert with a host system, will be a feature of this generation of data bases.

The key new concept in data bases is *relational*. The relational data base takes its name from the mathematical theory of relations. Simply stated, it is a way of arranging files that separates the user view of data (the language he or she uses to access data) from the physical representation of data, such that one can be changed without altering the other. The goals of relational data base are to construct the files so that the user sublanguage that is employed is easy to learn, has the ability to readily expand or alter files, and allows the flexibility to access data in formats that were not anticipated at file-development time, in either batch or spontaneous mode.

An important phrase heard more and more in the data processing industry is *ease of use*. With the widening circle of computer use as a result of distributed data processing, both DP and non-DP users demand a straightforward simplicity of operation. As someone has said, computer systems must become friendly, tranquil, and forgiving. Terminals must be operated by nondedicated users using simple menu selection and screen tutorial instruction. The user must be able to recover from seemingly out-of-control conditions with the press of a specified function key. Systems must be human-engineered to work for people and not the other way around.

Inquiry languages have been of the structured variety, which may be efficient for dedicated administrative users who have learned the structured language, but which are not useful for casual management users who desire system access. The advent of natural-language inquiry which, in the case of a U.S. installation, is the English language, will facilitate a much broader system use. Natural language allows nonexpert end users to access the company's data base in a language that is completely natural, free of form without regard to syntax, grammar, or spelling.

Finally, more attention will be given to protecting the user's investment in software, which far outweighs his investment in hardware. Vendors will become more conscious of compatibility and the ability to grow and upgrade without traumatic conversions involving serious interruptions in computer operations. Standardization of data formats and common languages will play a big part in this evolution.

One last comment on software is the need to develop better testing and quality methods. It is my opinion that software quality has seriously lagged the improvements in hardware. The fifth generation should see the development of improved quality and testing tools, not only to accelerate the development cycle, but to improve the final product.

Application

The object of this book is to focus on management, and it is a thesis that the fourth era only tapped the surface of management information systems (MIS). The fifth era will see the extended use of MIS. The distributed data processing concept will expand and will develop around a transaction-driven system, where events that trigger paperwork activity and supervisory actions will be processed as they occur. This will be coupled with new point-of-sale or point-of-transaction devices. In many cases the closed-loop type of operation employed in process-control operations will be applied to business information systems.

One emerging and quite important new application area will be the use of decision support systems, described in Chapter 9, which are just coming into use on a broad scale. Managers will be able to activate simulation models which have access to relevant portions of the data base to aid them in decision making. It will be an interactive, trial-and-error type of activity where the manager can experiment and see projected results of alternate action plans. This single application area may produce more benefits to a company than the sum of the other computer applications combined.

A major application growth area in the eighties will be office automation. Studies show that the investment in white-collar or office workers has not changed much over the past decade from the current $3000, while investment per factory or blue-collar worker is in excess of $20,000. A major increase in computer use in offices is forecasted for this period. Most medium to large companies are establishing office-of-the-future departments, and those concepts will trickle down to the offices of smaller companies as well. Figure 11.6 indicates a confluence of word processing, business data processing, and other office applications.

The word processor or smart typewriter is the cornerstone of office automation. Information keyed into electronic media can be easily edited, stored, indexed, and accessed for later use. Adjuncts are electronic mail, where, based on distribution indices, data can be automatically dispersed throughout a building or around the world. Also links to intelligent copiers can produce large-volume manuals or periodicals. Once installed, the computer used initially for word processing application can be upgraded to include management calendar/time scheduling, project control, information retrieval, and other business-related functions of the type discussed in Chapter 9. A. D. Little states that "the shipment of office information systems, taken as an aggregate, will be $15 billion a year by 1985." This is equal to total worldwide computer shipments in 1977.

Three other application areas will have significant influence on our lives. The first, robotics, will not affect the individual directly until the robots come out of the factory and into the home in the form of domestic robots. The second area, the personal computer, will affect us in both our business and our personal life. The third area of computer growth will be in the home, though it will be a while before this really takes off. The harbingers of the home computer are the TV games and the growing amount of microprocessor intelligence in appliances such as the microwave oven and the thermostat. A service that started in England under the name of View-Data allows subscribers to receive selected information and to make travel arrangements, restaurant reservations, and the like all via the home television screen. Home

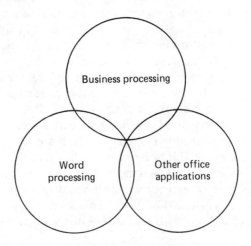

Fig. 11.6   Office automation

computers will expand from their current hobby use by engineers and professionals to uses in controlling environment and home security and providing interactive entertainment and educational modules via the video screen.

Robotics

Computer-aided manufacturing (CAM) and design (CAD) have already been mentioned as rapidly growing areas of computer applications; in fact Chapter 9 used a CAM application as an analogy to describe the changing management role of the computer. Robotics is an extension of CAM. CAM allows computers to control and drive manufacturing processes such as drilling, lathing, and milling. Robotics extends the range of machine-aided functions to die casting and welding, among others.

The Robot Institute of America (RIA) has developed a definition of robotics as follows: "A robot is a reprogrammable multifunctional manipulation designed to move material, parts, tools or specialized devices through variable programmed motions for the performances of a variety of tasks." This definition helps, because the public image of a robot is a device with anthropomorphic qualities that walks around on two legs, speaks, and emulates a human being in its actions. Most robots are used in factories, don't walk or speak, and don't look humanlike at all.

In industrial use, the robot must bring some form of intelligence to the work, have a form of power and control over the work, and be able to lend a strong and capable hand. In fact the latter may be the best way to think about the functions of a robot. A robot can emulate the functions of the hand, grasping, gripping, lifting, moving, and positioning items.

Many feel that computer-driven robots will mark the next significant stage in the industrial revolution. The Japanese have embraced robotics and currently have more robots than the United States. Sweden, which has always had a penchant for technology, is also among the leading robot producers. Robotics experts feel the next wave of robots will be more sensitive and more intelligent than those in use today, being able, for example, to employ an artificial sense of touch and to make decisions based on the texture of an object, also to use a complex vision system to recognize objects on the basis of their shape without the requirement of special lighting. Several leading-edge companies are developing what they call "factories of the future" based on advanced robotics.

The Personal Computer

One of today's most pervasive trends is the growth of the personal computer. A personal is defined as being used by a single person who has complete control over the system including the processor, files, printer, and display. Its price range is $1000 to $6000 (even less). It is possible to buy personals for less than $100, but their limited memory and peripherals place them more in the calculator class. It is obvious that a personal computer can have a communication link to a larger system and can share data, but primarily its use is in the freestanding mode.

In my thinking, there are four driving forces behind the explosive growth of the personal. The first is the obvious one of technology and the continued lowering of the entry price to the point where the power of a small to medium business computer ten years ago is now available in a personal. Of equal or greater importance is the proliferation of personal software. Today there are more people writing programs for personals than there are writing software for mini and mainframe computers. A program called Visicalc that provides an electronic spread sheet to do budgeting and financial analysis has sold over 300,000 copies and has made prosperous two young business school graduates named Daniel Bricklin (Harvard) and Robert Frankston (MIT).

A second force driving the business use of personals is the concern of executives, professionals, and administrators with the growing backlog of computer applications within their companies and their view of the central information service as lethargic and unresponsive. It has been said that business people are acquiring personals more from anger than analysis. The personals look very inviting to a data-hungry business audience.

A third force is the individual's innate curiosity and the search for self-improvement. Though it applies in the business use of personals, this motivation probably is more prevalent in the use of home personals. It is hard to cost-justify a personal computer for the home; usually the motivation must be present to experiment with new technology and to learn a skill that is fast becoming commonplace. Looking for strict labor-saving applications and use can cause disappointment, particularly to the nontechnical, non-gadget-loving individual. Under these circumstances the personal computer suffers ill use and may be relegated to a back shelf or retained merely as a status symbol. Of particular note is the involvement and enthusiasm of today's youth. Their fervor and motivation to use personals for almost everything represents a driving force in itself.

The fourth force, and maybe the most significant, is the high-powered merchandising of personal computers. Magazines, newspapers, TV, and radio are filled with ads telling would-be buyers what these compact, table-top machines can do for them. The airline magazines are typical of the media movement, each edition featuring ten to fifteen different electronic aids that promise quick and wondrous results ranging from maintaining personal budgets and bank accounts, to legal information retrieval, to solving complex financial models. The so-called merchandising "hype" is also evident in the youth or school market. Advertisements feature computer camps where children can "hike, swim, and run a computer" and an ad that states "Dad, can I use the computer tonight?"

There are three general markets for personals. By far the largest and fastest growing is the business market. In 1982 this sector accounted for approximately 60 percent of the 600,000 personals in use, with home/hobby and educational/scientific use splitting the remaining 40 percent. International Data Corporation predicts the 600,000 figure will grow to 1,600,000 by 1986, with business accounting for some 65 percent of the total. Many educators feel that future students will own their own personal computers and bring them to school as they previously brought slide rules and calculators. Computer literacy has become a popular educational objective, with computers entering the curriculum as early as the third grade. The combination uses of personal computers will make it a $10 billion market by the end of this decade, so state the market forecasters.

There are some important lessons for purchasers to heed in viewing the personal computer revolution. In a business environment a company must avoid repeating the often painful stages evolution, as explained earlier in the book. An unbridled contagion stage can lead to a period of control and retooling, necessitating standards, quality checks, and documentation which can slow progress until the proper techniques can be implemented. Thus, it would seem prudent to recognize early that personals may grow to communicate with each other and with the firm's main processing system(s) some time in the future. Establishment of a brand policy (for example, limit purchase to two or three different personal vendors who have software compatibility and a specified communication protocol for later networking) would seem a desirable initial step. Some type of security and back-up may become necessary for applications which grow to become integral parts of business operation. For example, a professional group may initially develop its own forecasting system which evolves to become the sole system for forecasting orders, inventory, and production for the entire company. Proper security, system back-up documentation, controls, and the like now become essential.

The Computerized Home Information and Control System

A home is a place where most of us spend over half our lives. Technology has influenced the home over the years—adding, for our ease and enjoyment, the gas and electric stove, the electric refrigerator, the washing machine, the telephone, the radio, and the television set. We are on the threshold of adding another device, which can have as great an impact as all the devices that we use today combined. I refer to the introduction of the computer into the home. My concept is the broad use of computer power throughout the home; I call it a *home information and control system.*

I envision a future scenario featuring an integrated home computer system, having internal communication links within the house and external communication links that will tie the outside world into our home as telephone and television do today. Some of the functions performed will be enhancements of current devices such as appliance and temperature control, while other functions will be new, such as security communication links to the police and fire stations and access to a variety of external information data bases.

The Subsystems

Figure 11.7 is a picture of the home of the future. From the outside you cannot detect any difference from the home of today. The difference lies inside, where an

Fig. 11.7   Home information and control system

electronic network accesses programs and data used by individuals to control their environment, ensure their security, and enhance their education, business, and entertainment.

The system features three integrated subsystems. The *home information unit* will normally be located in the den, living room, or family room. This subsystem handles the flow of information in and out of the house for business and leisure purposes and also serves as the educational and entertainment center. The second subsystem, the *household operation unit*, is located in or near the kitchen. Here, preset programs control the physical environment and home appliances. The third subsystem, the *master security unit*, is positioned in or near the master bedroom. It controls security intrusion, primarily from theft and fire. These subsystems, working in concert, form the core of the home information and control system.

Links to the Outside World

In addition to electric power lines, water pipes, and sewage pipes, a number of communication links connect the house to the outside world. Current communication links are the telephone line and radio/television waves, which are beamed through the air, sometimes via satellite. Also in certain areas coaxial copper cables are buried in the ground to bring television into areas remote from transmitting stations.

Much of tomorrow's home communication will be integrated into the cable television line. This system has long been able to deliver twenty or more channels into the home, something that is not possible via through-the-air television. Future enhancements will offer choices of hundreds of channels as well as two-way communication—the ability to send signals as well as to receive them. Fiber optics, utilizing optical or glass fibers produced from silicon (sand), which look like violin strings and upon which beams from light-emitting diodes or lasers can travel simultaneously in both directions, represents still another significant communication development. These optical fibers will replace copper wires both in telephone lines and in coaxial cable. Today silicon is plentiful and cheap when compared to copper.

Cable television or telephone lines, both using fiber optics, will be the vehicles for communication links in the home of the future.

Home Information Unit

The technology trappings in the home information unit include a large, flat, 5-foot plasma (neon gas) screen on a wall in the den or family room. The plasma telescreen provides better resolution than do current television methods. The surface can be split screened to allow multiple use or can be employed as a single large screen. In front of the screen is a microcomputer console with a series of function and typewriter keys as well as a desk-top work area. A disk storage unit next to the screen holds packaged individual video/educational programs plus computer programs written by members of the household. One of the console function keys activates a photocopier, which can reproduce the contents of any selected screen display. An alternate form of input-output is voice communication, where the computer can accept a prescribed set of verbal commands as well as synthesize verbal response.

Via the console control panel, TV interaction is available. The viewer can participate in game shows as well as give instant feedback on program content and advertising inquiries. A more significant element of interactive TV is the local or national instant referendums that can take place in the political world.

Television, through personal selection of programs and interaction, can begin to individualize rather than homogenize people as the standard TV formats and programs do today. For example, networks will carry libraries of educational, cultural, or sports modules that can be selected by the viewer. Interactive modules can be selected to produce programmed instruction courses, replete with instantly graded exams, enabling individuals to acquire educational degrees without leaving the house (a boon to the handicapped).

Additional packaged utility modules can be addressed in the interactive mode. An example is the income tax module, where a programmed inquiry and checklist approach enables an individual to fill in the requested information while the utility module does the necessary mathematical calculations. Other personalized utility modules are checkbook reconciliation and stock/asset portfolio analysis. In the former example, bills can be paid, automatically crediting the payee while reducing one's bank balance. Information-retrieval applications include insurance and legal response to inquiries, as well as listings for dining, theater, concerts, child care, or marriage counsellors.

Electronic mail is an adjunct to the home information unit, where letters can be typed and sent via satellite to worldwide locations. Also newspapers and magazines can be transmitted to the screen based on selected subscriptions.

The telecommunications center can be used as a business subset for either domestic business or business associated with the individual's company or corporation. Through a link to the company data base, he or she can make inquiries or employ simulation models to plan potential business strategies. The businessperson can originate individual meetings or full-blown teleconferences. This is a particularly desirable outlet in homebound individuals who cannot or desire not to leave the home; the concept is known as *telecommuting*.

Household Operation Unit

A related subsystem is the household operation unit, located in the kitchen. A panel located on a kitchen wall is the visual control governing the physical elements in the house. Function and numeric keys form the control console, while a separate disk storage unit holds programs for control of individual physical units within the home. Communication lines link the control center to the outside world, so that changes and alterations to the programs can be made via telephone or citizen band radio in the car.

The household operation unit controls total home environment including temperature and humidity. Programmed instructions control the temperature; for example, at 7 A.M., increase temperature to 72° in kitchen and 68° remainder of house, decrease temperature to 64° during the day, increase to 70° at 6 P.M., and lower to 65° at 10 P.M. Similarly, air conditioning programs can be established for the summer months.

Another major function is control of appliances including oven, toaster, washer, dryer, and dishwasher. Meat and vegetables placed in the oven in the morning will be ready for the table upon arrival home. Likewise, washing of clothes and dishes can be accomplished under program control.

Minor functions directed by the household operation unit include warming up the car in the morning and permitting cats and dogs to enter and leave the house and eat at programmed times via sensor-based door and cabinet panels. An outside weather station, either at a meteorological center or in the back yard, records high and low temperatures for the day, barometric pressure, rainfall in inches, wind velocity, and other statistical data as requested. This weather station can be linked directly to the thermostatic control of the home environment. Another function is the store ordering procedure, whereby the house manager can select from a variety of food, clothing, and merchandise displayed on the screen. Delivery service can be scheduled and an automatic debit made to the family's bank account.

One interesting and obvious sociological impact of this particular subsystem is that of woman's liberation. This unit certainly reduces the time and effort required for household tasks, and if these tasks are still primarily the role of the woman in the year 2000, they can be dispatched quickly, leaving time for work or other pursuits.

Master Security Unit

The master security unit primarily covers security and theft intrusion. Before retiring, the homeowner activates the sensors at each entry point into the house, the doors, windows, garage, and outside workshops. When the security seal is broken, a sensor automatically flicks on the inside lights, opens the window drapes, and emits an alarm. Simultaneously a telephone message is delivered to the police station.

The fire system detects smoke or elevation of heat, and its sensors trigger a siren, turn on the lights to facilitate escape from the house, and automatically deliver a phone message to the fire department. This particular system also has sensors that monitor gas and water leaks and furnace malfunctions.

An important function of the security unit is a telephonic medical jack, into which can be connected an electrocardiograph, pulse and blood pressure unit, thermometer, and bodily sensors to measure infection. Blood and urine samples can also be tested remotely. This medical link is to either a doctor's office or a diagnostic unit of a local hospital. The doctor can verbally and visually interrogate the patient via the television screen. Thus the concept of a house call is revived.

In addition to these functions, the individual can perform most of the functions available on the other units.

Social Feasibility

In addition to technological and economic feasibility, social feasibility is a most significant element in thinking about the above scenario. The possibilities of invasion of privacy and electronic eavesdropping are issues that must be addressed. A broader issue is the extent to which this type of system enhances the quality of life. The system is a boon to the handicapped and the elderly, but the question remains whether the positive aspects outweigh the negative ones for the remainder of the population. If we have become dependent on TV today, will this development make us complete captives? Will we become more homebound and ensconced in individually oriented activity, thus isolating ourselves more from the community? Will the plethora of movies and other entertainment features make for a more decadent, self-indulgent society?

Other concerns center on changes to the political process as a consequence of instant referendums and public opinion polls and the impact on the professions as a result of telemedicine, teleinsurance, and telelaw. The advent of electronic mail, electronic newspapers, and electronic magazines will have a significant influence on the printing and publishing industry, as will home shopping and the cashless transaction on the retailing and banking industries. Thus the emergence of the home information system could have the sociological impact of the telephone, radio, and TV set combined and then some. It is a sobering thought.

User Impact

This area summarizes the type of thinking that will probably direct the fifth era of data processing. Management people want information systems that produce results rather than promises and they want the system to aid them in the real money-making areas of a business—strategic decision making. Business operation relies on integration and unification of activities to optimize decisions across the functional areas, the type of result produced by efficient MIS and data-base systems.

Users want to see applications developed quicker, with the gestation period (the interval between application conception and successful implementation) cut down to reasonable limits. They want protection of their programming investment as they advance to the MIS and DDP stages. Users want the benefit of these advanced systems, but the systems must not be so complex and multifaceted that no one can understand, much less use, them.

A subtle but important development is occurring in MIS management with the full recognition of information as a resource. The distinction between the computer as opposed to information is analogous to the distinction between the railroad business as opposed to the transportation business or the telephone business as opposed to the communications business. Focusing, in each case, on the latter illuminates the scope and significance of the business. It puts things into proper perspective. The future MIS manager will become an information resource manager, having broad responsibility for maximizing the effectiveness of that most valuable business commodity—information.

Finally, cost/performance is still a major criterion for any business investment and particularly for MIS, which has fended off the normal ROI measurements for so many years. It can no longer be rationalized that computer technology and information systems are changing too fast to warrant strict cost justification; therefore cost/performance becomes a major criterion in the fifth era. Management wants the DDP transaction processing and the decision support systems, but these developments must pay their own way in a reasonable time frame.

Social Considerations

As national attention is drawn to the sociological and psychological implications of technological events these days, it seems appropriate to conclude with a discussion of this area. Sometimes these considerations are taken for granted, but both the computer professional and the non-MIS person who works with computers are remiss if they neglect this area, particularly when many of society's ills are blamed on automation. Sociological factors are pertinent to the broad spectrum of computerization. As in any area of automation, I believe that these factors should be heeded.

While societal issues were not that significant in the early decades, they may prove in this decade to be the most vital of all the environmental rings. The first major impact is that of governmental regulation. EDP has become so all-pervasive that it is a direct target for government surveillance. First, a single company, IBM, has held a 60-plus percent share of the computer market almost since its inception, and government suits against the company have marked the history of IBM. The last one lasted thirteen years and was finally dropped with no recommended actions. It is an example of government involvement if not intrusion. The government has instituted commissions to investigate computer applications with broad citizen impact such as electronic funds transfer and the use of the Universal Product Code in grocery stores. Probably the most significant area is communications. Communications has been a regulated industry, dominated by American Telephone and Telegraph, but recent decisions of the Federal Communications Commission have allowed independent companies to provide microwave and satellite communication services. The most recent decision requires AT&T to spin off its 22 operating companies, but allows it to enter the data processing market on a nontariff basis (in other words, the prices will be competitively determined) to compete with companies in the computer and information systems business. The proposal has major impact on the availability and costs of communication and terminal equipment. Not only the business office, but the individual who uses a telephone is affected as well. AT&T now competes with IBM, Honeywell, DEC, and Wang in the data communications and terminal business.

Individuals have feared the intrusion of the computer, in the guise of huge corporate and government data bases, creating a Big Brother type of society. The Privacy Act of 1974 provides specific safeguards by requiring federal agencies to permit an individual to examine his record, question and contest specific data, and ensure that the data is current and accurate for its intended use. Federal agencies are subject to damages if an individual's rights are violated.

In very general terms there have been three industrial eras. The first or pre-industrial era is characterized by humans' mastery of material (stone, iron, bronze, etc.), while the second or industrial era is tied to the invention of the steam engine around 1740 and is characterized by humans' mastery over energy (steam power, then coal, electricity, the jet engine, etc.) Peter Drucker, an authority on management and technology, has coined the word *knowledge worker* and states, "The substitution of knowledge for manual effort as a productive resource in work is the greatest change in the history of work." He points out that in 1900, 18 of 20 workers were manual workers, while by 1965, 5 of 20 of a vastly increased work force did manual labor, and this trend continues. Figure 11.8 points this out, and it ties the information era to the development of the computer around 1940.

In the information era, it behooves us to avoid the Luddite syndrome. The Luddites, led by Captain Ludd, were an organized band of English rioters who campaigned against and destroyed labor-saving equipment in the early 1800s as a protest against lost jobs and the poor quality of work produced by the machinery. The aftermath of this activity was a series of shootings and hangings and then strict legislative control before the movement finally came to an end. Today the term Luddites is used to refer to an individual or group who oppose automation or the use of machinery to replace people or even to augment individual effort.

Modern-day Luddites and Captain Ludds are prevalent in the computer age. The original Luddites attacked the initial products of the first industrial revolution, namely textile machines; modern-day Luddites find computers, and the information systems they power, targets for their twentieth-century fear and anxiety. Today's Lud-

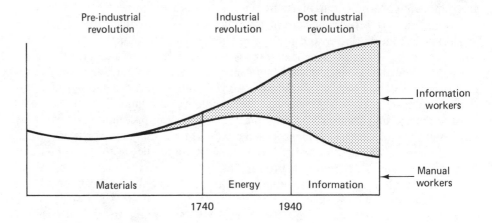

Fig. 11.8 Technology and the industrial revolution

dites do not use physical means (though there are still intermittent instances of computer destruction) but employ more subtle methods geared to the information era.

Other business people, including some high-level executives, secretly resent the intrusion of computers into their business sphere, changing the way they perform their functions and causing them to learn complicated new procedures whose effectiveness they question in the first place. The mode of battle here is often to avoid involvement altogether or to subtly withhold key information parameters that are vital to successful system operation.

It is obvious that we should be as interested in what computers can do for us as what they can do to us. The answer is not resistance, recalcitrance, and sabotage. Everyone is aware of what technology brings to a society, in transportation, communication, medicine, industry, education; yet there is urban blight, traffic jams, pollution, radiation, crime, juvenile delinquency, schizophrenia, depression, and loneliness. As Peter Drucker says, "The only positive alternative to destruction by technology is to make technology work as our servant. In the final analysis this surely means mastery by man over himself, for if anyone is to blame, it is not the tool, but the human maker and user. 'It is a poor carpenter who blames his tools' says an old proverb." Murray Laver, Director of National Data Service in London, stated it this way and very effectively:

> The falling cost and rising speed of computation could mislead us into substituting computing for thinking, but an ounce of insight remains worth a ton of processing. That we can type faster than he could pen, offers no assurance that we will write better plays than Shakespeare. There is a rather early limit to the substitution of good computers for bad mathematics. Computing mirrors the simplification of science; but in dealing with the real world we do well to heed Whitehead's warning "Seek simplicity and distrust it"; nothing can be safely left out. Progress in applying computing has so far been rapid; we have been advancing quickly over the

open plain. Now we are reaching thickly-wooded foothills, and our progress will depend more on genius and less on honest journeymen; more on good ideas, less on hard work. People can be paid to work harder, but good ideas cannot be forced, and above all else it is in the efficient application of ill-conceived ideas that computers could have their most troublesome effects in influencing people.

The feasibility of computer applications was discussed in Chapter 7 under the headings of economic, technological, and operational feasibility. These three categories consider whether an application is profitable, whether it can be accomplished, and whether it can be effectively installed. An additional feasibility consideration might be whether it is socially useful or acceptable.

A statement on a personal resume I received several years ago indicated that the individual's objective was to pursue a challenging, rewarding, and socially acceptable job in the computer industry. As businessmen, we expect an individual to be interested in challenging and rewarding work; we are a little surprised to see *socially acceptable* in a *resume*. It raises a valid question, one that we should all give more thought to.

There is a social difference between using computers in the aerospace industry and in the medical industry. We have learned the system and calculations for sending men into space, but we have not developed the calculations for diagnosing and curing illness. There are obvious reasons why it is easier to use computers in aerospace than in medicine; however, there is an imbalance in the amount of money devoted to each. There is more profit in developing computers for aerospace and for industry. It is reasonable to assume that profit was necessary when the companies were getting established. But the industry is maturing, and manufacturers and users should be expected to dedicate a greater portion of their resources to the more socially oriented industries, even if the profit is less assured.

Where should the application emphasis be in industries like medicine? I believe that there are things that men can do better (and probably always will) and things that machines can do better. The DP industry has wasted a good deal of money trying to tackle applications that were not technologically or operationally feasible. A computer can aid the medical profession in recordkeeping and in the business end of operations; hopefully, it can help reduce the spiraling medical costs. It can aid in scheduling scarce facilities and in assisting nurses and doctors in the administrative aspects of their jobs. The computer can maintain historical information about patients and act as an extension of the doctor's recall system to uncover similar cases. It can maintain an index and retrieval system for medical articles, books, and journals. The computer can aid in the initial testing and screening of patients who are either ill or undergoing routine checkups. I do not think the computer can accomplish surgery or develop the final diagnosis for a patient with neurological disease. I do not think a computer can replace a doctor or the major part of his job, which requires judgment, wisdom, experience, compassion, and manual dexterity.

Electrocardiograms by computer is a case where a computer is capable of measuring, calculating, and analyzing medical data quicker, more accurately, and perhaps more economically than a doctor. It is an area that deserves attention and investment. It is an area where the computer can be superior to man. This is the way the system, as developed by the TELEMED Corporation, works.

> A mobile electrocardiograph unit is installed at the location (hospital, clinic, nursing home, doctor's office, etc.) where the ECG is to be taken. While the signals from the ECG machine are being used to drive a conventional chart recorder, they are also used to frequency-modulate carrier signals which are in turn transmitted to the computer center over normal voice-grade telephone lines. Telephone lines transmit ECGs to the computer with no clinical distortion, and noise in the lines can be readily filtered out.
>
> At the computer center, the analog telephone signal is converted back into its original analog form, then converted into digital form and entered into the computer system for analysis. The computer will then perform an analysis which will: (1) measure all pertinent ECG amplitudes and duration; (2) characterize the wave forms from each of the twelve leads of the scalar electrocardiogram; (3) calculate such factors as rate and electrical axis; and (4) produce an interpretation of the status of the electrical function of the heart based upon these parameters. The resultant interpretation is then teletyped back to the location at which the ECG has been taken, in digital matrix format with a summary set of correspondent interpretive statements.

Extending this type of computer application to other types of diagnostic tests is a sound and feasible social usage of technology. It promises major advances in preventive medicine.

I remember reading an article that, in my opinion, illustrates the potential misuse of computer resources and is a classical case of working on the wrong problem. The article talks about surgery in the year 2001. I would like to think the article was science fiction, but I believe that the intent was serious. It describes a patient who receives a kidney transplant from the robot doctor using laser beams after his problem had been diagnosed and the size of the artificial kidney calculated by determining his weight and body volume, the latter by a system of photo-sensing devices. The computer calculated the patient's survival chances without the operation, versus his chances while undergoing the operation, versus his survival chances as a result of having had the operation, and then mathematically selected the best statistical course of action. The patient leaves the hospital with a new kidney five minutes after he enters.

I think investment of computer resources for computerized operations or for full computerized diagnosis is stretching reality. Although both the electrocardiogram application and operation by computer are socially useful, we must use intelligence and our knowledge of machines to direct their use to those applications that are technologically, operationally, and economically feasible. I intended that "socially useful" be a fourth feasibility consideration and not be used *in lieu of* the other three—in other words that computer applications be directed at socially useful purposes.

A FINAL WORD

In the long run, I feel the future role of computers will be dictated by the interplay of the four feasibility criteria. The first three criteria (technological, economic, and operational) were mentioned before. A fourth (social) was added in this chapter.

All four criteria must be met for a computer system to be a positive factor in our society. The industry has made great technological strides, and there appears to be little reason to doubt that from a technical viewpoint, most of our data processing requirements can be met. We must analyze the economics of each situation to see if the resulting benefits offset the added costs and produce a satisfactory return on investment. Operational aspects involve the ability to successfully install the system in the existing environment. A system that is technically and economically sound may fail because the human factors have not been reflected in systems design or implementation.

More and more, the social worth of something is increasing in significance. The social consequences of data processing and computers can rule out otherwise feasible applications. For example, there is a fear that using a single identification code (such as a social security number) will enable or encourage the government to hold all data about citizens within a massive central data base. This could lead to invasions of privacy and to situations where a minor criminal offense could remain a lifetime part of an individual's file to severely limit freedom and opportunity. Proper administration of the Privacy Act described in this chapter could alleviate this fear.

It is my belief that use of the four feasibility criteria discussed earlier will determine how the world of 2001 will differ from ours. When one criterion is ignored, growth is malformed and unhealthy. It takes consideration of all four to produce sound progress.

SUMMARY

Chapter 11 has taken a look at the future of computers and management information systems. The discussion centered on data processing developments over the past four generations and projected into the fifth. A plea was emphasized throughout for user involvement and proper reflection of user needs in planning for future computer products and product lines. The importance of management information systems was stressed as a cornerstone of user requirements. Whether the company is large or small, management seeks the real payoff from computers, and that payoff means aiding them in making better decisions and in giving them more analytical information to control costs, increase sales, and thereby improve the rate of return on investment. This is the promise of MIS in general and management-oriented MIS in particular.

Finally, the social and psychological values of computer automation were discussed. Although the major focus of the book has been on the economic, technologic, and operational feasibility of computerized information systems, it is appropriate to include the social feasibility criterion.

Although computers can do wondrous things and can materially aid management in conducting its business, I think we must retain the perspective to realize that the discipline of management still remains part art, part science. There are still things man can do better than machines, and still things that only man can do. It will always be that way. I think this point is made clear by a book called *The Analytical Engine*, in which the science writer Jeremy Bernstein recalled the career of Charles Babbage, the nineteenth-century English mathematician who invented the analytical engine that was the forerunner of modern computers. Bernstein mentions the time that Babbage wrote to Lord Tennyson as follows (from "The Assault on Privacy," *Newsweek*, July 27, 1970):

> Sir, in your otherwise beautiful poem "The Vision of Sin" there is a verse which reads
>
> > Every moment dies a man
> > Every moment one is born.
>
> It must be manifest that if this were true, the population of the world would be at a standstill. In truth, the rate of birth is slightly in excess of that of death. I would suggest that in the next edition of your poem you have it read—
>
> > Every moment dies a man
> > Every moment $1\frac{1}{16}$ is born. . . .
>
> I am, Sir, yours etc.

It is appropriate to end with a statement from the ultimate satirist, Art Buchwald. It was only a matter of time until he got around to computers and information systems.

THE GREAT DATA FAMINE*
by Art Buchwald

One of the major problems we face in the 1980's is that so many computers will be built in the next decade that there will be a shortage of data to feed them.

Prof. Heinrich Applebaum, director of the Computer Proliferation Center at Grogbottom, has voiced concern about the crisis and has urged a crash program to produce enough data to get our computers through the eighties.

"We didn't realize," the professor told me, "that computers would absorb so much information in such a fast period of time. But if our figures are correct, every last bit of data in the world will have been fed into a machine by Jan. 12, 1986, and an information famine will follow, which could spread across the world."

"It sounds serious," I said.

*Reprinted with permission.

"It is serious," he replied. "Man has created his own monster. He never realized when he invented the computer that there would not be enough statistics to feed it. Even now, there are some computers starving to death because there is no information to put into them. At the same time, the birth rate of computers is increasing by 30% a year. Barring some sort of worldwide holocaust, we may soon have to find data for 30,000,000 computers with new ones being born every day."

"You make it sound so frightening."

"It is frightening," Prof. Applebaum said. "The new generation of computers is more sophisticated than the older generation, and the computers will refuse to remain idle just because there is nothing to compute, analyze, or calculate. Left to their own devices, the Lord only knows what they will do."

"Is there any solution, professor?"

"New sources of data must be found. The government must expand, and involved studies must be thought up to make use of the computers' talents. The scientific community, instead of trying to solve problems with computers, must work on finding problems for the computers to solve."

"Even if the scientists really don't want the answers?"

"Naturally. The scientific community invented the computer. Now it must find ways of feeding it. I do not want to be an alarmist, but I can see the day coming when millions of computers will be fighting, for the same small piece of data, like savages."

"Is there any hope that the government will wake up to the data famine in time?"

"We have a program ready to go as soon as the bureaucrats in Washington give us the word. We are recommending that no computer can be plugged in more than three hours a day.

"We are also asking the government for $50 billion to set up data manufacturing plants all over the country. This data mixed with soy beans could feed hundreds of thousands of computer families for months.

"And finally we are advocating a birth control program for computers. By forcing a computer to swallow a small bit of erroneous information, we could make it sterile forever, and it would be impossible for it to reproduce any more of its kind."

"Would you advocate abortions for computers?" I asked Applebaum.

"Only if the Vatican's computer gives us its blessing."

CASE STUDY

COMPUTERS IN THE YEAR 2001

The turn-of-the-century Sam Curtis has reviewed his data processing needs with several vendors and has selected the Alpha system. Sam's manufacturing business had reached a stage where paperwork was beginning to pile up and he knew a computer system was required. The Alpha system features a customized turnkey system that requires no programming or systems personnel on the part of the user. Sam and his controller indicated their particular application requirements, and via a menulike selection process the relevant application chips were plugged into the processing unit and the system customized for Curtis's unique requirements. The chips are chosen from a program library and can be exchanged or updated as conditions dictate. This feature is important to Sam, as he anticipates growth from inside and also from acquisition. The application chips provide economical processing power that is optimized for Curtis's particular method of operation—thus the software is bent to serve the user and not the other way around. The application chips offset the increasing people and programming cost that has paralleled the inflationary economy since 1980. The Alpha system is customer-installable and comes equipped with self-diagnosis and maintenance routines such that the average machine failure is once per year. Sam is looking forward to the installation of his first computer system.

When the investment counsellor, Carole Harrison, enters her office one morning in the year 2001, her duty for the day is to review the customer portfolios assigned to her and the stocks under her surveillance. The portfolios of her clients are under continual computer control. The stocks were selected based on the individual investment profile, income status dependencies, future objectives, and the like. Each day the closing prices of the various stock exchanges are screened against the updated customer profiles. When change points are hit, automatic buy and sell orders are issued to maintain the desired profile of the portfolio. Harrison has access to a computerized econometric input-output model of U.S. business. The model immediately reflects the various investment factors, such as new housing starts and inventory positions. The model projects the impact of these elements on current and future stock market prices and investment decisions. In addition, Harrison can obtain a projection of future economic patterns based on her own judgment of what she thinks is likely to occur. The model can simulate the complicated interaction of many variables and can print out the results in a matter of seconds on Harrison's office terminal.

The twenty-first-century Dr. Lloyd Carson is able to spend far more time in medical research and in enjoying his family because of the patient monitoring system installed at his hospital. Every patient is continuously monitored for thirty different biological functions, from temperature and blood pressure to brain wave patterns and metabolic balance. Between visits a two-way video screen enables Dr. Carson to communicate with his patients. After reviewing the monitors, he then indicates the various medication and tests for each patient via a special terminal. To request a test or medication he need only point with a light pen to the name of the requested test or prescription. Dr. Carson's orders are transmitted immediately to the on-line terminal in the lab or clinic where they are queued by priority and then carried out. Patient records are automatically updated when the drugs are dispensed. Diagnostic tests also are conducted via an on-line telemonitoring system that projects the most likely diagnoses along with the statistical odds of each possible diagnosis based on case histories. The computer can suggest courses of treatment and project the duration of the illness.

Helen Swindell looks at the calendar and sees that today is May 26, 2001. Helen is an early riser and often sits down at the family computer control center with her first cup of coffee to get chores out of the way before the rest of her family stirs. The kitchen is already comfortable, because the house temperature has been programmed to respond automatically to the outside environment. First she asks the computer to list the notes and reminders for today on the display screen. (The family uses the computer as a message board.) Helen finds a note she left herself that she needs to buy a few clothing items for her daughter. Helen decides to order them via the terminal, since she has a business luncheon in conjunction with her job at the bank. Monday is grocery day, so Helen asks for a price update and then checks off the items she wants. Pressing a transmit button delivers the order to a terminal at a local supermarket. Because of the home computer control center, it is no longer necessary for one member of a family to devote full time to running the household. The Swindells are living in what was called the "cashless society" back in the 1980s. For every purchase made, whether at home or in a store, Mrs. Swindell inserts an ID card and her index finger into a special identifier unit. Her social security number and fingerprint provide the necessary identification. The computer checks her credit status and automatically debits or credits her bank account.

QUESTIONS

Relative to these four twenty-first-century information systems users:

1. Which seem to be the most likely to occur?

2. Why do you think they are most likely to occur?

3. Referring to the feasibility criteria mentioned in the chapter, which criteria are present or lacking in each instance?

4. Do you think the quality of life will be improved if the vignettes come to pass?

5. Are the information systems that are used in business harbingers of the type of systems to be used in people-oriented institutions such as the hospital, school, and home?

BIBLIOGRAPHY

Albus, James S., *Brains, Behavior, and Robotics.* Peterborough, NH: Byte Publications, 1981.

Diebold, J., *Man and the Computer—Agent of Social Change.* New York: Praeger Publications, 1969.

Dolotta, T. A., M. I. Bernstein, R. S. Dickson, Jr., et al., *Data Processing In 1980–1985.* New York: John Wiley, 1976.

Drucker, Peter F., *Technology, Management, and Society.* New York: Harper & Row, 1970.

Gruenberger, F., *Computers and the Social Environment*. Los Angeles, CA: Melville, 1975.

Herbert, Frank, *Without Me You're Nothing: The Essential Guide to Home Computers*. New York: Simon and Schuster, 1980.

Laver, Murray, *Computers and Social Change*. Cambridge, England: Cambridge University Press, 1980.

Lecht, Charles P., *The Waves of Change*. New York: McGraw-Hill, 1979.

Martin, James, *The Wired Society*. Englewood Cliffs, NJ: Prentice-Hall, Inc., 1978.

Naisbitt, John, *Megatrends*. New York: Warner Books, 1982.

Osborne, Adam, *An Introduction to Microcomputers*. Berkeley, CA: Osborne, 1980.

Tanner, William R., *Industrial Robots*. Dearborn, MI: Society of Manufacturing Engineers, 1981.

Webster, Tony, *Microcomputer Buying Guide*. Los Angeles, CA: Computer Reference Guide, 1981.

Weizenbaum, Joseph, *Computer Power and Human Reason*. San Francisco: W. H. Freeman, 1976.

Appendices

APPENDIX A

CASE STUDY: ROLCO

This appendix is an exercise illustrating system principles, design considerations, and trade-offs in the computerization of business applications. It is intended for the reader or student who desires to go a step beyond the discussion of Chapter 3, which presented an MIS framework for a company in the distribution business. The addendum looks at one of the major subsystems of the company in more depth. The case, although concentrating on order processing, should be viewed in light of its fit within the total MIS framework (see Fig. 3.8). Analysis will show the problems in designing a subsystem that is part of an MIS.

The case study is built around Rolco, Inc., a large supermarket chain. The company's organization and operational philosophy are described as a backdrop to the specific business system study. The case illustrates that a computer system cannot be viewed as an isolated entity but is embedded in the business environment and operational framework of the company installing the system. The trade-offs in information system design are not solely within the domain of the MIS department but are system-business trade-offs. The need for interaction between the system analyst and operating personnel and the management of both is clearly illustrated.

The reader or student is introduced to the principles of flow charting, input-output formats, file design, application timing, and the overall system considerations in computerizing a typical business application. The reader should be in a better position to understand the role of the system analyst, plus that of the businessman, who is becoming increasingly involved in system design.

Organization of Rolco, Inc.

Rolco is a large supermarket chain operating in the Midwest and Far West. With sales approaching $2 billion and with thirteen retailing divisions and one manufacturing division, it is one of the largest companies in its field. Rolco distributes a wide line of food items through its thirteen division warehouses. Each division operates as a relatively autonomous unit with its own general manager and its own merchandising, buying, personnel, real estate, warehousing, and accounting functions. The manufacturing division supplies about 10 percent of the overall items sold in the stores. The corporate offices of Rolco are located in Los Angeles, as are the manufacturing division and one of the largest retail divisions.

Figure A.1 is an organization chart of the company showing three regional vice-presidents and the manufacturing division vice-president reporting to the president. Each regional vice-president controls the specified number of divisions and has specific sales and profit goals. Rolco operates in a decentralized fashion under the theory that the best performance occurs when a manager has budget and profit goods and is rigorously measured against them. With this in mind, Rolco has established a profit-sharing program that operates at the individual store-manager level. Each retailing division controls from 40 to 90 supermarkets and each store manager receives a bonus at year-end based on his profit performance compared to the previous year and to the established profit plan. The percentage of this bonus as a proportion of the store manager's total salary has been steadily increasing.

The characteristics of the supermarket business are as follows: Supermarket chains operate on a low net profit to sales percentage, usually between 1 to 2 percent. The volume of transactions is extremely high; profitability comes from establishing economically sound store sites, providing products and services to the customer at competitive prices, developing merchandising policies that ensure a complete product line, and buying, warehousing, and distributing products in the most economical manner. A good proportion of the capital assets are tied up in inventory, for the business centers around procuring, warehousing, distributing, and selling the product. Inventory is maintained at the warehouse and also in lesser amounts at the individual store level. The "backroom" inventory (inventory carried at the store level) varies from store to store, depending on the policies and actions of the store manager. Rolco has 850 stores. The number of items carried in each division warehouse approximates 10,000 and includes grocery products (edible and nonedible), drug items, cosmetics, soft goods, hardware, and miscellaneous. In addition, certain perishables are shipped

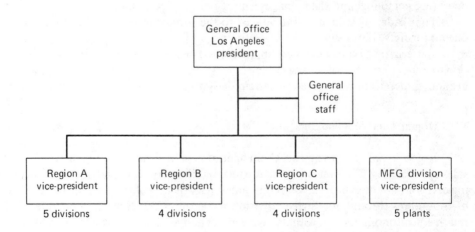

Fig. A.1 General organization of Rolco, Inc.

to the store directly from local bakeries, dairies, produce houses, and meat plants. A store receives perishables daily and orders grocery and other items from the warehouse three times per week. The trend is to increase the number of orders per week and to improve the ordering cycle so that the stockouts (not having items on the shelf or in inventory) are reduced while "backroom" store inventory is controlled.

Responsibilities of the Operating Levels

Figure A.2 lists the organization at the corporate office level, the division level, and the store manager level. The basic operating unit of Rolco is the division. The regional vice-president has a relatively small staff that coordinates sales, inventory, and accounting statistics; the major control and operating functions are handled at the divisional level.

The corporate office operates as a staff advisory group to the regions and divisions. In general, the control is loose, with major emphasis on coordinating financial reports, distributing general procedures and policies, and assisting the field operators in technical matters. The legal department works closely with the facilities group to select sites for new stores and negotiate store contracts (most stores are under sale and lease-back arrangements). The finance group accumulates and analyzes monthly region and division operating reports and consolidates profit-and-loss and balance-sheet statements. The planning department, in conjunction with top management, establishes one-year and three-year sales and profitability goals and is also responsible for evaluation and recommendation of new ventures, mergers, and the like. The merchandising group is mainly a competitive analysis service, continually monitoring and evaluating different products, assessing buying habits and trends, and relating these findings and recommendations to the field operations. They also coordinate nationwide advertising and promotion programs. There is a certain amount of central buying coordination to ensure that Rolco takes advantage of quantity purchases and has long-term contracts for items in critical supply. The MIS group handles the computer operation for the corporate office and acts in an advisory capacity to the MIS departments of the division. MIS decisions are decentralized, and although there are periodic meetings of the thirteen division MIS managers, each manager pretty much runs his own show. The engineering group oversees the physical facilities and is involved in new-equipment evaluation. The personnel department establishes general salary and job guidelines and also is heavily involved in nationwide union and labor contract negotiations.

The division office has an organization similar to the corporate office. The functions are analogous; however, the division operates as a highly autonomous profit center. In order to exploit this concept successfully, top management has given the division a high degree of local control. The division operates with minimum regional or corporate office restraint.

The division office in turn delegates profit authority and responsibility to each store. The store manager has a produce, grocery, and meat manager reporting to him, as well as a head cashier. His profit-and-loss statement is shown in Fig. A.3. Gross

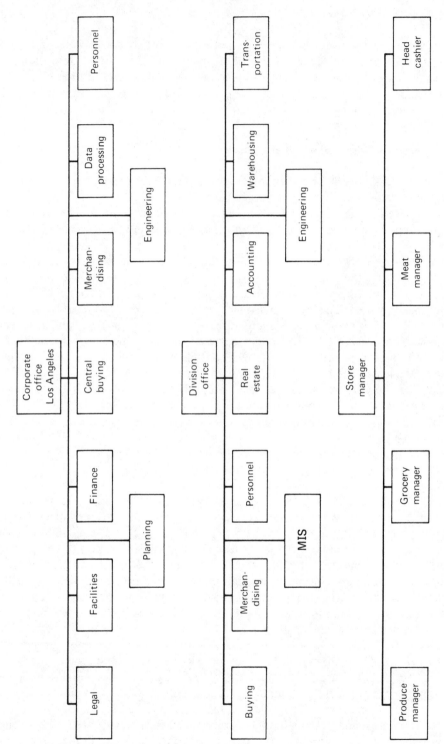

Fig. A.2 Functional organization of Rolco, Inc.

Meat sales
  — Meat cost of sales   _____
       Meat gross margin   _____
                                 _____

Grocery sales
  — Grocery cost of sales   _____
       Grocery gross margin   _____
                                 _____

Produce sales
  — Produce cost of sales   _____
       Produce gross margin   _____
                                 _____

Total gross margin   _____

Less: Labor expense   _____
        Facility expense   _____
        Inventory charge   _____
        Miscellaneous expense   _____

Total controllable expense   _____

Store net profit   _____

Fig. A.3   Individual store profit-and-loss statement

margin (sales, less cost of sales) is developed for meat, grocery, and produce. Controllable expenses include labor, 60 percent of which represents part-time personnel, facility charges, including rent, heat, and light, an inventory charge based on his average backroom stock, and miscellaneous expenses, such as cleaning supplies and paper bags. The total of these controllable expenses is then subtracted from the gross margin to give a net-profit figure for the store. To develop divisional profit figures, noncontrollable expenses (from the store's point of view), such as divisionwide advertising data processing costs, and warehouse operations, are reflected against the sum of the individual store's profit. The resulting figure becomes the division's monthly statement, which is submitted to the regional staff and consolidated there for submission to the corporate office.

    This, then, is a brief synopsis of the way in which Rolco operates. It is a fairly straightforward operation in that the prime purpose is to get food and related products into the hands of the consumer at a price that permits the company to remain competitive and yet allows for a reasonable profit margin after the costs of getting the product to the consumer are considered. The business is highly inventory oriented—

the major capital is tied up in inventory. Effective and efficient movement of that inventory through the division warehouses into the store's backroom and on to the shelves is a highly critical operation. It is here that data processing can make a significant impact in optimizing this flow and supplying valuable by-product information that forms the basis of an effective information system. The basic physical operation and flow of goods is depicted in Fig. A.4. The Rolco division warehouse is stocked by inventory that is purchased from a variety of vendors and manufacturers of food and related products. These products are then shipped to the various retail stores, where they are purchased by consumers who carry them out of the store in shopping carts, into their cars, and finally into their homes. The information system is built around this physical model.

Trade-Offs in System Development

When an information system for a company like Rolco is reviewed, it becomes obvious that there are a host of trade-off decisions in planning the implementation of the system. An illustration will show the trade-offs in designing a system that blends the following subsystems: order processing, inventory control, and transportation. In developing a set of decision rules for these subsystems, four key management objectives can be ascertained:

1. Increase customer service by reducing stockouts.
2. Keep inventory levels low, thereby conserving working capital.
3. Maintain transportation costs at a reasonable level.
4. Control data processing costs in the order processing cycle.

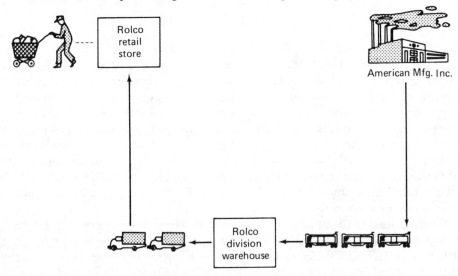

Fig. A.4 Basic flow of goods

Analysis shows that these four objectives are conflicting. For example, one way to reduce stockouts is to maintain higher-than-normal inventory levels so that there is ample safety stock to handle unforeseen emergencies or changes in buying patterns. Another way to reduce stockouts is to allow each store to order every day and to ensure one-day delivery service. This process, of course, is desirable from the store point of view and allows the store a great deal of ordering flexibility; however, transportation costs and data processing costs to handle the additional volume of orders will obviously rise.

The solution to these conflicting subsystem objectives is to select the decision rules that optimize the total order-processing cycle, based on the relative priority that management places on the four objectives. The point is that in many cases these decisions are made by the MIS manager, often by default. The design of the system makes it mandatory to face these issues. When the subsystems were functioning separately, each department manager (i.e., inventory control manager, transportation manager, sales administration manager, and store manager) designed the system to optimize around his particular requirements. This is not to say that each department ignored the needs of the other. The transportation manager serves the store manager and the order processing department serves both. Since the information system is often the catalyst that brings the conflicting requirements to light, it was the MIS manager who attempted to bring the various department heads together to agree on a system that came as close as possible to balancing the conflicting needs—to balance the four management objectives.

The way to develop a system that properly balances these and other management needs is to obtain management involvement from the start. The first step is to show management why they should be interested. There are techniques for assessing the trade-offs, for example, of customer service and inventory levels. Based on historical demand patterns of different items and the degree of fluctuation around an expected demand, a level of safety stock is predicated. The amount of safety stock can be based on a stated level of customer service. Thus a 95 percent level of customer service (stockouts would occur in 5 out of 100 orders) requires more safety stock than a 90 percent level. Also, an item that has a widely fluctuating demand pattern requires a greater amount of safety stock than a stable item with relatively stable demand.

It is also possible to develop the cost trade-offs in ordering more frequently, thus cutting down store backroom stock. For example, daily ordering and 24-hour delivery may completely eliminate backroom stock (items can be loaded directly from the truck onto the shelves at night). The inventory savings must now be viewed in light of the added transportation costs and costs of a nighttime store crew. It is here that the data processing department and the computer system can play a role and add a dimension to the trade-off decision. It may be possible to reduce the order-processing time by as much as 24 hours by putting communication terminals in the store. Thus, instead of being hand-carried at the end of the day to the division office, the orders would be fed directly into the computer each morning. The inventory records could be screened, the order processed, and the picking slip sent to the warehouse within an hour of receipt. The goods could be at the store that evening instead of the following evening. With this ordering flexibility, the store manager might still be able to eliminate backroom stock without increasing his number of orders per week. The communication equipment in each store will obviously add to the data processing costs, but it might be well worth the expenditure.

The foregoing is a classic example of the system trade-off decisions that must be resolved to optimize information systems. These are management decisions. The MIS manager can help resolve the issues by showing the pros and cons of one policy versus another and the relative risks inherent in following various policies. However, middle management must make the final decision, and often the issues are so basic and important to company operations that top management must also become involved.

This discussion illustrates the importance of management involvement in system design, frequently at the executive level. This is so because the system design and resultant system trade-offs often impact and raise questions of top-management strategies and objectives. Thus, while a system trade-off might optimize a conflicting set of costs, the decision reached might run counter to an important company policy, possibly not a short-term but a longer-range one of which the people working on the system are unaware.

The Order-Processing Cycle

The current method of ordering involves a store catalog that lists the 10,000 inventoried items at the division warehouse. The order catalog is illustrated in Fig. A.5. The punched cards correspond to the items ordered, and a special pencil is used to mark the quantity desired. The cards are prepunched with the store number and catalog page number. The combination of the page number and the mark-sense quantity in one of 25 card columns designates a specific item number. The computer is programmed to convert the page and line number into an item number so that the system can look up the inventory record, multiply the quantity ordered by weight, price, and cost, and print the extended store order. It does not take a system designer long to see that although this system is effective, it can be improved. The store manager or his delegate must make the rounds through the store, look at the shelves, and order what he needs for the next few days. In actual practice, because doing so takes considerable time, the store manager will order half the items in his store for one order and the other half the next order. Since most of the items ordered are fairly stable in demand and the computer extends each order, why cannot the computer automatically produce the order and eliminate a good deal of effort? There are some problems to be worked out, such as how the computer can spot trends in item movement. However, the store manager could still have the option of overriding the system to handle changes in the automatic order quantity due to changes in buyer demand, special promotions, and seasonal influences. The computer system with the required decision logic could also be programmed to accomplish this step.

The more important question in the preceding system trade-off is what effect it will have on the company policy of autonomous operation with profit-center respon-

Match item number with card item number

SHIP WT.	PRT. LIST	DESCRIPTION	ZONE 1 RETAIL	ZONE 2 RETAIL	ZONE 3 RETAIL	PRICE CHANGE	LINE NO.
		12 2LB STRAWBRY PRSV	65	65	65		7550
		12 2LB BLKBRY PRESV	59	59	59		7551
		24 10 OZ STRW PRS TMB	29	29	29		7566
		24 1LB 4OZ PEACH PRES	39	39	39		7567
		24 1LB 4OZ STRAW PRSV	49	49	49		7568
		24 1LB 4OZ PLUM PRES	35	35	35		7569
		24 1LB 4OZ GRAPE PRES	35	35	35		7570
		12 1LB4OZ BLKBERYPRS	45	45	45		7581
		12 1LB 4OZ APRICOT PR	45	45	45		7580
		12 1LB 4OZ CHERRY PRS	49	49	49		7582
		12 1LB 4OZ PINAPL PRS	45	45	45		7583
		12 100Z K CHERRY JELLY	25	25	25		7765
		12 100Z ELDBERY JELLY	25	25	25		7766
		12 100Z APPLE JELLY	25	25	25		7767
		12 100Z BLKBRY JELLY	29	29	29		7768
		12 100Z BL RASP JELLY	35	35	35		7769
		12 100Z STRWBRY JELLY	29	29	29		7770
		24 200Z AP BKRSP JEL	35	35	35		7771
		24 200Z AP BKBY JELY	35	35	35		7772
		24 200Z AP STRW JELY	35	35	35		7773
		24 200Z AP ELDR JELY	35	35	35		7774
		24 200Z APL GRP JELY	35	35	35		7775
		24/1LB ORANGE SLICES	25	25	25		6302

Order guide and price book

Fig. A.5

393

sibility at the store level. The system, theoretically at least, would save the company a considerable amount of money but might have an unfavorable impact on the store manager. This is a decision that must be made by top management. Rolco management firmly believes in the profit-center concept and that performance is optimized when the store manager acts as an entrepreneur who owns his own store. The dollar savings of the system must be carefully weighed against the potential impact it will have on the store manager, who may feel that he has lost control of the ordering function—something he has always controlled and used as a tool to serve his customers better. This feeling may be the governing factor, even if the automatic ordering system can be proven more effective in a majority of cases. The answer to this dilemma, perhaps, is to pilot-test the system in several stores. Then the store managers can help sell the others on the merits of the system if the system works out in practice.

The store bill, which is the output of the system, shows the store header information at the top. Each line of the bill lists the item description information and shows the extension of the quantity ordered times the unit price. A copy of the store bill is used as a warehouse picking document that tells the order pickers what items to pull and assemble for shipment.

Rolco currently utilizes magnetic disk for its storage medium. Each inventory item includes the information shown in tabular form.

Disk records are used to carry the store header information and consists of the following items.

The batch-order processing cycle is as follows:

1. The store order data is converted from cards to disk, and in the process the page and line number for each item is translated (by a formula) to the item number as carried on the inventory master file. Each store orders three times a week, an average of 2000 items each time. The total order deck consists of 200 cards, although some cards will have no quantities ordered on them.
2. The orders (a store at a time) are screened against the master file to see if there is inventory on hand, extended (quantity extended by price), and sorted by warehouse slot number. (The warehouse slot number is the sequence in which the order is picked.)
3. The orders are then printed and sent (a) to the store ordering the items and (b) to the warehouse to pick the order for delivery to the store. The store can then match the physical receipt of the order with the paper invoice.
4. Out-of-stock items and order totals are stored by the disk for later printout.

The reader should be able to describe the receiving process, which in many ways is the reverse of the billing process. Receipts are entered daily. A record is made for each item received, with the item number, quantity received, and vendor identification. Receipts average 1000 per day.

Rolco desires to investigate automating their checkout facilities with the new scanning equipment currently on the market. They realize they have been slow in

MASTER FILE (10,000 ITEMS)

Data for Each Inventory Item	Length of Field
Item number	5 Numeric
Item description	32 Alpha
Warehouse slot number	3 Numeric
Zone 1 retail price	6 Numeric
Zone 2 retail price	6 Numeric
Zone 3 retail price	6 Numeric
Zone 4 retail price	6 Numeric
Beginning balance (cases)	6 Numeric
Beginning balance (dollars)	8 Numeric
Receipts (cases)	6 Numeric
Receipts (dollars)	8 Numeric
Shipping weight (gross)	6 Numeric
Shipping weight (net)	6 Numeric
Shipments (cases)	6 Numeric
Shipments (dollars)	8 Numeric
Miscellaneous data	24 Numeric

STORE HEADER INFORMATION

Data for Each Store	Length of Field
Store number	4 Numeric
Store address	32 Alpha
Pricing zone	2 Numeric

evolving their business information systems, and management would like to include the new concept of transaction processing as a foundation leading to a true management information system.

STUDY GUIDE

The study guide lists questions under five headings, ranging from the overall organization philosophy of Rolco through the development of system specifications to future system considerations. These questions can be used either as a checklist for the reader or as a guide for general discussion and work assignments by an instructor. Although the questions center on developing the system much as Rolco now operates, the reader or student should be able to see where he could improve the system and expand the application to accomplish more for Rolco. Doing so, of course, could be an additional assignment.

A. Rolco Organization and Operation

1. Describe the organizational philosophy and type of business engaged in by Rolco.
2. Do you think this organizational philosophy is sound, considering the type of business?
3. What potential MIS problems are raised by this type of organization?
4. As a store manager, what would be your major concern under this type of operation?
5. What are the key controllable elements in profitable store operation?
6. As a newly appointed vice-president of a region, what are your main concerns?
7. Discuss the pros and cons of centralization and/or decentralization on a function by function basis (i.e., buying, merchandizing, MIS).

B. Trade-Offs in System Development

1. What considerations would cause management to place heavier priority on one or more of the four management objectives listed?
2. What are the relative pros and cons in computerizing the three mentioned subsystems as a single entity? What are the system analyst-operating personnel interaction considerations?
3. Do you think the MIS manager might have a built-in predisposition to install communication terminals in each store?
4. Who specifically (i.e., what departments and what level of management) would be concerned with computerizing the subsystems mentioned?
5. Can you visualize what the ordering procedures of the grocery store of the future might be? What impact would future considerations have on designing of the current information system? How much built-in system flexibility should there be?
6. What advantages does Rolco have because it is a chain operation and owns the individual stores?

C. Initial System Assignment

(Assume that the system is for a single division.)

1. Write a simple English narrative of the order-processing system, including the objectives and purpose.
2. Assuming that the basic file storage medium is magnetic disk, flow-chart (a) the billing system and (b) the receiving system.

3. Block out the item records on disk.
4. Lay out the store-invoice form.

D. Point-of-Sale System Assignment

1. Write an English narrative and flow-chart a proposed automated front-end system.
2. Present a cost/benefit/savings analysis of your system.
3. Describe an implementation plan for installing the system.
4. Analyze and resolve, if possible, the major risks of such a system.
5. Prepare a management presentation of the system justification.

E. Further Study Questions

1. What factors would determine whether you proposed a computer configuration that had higher-speed disks and central processor and/or greater capacities?
2. Speculate on what extensions could be put into the system to handle (a) inventory control and (b) truck dispatching. Lay out a sample inventory control report that might emanate from the system.
3. Discuss the desirability of installing communication terminals in the individual stores.
4. How would the system handle items that, although they were listed in inventory, were unavailable in the warehouse?
5. What type of internal training would be necessary before installing the system?
6. What impact would the future plans of Rolco have on the initial system design?
7. How long do you estimate it would take to install such a system?
8. Do you think Rolco is wise in wanting to incorporate automatic checkout equipment? Are they ready for such a step?
9. What should be Rolco's approach to point-of-sale and transaction processing?

POINT-OF-SALE SUBSYSTEM

An evolution has been taking place at the checkout counters of grocery stores. Though to some, it is revolutionary, I am personally familiar with the effort that has gone into automating the point-of-sale area within the retail industry, and it has been a long gradual evolution spanning the last fifteen years. The advent of point-of-sale

Article	Name	Content
1	Revolution at the Checkout Counter	Description of the automatic checkout equipment available for supermarkets.
2	Checkstand Configuration for a Bottom-Slot Scanner	Picture and schematic of an automated checkout unit.
3	UPC Has Antitrust Angle	Brings out the government/legal issue.
4	POS Could Cut Super-market Job 25%	Brings out the union issue.
5	New Checkout Systems Anger Consumer	Brings out the consumer issue.
6	Supplementary Cost Data	Enables student to develop a cost/benefit/savings analysis.
7	Retail Merchandise Information Systems for the 1980's	Status and future of POS

devices plus the concept of transaction processing whereby customer or event transactions are recorded and handled at the time they occur are key areas of future system growth. The point-of-sale system assignment (see D in the study guide) will give the reader or student an opportunity to analyze this technology and determine whether it is feasible from a technological, economical, and operational viewpoint for a company like Rolco. It makes for an interesting and provocative exercise because the elements of risk are present as well as outside influences such as consumer acceptance, antitrust considerations, and union concerns. The following articles and references give additional information enabling the student to complete assignment D.

ARTICLE 1

REVOLUTION AT THE CHECKOUT COUNTER*
by Tom Mahoney

If you live in one of a few scattered areas of the United States or Canada, you may already have experienced something new in your grocery supermarket—a novel change on the shelves and packages and at the checkout counter, which marks a revolution in electronic retail marketing and accounting systems.

On the self-service shelves, prices may not appear on each package, but simply be posted on the shelf. Each package has a weird set of symbols printed on it by the packager—a bunch of vertical lines of varying thickness with numbers under them, all crowded together in a little patch about 1½ inches long and one inch high, with another number off to the left. Each packaged item has a distinct set of these lines

*Reprinted with permission from *The American Legion Magazine*, Nov. 1974.

which identifies it for what it is, by maker, product, size and weight. The size of the symbol can vary, Wrigley's chewing gum will use a miniature version. The little patch can separately identify 100 billion different items.

Millions of people have already seen these symbols on packages in stores and some have seen them in use. They are known as the Universal Product Code. Nearly half of all prepackaged food store items will soon bear the code. By the end of next year, about 70% of them will.

In a store that uses the symbol, when you take your purchases to the checkout counter the checker exposes the symbol on each package to an electronic scanner, instead of turning it every which way to see what price is marked on it. The scanner is hooked to a computerized cash register. The checker doesn't punch keys to register each item. Instead, the scanner-computer identifies the package on sight from the symbol, reads a program of its own to find the price, and flashes the information for each package in turn on a lighted read-out screen, visible to you. The checker can bag most of your items in the time she formerly used to punch keys.

Was it a 39¢ can of Alpo dog food? The screen may flash .39 ALPO DOG FOOD. Or perhaps just .39 DOG FOOD, without the brand name. No more just GR for groceries or MT for meat. As fast as the checker can expose each package to the scanner, the price and item flash on the screen. At the end of the sale the computer spits out your sales slip, with a printed record for every item, the name and address of the store, the checkout lane, the checker, the date (and possibly the hour and minute), the sales tax and the amount of change due you.

Internally, the computer records the sales—and the changes in store inventory and cash supply—in the accounting system of the store and perhaps of the central office of the chain of stores, as fast as the symbols on the packages can be viewed.

A pilot model of this type of checkout was run for 15 months, a while back, in a Kroger store in Kenwood, Ohio, outside of Cincinnati. A later version went into brief use last February 26 at the Finast Big Buy store on Route 30 in Framingham, Mass. On June 26, a Marsh supermarket in Troy, Ohio, put six checkout lanes on a scanner-computer system. Last August, Steinberg's, Ltd., Canada's second largest supermarket chain, started using such a scanner system in a Montreal store, printing the sales-slip information in both French and English. Earlier last summer, a big Pathmark store in South Plainfield, N.J., put one in service, while nine checkstands went on scanners in a Brockton Public Market at Stoughton, Mass.

By next spring, many more major food chains will have tested scanner checkouts in some of their stores, or have them well under way. By 1980 or so virtually every food store that is big enough to afford the expensive equipment may be pushing its customers through electronic scanner checkout lines.

There is more in this for the stores, perhaps, than for the customers, but there's something in it for everyone. You will see more clearly what you are being charged for and get a better record of it. Once the computers are working smoothly, there should be less chance of error in charging you for your purchases, or of ringing up items you didn't buy. The big stores are counting on running you through the checkout counters almost twice as fast as you go through them today.

How to Read a Can

The zero at left says the item is one regularly retailed in grocery stores. The 11132 says it is a product of Allen Products Co., Allentown, Pa., when read at the same time as the zero at left. The 00012 says the item is a 14½ oz. can of Alpo Chicken and Liver Dinner "for dogs and puppies," when read at the same time as the zero and the 11132.

The item sold for 39¢, and the computer was programmed to read the symbol as a 39¢ item, and sales-taxable.

If the price changed, the computer would be reprogrammed to assign the new price on "seeing" the symbol. The vertical lines are what the scanner reads to "see" the numbers under them.

The lines at the extreme ends and in the center orient the scanner, telling it that when it sees them as vertical lines it sees the symbol correctly. The second pair of lines from the left are what the scanner reads for the zero at left.

The imperfections in the lines over the 2 at right were caused in handling or shipping. The scanner can read any hairline path across the symbol, and wouldn't be bothered by these imperfections. If it couldn't get a good reading, it might beep or not beep, depending on the system used in the particular store.

Finally, the food merchants expect large operating cost reductions. This should help hold back food prices, as they compete for your trade with reduced overhead for themselves. The scanner system may be bad news for small merchants who can't afford it, if the savings are as great as the big merchants expect.

An obvious saving may come from eliminating labor now used to mark prices on every package on the self-service shelves. Some stores carry 8,000 price-marked items at any time. If Alpo dog food is 39¢ today, the computer is programmed to charge 39¢ for it on reading its symbol on the package. If the price goes to 42¢, each item needn't be marked with the new price. The price posted on the shelf is changed, and the computer is reprogrammed to charge 42¢ when it reads the symbol.

The scanners will be able to handle every prepackaged item except for those of unusually large size. The system does not provide a universal way of scanning things like bunches of bananas, heads of lettuce or cuts of meat that vary in weight from package to package. But it has a built-in method to allow the stores to affix scannable stickers of their own to such things.

The stores expect enormous advantages from the record-keeping aspects of the computer-scanner-registers. It should be possible for the transactions of every checkout counter to be instantly available to the store itself, to its chain's district office and its central office, on a minute to minute basis—to show what's selling where, and to keep instant inventories of every store and the whole chain. In effect, the moment you buy your Alpo dog food, the bowels of the computer system tell the store and the whole chain to "scratch one can" of that particular Alpo item. From this it is a simple jump to the computer telling the chain how much of what to buy and which stores to send how much of it—or even placing the orders itself. The information will also give rapid data to indicate the sales results of advertising and special pricing.

ARTICLE 2

CHECKOUT CONFIGURATION FOR A BOTTOM-SLOT SCANNER

Checkstand Configuration for a Bottom-Slot Scanner

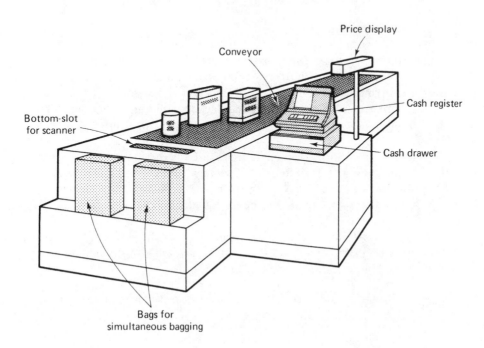

ARTICLE 3

UPC HAS ANTITRUST ANGLE*

WASHINGTON, D.C.—The use of computerized supermarket systems using the Universal Product Code (UPC) has antitrust as well as consumer protection aspects.

And a leading UPC consultant said last week the supermarket systems can be profitable even with price marking.

There are antitrust ramifications of the UPC systems in the area of food manufacturing, according to a Federal Trade Commission (FTC) staff member. About 1,800 food processing manufacturers have adopted the UPC symbol for source marking and, by the end of 1975, 80% of the items going through supermarkets will be marked.

But there are almost 30,000 food processors and manufacturers representing the remaining 20% of items in supermarkets. And there will be increasing competitive pressure on these firms to convert to UPC marking if they want to survive in the supermarket environment.

Many of these suppliers are small firms for whom the UPC conversion could be prohibitive in cost. "This could have significant competitive implications for smaller food chains and independents," the FTC staff member said.

It costs an estimated $1,000 to redesign a labeling machine for the UPC marking method and this could be prohibitive for smaller suppliers, he added.

Potential Savings Promising

On the plus side, the potential savings of the UPC systems seem very promising, the FTC source said. Even with the retention of price marking, there are savings for the average supermarket that installs a UPC check-out system.

A spokesman at McKinsey & Co., Inc. agreed with this evaluation. McKinsey has been consulting for the industry since the supermarket marking systems were first developed.

The savings, even with prices on the items, are still there, the spokesman said. In a $60,000/week store, the projected "hard savings" are about $34,000/year.

If prices had to be put back on "dry grocery products," the savings per year would be lowered by $6,000 to $8,000, he estimated, adding this is still a good return on the investment in UPC equipment.

One result of retaining individual price marking will be to slow down the rate of UPC supermarket installations and the smaller, medium-size stores may no longer find the new systems effective from a cost standpoint.

*Reprinted by permission. Copyright by *Computerworld*, Newton, Mass. 02160, February 19, 1975.

"We really don't yet know whether the communication of price information can be accomplished in some way other than pricing each individual item," the consultant said.

Most of the opposition thus far evidenced at UPC supermarkets is coming from consumerists instead of the average consumer, the consultant said. Asked for a definition, he defined consumerists as those spokesmen who say they speak for the average consumer.

But these spokesmen may not accurately portray the concerns of the typical supermarket shopper, he said.

The supermarket industry plans to survey shoppers carefully in UPC stores to assess their feelings on the absence of pricing. These surveys will be very important in determining how the UPC installations will evolve.

In the meantime, it is unfortunate that several bills are being proposed that require items to be priced, the McKinsey spokesman said.

"If the retail clerks afraid of being put out of work combine with the consumerists, there is a reasonable chance that some premature legislation gets passed. This is particularly true on the state and county level," he said.

The supermarket industry is now considering about four different market research proposals to survey shoppers and some of these surveys are being formulated with the assistance of consumer protection groups.

"We have to determine what is an adequate level of price information," the consultant said.

ARTICLE 4

POS COULD CUT SUPERMARKET JOBS 25%*

WASHINGTON, D.C.—The installation of point-of-sale (POS) systems in supermarkets could eliminate 25% to 30% of the jobs in those stores, according to an official of the Retail Clerks International Association. But at least one supermarket chain official has refuted the layoff charge.

Clerks now involved in such functions as check-out and price marking will be displaced if the POS systems come into widespread use, the union official claimed.

Commenting on attempts to justify the installation of terminal systems using the Universal Product Code (UPC), he said, "The supermarkets will try to educate the consumer to do without a price on every item. They did the same thing with trad-

*Reprinted by permission. Copyright by *Computerworld*, Newton, Mass. 02160, January 22, 1975.

ing stamps. First they told the customer they were out, then they were pushing them to spur sales and now they are out again.

"Over the next two to three years, the stores will have a running inventory on the computer and this will do away with some manual stock counting operations.

"And with just shelf marking instead of individual item marking it will do away with markers and stockers. [The supermarkets] will be able to cut open a case and put it right on the shelf instead of marking and stacking each item. One clerk will be able to do what two did previously," he suggested.

Many stores have not reduced their personnel because the full effects of computerization in the food industry have not yet been felt, the official said. Most stores are still in the initial test phases with UPC terminal systems.

'Old Propaganda Gimmick'

"We see a substantial loss of jobs in the supermarket industry with the installation of these computer terminal systems. We are not opposed to automation but we will protect our members from loss of jobs through collective bargaining and other means at our disposal," the official stated.

As a side effect of having fewer clerks doing more work in a store with POS systems, customers could experience a reduced level of in-store help with items such as perishable produce, meat and other items which typically require service, he added.

One of the claims often made by supermarkets is that they operate on a very small profit margin of less than 1%. They justify the installation of POS systems as a means to improve this profit margin.

But the Retail Clerks official called this "an old propaganda gimmick they have used for years at the bargaining table and other places.

"It might be true that they only earn a fraction of a cent on every dollar of sales, but the real measure comes on the return on their capital invested. And these ratios typically show 14% or more return as net profit," the union official claimed.

"We have been testing POS terminals since June without any adverse effects on our clerks," according to Clyde Dawson, director of research and development for Marsh Supermarkets. The chain has NCR terminals at its store in Troy, Ohio, and it has thus far experimented with the removal of item prices on only a limited scale.

The supermarket firm plans to increase its price removal operation in stores "on the assumption that our customers are adults," Dawson said.

"The employees of Marsh supermarkets have never lost a job because of modification of existing programs or installation of new equipment. At this point we don't anticipate anyone losing their job but we do anticipate being able to offer a higher level of customer service and to be more efficient in our operations," Dawson said.

Clerks no longer required to price items would be used to improve "housekeeping and other merchandising tasks."

Dawson said he understands some stores will rationalize the pay-back of POS equipment with reduced manpower, "but I don't see it that way."

ARTICLE 5

NEW CHECKOUT SYSTEMS ANGER CONSUMER*

NEWTON, Mass. Now that computer-based supermarket checkout systems are a reality, consumer opposition and demands that consumer needs be considered are springing up.

Many bugs still need to be ironed out, despite the seven or so years of testing which have gone into the systems, according to a consumer advocate here. Consumers, in her opinion, should have been consulted in the planning stages—but they weren't.

In those systems, item prices are marked on the shelves, but the products themselves are marked only with a standard product code which is optically scanned at the checkout stand. The system automatically adds the cost of the item to the customer's bill by accessing a file of prices stored in the computer.

The legality of the supermarket systems has yet to be tested, the consumer indicated, an eventuality which she feels could well arise.

"If the system should fail a court test for some reason after all the equipment is installed—what a waste of money," she said, indicating that the situation might have been avoided if consumers had been in on the earlier planning.

The consumer, who wished to remain anonymous because of annoying letters she has received in the past, said she spoke for hundreds of women in their areas of concern.

Removal of Prices

One of the major problems is the removal of prices from packages. This, she said, will in many cases eliminate the possibility of comparison shopping, a mode many shoppers have been forced into in the last year or so by spiraling prices.

"Once you take a box off the shelf and turn your back, you no longer have any idea what that item cost," she stated. "And since most stores have their 'specials' set up at the end of aisles, you'd have to run back each time to check if it really was a good buy."

In addition, there is no way of telling whether the person who posted the prices on the shelves marked up the up-to-date ones. "Human error is great. Even today in almost any supermarket you can find two identical cans of juice, for instance, with different prices. And when the prices are changed within the machine itself, you'll never know if there is a mistake," she said.

How Much Left

Consumers will also have to change their way of shopping in terms of the amount of cash they carry. Many people today bring a fixed amount of money, say $10, with them. Now, the consumer spokeswoman said, you can no longer look down in your cart and see how close you are to that amount of money.

"This is like sticking the housewife's head in the sand—saying, 'listen, bring your blank check, get what you need and that's the way it is because prices are going up and we're going to help you out by not frustrating you by showing you the rising prices.'"

Another complaint, she said, is that a shopper can no longer look in the refrigerator and know whether to give Johnny 50 cents or $1 to go buy a pound of butter.

Furthermore, the shopper can no longer look at last week's box of cornflakes and see how much it has gone up this week.

Useless Data

"Only about one out of 30 shoppers checks his register tape with packages now, so the added information the computer will give him or her is really useless from the consumer's viewpoint," she stated.

The laser beam used to read the Universal Product Code is another area of concern. Will it have any effect on the food?

"This isn't a once in a while thing," the spokeswoman said. "Every item of food that goes into your body will be exposed. Maybe the laser will kill bacterial growth in dairy foods, but I have to believe that different foods may be affected differently. And I haven't seen any documentation in any articles published so far."

Who Cares?

"The idea of this thing is fine. I think it's a very workable solution to a lot of problems," she said. "But I think that they have been so interested in the wholesaler and the retailer, and the manufacturers that they completely neglected the consumers and their feelings."

Consumer commissions are currently being set up throughout the Commonwealth of Massachusetts to look at supermarket systems among other things, she said. As a legal board, the commission will have more power than an irate group of consumers, and perhaps, she hopes, get some consumer input into the development of computer systems.

ARTICLE 6

SUPPLEMENTARY COST DATA

DATA PROCESSING COSTS AND OTHER COST DATA ON ROLCO, INC.

Typical Data Processing Annual Costs (for average retailing division)

Computer hardware rental	$140,000	35%
Systems and programming salaries	112,000	28%
Operating personnel	100,000	25%
Supplies and outside service	36,000	9%
Operating overhead	12,000	3%
Total Yearly Costs	$400,000	100%

Value of Typical Inventory Carried (for average retailing division)

Store backroom inventory	$ 60,000
Retailing division inventory	$4,000,000

Typical Store Operating Budget

Sales	$2,500,000	
Cost of Sales	2,000,000	
Gross Margin		$500,000

Store Controllable Expense

Labor and fringe	$ 22,500	
Facility expense	52,500	
Inventory charge	12,500	
Supplies	37,500	
Transportation/warehousing	20,000	
Other	27,500	
Total	$ 375,000	
Income from Store Operations		$125,000
Allocated Regional and Corporate Expense		87,500
Income Before Taxes		$ 37,500

Costs of Point-of-Sale Devices

1. Conventional cash register	$ 2,000	
2. Electronic cash register	$ 4,500	
(provides 100 total and subtotals)		

DATA PROCESSING COSTS AND OTHER COST DATA ON ROLCO, INC. (cont.)

3. Complete electronic terminal system. $48,000
   Includes:
   - Optical scanner terminals (5)
   - Communication link to central computer
   - Cash register terminals (5)
     (Claims are that this device can save up to
     15% of checkout labor)
4. Minicomputer with necessary peripherals $30,000

ARTICLE 7

RETAIL MERCHANDISE INFORMATION SYSTEMS FOR THE 1980's*

J. Barry Mason
Board of Visitors Research Professor
Graduate School of Business
The University of Alabama
University, Alabama

Morris L. Mayer
Professor of Marketing
Graduate School of Business
The University of Alabama
University, Alabama

This article explores the dynamics of hardware and software developments as the keys to retail merchandise information systems for the 1980's. Such systems will become a reality during this decade for many progressive retailers. Prototype systems are now being developed and tested. Experiments in data generation also show the promise of timely information feedback on consumer reactions to retail price changes, advertising, shelf-face changes, and a variety of similar variables. The assets of information and communications are being added to the traditional land, labor, and capital assets that scientifically based retail management will regard as the foundations of retail success in the 1980's.

SUPERMARKET SYSTEM PROGRESS

The technology for scanning merchandise tickets in the food and nonfood sectors is about equally advanced. However, the technology for printing tickets in general merchandising lags behind that in the food sector. Quality control remains a problem. Vendor marking of merchandise is further advanced in food than in nonfood retailing.

Journal of Retailing, Vol. 56, No. 1 (Spring 1980). Reprinted by permission.

Scanning at the supermarket checkout allows the capture of detailed sales information on an item-by-item basis for each scanning store. Such systems thus allow management to maintain perpetual inventories on each item and to implement an automatic reordering system based on timely item-movement information. This kind of routine, repeat ordering is less practical in general merchandising except for staple, nonseasonal items.

Giant Foods expects by the end of 1980 to have the entire chain locked into a single, computerized cash register-to-distribution center network. Chainwide uniformity will allow companywide automation of the stock replenishment process. Giant anticipates that the systemwide, scanner-linked reordering process will save the company more than $1.6 million annually.[8]

Headquarters management during the 1980's probably can begin to develop unique store setups reflecting the demographics and buying patterns of each store, since scanning produces detailed information on a store-by-store basis. The scanner-generated information can also be valuable in new item and product discontinuation decisions. Management, under the new technology, can require each product to stand on its own and justify the space which it has been assigned. Management can also more precisely define its requirements for new store setups and departmental reset-ups. Essentially, departmental layouts, including even shelf facings by item, can be compared against preestablished sales criteria. The detailed sales data can also be used for better control of inventory at the store level. Studies have shown that some departments now carry as much as 20 percent excess merchandise.[9] Other advances in inventory control will include maintenance of perpetual inventories and automatic reordering by store.

Experiments in Data Generation

Experiments in data generation and use as a result of the new electronics technology are also making rapid progress among food merchandisers. However, data capture for use in systems input at this point still represents only the smallest beginning of the development of a management resource. Management is still seeking to determine the types of information available through scanning that are needed for making business decisions.[10]

The research applications thus far have largely been in tracking and experimentation. Some supermarket chains, however, now use scanner data on a limited basis to provide weekly sales feedback for their own brand and for competitors' brands. Nielsen, for example, has recently introduced its first scanning-based service—

---

[8]"Giant Shoots for 100% Scanning," *Chain Store Age/Supermarket*, May 1979, p. 91.

[9]Willard R. Bishop, "The Age of Scanning: What's in It for Brokers?" *MRF/Broker*, December 1977, p. 4.

[10]D. R. McCurry and R. E. Shaw, "Turning Scanning Data into Information," *The Nielsen Researcher*, No. 2 (1979); "Scanning Data . . . The Real World Applications," *The Nielsen Researcher*, No. 4 (1978).

ScanTrack. The service consists of weekly sales data for all products within a category that are UPC marked. The reported data consist of unit sales, dollar sales, selling price, and the percentages of stores selling, of stores with local advertising, of stores with displays, and of stores that feature prices. The service currently reports activity in the Rochester, New York, and Seattle, Washington, areas and is designed to provide manufacturers with a facility for evaluating promotional and test-marketing activities. Efforts are also underway for a national ScanTrack service.[11]

Essentially, Nielsen has equipped 2,100 to 2,200 households with electronic diary identification cards. SAMI (Selling Areas-Marketing, Inc., a subsidiary of Time, Inc.) has also developed an electronic diary capability around four Milgram stores in Topeka, Kansas. Behavior Scan (a firm in Barrington, Illinois) has a similar electronic capability. A unique dimension of the system is that the sample households receive all TV programming by a cable service. The company has developed a device operated by a minicomputer that allows it to send different TV ads to different cooperating households at the same time on the same program. The Data Checker Company and IBM have also developed software that can be added to scanning systems to allow the tracking of individual household purchases. However, the equipment must be used in conjunction with a recruited consumer panel.[12] Finally, NABSAN (National Advertised Brands Scanning, a service of the Newspaper Advertising Bureau) has recently announced the availability of national grocery scanner data. Subscribers receive week-by-week product movement and retail price data for all UPC-coded items in the 206 participating stores in 36 different markets, delivered either as a hard-copy printout or on magnetic tape.

The future for the use of these kinds of data bases as part of a retail merchandise information system for supermarkets is truly exciting. Store experiments on price changes, end-of-aisle displays, newspaper coupons, and shelf restocking patterns will continue to be based on the provision of weekly item movement and brand share data from scanner stores by such firms as Nielsen. The sophisticated systems in the future will involve integrated systems for consumer and product tracking that will allow static and time series measures of consumer attitudes, demographics, psychographics, and family purchase behavior, all related to UPC-coded items.

MARKET PENETRATION OF POS SYSTEMS

Basic information on current and projected sales levels for electronic cash registers and POS systems yields some insights into the rate of diffusion of modern merchandise information systems capabilities in various retail sectors. Sales of equipment

[11]P. M. Schmitt, "Impact of Scan Data on Marketing Research" (Presentation to the FMI Scanning Conference, Boston, July 12, 1979), p. 8.
[12]"New Behavior Scan System Ties Grocery Sales to TV Ads," *Marketing News*, September 21, 1979, p. 7; "Checkout Scanner Ultimately a Marketing Data Goldmine," *Marketing News*, May 18, 1979, p. 1.

have greatly accelerated in the last two or three years and softwear capabilities have expanded at a comparable rate.

Supermarkets

As shown in Table 1, the forecast by the A. C. Nielsen Company is for 3,000 scanner-equipped food stores by the end of 1981.[13] The forecast is based on the assumption that scanners are feasible in food stores doing $80,000 per week. The potential, based on present census information, would indicate that scanners could be used in approximately 7 percent of the food stores in the United States that currently account for slightly more than 47 percent of the total food store dollar sales. A much larger number of stores are now equipped with electronic cash registers that can be upgraded to scanning.

Supermarkets installed more scanners in 1979 than in the previous five-year history of the system. During the past 12 or so months, management has started to realize the extra profit possible by scanner-assisted electronic checkouts. The first full-store scanner tests did not occur until 1974. Marsh Supermarkets, based in Yorktown, Indiana, installed an NCR scanning system in a Troy, Ohio, supermarket at that time.[14]

Higher levels of UPC source-coded items have made the systems more cost-efficient today. Supermarket trade groups have also been working out arrangements that will allow individual item-price removal, a major saving in labor costs. Today a profit of $100,000 can be realized by an $8-million store after two years of scanner installation.

Industry forecasts are for the addition of approximately 1,000 POS systems annually throughout 1990 at a cost of roughly $150 million each year. Advances in technology will yield cheaper and less bulky systems ideal for small, high-volume convenience units and limited assortment units. Widespread use of scanners will permit conversion to computerized ordering that will allow management more time to de-

TABLE 1   Scanner-equipped Food Store Universe

		Number of stores
	End of 1977	209
	End of 1978	535
	End of March 1979	704
	End of June 1979	903
Future estimates		
	End of 1979	1,200
	End of 1980	2,000
	End of 1981	3,000

[13]Paul M. Schmitt, "Promotion: It Does More than Anyone Ever Thought" (Presentation to Advertising Age Promotion Workshop during Advertising Age Advertising Week, Chicago, August 22, 1979), p. 2.

[14]"Progress Is Spectacular," *Chain Store Age/Supermarket*, May 1979, p. 66.

velop and implement sophisticated merchandising programs, including changes in the product mix and in the assortment and presentation of displays as management learns more about product movement.[15]

THE ROLE OF ELECTRONIC FUNDS TRANSFER

A still-to-be-realized advancement in POS systems is the elimination of many paper-based financial transactions.[21] Electronic funds transfer is now offering this possibility. An EFT system is operational when POS terminals are connected by telephone lines directly to financial institution computers. The computers of several different financial institutions may be linked together through an automated clearinghouse or electronic switching network. Electronic point-of-sales terminals are activated by a plastic card and a customer's personal identification number. When a point-of-sale terminal operation is used, funds can be transferred immediately to the retailer's bank account for the amount of sale, either from the customer's bank account (debit transaction) or through the extension of credit by the financial institution (credit transaction). When POS equipment manufacturers and the banks have developed the necessary EFT systems and when state laws support the concept of EFT, retail management will press ahead quite rapidly, thus leading to the replacement of older POS systems and related communications hardware and networks.

Further standardization of third-party account-number formats will also be necessary to allow the EFT system to work efficiently. VISA and Master Charge are developing a standard length and formulation for their cards. The new standardized formats, however, are longer than the ones accepted by many POS terminals today. This problem will also cause some older equipment to become obsolete.

The integration of POS, credit authorization, and EFT systems probably will be implemented first in national merchandise chains such as Sears and Penney's. Many of the experiments thus far, however, have been made by the financial community in utilizing EFT systems for credit or check authorization. Banks have been quite aggressive in seeking to eliminate their burden of paperwork by the use of the new technology. The benefits to the retailer and to the consumer from the technology have been limited thus far.[22] Further development needs to give explicit consideration to the day-to-day problems of the retailer, particularly the need to provide good customer service at the point of sale and to minimize delays and inconveniences.

General merchandise retailers have relatively small problems with check cashing but an ever-mounting problem with credit cards and the need for on-line credit authorization. Authorization alone, however, does not resolve the credit card problem. Also, the savings from on-line credit authorization may not have a sufficient short-term payoff to justify the installation of on-line networks and terminals that would be needed to support the system.

[15]"What's Ahead in 1990?" *Chain Store Age/Supermarket*, May 1979, p. 100.

[21]J. Barry Mason, "The New Technology of Retailing," in Neil Beckwith et al., eds., *1979 Marketing Educators Conference Proceedings* (New York: American Marketing Association, 1979), pp. 396–400.

[22]Sheldon Koplan, "EFT: How the Public Views It," *Administrative Management*, October 1979, p. 35.

APPENDIX B

CASE STUDY: THREE B'S INC.

On October 5, 1982, Bob Perry reported for his first day's work as staff assistant to Warren Coolidge, vice-president in charge of production, at Three B's Inc. Coolidge had hired Perry as a special staff assistant to assume general responsibility for all production and inventory control activities in the company. Perry understood that Coolidge expected him to improve the production organization's performance in meeting customer demand while maintaining a more balanced inventory position. He was also to concern himself with rising production costs. One of the first things Perry did upon joining Three B's was to review the overall company background and organization.

Company Background

The principal products of Three B's are bicycles of all types and sizes, ranging from the basic single speed model to the Italian-style ten-speed racing bike. They also manufacture motor bikes and other power-assisted bikes as well as tricycles, scooters, and kiddie cars.

The year 1981 marked the tenth year of business operation for Three B's. The company was founded by the Barrett Brothers and is still operated as a tightly controlled family organization. Bill Barrett is president and chief executive officer; his brother Sam is chairman of the board. Several of the Barrett's sons and sons-in-law hold positions with the company. Sales in the first year were less than a million dollars and have risen substantially each year to the point where the sales volume in 1981 was $145 million. The Barrett brothers expect sales to continue to grow in the future. They feel that they produce the highest-quality bicycle on the market, and their reputation is second to none. Of concern to the Barretts was the fact that although sales were rising, profit margins in their opinion were not rising proportionally.

The Three B's line is handled by company salesmen and jobbers throughout the country. All bicycles are manufactured in the main plant in Cleveland, Ohio, and are shipped directly from Cleveland. Salesmen take orders from large department stores and bicycle shops as well as from smaller outlets, and mail the orders to Cleveland where they are processed and filled. Figure B.1 presents a profit-and-loss statement for the year 1981 and a balance sheet as of year-end. Cost of sales is comprised of 35 percent labor, 50 percent material, and 15 percent expense.

Company Organization

There were no organization charts at Three B's, as the Barretts didn't believe in them. However, Perry sketched out his own rough chart (see Fig. B.2). Warren Coolidge, vice-president in charge of production, and Paul Peters, vice-president in charge of sales, are the senior officers of the company and have considerable influ-

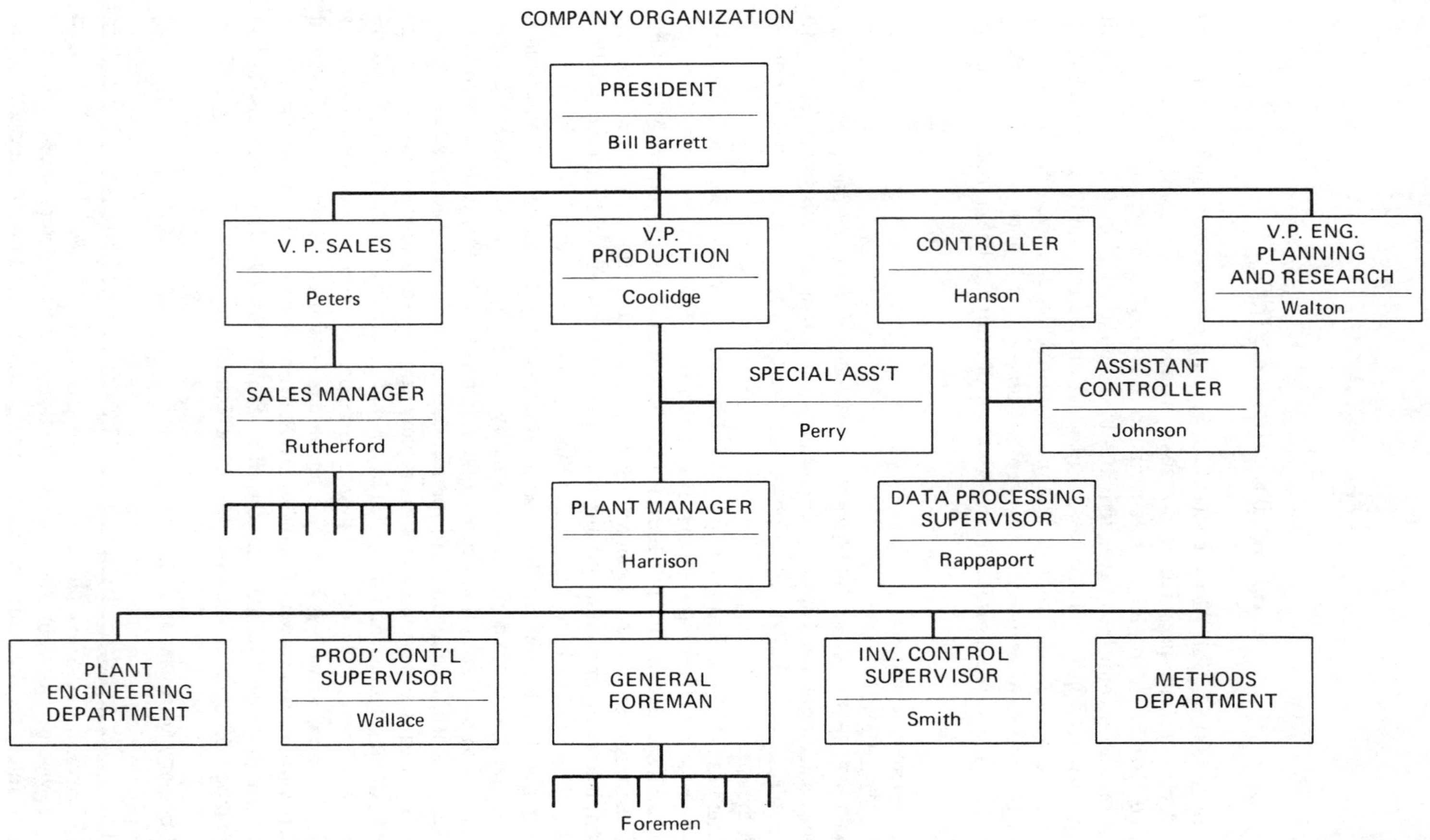
COMPANY ORGANIZATION
PRESIDENT
Bill Barrett
V. P. SALES
Peters
V.P. PRODUCTION
Coolidge
CONTROLLER
Hanson
V.P. ENG. PLANNING AND RESEARCH
Walton
SALES MANAGER
Rutherford
SPECIAL ASS'T
Perry
ASSISTANT CONTROLLER
Johnson
PLANT MANAGER
Harrison
DATA PROCESSING SUPERVISOR
Rappaport
PLANT ENGINEERING DEPARTMENT
PROD' CONT'L SUPERVISOR
Wallace
GENERAL FOREMAN
INV. CONTROL SUPERVISOR
Smith
METHODS DEPARTMENT
Foremen

Fig. B.1

PROFIT AND LOSS STATEMENT
(000 omitted)

Sales		144,690
Variable costs	82,025	
Fixed costs	41,015	
Administration costs	7,230	
Cost of sales		130,270
Net profit before taxes		14,420
Federal income tax		6,054
Net profit after taxes		8,366

Balance Sheet

Assets		Liabilities	
Cash	9,350	Accounts payable	7,930
Accounts receivable	14,465	Accrued expenses	3,000
Inventory	48,230	Short term debt	625
Other current assets	5,845	Other current liabilities	750
Total current assets	72,890	Total current liabilities	12,305
Plant	36,215	Stockholders equity	73,430
Equipment	27,425	Retained income	60,930
Other fixed assets	9,220	Other liabilities	4,085
Total assets	150,750	Total liabilities	150,750

Fig. B.2

ence in the decision-making process within Three B's. The controller, Henry Hanson, has been with Three B's since its inception and is a brother-in-law of Bill Barrett. Hanson is 62 years old, and expects to retire in a year or two. His assistant, Dexter Johnson, is a recent graduate of the Harvard Business School, and joined Three B's a year ago as the result of an accidental meeting with Bill Barrett on a flight from Cleveland to Los Angeles. Barrett considers his company's data processing operations extremely backward and was most interested in Johnson's MIS background. Johnson was a data processing specialist for a manufacturing company and also served as a systems manager and salesman for IBM. The plant manager, Burt Harrison, is the man who really keeps Three B's production lines running. Harrison has 25 years of varied production experience starting as a milling machine operator and working his way to night foreman, general foreman, and finally plant manager. He is considered a rough customer to deal with, but he has a reputation for getting his job done. He is adamant in his feelings toward computers and so-called sophisticated system approaches. Although he complains about the inaccurate production and inventory records, he is very skeptical about introducing a computer into their operations. He has friends in other plants in the city who say that their computer installations have fallen flat on their face. Harrison always refers to this whenever the word computer comes up at their weekly staff meetings. His idea is that the best system is the simple system. When it comes to computers, Harrison defiantly proclaims "My theme is the KISS theory—Keep It Simple, Stupid."

Perry began to gather statistical information concerning the finished products, assemblies, and piece parts manufactured and assembled by Three B's. He discovered that there are approximately 300 finished-goods items, of which approximately 200 are active items that are produced on a regular basis and carried in stock. Approximately 8000 assemblies and piece parts support the 300 finished-goods items. There are an average of six parts per assembly. On the sales side, Three B's receives about 1200 sales orders per day, the typical order containing eight items. Even though a good amount of Three B's business is in the southern and western part of the country, there is still a strong seasonal influence on sales. Of the 8000 piece parts, approximately two thirds are inventoried. Purchase orders average 100 per day, with a typical purchase order containing four items. There are approximately 40 machine centers, split about evenly between fabrication and assembly operations. Since most of the products are produced on a repetitive basis, large production runs are the rule.

Data Processing Background

The data processing department reports directly to Harry Hanson, controller of the company. It is run by Dennis Rappaport and has an annual budget of just under $1 million. Recently, Hanson and Rappaport had a lengthy discussion with Bill Barrett, in which the latter was quite critical of their operation. Barrett had just returned from an executive session on computers and was impressed by the strides that the EDP industry was making; at the same time, he was rather disappointed in his company's own use of data processing. His general feelings were that with Three B's rapid growth, it was time to take another look at where the company was headed in the area of information processing, to develop a long-range plan for some type of management information system, and to explore the use of on-line, real-time techniques. Hanson had conducted a computer feasibility study five years earlier aimed at initiating the MIS concept for Three B's. The conclusion was that Three B's should first get its existing system and installation running efficiently before considering a more advanced system. To Hanson's way of thinking, the system had not lived up to the promises of the computer vendor, who in reality provided the leadership and direction to their current approach. Rappaport did the majority of the fact finding for the feasibility study.

Company Interviews

During the first month of employment with Three B's, Perry spent a good deal of time with the sales manager, the inventory control supervisor, and the production control supervisor. He started with the sales manager, Bill Rutherford. In reviewing the sales picture, Perry discovered that two weeks prior to the beginning of each month, Rutherford would project the expected sales activity for the coming month. He based this primarily on previous months' sales, his own ten years' experience with Three B's, and his monthly meetings with key company salesmen. The sales manager was also responsible for a six-month forecast twice a year. Order turnaround time was approximately 60 days. In other words, a salesman mailing an order to Cleveland could expect his customer to receive the goods 60 days from the time he mailed the order. This caused a good deal of customer dissatisfaction, as certain customers needed merchandise quicker than 60 days from placing an order, particularly in areas that had a short spring selling season. The salesman had to explain that this was the best he could do. On rush orders, salesmen were bothered by the fact that although the inventory records showed certain bicycles were in stock, when they placed the order they were informed that they actually were not in stock. The salesman would then have to relate this back to his customer. More and more, salesmen were beginning to hear the story, "If you didn't make the best bike on the market, we'd certainly place our business elsewhere." Rutherford was seriously concerned, because two other major bicycle manufacturers were improving their bikes, and the quality edge that Three B's enjoyed was narrowing.

The inventory control supervisor, Jay Smith, was continually besieged by the production people, who claimed they had to shut down production lines due to unavailability of particular parts and assemblies. At the same time, the controller was pointing out the increasing amount of capital that Three B's had tied up in inventory. One of his basic concerns was the lack of a system which could take the sales manager's forecast and rapidly obtain the necessary piece parts and assemblies to produce enough bicycles to meet the forecast.

About 60 percent of piece parts and assemblies used in production were purchased. The other 40 percent were fabricated from base metal stock. Smith indicated his major problems were connected with purchased parts and assemblies. The number of parts had risen substantially with the addition of bike styles and new product lines. He could obtain certain parts with short lead time, but others came from plants which had a bad reputation for meeting delivery schedules. Unfortunately, these were the only plants producing the quality of parts that Three B's demanded. Smith also knew his inventory records were unreliable. In some cases, production lines were shut down for lack of parts when the parts were actually available in another part of the plant, but were not recorded as such. Some departments had built up their own staging areas where they maintained a day or two's supply of piece parts and assemblies in order to ensure a full day's production run.

The inventory control department kept a record of price breaks for each of the vendors. When a particular part or assembly hit a reorder point (the reorder point was a month's projected usage plus an additional half-month's buffer stock for items ordered from the "unreliable" vendors), the inventory clerk handling that item would initiate a purchase requisition. It usually took two to three days from the time a purchase requisition was prepared to the time the purchase order would be written. The order quantity was based on the price breaks. The quantity ordered was at the price-break point where the quantity ordered would not exceed eight weeks' usage. Usage figures were maintained on cardex files in the inventory control office. The files were posted from the weekly inventory reports issued by the data processing department. Smith knew these usage figures were historical and did not reflect changes in buying habits or seasonal factors. He had no way of obtaining a product explosion of piece parts and assemblies based on current sales trends.

J. B. Wallace, production control supervisor, indicated that his main problem was the constantly changing order requirements. He placed little faith in the sales manager's forecast and knew from experience that he must adjust it himself in order to anticipate the changes that inevitably occurred during the month. He realized that an important company asset was its highly skilled labor force, which was one of the key reasons for the high-quality bicycles produced by Three B's. A prime consideration from the president on down was to level out production so that there would be minimal fluctuation in the labor force. "Accomplishing this, while keeping costs and inventory balanced, is all there is to do," facetiously stated the production control supervisor. Wallace felt that he was doing a good job, considering the rapid growth of operations over the last five years. He was gravely concerned over the effect further expansion would have on production operations.

Wallace continued to elaborate on the problems as he saw them.

> Three B's is not the small company it was five years ago, but in many ways it still acts like it; we're literally breaking out at the seams. Our labor costs are extremely high. This relates back to the scheduling problem and the inventory problem. We've had to shut down lines and have expensive help sitting around idle while we're hunting around for parts. I've been able to adjust by rescheduling these men, but the work then is below their skill level. We not only incur high costs, but we run the risk of a morale problem if we continue to do it.

Wallace related the decision rules he used to schedule production.

> My primary consideration is keeping a level work force. This puts a greater burden on the availability of piece parts and assemblies. I always shoot for long production runs to minimize set-up costs. We have outside storage facilities which I can use for temporary overstocks. If I had a forecast I could rely on, I could do a better scheduling job. Some of our unskilled help is part time, so we can call on them as needed. This gives me a way to increase or decrease production at relatively short notice; however, even in this situation, I'm beginning to hear about it from the union steward. The key to our problem is getting a more accurate long-range forecast to work from—then I can level off production while keeping costs down. For example, we've incurred major overtime last month because of several urgent rush orders from our two largest customers.

At a recent meeting attended by Warren Coolidge, Paul Peters, Henry Hanson, and Bob Perry, Bill Barrett indicated that the time had come to take some action to resolve the major problems of the company and to improve the profit picture. Barrett was convinced that the answer was an improved information processing system, which could start from sales forecasting and go right on to improve inventory and production control and to reduce production costs. He wanted a management information system. He specifically stated that Perry should get together with Dexter Johnson and bring in whatever and whoever was needed to develop a system and a plan for utilizing more advanced electronic data processing gear to improve the situation.

STUDY QUESTIONS

1. How do you assess Three B's use of computers up to now? What are the main reasons for the situation?

2. What kind of business is Three B's in, what is the background, company organization, management perspective and capability, and, in general, the environment for future DP and MIS growth?

3. Give an analysis of the following executives and their receptiveness to MIS development: Bill Barrett, Warren Coolidge, Paul Peters, Bill Rutherford, Henry Hanson, and Burt Harrison.

4. Comment on the organization of data processing within Three B's.

5. Do you think Three B's is spending too much or too little for data processing?

6. Do you think Jay Smith and J. B. Wallace have reflected an accurate picture of Three B's inventory and production control system?

7. Do you think Barrett was wise in pushing the hiring of Dexter Johnson? What did this say about his attitude toward MIS at Three B's?

8. What role should Perry have in the design of an MIS? How should he and Johnson work together?

9. Do you think Three B's should resort to outside consultants?

10. Do you think Three B's will have the proper level of management involvement and leadership? Is there a danger that they could have too much?

11. Does the profit-and-loss statement give you any indication of the priorities that you would establish for computer applications?

12. Do you think Three B's can continue on their present course, or is there danger of extinction if they don't change their strategies?

13. Assume that you are Bob Perry. Outline the steps you would take to develop an effective plan for obtaining maximum benefit from a computer at Three B's Inc.

14. State three keys that you consider most significant to computer success at Three B's and explain why.

15. List and describe the pros and cons of an integrated management information and control system for Three B's Inc.

16. Bill Barrett of Three B's Inc. requested that his staff explore the use of advanced communications techniques. Describe areas where this approach might be advantageous to Three B's Inc. and point out potential benefits—also potential pitfalls.

17. Establish a schedule of events and milestones that might be established for Three B's after the meeting of Coolidge, Peters, Hanson, Perry, and Barrett.

APPENDIX C

CASE STUDY: GENERAL AUTO INC.*

A TIME-SHARING APPLICATION TO AUTOMOTIVE
MAINTENANCE PROBLEMS

System Background

About 850 General Auto dealerships have access to United System's (US) Tack III Information Services Network. The primary function of the system is to trace the status of new car orders. A dealer can locate a car that is on order, or learn delivery times instantly. A secondary function of the system is to process replacement-parts orders.

It is the third application of the General Auto system with which this paper will deal. The time-sharing application programs have been expanded to deal with a group of new and particularly difficult maintenance problems.

Beginning in 1979 General Auto's automatic temperature-control systems and cruising-speed controls were made increasingly complex, to the point that mechanics were not really capable of fixing them without specialized help. Vehicle vibrations, a problem whose cause is usually complex, added to the need for outside help.

Working with General Auto headquarters' maintenance people and system analysts, US people flow-charted these diagnostic and maintenance systems. Programs were developed which worked through each system in a step-by-step fashion to identify each problem for the mechanic.

When a vehicle has a problem in one of these areas, the serviceman accesses a local phone number from the terminal in the dealership. When connected to the network, he types in his user number, a password, the vehicle identification number of the car he is working on, and the area with the problem.

The terminal prints the diagnostic equipment he will need and asks some progressively detailed questions isolating the malfunction. Once the specific location of the problem is found, the serviceman goes back and makes the repair.

Economic Justification

With this system, economic justification is simple. The terminal, telephone modem, and initial US time-sharing fee are considered sunk costs, as they were incurred

---

*This paper was submitted by Roger Bentley as part of the requirement for the course "Management Information Systems," which I taught at Northeastern University.

for the previous new-car tracing and parts-reorder applications. The cost for the new application includes only the central processor time and the time required for each connection. The way General Auto evaluates the cost, it does not include programming time because that involved staff personnel whose time is not charged to components or functions, but is simply lumped into overhead.

To justify the system, these costs are weighed against the savings in mechanic time and parts. First, as these repairs were most frequently done on cars under warranty, the mechanic's time was charged to General Auto rather than to the customer—thus the saving was direct to General Auto. If the car was not under warranty, time for the repair was charged on the basis of standard "book time" normally required by the mechanic to repair the car. For example, if the "book time" for repairing a cruise control was one-half hour, that was what the customer was charged, even if the mechanic actually took ten minutes or four hours. This system should have substantially reduced the number of jobs that required more time than the customer could be billed for.

Before development of the time-sharing application, the mechanic often found it easier to rip the entire troubled system out, sending it back to General Auto, and installing a new system. This resulted in a higher warranty charge to General Auto. On many of these occasions, General Auto found that a $200 warranty charge was made when the mechanic could have fixed the system in 15 minutes with a 10-cent resistor—if he had known the nature of the problem. In some rare instances involving unsolvable vibration problems (and, I would presume, preferred customers) dealers returned entire cars to General Auto for replacement.

The "rip out rather than repair" procedure also existed in other systems that were slated to be added to the maintenance program. If, for example, a car under warranty had a carburetor problem, a new carburetor would be installed; if the car had a generator problem, a new generator would be installed. Both of these parts can be repaired cheaper, quicker, and at substantially less cost to General Auto than they can be replaced.

The dollar costs for each of these kinds of repairs obviously varies, but when balanced against the computer cost, the time-sharing approach represents significant savings. During the first six months of use, the average cost per program use was about $2.10. At $30 an hour for service, plus the cost of unnecessarily replaced parts, the savings represented by the system are significant.

The Tack III Time-Sharing Network

United System's Tack III network is composed of more than 50 interconnected computers. It is tied to users in eighteen time zones by 100,000 miles of communication lines, including transoceanic cables and communication satellites. As the communications part of the system is owned or leased by US, a customer can access the system with a local telephone call. Each General Auto dealer has at least one terminal in his dealership, usually in the parts office, where its heaviest use, parts reorder, occurs. A few large dealerships also have a terminal in the new-car sales area for ordering and tracing new cars.

The application is written in BASIC, which, although not a particularly efficient language, easily handles the comparatively simple maintenance programs. Output parameters have been carefully designed to be simple for the service people. Questions are put out in simple English, and, wherever possible, require only a yes or no answer to be typed in by the mechanic. The programs are stored on disc for immediate response.

Interview With the Maintenance Manager

One of the first questions I asked the General Auto maintenance manager, who was instrumental in developing the system, was whether or not these same savings could be incurred by using a programmed approach in the service manual. For example, referring to the sample printout, Fig. C.1:

"Does starter crank?" If yes, turn to Instruction 14
If no, turn to Instruction 22.

This is basically what the computer does—and its simplicity seems to suggest that it could be done through the manual.

The answer to that question was: "The servicemen do not use the manual, so putting this material in it wouldn't have any effect." The intent, apparently, of the manual is to tell the mechanic *everything* about the system or component he's work-

```
DOES THE STARTER CRANK (YES/NO)?   NO
1.   CONNECT TEST LIGHT TO GROUND AND, WITH IGNITION SWITCH IN "START"
     POSITION, CHECK FOR POWER AT BOTH YELLOW WIRE TERMINALS IN
     CONNECTOR AT NEUTRAL START SWITCH.
     A.   IF POWER AT ONE ONLY, ADJUST OR REPLACE SWITCH.
     B.   IF NEITHER TERMINAL HOT, REPAIR OPEN BETWEEN BATTERY.
     C.   IF BOTH TERMINALS ARE HOT, CONTINUE.
2.   PLACE SHIFT LEVEL IN "P" AND TURN IGNITION SWITCH TO "RUN" POSITION.
3.   UNPLUG BYPASS RELAY (UNDER HOOD—IN PURPLE CONNECTOR).
4.   TEMPORARILY CONNECT JUMPER WIRE TO 24-VOLT SOURCE AND TOUCH TO
     YELLOW WIRE (THE "B" TERMINAL) IN THE PURPLE BYPASS RELAY
     CONNECTOR.
DOES THE STARTER CRANK (YES/NO)?   NO
YOUR PROBLEM WITH THE STARTING CIRCUIT DOESN'T SEEM TO INVOLVE THE
SEAT BELT STARTER INTERLOCK SYSTEM. PLEASE CHECK THE STARTING CIRCUIT
DIAGNOSIS SECTION OF THE SERVICE MANUAL FOR ASSISTANCE IN FURTHER
DIAGNOSIS.
AFTER CORRECTING THE PROBLEM BE SURE TO RECHECK THE WHOLE SYSTEM TO
BE SURE IT IS FUNCTIONING PROPERLY. I HOPE I HAVE BEEN OF SOME ASSISTANCE.
GOODBYE.
```

Fig. C.1

ing on. For example, I was told that if a mechanic wanted to look in the manual to find out which side of the battery should be grounded, he would have to wade through a theoretical discussion of how a battery works, complete with information on ion discharge, before he could find the answer. First, this approach intimidates the mechanic. Second, a lot of them don't have the reading-skimming skills to wade through bushels of chaff to get at one kernel of wheat. As a result, they do not use the manual. If they don't know how to fix something, more often than not they simply replace it, because that is something they can easily handle. Further, they are probably encouraged to do that, because the more work they do, the more money for the dealership, regardless of whether the work is paid for by a customer or by General Auto under a new-car warranty.

The Problem With the System

There is only one problem with this application—it does not work. This interesting fact was agreed to both by General Auto's system designer and the US sales engineer. The application was installed in late 1979, coinciding with the introduction of 1980 models. In the last nine months, not one mechanic at any of the 850 dealerships has accessed the system. The application considerations that render the system worthless are crucial and were apparently overlooked by everyone involved. And it is this aspect of the application that prompted me to center my paper on it.

First, the terminal that the mechanic uses is located in the parts office. That means that he has to put down his tools, leave the maintenance bay, and walk into the parts office before he even begins. And, as if that isn't enough, he probably has to stop on the way to scrub his hands because the secretary in "parts" complains of grease and dirt all over the terminal and the telephone. Next, he has to use a typewriter keyboard—with which he probably is not comfortable. Let's presume he remembers the local number to call, his dealer identification number, and his password. He types these in without making a mistake. The first thing the terminal asks him for is a 13-or-so digit vehicle identification number. He signs off, replaces the phone, goes back to the car, writes the number down, goes back, gets an available phone, reaches the number, and types in his dealer identification number and password and vehicle identification number. The terminal asks him a question which he has to go back to the car to answer.

He usually doesn't come back. If he does, at some point the terminal will ask him to get a particular diagnostic instrument out, connect it, and come back with the reading. The mechanic simply won't do it. Studies of the early usage of the application indicated that most sign-off's occur when the mechanic is asked to go back to the car for something—he doesn't come back to the terminal.

Given that the program will yield substantial savings if used, and that those savings can be increased when programs are added to include other usually replaced automotive parts, how can General Auto get them to be used? Before I discuss my suggestion, I want to discuss one approach that General Auto rejected, and another that they are pursuing.

First Approach (Rejected by General Auto)

The one that was rejected involved US's Telephone Data Process (TDP). This is a computer voice-response system in which, instead of communicating through printed words from a terminal, the communication is by voice, prerecorded on tape. The user talks to the computer either through pressing buttons on a touch-tone phone or, with a dial phone, tone buttons on an acoustical pad. The advantage of using this system is that the mechanic won't have to go all the way into the parts area and is faced with a much less imposing keyboard. Also, no one will care if he gets grease on it. However, TDP will not solve the "connect-reconnect-reconnect again" problem which made the mechanic shy away in the first place. Besides, this system requires much more connect time because the voice tape obviously goes a lot slower than the teletype.

Second Approach

General Auto is discontinuing the time-sharing application and, beginning with the introduction of the 1982 models, is initiating a special diagnostic package including a minicomputer that plugs into the new model cars. It is virtually identical to the International Motor's diagnostic center. Dealer cost for the computerized diagnostic set-up will be about $12,000, and will enable 55 diagnostic tests to be performed on each car.

I suggest that this substantial, more expensive system will not work satisfactorily for the same basic reason that the time-sharing system will not work at all. That basic reason is "inside-out" rather than "outside-in" application engineering. The time-sharing system is not effective because no one thought of the needs, habits, and prejudices of the user in respect to the system. The diagnostic-center approach will not work because it is not sensitive to those needs and can't even listen to the mechanic. Remember, all the mechanic does is plug the car into the computer and read the resulting printout. I will elaborate by indicating some of the problems with International Motor's system. Remember, also, that for virtually every measurement, a sensor has to be built into the car, as the computer only reads out sensors—few, if any, are in the diagnostic center itself.

Part of International Motor's system checks headlight alignment through photo sensors on the back of the diagnostic bay. If the lights don't hit the right spot, the mini tells the mechanic to adjust them. If, however, the air pressure in the front tires is low, and the lights are adjusted right, the computer will think the lights are out of alignment. The computer cannot ask the mechanic, "What is the pressure in the front tires?" The result is, the next time the tires are properly inflated, the diagnostically repaired International Motor's car will blind you on the highway.

Also in the International Motor's system, there is some way of checking valve adjustment. (I don't know if there is a sensor in one of the valves or if the clearance is somehow computed from other measurements.) It is imperative that valves be set while the car is absolutely cold. (Some good mechanics even bring the car into the service bay the night before and set the valves the first thing next morning.) When the car is warm, the valves will measure looser than they actually are. When a minicomputer diagnostic center sees the warm, correctly set valves as loose, it tells the mechanic to tighten them. I am familiar with a case where this caused the failure of the engine less than 500 miles later—it cost International Motors a new engine. Of course that's not the way the system should have been used. The mechanic should use discretion in interpreting the printout. But the point is that there is no way the mini can insure that this is done. As a result, it is my opinion that General Auto's new system to hold down warranty maintenance costs will not be effective. Even with 55 sensors, there will be many interrelated parameters not monitored, and there is no way to ask the mechanic to read them. The system has to presume they are correct. It has to presume that the tires are fully inflated or that the engine is cold. With a good mechanic, those presumed parameters will be correct, but if he is not conscientious, he will be told to repair many things that don't require repair.

A Suggested System Approach

My solution to the situation is to pull the mini out of the diagnostic center and replace it with a simple telephone hookup into the time-sharing system. By throwing a switch, the mechanic turns on the machine, automatically dials the local number, and gives the code number and the other housekeeping chores. To reduce connect time, the system automatically connects when needed, retaining previously supplied information on magnetic tape in the diagnostic center. When the mechanic has another entry to make, the diagnostic center reconnects and relates to the computer the entire conversation that occurred up to that point. This data will not be stored that in the time-sharing computer because the computer has no way of knowing if that diagnosis is complete. The data on a particular car is erased after the final printout is complete and the car is disconnected from the diagnostic center. Through "yes" and "no" buttons, the mechanic can provide all required data, including instrument measurements. The computer can ask all its questions so they are answered in that fashion—"Is voltage between 10 and 12V? Is it below 10V?," etc.

Advantage of the Approach

There are three advantages to my proposition. First, it allows inputs from other than the 55 (or less) sensors in the car. These inputs can either be measurements made by the mechanic, or observations by the mechanic. Second, my system is more easily modified and updated. To change General Auto's system, a new program has to be sent to each mini, and entered somehow by somebody. My proposed system can be modified by a change in the program stored at the time-sharing center. Third, I think my system would be cheaper. My proposed system eliminates the mini at $10,000, substituting some local storage device and some time-sharing time. At $2 per connection in the original time-sharing system, a lot of cars could be diagnosed for less than the price of the mini computer.

STUDY QUESTIONS

1. Do you think General Auto is wise in using the Tack III service? What are the advantages? Disadvantages?

2. Do you agree with the way General Auto went about its economic justification of the original system? How effective is its method of including programming time into overhead?

3. Does the original system reduce the number of times the mechanic resorts to the "rip out rather than repair" solution? In theory would you say the original system's approach made sense?

4. What do you think of the maintenance manager's role in the development of the system? What do you think of his attitude toward his mechanics' preference to replace rather than repair?

5. Do you think it could have been anticipated that the system wouldn't work? Is it possible that a different implementation approach could have made the original system effective? What kind of approach?

6. Do you agree with the major reasons the original system failed?

7. Do you think the rejected system would have worked? In your opinion, did it have more chance of success than the original one that was installed?

8. Do you agree with the author that the proposed new system won't work? Why do you agree or disagree?

9. Do you think it is a good idea to adopt a system used by a competitor? What are the pros and cons?

10. Do you think there is validity in the author's feeling that the diagnostic tests should be integrated in the International Motor's system?

11. What do you think of the author's suggested approach? What are the potential advantages and disadvantages? What are the risks? Do you agree with the advantages that the author lists?

12. Do you agree with the author's claim that his system will be cheaper?

13. What are the main lessons to learn from this experience?

APPENDIX D

CASE STUDY: DEACONESS HOSPITAL'S REAL-TIME HOSPITAL INFORMATION SYSTEM*
by Harry N. Valentino, Deaconess Hospital

Hospitals, as well as other industries, traditionally have utilized computers primarily for payroll and financial applications. In recent years, however, an increasing number of hospitals have begun utilizing computers for a wider variety of patient-oriented medical uses, such as scheduling, admissions, medical records, message switching, inventory control, medication charting, drug control, and laboratory reporting. All evidence seems to indicate that the trend of the future is increased utilization of computers for clinical applications.

Choosing a Turnkey HIS

The decision by Deaconess Hospital, Evansville, Ind., to install a real-time, on-line hospital information system was made after two years of extensive systems study and evaluation in which the present and the future information processing requirements of the hospital and the means to meet these needs were analyzed thoroughly.

The hospital previously operated a very sophisticated off-line batch processing system whose applications were concentrated mainly in the financial and payroll/personnel areas. After the clinical information processing needs of the hospital were analyzed, it was quickly realized that the off-line batch method of data processing was limited in its applications and could not meet these needs. As the hospital systems analysis continued, management became increasingly convinced that real-time capabilities (instantaneous data input and retrieval) were needed for clinical information processing.

The management at Deaconess Hospital made an intensive effort to involve the board of directors, the medical staff, and key hospital supervisory personnel in the systems project analysis. Broad personnel involvement mandated an extensive educational effort; nevertheless, it was believed that this broad involvement was essential for a meaningful project evaluation. A computer system is a very sensitive element in most organizations, and it can be utilized optimally only by personnel who are committed to its purposes.

The hospital management further realized that the basic turnkey system that finally was acquired would have to be modified to meet the unique processing needs of Deaconess Hospital. It is not realistic to think that a complex turnkey information system can be overlaid on an organization without some basic program modifications. However, the decision to acquire a turnkey system in lieu of building our own

*Reprinted with permission from *Hospitals, Journal of the American Hospital Association*, Vol. 48, No. 22.

system was predicated on the belief that acquisition of a turnkey system would be the less expensive alternative and that such a system could be implemented in a relatively short period. It is beyond the resources of many hospitals, even the larger ones, to build a comprehensive real-time information system to meet their individual needs. Because the system was to be unique to Deaconess Hospital, it was named the Deaconess Hospital Medical Information Processing Services (MIPS).

Benefits of a Real-Time System

The benefits of a real-time hospital information system have been documented frequently in the professional literature. Some of the more commonly stated benefits of a real-time information system are:

- Reduction in the number of personnel.
- Reduction of clerical work required of professional personnel.
- Reduction in the number of lost charges.
- Instantaneous input and retrieval of clinical information from numerous remote sites within the hospital.
- Centralization and consolidation of the patient care data base.
- Reduction in the number of ordering forms needed.
- Improved accountability and accuracy of information.
- Improved cost accounting and cost containment.
- Possible reduction in the length of patient stay.

The most obvious question that management must ask is, "Are there identifiable cost benefits of a real-time system that make the investment cost justifiable?" The answer to this question is exceedingly complex and beyond the scope of this article. Cost-benefits analyses are meaningful only in the context of a specific organization. Many of the benefits of a real-time system, such as increased managerial control and instantaneous availability of needed clinical data, also are very difficult to quantify.

A thorough cost-benefit analysis was done prior to making the decision to install a real-time system. The cost benefits of the system were divided into two major areas: (1) known, quantifiable savings, such as reduction in the number of personnel, saving of forms' costs, and elimination of existing equipment and systems, and (2) savings for which assumptions had to be made to quantify, such as saving of professional time and lost charges and increased managerial control for staffing and inventory control. Three cost savings projections were made based on assumptions that were classified as pessimistic, expected, and optimistic. All projections indicated that sufficient cost savings could be recognized to justify implementation of a real-time system.

Our operational experience with MIPS has not been sufficient to totally analyze the impact of the system compared to the projections. However, savings have been realized in the areas of manpower, lost charges, and the number of ordering forms needed. Probably one of the most important benefits of MIPS has been that the real-time applications have ensured standardization of all catalogs, charges, and operating procedures. This required standardization has enabled administration to maintain tight managerial control and to establish mechanisms for excellent procedural accountability that was not previously possible. The increased availability of needed clinical information also has enabled the hospital departments to more efficiently coordinate their activities.

Patient Data Base

The conversion from a manual patient ordering system to a real-time computerized patient ordering system is not easy; it demands a great amount of planning. However, once all patient ordering and results reporting are implemented in real time, a comprehensive data base, which includes personal data, insurance coverage, all orders placed, treatment profiles, nurses' notes, and other needed narrative reports, can be established for each patient. The system is centered around the ordering process. Most of a hospital's resources are connected with the patient order, and, as a result, virtually every area is affected, from billing and inventory control to tests and treatment.

The process of bringing all clinical information on-line is very difficult and requires time and reorientation from traditional ways of viewing information. The point probably will not be reached in the near future when the traditional patient's chart will be eliminated completely, but there is much information from the chart that is valuable when available in real time. Such information may include a patient drug profile, results of clinical laboratory tests, nurses' notes, clinical narratives, and consultations. MIPS has the capability to hold narrative reports on-line for a specified period; however, this is not yet being done. It is expected that some applications in this area will be implemented within the next year.

The direct patient care benefits of MIPS result from the increased availability and accuracy of clinical data. The accountability of the system further ensures that laboratory tests are completed, that medication orders are filled accurately, that pertinent drugs are noted on ECG requests, and that needed medical data are available for departments such as radiology, physical therapy, and clinical laboratory.

Operation, Implementation

The central processing area is located in a high-security area in the basement of the hospital. The basic hardware configuration was designed to accommodate the hospital's expected growth over the next five years. The system has several features that significantly increase its reliability and operability. The central processing units are readily interchangeable between real-time processing and batch processing. There are two strings of system disk drives; each string contains seven drives and is a mirror image copy of the other, thereby providing reliable backup in case of disk failures.

The duplication of information on disk also improves the response time for the input and the retrieval of real-time information via a cathode-ray tube (CRT). All data inputs are corded on tape for further system backup and data storage.

The static inverter with battery backup ensures an uninterrupted supply of electrical power to the system. The backup batteries will provide approximately 15 minutes of electrical power to cycle the system without loss of data. The hospital's auxiliary generators can be used to keep the system operating if outside commercial power is interrupted. MIPS must operate seven days per week, 24 hours per day; consequently, system reliability is essential. And unexpected, extended downtime of the real-time system beyond one hour will lead to some organization disruption. Because some unexpected downtime is inevitable, a well-documented backup paper system must be maintained in every department. However, the computer system routinely is down each day between 2 and 3:30 A.M. to allow duplication of disk copies and preventive maintenance. Over the past six months, MIPS has averaged less than 30 minutes of unexpected downtime per week.

Each nurses' station has at least one CRT and one attached printer. Larger nursing units, which typically have 45 or more beds, have three CRTs and one attached printer. Access to the system is accomplished by means of a precoded badge identifying each employee to the system. The badge indicates the job of the employee and enables the user to perform only those tasks that are within his normal responsibility, as outlined in his job description. Complete integrity of the system is maintained by identifying all entered information by means of the employee's badge number. The CRT is the only input device for MIPS that is utilized by hospital personnel; therefore, the requests for all patient orders and services must be initiated through a CRT.

The attached printer is used to print routed messages or other types of requested hard copy information. Because the attached printers are comparatively slow (10 characters per second when attached to a CRT), lengthy reports from the real-time system and the batch system are printed, whenever possible, on the high-speed line printer located in the computer room. Presently, there are approximately 400 different reports that are printed on the high-speed line printer.

Implementation of MIPS began with the loading of accounts receivable, general ledger, and general accounting. Patients were admitted to the hospital on MIPS through a floor-by-floor phase-in approach. Within six weeks, all inpatients were on MIPS. Trained educational coordinators were available throughout the hospital to assist supervisors in answering questions, solving problems, and educating personnel during the initial stages of the implementation. These coordinators were retained by the hospital for about two months and then were gradually withdrawn from the departments, as the hospital supervisors became increasingly proficient on MIPS and could answer most questions.

The first three to four months, however, were an exceedingly difficult period. A tremendous burden was placed on the organization in a relatively short period because of the vigorous implementation schedule. Some reorganization was necessary to coordinate needed lines of communication. During the early stages of the transition, personnel were frightened of the unknown and were frustrated with the new requirements placed upon them. Attitudes gradually changed, and acceptance grew, as familiarization with and proficiency in the use of MIPS increased.

Personnel Attitudes, Education

One of the major challenges of the system implementation was to obtain hospital employees' acceptance of the fact that change was imminent and desirable. Department directors were required to look beyond the specific needs of their areas in order to associate their departmental functions and requirements as intricate components of the total hospital information system. MIPS did not reduce the work load in every area; as a matter of fact, it increased the work requirements in some departments, because it redistributed the input requirements of the previous information system and created many additional capabilities for data gathering.

The initial reaction of many personnel was that the new computer system would rectify all of their previous operational problems and automatically would perform all of their disliked record-keeping functions. These personnel had to be cautioned that a computer is only a tool for efficiency, not a panacea for all organizational problems. Even though this tool has tremendous capabilities, it also has limitations; therefore, it cannot be used successfully to solve every problem or to meet every demand.

Many personnel with diverse skills and talents must utilize the computer via CRTs. The reliability and integrity of the information in MIPS depends on the skill, the knowledge, the proficiency, and the cooperation of these various personnel. The administration recognized that inservice education for employees was one of the most important factors in implementing effective utilization of a real-time system. An intensive educational program was undertaken several months before implementation of MIPS.

Five CRTs were placed in a classroom and were used for inservice education of key hospital personnel, who were able to use the actual system software to perform their tasks on a CRT. These sessions were one and one-half hours in duration and were conducted on a 24-hour per day schedule for approximately two months. Employees could take as many training sessions as they deemed necessary to familiarize themselves with MIPS.

Approximately 500 employees were exposed to the initial familiarization sessions during the first two-month period. These employees were expected to assist subsequently in the hospitalwide inservice education program, after the implementation of the system began. All questions were to be directed to an employee's immediate supervisor, and each supervisor was responsible for answering these questions, and for training the personnel under him in the use of MIPS. This arrangement required that the supervisors be extremely skilled in the specific requirements of the system relating to their areas of responsibility. It was fortunate that the hospital realized that continuing education was the key to success.

The hospital's educational coordinator developed a three-step educational program to which all new employees were to be exposed in varying degrees, depending on their jobs. The first step utilized a 24-minute color film on MIPS, produced by the hospital's audiovisual department. The goal of the film was to provide a general overview of MIPS and to introduce the viewer to the basic concepts and principles of a real-time computer system.

The second step required that each employee complete a 36-page instructional manual, which was developed and written by the hospital's educational coordinator. The primary purpose of the instructional manual was to assist hospital personnel in learning how to operate a CRT. This manual also included terminology, definitions, visual displays, and computer concepts that were helpful to anyone using a CRT.

The third step required that each hospital department develop its own manual for on-the-job-training. Personnel were required to complete the appropriate, departmental, on-the-job training course. The educational coordinator's office kept records to ensure that all personnel who used a CRT had successfully completed all three phases of the inservice education program.

Few devices in our complex society have the mystique and evoke the misconceptions that computers do. Deaconess Hospital attempted to overcome some of these attitudes and concerns among its employees by offering a basic six-hour computer concepts course. This course was given to approximately 400 hospital supervisors over an 11-week period. The course highlighted computer terminology, basic principles, applications, and the psychosociological impact of computers on our society. This course enabled the supervisors to gain insight into automated systems technology and future trends in computer applications. Not only the capabilities and the benefits of computers but also the limitations and the disadvantages were indicated. The course stressed that computers do not replace man but only augment his abilities.

Medical Staff Attitudes, Input

A hospital's management should rely heavily on physician input when evaluating a real-time hospital information system. Physicians frequently are not computer experts or systems experts, but they know better than anyone else the medical information needed for effective disease management. It is wise for a hospital to spend resources on computer educational programs tailored to the particular needs of the medical staff so that the physicians can give the intelligent, well-planned guidance needed in the decision process.

Deaconess Hospital attempted to change as few operating procedures as possible for the physicians, because the established goal was to get the system operating reliably before involving the medical staff with MIPS. The area of particular sensitivity to the medical staff was clinical laboratory reporting, including laboratory summaries. The hospital decided to refrain from laboratory reporting until the medical staff's confidence in the system was increased and all administrative programs were implemented. Progress with the medical staff has been steady, and the physicians are becoming much more comfortable with the presence of the system in the hospital environment. The administration and the medical staff agree that many clinical capabilities are present but that intelligent medical staff guidance is essential to make them realities.

Conclusion

A real-time hospital information system is not recommended for every hospital. Moreover, there are hundreds of types of real-time systems, differing in requirements and capabilities, that hospitals can consider.

The extent of a hospital's real-time computer involvement should depend on the institution's system requirements, resources, and philosophy of management. Before it even considers the possibility of real-time computer applications, a hospital must be administratively strong; have firm, established operating procedures; and have commitment from all levels of management. It is easy to make the costly error of thinking that a highly sophisticated, turnkey, hospital information system will quickly and efficiently correct the problems of an existing poor operation. Such a decision, more frequently than not, compounds and magnifies the existing deficiencies. This failure then is attributed to an inflexible computer system. Such a serious mistake is, unfortunately, most difficult and costly to rectify.

The basic management philosophy of the hospital must support the concept of centralization of functions and standardization of operating procedures. A real-time information system removes many operational flexibilities that exist under a paper ordering and reporting system, and it demands that ordering and results reporting occur through input/output devices in a standardized manner. However, with this standardization, the hospital gains superior accountability and managerial control. The initial response of hospital personnel toward such increased accountability is fear and distrust. The personnel must be reoriented through education to have confidence and excitement about the many ways in which a real-time information system can help them work more efficiently and accurately.

STUDY QUESTIONS

1. What are the relative pros and cons of utilizing a so-called turnkey system? Was Deaconess wise in going this way?

2. What do you think of the way Deaconess conducted its cost/benefit analysis? What additional factors do you think they should have considered? Is it possible to quantify elements such as better controls, savings in professional time, less confusion, and the like?

3. Comment on the role of computers as catalysts to bring about required discipline and standardization?

4. What are the potential pitfalls and risks in having all patient information in a central data base?

5. Do you think the redundancy and duplication of computing equipment and data files is necessary in this instance? What do you think of their back-up system?

6. What potential data security problems are there in the system? Do you think the employee badge number is sufficient security? Is there a risk of unauthorized people gaining access to the data files?

7. Do you think the trainee educational coordinators were a justified expense in converting to the new system? Should anything more have been done in this regard?

8. How do you evaluate the in-house educational effort? Was it complete enough? Was the timing correct? What more could have been done?

9. Do you agree that a heavy reliance should be made on physician's input when evaluating and implementing a hospital information system? How can you obtain this input? How can it be analyzed and evaluated?

10. Do you think Deaconess made the right decision not to change existing operating procedures and to go slowly with the medical staff? Would a management steering committee be helpful in this regard?

11. The author states that real-time information systems are not recommended for every hospital. What are the criteria for determining if a hospital can benefit from such an approach?

12. Is the on-line approach applicable to other industries? Which ones are, and why?

13. How have current data processing developments made on-line systems like the one Deaconess has implemented more feasible?

WILLIAMSBURG CLOTHIERS*

From her new glass-enclosed office, Wendy Kelley had a good view of the rolling Virginia hills and the spring flowers that were just beginning to dot the landscape. She found, however, that she had little time these days to take advantage of the scenery. During the winter of 1980 the company had been gearing up to move its headquarters staff to a new building in Williamsburg, Virginia. Wendy had been involved in planning and preparing for the move in addition to her regular operating responsibilities as manager of the office services department, a centrally located group who handled all the company's typing and correspondence needs from a one-page letter to lengthy reports. The department also helped design forms, type labels for files, and make travel and airline reservations for the managers at company headquarters. Wendy had felt that once the move to the new building was completed and the department was in its new home, she would have more time and find work less hectic. The pace, however, did not seem to let up, as demand on office services continued to increase dramatically.

As she was preparing for a budget meeting with her boss, Earle Jordan, vice-president of personnel and administration, and company president Don Deprez, she thought about the growing demands placed on office services. Part of this was due to the rapid overall growth of the company, but part was due also to the fact that users were making new requests and continuing to expect fast turnaround and quality output.

Don Deprez had requested that Earle Jordan and Wendy meet with him to work on budget and staffing requirements for the following year, in light of this rising demand. They were interested in discussing the company's long-term needs for office services, and information management in general. As she was preparing her report, Wendy thought about the areas of staffing, budget, technology, and organization, which she knew would be topics at the meeting.

History

Williamsburg Clothiers was founded in 1945 by Mary Flavin shortly after her husband was killed in action during World War II. Mrs. Flavin and her daughters began operating a small specialty shop in the two front parlors of their gracious colonial home in historic Williamsburg, Virginia. When Mrs. Flavin died suddenly in 1950, her oldest daughter, Elizabeth, and son-in-law John Alden took over the business.

In 1955 the company moved to a large, well-appointed store in downtown Williamsburg and opened another store in Charlottesville, Virginia.

*Adapted from a Harvard Business School case.

In conjunction with their successful store operations, the Aldens embarked on the development of a mail order business, distributing flyers and placing ads in several national magazines.

During the ensuing years, Williamsburg Clothiers enjoyed a modest rate of growth, a high rate of profitability, and a strong reputation for quality and service. This combination of assets made the company an attractive candidate for acquisition, and in 1973 John and Elizabeth Alden sold it to a large conglomerate. Williamsburg now operates as a wholly owned subsidiary of that firm while enjoying relative autonomy in its day-to-day operations. Since its acquisition, the company has pursued a more aggressive growth strategy. By 1980 the mail order business had expanded from 3000 black-and-white flyers to a total of six major full-color catalogs with a circulation of over 15 million annually. In addition, the company has fifteen stores throughout Virginia, Maryland, and the fast-growing Piedmont region of the Carolinas.

The Company's Business

Williamsburg Clothiers is a retailer of high-quality classic clothing for women and men. The company has no manufacturing facilities and buys its merchandise from about 500 leading vendors. It distributes its merchandise through its fifteen retail stores and through the six major catalogs mailed annually. Although the business had grown dramatically since the early days when Mrs. Flavin and her daughters personally knew most of their customers, Williamsburg Clothiers still prided itself on an exceptional degree of personal service. Maintaining a close relationship with customers, and responding to unusual or unique requests, was an integral part of Williamsburg's strategy, which the company felt was an important complement to its high-quality merchandise. This high degree of personal service characterized operations, both in the retail stores and at the catalog level.

As an example of the company's commitment to meeting customer needs: A Contessa in Spain sent a linen handkerchief with her embroidered crest on it, and asked if Williamsburg's monogramming department could copy the unique pattern, a crown with a large Olde English initial underneath, on six oxford cloth shirts to wear horseback riding. The company's skilled artists did these for her, making sure to heed her directions, "Remember, nine points on the crown for a Contessa!"

Organization and Operations

With the exception of the fifteen retail store managers and their sales staffs, all of Williamsburg's personnel are located at company headquarters. Operations at headquarters can be broken down into three general areas: (1) management and support personnel, (2) catalog order processing, and (3) receiving and distribution of merchandise.

The Williamsburg, Virginia, headquarters houses about 80 management personnel charged with the various line and staff responsibilities outlined in Fig. E.1. Administrative and clerical support is provided by the office services department and by one receptionist and two telephone operators, who greet all visitors and route all incoming calls. No one has a personal secretary.

The office services department has a staff of seventeen people, day and evening shifts, who provide all the typing and clerical support for the executive staff, in addition to handling large-batch correspondence for other departments, such as mailings to catalog customers and customer service letters.

Since Williamsburg Clothiers receives about a million catalog orders per year, a large proportion of headquarters staff is involved with processing those orders. Catalog orders are received either by telephone or by mail. The order process is triggered, typically, when a new catalog is mailed out. For a telephone order, the customer calls the number listed in the catalog. The company handles as many as 2500 telephone orders per day and strives for one-day response time.

Information Systems

The current mail entry and processing system was implemented in November 1978. The new system allowed Williamsburg to keep pace with the rapidly increasing mail order business.

There are now about fifty people working in data processing, with an active system development group preparing for the future and an on-line order entry system and purchase-order management system planned for the fall of 1982.

Williamsburg's experience with word processing was much more recent. Until 1978, when the company began to expand, the headquarters staff had managed the company's correspondence with one or two typists and the occasional help of a printing service for large mailings. As the company began to grow and the availability of word processing machines increased, it was decided in 1980 to purchase a small Wang system word processor. The system began with one work station and one Diablo character printer.

The manager of customer service had recommended the purchase of the machine primarily for "merge letters," providing correspondence for customer service and accounts receivable and replies from personnel to applicants for employment. The Wang system was chosen because the quality of output most closely resembled an IBM Selectric, which the company felt was important, as the customer must feel she was receiving customized responses not computer printouts. Gradually new applications were added. Since the company had no personal secretaries, reception of word processing into the organization was generally successful, for the following reasons:

1. Good equipment.
2. No alternatives for users.
3. Good service.

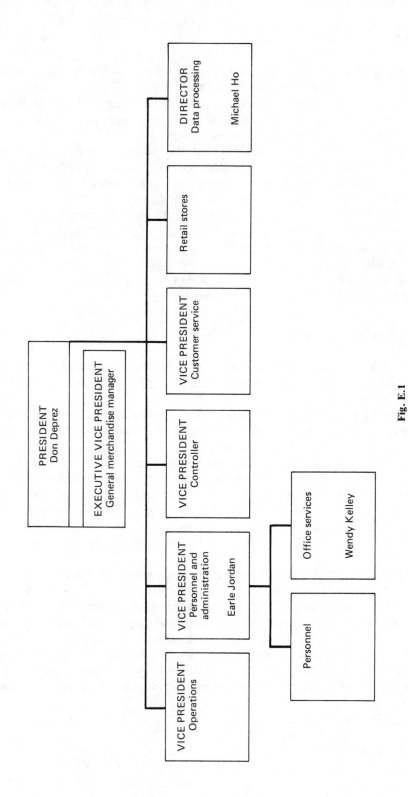

Fig. E.1

438

4. Few constraints on use of the service.
5. Technically capable operators with good proofreading and writing skills.

By 1982 the equipment had been upgraded to a larger Wang System consisting of five CRT's, two printers, and 10 megabytes of memory. A full night shift was added to handle customer service correspondence, the original reasons for purchasing the equipment! Other applications kept the equipment fully utilized between 8:30 and 5.

When the company was designing its new headquarters space, Wendy had requested that the office services department remain visible and accessible rather than closeted off in a corner of the building. She felt that, in maintaining worker morale and the department's level of quality and service, it was important that the operators and users know each other and develop a sense of teamwork.

From the beginning, the office services staff provided high quality and fast turnaround in the work they performed for the headquarters staff and customer service. This success, combined with expanding sales, resulted in the department's being swamped with work, as users learned the capabilities of word processing and made more demands upon office services. Wendy was concerned about how the department would continue to maintain its quality service and at the same time control the growing costs of personnel and equipment. She knew that this would be one of the major issues at the budget meeting.

The Decision 1982

In preparing for the budget meeting, Wendy felt that the first issue discussed would be the question of capacity. There was no doubt in her mind that Williamsburg would need more word processing capacity, both in the short run and in the longer term, if the company continued to pursue its ambitious growth goals (see Fig. E.2). Each new store that was added generated an increase both in retail sales and in catalog orders. In addition, the headquarters staff had been growing to meet the needs of a larger and more complex business. Both these factors meant an increase in the amount of work demanded of office services.

With the present five machines, Wendy was already having to queue projects and ask users to cooperate by specifying the longest acceptable turnaround time on work done. She knew that the operators were doing their best to get quality work out quickly, but sometimes, if a report or memo had to be redone five or six times to incorporate minor changes that the author wanted, it seemed as though the capabilities of the system were being abused by unnecessary revisions. It was, however, almost impossible to determine how much of the system's capacity was devoted to "excessive" or unnecessary use. At present, users were not charged directly for their use of office services, and this made it seem like a "free" resource to some departments.

Wendy and her boss, Earle Jordan, had discussed setting up a list of "standard" and "urgent" turnaround times for different projects. For example, a "standard"

	($,000) Actual					($,000) Plan		
	1976	1977	1978	1979	1980	1981	1982	1984
Current Assets	1702	1557	1772	3981	6336			
Current Liabilities	941	612	2208	3026	6233			
Long-Term Debt	302	292	281	271	260			
Equity	2231	2622	3861	5674	7565			
Fixed Assets (Net)	2068	2059	2542	4329	11228			
			($,000,000)					
Retail Sales	3.0	3.8	4.7	8.0	12.5	19.0	25.7	57.0
Catalog Sales	6.6	7.0	13.7	22.3	28.0	34.2	40.4	54.0
Total Sales	9.6	10.8	18.4	30.3	40.5	53.2	66.1	111.0
Return on Sales	7.6%	5.5%	10.4%	9.2%	6.4%	7.4%	7.9%	7.9%
Retail	17.6%	17.0%	19.5%	20.4%	18.6%	16.5%	15.8%	14.3%
Catalog	10.4%	7.9%	13.4%	11.6%	8.8%	10.0%	10.5%	10.5%
G and A	5.0%	5.7%	4.6%	4.8%	5.4%	4.9%	4.7%	4.6%
Number of Retail Stores	5	5	6	8	11	17	25	49

Fig. E.2

turnaround time for a business letter might be one full day, while an "urgent" request would be met within four hours. In addition to this priority scheme, they had discussed setting up some kind of charge-out system that penalized users for too many "urgent" requests.

They had also discussed the idea of decentralizing some of the word processing functions of office services into the individual departments and giving those users responsibility for priority setting and cost control. Although decentralization would ease the problems of priority setting and resource allocation, it tended to encourage the proliferation of equipment throughout the organization. Ultimately, this kind of a system could be more costly than a well-managed central facility. Decentralization also meant that the consistent quality of writing and output that office services provided might be compromised.

Finally there was the question of technology. The company had already been forced to upgrade their original Wang less than a year after the initial installation. In expanding capacity, they wanted to adequately take into account the company's future needs as well as what technological options would be available.

Wendy and Mike Ho had recently attended an IBM presentation on merging data and word processing capabilities. The IBM distributed word processing system could be linked with the company's present IBM mainframe. Electronic mail, calendar management, phone logging, and other more sophisticated applications such as market simulations could be done on the system much more quickly. The aim of these large-scale integrated systems was in improving managerial productivity. IBM-sponsored studies showed that an integrated information system could improve executive productivity by as much as 15 percent.

Williamsburg's management emphasized the importance of keeping correspondence and communications as simple as possible. The company had one receptionist and two telephone operators who received and directed all incoming calls and visitors. Managers answered their own telephone calls and were responsible for keeping their own files. Wherever possible, memos were handwritten rather than typed, or people talked to each other in person or on the phone.

The issue of managerial productivity was difficult to get at. Increased effectiveness was hard to measure. Williamsburg could, however, measure some hard dollar savings from office services just in terms of secretarial help that they didn't have to hire. After all, Wendy thought, we have a management group of 80, whose work we handle with 17 people! Even if we do add some staff and additional equipment, we are still way ahead of where we would have been without a centralized word processing function.

QUESTIONS

1. What do you think of the organization at Williamsburg that has office services as part of personnel rather than data processing?

2. Should word processing be centralized or decentralized?

3. Describe the culture of Williamsburg Clothiers. How unique do you think it is?

4. What is the impact of the projected growth in sales on office automation and data processing?

5. What are the critical service factors for this company? For example, how important is customer service?

6. Discuss and evaluate Williamsburg's experience with word processing.

7. What do you think of Wendy Kelley's stress on morale and teamwork?

8. Is it timely to institute a charge-out system for office services?

9. Should word processing and data processing be combined? What are the pros and cons? What are the risks?

10. Which is more important, managerial productivity or clerical/secretarial productivity? What is the relative degree of difficulty in automating each?

11. Should Williamsburg reorganize and combine the Ho function and the Kelley function? Do you think either party understands the other? Would this be a difficult merger?

Index

Note: In this index, the acronym MIS stands for management information systems.